Elusive Dove

Elusive Dove
The Search for Peace During World War I

Neil Hollander

McFarland & Company, Inc., Publishers
Jefferson, North Carolina

LIBRARY OF CONGRESS CATALOGUING-IN-PUBLICATION DATA

Hollander, Neil, 1939–
  Elusive dove : the search for peace during World War I / Neil Hollander.
      p.   cm.
  Includes bibliographical references and index.

  ISBN 978-0-7864-7891-0 (softcover : alkaline paper) ∞
  ISBN 978-1-4766-1410-6 (ebook)

  1. World War, 1939–1945—Peace.   2. Peace-building—History—20th century.   3. World War, 1939–1945—Moral and ethical aspects.   4. World War, 1939–1945—Social aspects.   5. World War, 1939–1945—Biography.   I. Title.
  D613.H66 2014
  940.3'12—dc23   2013048084

BRITISH LIBRARY CATALOGUING DATA ARE AVAILABLE

© 2014 Neil Hollander. All rights reserved

No part of this book may be reproduced or transmitted in any form or by any means, electronic or mechanical, including photocopying or recording, or by any information storage and retrieval system, without permission in writing from the publisher.

On the cover: flags from the Allied Powers and Central Powers of World War I (dove © 2014 iStock/Thinkstock)

Manufactured in the United States of America

McFarland & Company, Inc., Publishers
  Box 611, Jefferson, North Carolina 28640
  www.mcfarlandpub.com

For Régine

Table of Contents

Preface	1
ONE • A Prelude for Peace	3
TWO • "Peace Before Christmas…"	77
THREE • The Long Road to Peace	147
FOUR • Peace—with a Vengeance	239
Conclusion	255
Chapter Notes	259
Bibliography	287
Index	299

... a day will come when a cannon will be exhibited in a public museum, just as an instrument of torture is now, and people will be astonished how such a thing could have been. —Victor Hugo, 1849

Preface

Most histories of World War One revolve around gruesome battles, ribboned generals and feats of military heroism. All too often the acts of those who tried to stop the fighting by word or deed have been drowned out by the roar of cannons. Yet there were moments when reason and justice prevailed, when men spoke instead of fought, and when peace was the victor and not the vanquished. Even in the heat of battle individuals of courage have stepped forward and attempted to bring the better part of man out of darkness and revive the phoenix of peace.

These are the real heroes of the conflict, and in the battle of right and wrong the righteous have been the peacemakers and the wrongdoers those who pursued the conflict no matter what the human cost.

As a journalist I had the unfortunate privilege to witness the brutalities of war on several continents, the burning homes, the mass hysteria and the murdered, mutilated, and molested. What I saw still haunts me and it changed the way in which I perceive the world.

When the Smithsonian Institution asked to me to write and direct a program about the recipients of Nobel Prizes I readily accepted. After interviewing in depth several Peace Prize winners I came to the realization that history has largely overlooked the efforts of peacemakers. For every man and woman who received international recognition and acclaim, hundreds, if not thousands, of others tried desperately to kindle the spirit of peace. Very few succeeded; most failed, often at the cost of their own lives. For the most part their efforts have been glossed over, lost, or perhaps at best relegated to the fine print of a footnote.

For years I have collected information about these peacemakers. I have combed the archives of many newspapers that were widely read at the time, examined speeches, treaties, prose and poetry, and of course consulted the works of academics who have studied in detail one aspect or another.

The result is this book. It makes no attempt to deal with warfare per se, that is, the battles and the tide of carnage. Nor does it try to probe into the minds of the generals who were quite willing to let men die uselessly by the million. Instead, it focuses on the forces of peace, compromise and reconciliation. I sincerely hope it will be a tribute to the peacemakers of the world, in all their diversity, be it in terms of means and results, nationality, or even social origin and standing. As such, it is an incomplete mosaic, more of a humble beginning than a definitive end. It attempts to bear testimony to the efforts of those on both sides of the conflict who did what they could to end what was then the world's most devastating war. To my knowledge, no similar volume exists.

I have defined peacemakers in the widest sense possible, anywhere on a continuum from advocacy to action—in other words, not just those who tried to broker an end to the conflict or sought a unilateral cease-fire, but also those who believed that peace began by example, with the courage of one person who stood up and refused to fight, theoretically compelling others to follow, individual after individual, until the generals found that they no longer had an army to command. Also included in this definition are those anti-war activists who used the pen, and whose stories, poetry, plays and tracts encouraged others to reject the violence of modern warfare.

The quest for peace has always been a difficult one, so full of obstacles and hidden pitfalls that it appears to be an impossible task. Yet whenever warfare or the threat of bloodshed appeared on the horizon courageous men and women have often risked everything, even their lives, so that those around them could live in a world without violence.

As the world becomes increasingly threatened by the balkanization of some countries and the redefinition of their borders—many set arbitrarily at the end of the First World War—there is an ever-growing need for peacemakers to come to the fore and prevent further strife and slaughter. Perhaps this book will help today's men and women of conscience realize that should they step forward, speak words of reason and act accordingly, they will be following a long tradition. Many of the problems they are facing today were also confronted when the peacemakers of the First World War desperately tried to calm the maelstrom of hatred and violence. Unfortunately, their efforts were to no avail. But if we all ponder on why and how they failed, maybe this time we will succeed.

ONE

A Prelude for Peace

More than 40 years of European peace ended in the summer of 1914. A whole generation had grown up without witnessing the horrors of war and its legacy of broken lives. Generals trained armies that never fought. Battleships were built and became obsolescent without firing their guns in anger. Year by year trade between nations was increasing. The global economy had become a reality. Modern tourism was born and the traditional fear of the foreigner appeared to be fading.

Millions of Europeans were even beginning to speak the same language, Esperanto, a mix of Romance, Germanic and Slavic tongues. In 1907 over 20 countries sent representatives to the first Esperanto congress, which was held in France. Twenty-seven different magazines were published in Esperanto and every year their circulation increased. And there were more and more people to read them. Literacy in Northern Europe passed 90 percent. Communication between peoples of different nationalities seemed to be getting easier, and, it was widely believed, once they could speak with one another they might perhaps debate their disagreements instead of reaching for their weapons. It was not unreasonable to declare that real world peace was clearly on the horizon.

In the halcyon days before the war, the average citizen, wherever he might be, the Americas, Europe, or Asia, might look about him and conclude that, in general, the world was becoming a safer, saner place in which to live.

A worldwide network of more than 400 peace societies led the struggle for the creation of a world without war. With memberships in the hundreds of thousands, they agitated, lobbied, and published a steady stream of tracts and pamphlets, which were studied, discussed and debated in detail. Heads of state often addressed their yearly congresses.

In America, for instance, peace had become part of the fabric of society. Never before had the concept carried such importance. Drawing upon the 19th-century faith in human reason and inevitable progress, peace societies bloomed as never before.

Lawyers belonged to groups such as the Inter-Parliamentary Union and the American Society of International Lawyers. Educators supported the World Peace Foundation and the Carnegie Endowment for International Peace. The man and woman in the street were members of the American Union Against Militarism, the National Council for Prevention of War, the Woman's Peace Party—which was succeeded by the United States Section of the Women's International League for Peace and Freedom—the Fellowship of Reconciliation, the American Friends Service Committee, the Church Peace Union, just to name a few.

Like a kind of new religion, peace societies frequently became the defining group for a person, his or her raison d'être, and an individual's devotion to the cause could become almost messianistic. To attend a meeting, a lecture or a discussion group about peace became a duty and a pleasure, a way to greet the future of humanity. When the wealthy died, it was not uncommon for them to leave their fortune to a society that would further the cause of peace. Alfred Nobel (1833-1896), Andrew Carnegie (1835-1919) and Edwin Ginn (1838-1914)[1] led the way and set the example.

At roughly the same time a new word, "pacifist,"[2] meaning the antithesis of a militarist, came into use, both in French and in English, and referred to an advocate of peace rather than to an enemy of war. Those who, with pride and pleasure, called themselves pacifists declared themselves members of a new, very rational religion of man, one based on knowledge, research and study.

Many peace societies cut across class, ethnic and economic lines, joining like-minded men and women who were committed to finding the way to world peace. Their meetings, lectures and congresses became important local and national events, well covered by the press, for it was widely acknowledged that they were the vanguard of society, the voice of the future racing ahead of the politicians, preparing for a new world that would arrive soon, perhaps not tomorrow but certainly well within the life span of the young.

At their meetings the agenda was always full, for there was a great deal to discuss. For example, did "peace" mean merely the absence or the avoidance of war, or did it entail the creation of some international structure to enforce it? What would such an entity look like? Was it to be guided by a philosophy or program of social justice? If so, which one, religious or secular, existent or yet to be devised? Was all violence morally wrong? There was more than enough grist to keep the lecturers and congresses and authors busy for years. Peace leaders such as Bertha von Süttner (1843-1914), Frédéric Passy (1822-1912) and Jane Addams (1860-1935) graced the headlines and commanded wide, popular respect. Whenever they spoke, the halls were often full to overflowing. People would gather at the windows to hear the latest news on the progress of peace.

This enormous wave of words seemed to be producing results. More and more people joined the ranks of the committed. It was a unique moment in history. For once, Prime ministers, Presidents, parliamentarians and the people on the street all seemed to be speaking the same language.

Reflecting this spirit of optimism, at the turn of the century the British Prime Minister, Lord Salisbury (1830–1903), announced in the House of Commons that the future would see an inevitable "federation of Europe."[3] And for proof, he declared, one only had to look across the Channel to the Netherlands.

There, at The Hague, in 1899 and 1907, the world witnessed truly unusual events. Twice a peace conference was held without a war to precede it. Czar Nicholas II of Russia (1868–1918) had started the process by summoning the most powerful nations of the world to a meeting. At The Hague they took the first steps toward the creation of a rational international community where discussion and negotiation would replace arms and armies.[4] They also agreed that a third peace conference would be convened in the near future to further reduce the possibility of international conflict. This was an unprecedented step toward world peace and, for those who took a positive view of the future, ample evidence that warfare would soon be banished to the history books.

The Hague Peace Conferences were the most discussed international events of their time, receiving unprecedented popular attention and support. In England over 750 resolutions endorsing the conference were sent to the Foreign Office from peace societies, religious groups, and town and county councils. Belgium produced a petition with more than 100,000 names in support of the conference, and Holland sent one with more than 200,000 signatures. In Tokyo a Japanese princess forwarded 6,741 signatures on behalf of the Japanese Ladies Peace Association.[5]

One often-cited explanation for the Czar's peace initiative is that he was influenced by *The Future of War*, a six-volume study by the Polish pacifist and economist Jan Bloch (1836–1902).[6] Nicholas II was certainly acquainted with the work and its central thesis, and he may even have read parts of it.[7] Some sources contend that the Czar met privately with Bloch and the two men discussed the book and its dire predictions about Europe's future.[8]

Despite its prodigious length, a total of 3,084 pages, and wealth of details, *The Future of War* was extremely popular in Europe near the turn of the century and was republished in several languages. Bloch became an international celebrity and was even nominated for the first Nobel Peace Prize.[9] He was one of a long line of people who thought that they could write the way to peace, amass enough data and logic so that even the most hardened skeptic would be convinced. Bloch believed in the inherent rationality of man and thus "the impossibility of war." This placed him at the forefront of those seeking a legalistic solution through the creation of an international court. For Bloch, it was not a question of whether international adjudication *could* be used to avoid war, but rather that the nations of the world had to understand that a court *must* be used to prevent war.

With incredible clarity Bloch realized more than anyone else at the time the nature of a future war among the Great Powers. After amassing a huge quantity of statistical data, from the price of artillery shells to buttons on uniforms, he calculated exactly what a war between the European powers would cost. He arrived at the conclusion that militarism was gradually impoverishing all modern states and the next European war would pauperize most of them. He accurately predicted the First World War would be a horrendous bloodbath, stagnate into trench warfare and produce a stalemate that would have revolutionary consequences.[10] It is this latter dire conclusion that probably caught the Czar's attention, for, in effect, Bloch spelled out Nicholas II's nightmare, the exact conditions that would cause the fall of the Romanoffs 20 years later.

Backed up by a vast array of maps, statistics, graphs and tables, Bloch concluded:

> Will the armies of western Europe, where the Socialist propaganda has already spread among the masses, allow themselves to be disarmed, and if not, must we not expect even greater disasters than those which marked the short-lived triumph of the Paris Commune? The longer the present position of affairs continues the greater is the probability of such convolutions after the close of a great war [...]. Not long ago the advocates of revolution were a handful; now they have their representatives in all parliaments, and every new election increases their number in Germany, in France, in Austria, and in Italy [...]. Such are the consequences of the so-called armed peace of Europe—slow destruction in consequence of expenditure on preparations for war, or swift destruction in the event of war—in both events convulsions in the social order.[11]

If indeed Nicolas II was influenced by *The Future of War*, then the inception of The Hague Peace Conference is one of the rare moments in history when the head of a great power and a peace movement have been so close together.

Thousands flocked to The Hague with their dreams and schemes, among them probably every well-known peace activist in Europe. The press and bystanders far outnumbered the delegates. Bertha von Süttner, by then the most famous peace activist in Europe, rented a suite in a hotel nearby where she kept an open bar and regularly entertained delegates.

Samuel Gompers (1850–1924), head of the AFL (American Federation of Labor) representing a million American workers,[12] pledged his support and declared that soon the time would come when workmen would refuse to handle "the machinery of death for one another's destruction at the bidding of men who, for their own gain, wish other men to wade in blood."[13]

In Europe the peace movement had suddenly emerged from the obscure and irrelevant margins of society. Delegates and diplomats were consulting peace advocates and journalists were quoting their opinions. One British activist wrote: "I, for one, feel the awkwardness of my position, for [...] now [...] daily [...] my opinions on subjects connected with the Movement are asked, and [...] more than once, I have actually been treated with respect."[14]

It was the birth of a modern, lobbying public opinion and it began with a dramatic cascade, a sudden flood of mail, to peace societies, to newspapers and magazines, and above all to the delegates themselves. A member of the American delegation complained: "The number of people with plans, schemes, notions, nostrums, whimsies of all sorts [...] is enormous."[15] Nonetheless, the head of the American delegation, Andrew D. White (1832–1918), recorded in his diary that he was impressed by "the depth and extent of the longing for peace."[16]

A British weekly, *War Against War*, was created specially for the Hague conference and immediately attracted a wide public. Mark Twain (1835–1910) quipped in one of the opening editions: "The Czar is in favor of disarmament and so am I. There ought to be no difficulty about the rest of the world."[17] The magazine aired a number of the schemes presented at The Hague, some wildly impractical but many realistic, simple and perhaps easy to implement, for example, the proposal to spend 1 percent of all sums devoted to arms and armies on peace. The idea caught on and was seriously discussed by those in power. At one point bills favoring it were introduced into the British Parliament and the American Congress.[18]

For the thousands of members of peace societies all over the world, the conferences at The Hague represented the germ of a true "Parliament of Man,"[19] and, for them, its opening day, the 18th of May 1899, Czar Nicholas II's birthday, marked the beginning of a new era of human history. The nations of the world had come together and created a forum, the first of its kind, a place where countries could discuss virtually any subject that threatened to violate world peace. What had once been a utopian dream had suddenly become a reality. One American enthusiast proclaimed: "[The Hague] transcends any human event which has taken place. It is the first step toward the federation of the world."[20]

The press carefully tracked the debates and reported on them in a dozen or more languages. The Hague Peace Conferences became the prototype for all League of Nations and United Nations meetings ever since.

* * *

The decades preceding the First World War were a golden moment of peace advocacy, a high point of hope and pacifism. It was widely believed that universal peace, the possibility that the nations of the world might finally renounce war, seemed to be on the horizon.

The most popular method for the elimination of armed conflict could be summed up in a single word—"arbitration," the concept that disputes between individuals or countries could be given to a third party, the disputants agreeing in advance that whatever decision the third party thought was equitable would definitively settle the issue. It was not a complicated theory that needed textbooks to explain it. And it was widely believed that once it had been fully introduced into international law its scope might be expanded, little by little, until it became *the* method, the only method of resolving conflicts between nations.

Should one or both parties disagree with the decision, how would the result of an arbitration be enforced? How could the arbitrator compel the conflicting parties to accept his judgment? This had always been a weak and contested point. Many schemes had been put forward, but in one way or another most came to rest on convention, morality, respect, and common sense, in other words, a force of will and reason, not arms. And perhaps that was enough. Over 2,000 years ago, Thucydides recorded the declaration of the King of Sparta: "It is impossible to attack as a transgressor him who offers to lay his grievance before a tribunal of arbitration."[21]

Whenever a violent conflict did threaten to push the European powers onto the field of battle, such as the Agadir Crisis of 1911 or the struggle for Norwegian statehood, men of reason stepped in front of the generals. The drumrolls ceased. Swords were sheathed and cannons muzzled. The affairs of nations retuned to rationality, and it seemed like man was learning to control his martial instincts.

When armed conflict did break out, such as the Russo-Japanese War of 1904–1905, it was ultimately settled at the conference table. The American President, Theodore Roosevelt (1858–1919), stepped between the two antagonists and brought them to Portsmouth, Maine, where they negotiated, then signed a peace treaty.

Words had proved to be stronger than bullets. A precedent had been set, a lesson learned. The years passed often without a single threat to international peace even though the European powers continued to arm themselves, perfecting their killing machines with new technology.

The year 1910, for example, began quietly, one of the few moments when the entire world was basically at peace. The previous year had been relatively non-violent. Only a few small wars had marred the horizon as the century turned into its second decade, a civil war in Nicaragua and two small colonial conflicts: France was fighting the Wadai war[22] in the remote, arid mountains of Chad, and Spain was skirmishing with Moroccan Rif tribesmen near their enclave at Melilla. But by the end of January the Spanish and the Rif had come to terms. The Nicaraguan war simmered on sporadically and unresolved, while, largely out of sight, the French fought a few minor skirmishes in the heart of Africa.

A world without war, or at least almost: that was something to celebrate. On New Year's Eve 1910, in the capitals of the world, the champagne flowed and the mood was decidedly effervescent.

For once, the grandiose toasts were not empty and the pompous speeches filled with platitudes of peace and prosperity mirrored reality. The nations of the world were learning to behave with rationality and respect. On January 1 the *New York Sun* boldly predicted: "At the close of a year of unusual peace throughout the world nothing is to be seen ahead likely to create serious disturbance among the nations [...]. The general feeling of peace in Europe has pervaded the Latin republics of the New World as well."[23]

Optimism soared, and it was not unreasonable to believe that the dawn of a new age might finally be just over the horizon: indeed, a world without war.

As 1910 advanced, a *New York Times* editorial waxed: "I believe we will live to see the day when the greatest men will be those who stand for peace and good will, and not the victors of many battles [...]. No question. Before we reach 1950, the apostles of peace will be out of a job."[24]

Another prominent American newspaper did not hesitate to declare: "The past century [the 19th] has seen man bound closer to man; the new one shall bind nation to nation; new inventions shall make war impossible."[25] That seemed to be a perfectly reasonable conclusion, and not just to dreamy utopians. Even hardened politicians and wily diplomats were pondering the same thing. Do away with war, once and for all, everywhere? Cleanse the world of a scourge that had plagued it since the dawn of history? Why not? The ideas were on people's lips, not as flights of fantasy, but as goals that were well within reach. Peace was popular and fashionable, a subject to be discussed at dinner tables, argued in bars, debated in lecture halls, schools and churches, and seriously considered in the corridors of power. After all, other social evils had been condemned to the trash can of civilization. Why not war?

Slavery, for example, the source of immeasurable suffering, had been largely abolished. By the beginning of the 20th century it had been eliminated from the so-called civilized world. No one then, or today for that matter, would stand up and argue that slavery is and should be a part of the fabric of human society. Yet when it was in full flower only a few centuries ago, slavery was regarded as inherent in the natural order of things, an institution that had existed since man formed society. Philosophers justified it, the clergy defended and praised it, and politicians reasoned that it was a necessary part of any state. After all, civilization's greatest monuments had been built by slaves: the pyramids of Egypt, the temples of Greece and Rome, the Great Wall of China and the massive city of Angkor, to name but a few.

Yet within the space of a few generations slavery had been abolished. So why not war, now, at the dawn of a new century? The moment was ripe to discard physical combat as an archaic and vicious behavior. According to the European and American press, humanity was finally growing up, coming of age, and leaving its tumultuous adolescence behind. "Man was learning from his past" was the common theme, and finally non-violence was becoming the law of our species; violence, the law of the brute. A British newspaper commented: "A warless world is, then, a state of things that it is not unreasonable to discuss [...]. Private war, they tell us, has ceased; the duel is dead,[26] or dying; and yet mankind has not degenerated but improved, physically and morally. Why, then, should not the stoppage of public war be as little detrimental to character?"[27]

Many people were firmly convinced that war was a disease that could be treated and eventually cured. As the new century advanced, the man in the street believed that it was possible, even highly probable, that soon the world would witness the elimination of humanity's greatest source of cruelty and suffering. A London newspaper announced: "There is a deep-seated and ineradicable conviction that eternal peace must be established."[28]

Even many military leaders publicly acknowledged that one day soon they might be eclipsed by diplomats armed with only wisdom, reason and a handshake. Speaking at a meeting of the Peace Society in New York, Admiral Tōgō, the hero of the Battle of Tsuhima, declared that "peace hath its victories, more renowned than those of war."[29]

Peace was stylish, the social currency of the moment, and front-page news. Proposals, counterproposals, and critiques for arms limitations, international courts, and arbitration procedures rippled through the world's press. Politicians and diplomats also spoke seriously about the creation of an international police force and a movement to re-examine schoolbooks to eliminate the so-called glory of war. In this spirit, the International School for Peace was created in 1910 in the United States with its sole purpose to disseminate books and pamphlets against the military spirit. The American textbook magnate Edwin Ginn,[30] who started it, became the first person to donate a million dollars directly to the cause of peace.

The average man or woman had a right to feel that the world was becoming a better, safer place in which to live, that peace was linked to progress, and that reason was speaking louder than hatred. Proof was not hard to find. More and more people were speaking to each other across borders. Over 1,500 international conferences were held between 1899 and 1914.

And tangible results were not hard to find. Many international disputes were being resolved in a peaceful manner. Between 1794 and 1900, 477 cases of arbitration were recorded. And in the following 15 years there were at least an additional 200. When war broke out in 1914, 209 arbitration treaties were in force.[31] Many of these agreements were well reported in the press, each regarded as a benchmark on the road to world peace.

The United States and Great Britain, for example, amicably settled a dispute that had lasted nearly a century and had been a constant source of friction. The argument over who had what rights to the rich fishing grounds in the North Atlantic had seriously strained the relations between the two countries on several occasions. A decision by an arbitration council at The Hague essentially granted the legislatures of each country the right to set their own laws for the fisheries, with the proviso that it must always provide free and equal access to all competing factions in the fishing industry regardless of their country or origin.[32]

At roughly the same time, 1910, another decision at The Hague fixed the maritime boundary between Norway and Sweden, which had not been set at the time of Norwegian independence in 1905. Russia and Turkey settled a dispute, so did the Netherlands and Portugal, Italy and Peru, France and

Germany.³³ Case by case, a strong precedent was being set and a body of international law based on pacifist principles was being created.

The Court of Arbitration at The Hague had become a classroom for nonviolence, and humanity was slowly learning its lessons. Like most students, when put to the test, the score was not perfect. Frédéric Passy, who was often called the apostle of peace, admitted that it would take time. Mistakes would be made and errors would be costly and, unfortunately, measured in human lives. Passy once objected to a congress being called the Universal Peace Congress. Instead, he suggested it should be called the Universal Congress OF Peace. He went on to say: "I have never met any person who started with the notion of once and forever, today or tomorrow, abolishing the art of warfare. We are called upon to do what we can to better humanity, but to flatter ourselves that we are going to make her ever quite perfect is a snare and a delusion."³⁴

Passy was a dynamic orator, tireless, impassioned and persuasive. All his words, years of them, were focused on one subject, one concept, arbitration. It became a mantra that he never tired of repeating. When he was asked, as he often was, why, after all of the arguments set forth by pacifists, all the speeches and debates in congresses, the meetings of parliamentarians, and the treaties of arbitration, the world was still plagued by warfare, Passy always replied that in his lifetime he never expected war to be totally vanquished. Violent conflict had been a part of man's culture for thousands of years. It would not die out easily or quickly. To expect otherwise, he often explained, was like telling a farmer that "because too frequently hail and rain destroyed his crops, there was no use in sowing, and that he was only exposing himself to inevitable disappointments."³⁵

* * *

On the other side of the Atlantic William Howard Taft (1857–1930) became President of the United States in 1909 and immediately raised the flag of peace. A former Secretary of War under President Roosevelt, Taft paradoxically was also an ardent advocate of arbitration, and he didn't hesitate to say so: "I shall look forward with confident hope to the signing within a few decades, or a half-century [...] of a general treaty or convention by all the great powers in which they shall agree to submit all justiciable controversies to this tribunal [The Hague Court of Arbitral Justice] [...]. Why do I hope for this? Am I overenthusiastic? It may take time, I admit, but not so many years as scoffers suppose."³⁶

President Taft believed that he was just following the natural course of history. He saw himself not as a visionary, merely as a realist, an internationalist who was quite willing to see the United States absorbed into a larger federative state that would eventually include all the great powers. He wrote: "The nations of the world are growing closer and closer to each other. Facility of transportation and facility of communication have developed a knowledge and an interest among the people of one country in the doings of the people of another that was never known before."[37]

To draw the world closer together, President Taft focused on treaties of arbitration, using the Anglo-Saxon juridical system *writ large* as the means of preventing war. He proposed that the United States would lead the way. While addressing the American Peace and Arbitration League in March 1910 the President declared that thus far the United States had avoided a number of wars by the simple fact that "God looks out for fools, drunkards and the United States."[38] That could not last forever and whereas the previous President, Theodore Roosevelt (1858–1919), had agreed to arbitrate issues not involving national honor or vital interests, Taft favored unlimited arbitration; that is, he proposed that any dispute between the United States and another country should be given to a panel composed of impartial experts from other countries and their decision would be final and binding.[39]

Taft went right to the weak point of arbitration theory and posed the difficult question of enforcement himself:

> How will judgments of such a court be enforced: what will be the sanctions for their execution? I am very little concerned about that. After we have gotten the cases into court, and decided, and the judgments embodied in a solemn declaration of a court thus established, few nations will care to face the condemnation of international public opinion and disobey the judgment. When a judgment of that court is defied, it will be time enough to devise methods to prevent the recurrence of such an international breach of faith.[40]

In April 1911 President Taft told his friend and advisor Archibald Butt (1865–1912)[41] that a treaty of arbitration with Great Britain "will be the crowning jewel of my administration [...] but also the greatest failure if I do not get it ratified."[42] Ultimately the treaty was not ratified, at least not in the form that President Taft had proposed it. Although it was initially greeted with applause when he presented it to the Senate, the Senators proved to be extremely jealous of their treaty-making prerogatives and refused to surrender any of them. The Senate Foreign Relations Committee deleted a key paragraph permitting the referral of arbitral matters to an international commission apart from the Senate.

President Taft embarked on a lengthy speaking tour hoping to use public pressure to force the Senators to change their minds, but it was to no avail. The Senate remained intransigent. The treaty was rewritten and its arbitration teeth extracted. An opportunity for peace on a grand scale was lost. William Howard Taft had hoped that America would be an example for the world. More than any other President, for the sake of peace he was willing to surrender national sovereignty and lead the country into some sort of new world federal order.

In 1913, on the eve of World War I, Taft, now a former President, had become a professor at Yale University. Still optimistic, he delivered a lecture that linked the "federative trend in international affairs" to the movement toward universal peace. He traced federative politics in Western civilization from the Achaean League[43] of ancient Greece to the dominions of the British Empire. Within the next 50 years he believed that the Great Powers would sign a convention requiring that all justiciable disputes would be submitted to a permanent tribunal. The future, Taft predicted, would witness the creation of a Tennysonian "Parliament of Man," a phrase taken from the poem "Locksley Hall," written by Lord Alfred Tennyson (1809–1892) in 1835:

> Till the war-drum throbb'd no longer, and the battle-flags were furl'd.
> In the *Parliament of man*, the Federation of the world.
>
> There the common sense of most shall hold a fretful realm in awe,
> And the kindly earth shall slumber, lapped in universal law.

* * *

By 1911, however, for many, the honeymoon of peace was over. Despite the efforts of politicians, journalists and peace activists, war, one that could possibly involve all of Europe, was looming large on the horizon. The flashpoint appeared in an unlikely place, North Africa. Germany sought to extend its colonial empire and the Kaiser sent a warship to Agadir, a small seaport in Morocco perched on the edge of the Sahara.

The gunboat anchored in the harbor, theoretically to protect German business. France became alarmed, afraid the Germans were trying to establish a toehold in Morocco, one that could easily grow to fit the Prussian boot. When the Germans sent a second warship, the French protested vigorously the intrusion into what they considered to be their sphere of interest.

The British rallied to support the French even though they were not bound by treaty to do so. In British eyes, the Germans were trying to obtain an Atlantic port for their fleet. That would be a clear threat to British communication with the colonies. Even the noted opponent of war David Lloyd George (1863–1945) railed: "If Britain is treated badly where her interests are vitally affected, as if she is of no account in the cabinet of nations, then I say emphatically that peace at that price would be a humiliation intolerable for a great country like ours to endure."[44]

Sabers began to rattle. The entire British fleet steamed southward. Meanwhile, France mobilized its army to protect its interests.

All over Europe newspapers headlined the preparations for war. The French press accused the Germans of behaving like Dick Turpin,[45] the legendary English highwayman, and willfully disturbing the international peace.[46] Germany refused to withdraw unless it received concessions elsewhere in Africa. The drums of nationalism began to roll and their cadence grew steadily louder. The stage was set for a major conflict. A few German shops in a Moroccan backwater could easily have been the spark to ignite a European war.

However, Jules Cambon (1845–1935), the French ambassador to Berlin, was determined that this would not happen. He immediately met with his German counterpart, Alfred von Kiderlen (1852–1912), the Deputy Secretary for Foreign Affairs, and the negotiations began.

The two men had known each other for years, and, from the moment he took up the post in 1907, Cambon had always stood for a Franco-German détente. Even with the nationalist press in Paris calling for military action, Cambon quietly pressed on with the negotiations and a peaceful settlement of the conflict.[47]

During one of their meetings, von Kiderlen is reported to have said that "we will both decide whether war or peace."[48] Seldom have two men held such power.

Meanwhile, British warships sailed toward an almost certain confrontation, and on the Continent French and German soldiers marched toward their frontiers.

Newspapers in all three countries fanned the fires of hatred and retribution. In London, the *Daily Chronicle* ran the headline "Great Britain Warns Germany—National Honour at Stake."[49] The *Times* announced that "the German demands are [...] so extravagant that we are slow to regard them as seriously made [...]. No British government could consent to suffer so great a change in the distribution of power in Africa."[50] In Germany the press announced that the government intended to claim part of southwestern Morocco.[51]

In England, fuel for the flames of insult and injury was provided by the German "demands," which were immediately taken to be Prussian arrogance and intransigence. There were, in fact, no demands at all. What the German Foreign Secretary had said in French was, "*Voici ce que nous demandons.*" But *demander* in French is not to demand, but simply to ask. Contrary to the common stereotype, the Germans were being reasonable and simply saying, "Here is what we are asking."[52] The mistranslation went uncorrected in the press.

Encircled by an enraged public who shouted for bombs and bayonets to save national pride, Cambon and von Kiderlen desperately tried to find a compromise. On both sides of the frontier the generals waited for the order to load their weapons and fire.

But the voices of peace were not silent. In both France and Germany, thousands of mothers and wives of soldiers wrote to both von Kiderlen and Cambon pleading with them to avoid war. When the two diplomats met, they exchanged letters and read aloud some of the passages.

The threat of a vast human tragedy hovered over the negotiations. Yet both sides played their cards as if the next one was a declaration of war. Von Kiderlen wrote to the Kaiser that Germany had to give the French the impression that, if necessary, they were ready to resort to arms: "It could happen in the course of negotiations, if they are pursued seriously on our part, that such tension was created that we must positively say to the French that we are determined to take the ultimate step. And if this is to be effective we must be mentally prepared for it."[53]

Later von Kiderlen wrote in his memoirs: "If the intermediaries had been anybody but Jules and I, there would have been war. It is always a meritorious thing to have avoided it without humiliating either of our two countries."[54]

Jules Cambon entered into his journal that "the only thing of which I am proud is that I avoided war in 1911."[55] Few men are able to make such a dramatic and vital claim.

When they parted after signing the final agreement settling the crisis, they exchanged photographs with the inscriptions "À mon terrible ami, À mon aimable ennemi. [To my dreadful friend, to my likable enemy.]"[56]

War was avoided. Germany withdrew its warships and was compensated by a strip of jungle in Central Africa, roughly half of what had been the French Congo, approximately 100,000 square miles of Central Africa that had hardly been explored. A number of economic issues were settled and, in keeping with a spirit of peace, it was agreed that all future disputes were to be settled by the Hague court.[57]

National pride had been saved and with it thousands, if not millions, of lives.[58] The solution of the Agadir Crisis seemed to prove that the sparks of conflict could be extinguished. The armies unloaded their weapons and were demobilized and the fleets of warships returned to their home ports. The most well-armed nations in the world had come to the brink of conflict, then stepped back. There was real cause for celebration. Peace had won. One more example had been set for the future.

* * *

While the British, French and Germans were squabbling about the western end of the Sahara, Italy was poised to grab a piece on the other side. The Italians had come late to the scramble for colonies and found very little left. In North Africa, Turkish rule was waning. The Italians sought to replace it, invading Libya on the thin excuse of protecting Italian citizens and their property.

However, not all Italians were in agreement. The anti-war and anti-colonial movement was strong and vocal. When the government announced its plans to seize Libya, the socialists called for a general strike by the working class.

The motivations of peace warriors were not always self-sacrificing and pure. Peace could also be a stepping-stone to power. Standing in the front ranks of those who marched against an Italian war of conquest was an unlikely leader, Benito Mussolini.[59] He called the invasion of North Africa "the mock-heroic madness of the war-mongers,"[60] and, true to socialist dogma, he claimed that the working man has no homeland and no interest in fighting wars for the profit of a few and the enslavement of many. He wrote in the local newspaper: "So long as there are Fatherlands, there will be militarism. The Fatherland is a spook [...] like God, and like God it is vindictive, cruel and tyrannical [...]. Let us show that the Fatherland does not exist just as God does not exist."[61]

At the head of the strike, Mussolini tried to stop the war by preventing the Italian army from boarding ships to Libya. He proclaimed that "the national flag is for us a rag to plant on a dunghill."[62]

Convinced that they had the support of millions, the workers of Forli tore up tram and railway lines, disconnected the telegraph and confronted the trains full of soldiers, calling on them to disobey their orders, take off their uniforms and join the strike. For two days the workers occupied the city. Mussolini stood at the head of the strikers, unarmed and defiant, a warrior against war. He wrote that "the proletariat of Forli has set a magnificent example. The general strike has fully succeeded."[63]

In fact, the general strike was less than general and quickly crumbled elsewhere in Italy. While Mussolini was having his morning coffee in a café in Forli, the police arrived and politely arrested him. Mussolini went quietly. He knew what was coming. It would be his fifth time in jail. Fame had its price.

He was tried for vandalism and fomenting acts of violence, and despite an eloquent self-defense—for example, he referred to himself as "a soldier of faith"—he was found guilty. Mussolini spent five months in prison. While he languished behind bars and became a nationally known martyr, Italy conquered Libya and quickly turned it into a colony.

Mussolini emerged from jail and onto the national stage. Once in the spotlight, he quickly shed his pacifist's coat for one of armor. Overnight, the man of peace became Il Duce, the brazen prince of bravado. His pacifism was soon sacrificed on the altar of self-promotion.

A Russian nihilist, Anna Kulishov (1857–1925), who knew Mussolini at the time wrote: "He is nothing of a Marxist. In fact he is not really a socialist at all [...]. Nor is he really a politician. He is a sentimental poetaster who has read Nietzsche."[64]

Less than two years later Mussolini's transformation was complete. He wrote in *Popolo d'Italia*: "Who has iron has bread. Revolution is an idea that has found bayonets [...], WAR!"[65]

* * *

In the United States, the same year, 1911, marks the end of one of the longest wars in recorded history, that between the Native Americans and the white settlers. After more than 250 years of almost continuous warfare, peace arrived on the western frontier.

The last battle was a small one, insignificant in terms of numbers, but a tragic and symbolic final chapter, and while the Indians may have lost the war, they were responsible for the final peace.

In the desolate mountains of Nevada, a dozen nomadic Shoshones, known as Rock Well Mike's band, were camped in the snow. According to the white ranchers of the area, the Shoshones were caught red-handed stealing cattle. The Indians tell a different story. In their version they encountered a group of white cattle rustlers. A short battle followed and one of the Indians was killed. Then the Indians went looking for revenge and found a group of four cattlemen whom they took to be the rustlers.

In any case, knives and pistols were drawn and, when the air cleared, the four cattlemen were dead. The Shoshones stripped the men of their clothes and weapons, took their horses, then fled into the hills.

Rock Well Mike's band were perhaps the last to live outside a reservation and follow Indian traditions. They had little contact with the white man and his ways and existed as their ancestors had, hunting for food, making their own tools and building willow-frame tepees as their homes.

For weeks, a sheriff's posse tracked them through the snow across northern Nevada. A reward of $15,000 had been placed on Shoshone Mike's head, dead or alive. Finally, after a 200-mile chase, the Indians were cornered in a canyon called Kelley Creek.

While the posse encircled them on horseback, an Indian guide called out to them to surrender. He told them they were outnumbered two to one, but the Indians had no intention of giving up without a fight. They painted their faces and did a war dance.

Shoshone Mike, a toothless old man, put on his feathered war bonnet, and his squaws began beating tom-toms. During the battle that followed, the Indian braves used rifles; and their women, bows and arrows. In the end, when the horsemen drew near, the Indians threw tomahawks.

The struggle lasted for more than three hours. When it was over, eight Indians and one member of the posse had been killed and another cattleman wounded with an arrow in his chest. Shoshone Mike had been the first to die, proud and defiant to the end. He went down with at least ten bullets in him. The Indians were buried where they fell.

The victors marched the few Indian survivors into the nearest town, a young girl of 17 and three frightened children aged 7, 5, and 2. The girl had kept firing until she used her last bullet. All the captives except the youngest one died of tuberculosis within a year.[66]

Word of the chase and battle spread throughout the state. Stores sold out of guns and ammunition. Nevada became an armed camp and every farm and ranch an arsenal. Any Indian in the state became a potential target. For safety, they tended to travel and hunt in groups, which only made them seem more suspicious. Ranchers were afraid that the Shoshones on the reservation would go on the warpath to avenge Mike's death. There was grave danger that the battle of Kelley Creek would escalate into racist rounds of revenge and counterrevenge.

A full-scale Indian war might have developed had not Harry Preacher, Chief of the Shoshones, stepped forward. While the Indians simmered, spoiling for vengeance, and cattlemen armed themselves to be ready for it, Chief Preacher was determined to prevent further bloodshed. Unarmed and alone, he faced the weapons of both communities and tried to keep the peace. As the spokesman for the Shoshones in the Brotherhood of the North American Indians, he went to the local newspaper and made a statement that was printed across the front page: "I've heard that some of the white people are afraid the Indians might go on the warpath [...]. But I don't believe that there is a danger of any of the Shoshones making trouble for the whites. I tell you it will not happen."[67]

Then Chief Preacher returned to the reservation and spoke to his fellow Shoshones: "We must be friendly to the whites [...]. We have no choice. Be very careful what you do. Don't do anything to offend them, for no good will come from their hatred and, as we all know, we will suffer for it in the end."[68]

Chief Preacher made peace. The war was over. The battle of Kelley Creek became the final chapter of the American West. From the moment the first settlers had encroached on Indian land on the eastern seaboard until this last stand in the barren mountains of Nevada, the native American population had declined by over 90 percent.

* * *

In London, at roughly the same point in time, Norman Angell (1872–1967), a correspondent for the London *Daily Mail*, published *The Great Illusion*, which instantly became an anti-war classic. Its central thesis was simple: modern wars had become economically irrational. Angell argued that the increasing internationalization of credit, industry and communications was rapidly forcing nations to become economically interdependent. Should there be a war, victor and vanquished would suffer equally.

It was the right message at the right moment, a persuasive antidote to the massive arms race that was consuming the Great Powers of Europe. Angell assured the public that no matter how many battleships a country built war would be impossible.[69]

A passionate speaker and remarkable propagandist, Angell tirelessly pumped the lecture circuit and issued tract after tract. He tapped all levels of society, drawing in workers, industrialists and politicians and uniting them under the slogan "war does not pay!"[70] He generated so much enthusiasm for his argument that his position was often referred to as "the new pacifism" to separate it from the older, more traditional Quaker-Tolstoyan attitude.[71] He was able to reach into the mainstream of society, those he called the "unconverted," who "confuse war-making with patriotism." He spoke before such diverse organizations as the Navy League, the National Liberal Club, the Cambridge Union and the London Institute of Bankers.

A tireless activist as well as an author, Angell virtually became a one-man political movement who devoted himself to trying to stop the conflict he saw looming ahead. Whereas President Taft put his faith in the law, a growing body of international legislation based on arbitration, Angell was a peace populist, a democrat who believed in the power of the masses. He was convinced that if enough people realized that war was futile, then their will would manifest itself. Politicians would have to listen to the growing and strident voice of public opinion. In the years before World War One *The Great Illusion* sold over 2 million copies and was translated into 25 languages. The *Times* of London stated in an editorial that "few writers have stimulated reflection upon International Politics more than Mr. Norman Angell."[72]

In *The Great Illusion* he argued vehemently:

> War has no longer the justification that it makes for the survival of the fittest; it involves the survival of the less fit. The idea that the struggle between nations is a part of the evolutionary law of man's advance involves a profound misreading of the biological analogy [...]. The warlike nations do not inherit the earth; they represent the decaying human element [...]. Are we to continue to struggle, as so many good men struggled in the first dozen centuries of Christendom— spilling oceans of blood, wasting mountains of treasure—to achieve what is at bottom a logical absurdity, to accomplish something which, when accomplished, can avail us nothing, and which, if it could avail us anything, would condemn the nations of the world to never-ending bloodshed and the constant defeat of all those aims which men, in their sober hours, know to be alone worthy of sustained endeavor?[73]

The Great Illusion became the subject of public debates, discussions and lectures. The book was read by members of the House of Commons and even brought to the attention of the King. However, some of the strongest support came from the political left, the Social Democrats and labor organizations of the Second International, which had socialist parties in every European country.

After the British, the German public was the audience Angell wished to reach. Germany was thought to be the most hostile to pacifism, but in fact in Germany there were nearly 100 peace societies, half a dozen in Prussia, the heart of German militarism.[74] Outside of England *The Grand Illusion* sold more copies in Germany than anywhere else. Angell was convinced that every copy sold, or read, was another vote for peace. Eighteen months before the war began Angell traveled to Germany, where he was received like a celebrity. He was supported by a secret $36,000 subsidy from the Carnegie Endowment for International Peace,[75] which, among other things, paid for the publication of 40,000 15-page pamphlets in German that were distributed by mail.[76] Focusing on students, Angell toured universities, lecturing and winning converts wherever he went. According to one historian: "The tour probably did as much as any single effort to stir the interest of German youth in the peace movement."[77]

Angell's message to German youth was twofold: first, new ideas, no matter how valid or valuable they might be, generally had difficulty being accepted—witness the examples of Galileo and Darwin—and second, it was long overdue that the nations of Europe realized that war was not a solution to their problems. A new war could only mean a disaster for all.

At one point during his German tour Angell put forward the proposition that British and German Members of Parliament should send delegates to sit in each other's legislative chambers and lobby for armament restraint. It was one of many proposals that sought to interlace the two cultures and provide a firm riposte to the rattling of sabers.

In his wake Angell left a stream of glowing articles claiming that Germany, and particularly the generation that would bear arms, did not want war. After the First World War Angell wrote that "if we would have had five years in which to work among young Germans, we would have diluted Prussianism sufficiently to have rendered it much less dangerous."[78]

* * *

Reaching beyond the spoken or written word for a method to end war and civil strife, the French banker Albert Kahn (1860–1940), a dedicated pacifist, put his faith in a kind of existential lesson. He believed in the transformative power of knowledge, that education in all its various forms changes a person and his ideas of the world. For example, if young adults could learn for themselves that beneath the veil of culture men are essentially the same, that they all belong to the family of man, that realization would be enough to put an end to warfare.

Kahn's ideas were strongly influenced by his lifelong friend Henri Bergson (1859–1941), a philosopher who was extremely popular at the time. Bergson believed that in order to understand reality, immediate experience and intuition were more important than rational thinking and science or, put in a less abstract fashion, travel, coping with other cultures and seeing the world through another's eyes were far more valuable than information that could be learned from a book or the classroom. The new generation, the young men of the decade prior to the war, Bergson believed were "a miracle," a rare mutation in temperament that seemed to have left behind the negative and destructive tendencies of the previous generation.

Kahn had made a fortune financing South African gold and diamond mining, and he put it to work to further the cause of world peace. Convinced that travel would foster pacifistic relations among peoples, he created *bourses de voyage autour du monde* (scholarships for trips around the world) for students who had passed the Agrégation, an entrance exam into academia. Kahn wanted the future leaders of France and, importantly, their teachers to be well versed in what he called "the book of the world." He offered them an all-expenses-paid 15-month tour of the world. There were few conditions. The candidates had to be in good health, speak English, and be willing to travel alone or in pairs. They could establish their own route.[79]

Kahn put his faith in the world as a teacher of life, whereas most other philanthropists of the day believed in the superiority of their own culture. Cecil Rhodes (1853–1902), for example, who also made his fortune from South African mining, created his scholarships to bring young men from other countries to England to study. Rhodes said of the British: "I contend that we are the first race in the world and that the more of the world we inhabit the better it is for the human race."[80]

Thus he wanted to bring Anglo-Saxons, who he defined as including Americans and Germans, to Great Britain to study and learn how to rule the empire, and, he hoped, with time, the planet. Rhodes believed that eventually the United Kingdom, the United States and Germany together would dominate the world and thus ensure peace.

Whereas Rhodes was ethnocentric, Kahn was an egalitarian and assumed the opposite strategy. He sent his travelers out into the world to "see with their eyes the different faces of the world [...], learn something about social life in diverse parts of the world, how governments form public spirit, the means used to develop the genius of each nation, and how in particular domains, particular groups realize their potential."[81]

Not everyone could make a world trip, so to encourage others to take a virtual voyage Kahn sent photographers to 50 countries to bring back a cultural record that could be exhibited in museums or galleries. Seeing is tantamount to experiencing, he believed; thus the exposure to man's diversity, at home, at work, at play and at worship, also revealed his uniformity, the sameness of us all. This realization, Kahn was convinced, would compel the viewer to think and behave rationally and positively, especially when dealing with his fellow man. In short, one could trace a path from pictures to pacifism, communality to compassion, empathy to goodwill.

The photographic collection became known as *Les Archives de la planète* (the Archives of the Planet) and Albert Kahn spent tens of millions of dollars creating them. For him, it was a way of visualizing the entire world, creating the family of man, capturing the essence of many traditional societies that were about to be swept irrevocably into the industrial age.

Eventually the archive contained 75,000 still photographs, most using the first color photography, *autochrome* plates, and more than 450 kilometers of film. Kahn purchased a home for his collection at Boulogne-Billancourt, a suburb of Paris (where it remains to this day), and held regular screenings there as well as at the Sorbonne. At least once a year the President of the Republic came to witness new additions to the collection. And, just a few months before the First World War began, Kaiser William II (1859–1941) came to Paris and had a private viewing.[82]

The Kaiser was apparently fascinated by the unusual images in the archive, but he failed to see, or heed, their inherent message. When confronted by perhaps its most important and influential audience, the Archives of the Planet unfortunately failed to accomplish their purpose.

William II was, however, impressed by another man who put his faith in pictures over words, the Russian artist Vasily Vereshchagin (1842–1904), a pacifist who painted with an extreme realism that tried to strip war of romance and glory. At one point the Kaiser reportedly told the artist, "Pictures like these are our best guarantee against war."[83] Vasily Vereshchagin had taken part in the Russo-Turkish War of 1877–1878, and afterwards, employing a style that was almost photographic in its precision, he depicted the horrific realities of the battlefield. The inhumanity of war became the subject matter for his life's work. He once wrote to a friend that "facts laid upon the canvas without embellishment speak eloquently for themselves."[84] His pictures were widely exhibited in both Europe and America. In Germany, General von Moltke forbade his troops from seeing them, while another general urged the Czar to buy and destroy them. Knowing the inherent moral message of Vereshchagin's pictures, the British government denied him access to the Boer War.

Yet several million people saw Vereshchagin's art, most of which detailed the gruesome effects of war, even though there is no way of knowing or judging to what extent they had an effect. When the paintings were exhibited in Chicago, for example, over 100,000 people came to the gallery. While gathering material for a series of paintings about the Russo-Japanese War of 1904–1905, Vereshchagin died on board the Russian battleship *Petropavlovsk* when it struck a mine near Port Arthur (known today as Lüshunkou, at the southern tip of the Liaodong Peninsula).

* * *

The years prior to World War One witnessed a desperate arms race, with the two largest naval powers, Great Britain and Germany, leading the pack. The naval budgets became bloated as both countries built more expensive dreadnoughts[85] every year. "The whole world," Britain's Foreign Secretary Sir Edward Grey (1862–1933) told the German ambassador in 1908, "was now watching the rivalry between German and English shipbuilding."[86]

Some of those "watching" saw clearly where the arms race could lead and did their best to defuse a European war and the economic collapse that could easily follow it. A number of private citizens decided that if the government could not launch peace proposals, they would. Albert Ballin (1857–1918),[87] for example, was a successful German businessman and a pacifist who believed that, in spite of the increasing amount being spent on arms, a pragmatic peace was still possible. He set out to construct it piece by piece, starting with a reduction in the number of warships each country intended to build. An Anglophile and a friend of the Kaiser, Ballin was known as "a man of compromise."[88] And he tried to open a dialogue between German and British naval experts who he hoped would discuss the means to gradually reduce naval expenditures. When that didn't succeed, he tried to organize a preliminary peace conference between British and German statesmen. That also did not succeed, but more than likely his efforts planted a seed that several years later matured as the Haldane Mission.

Shortly after the Agadir affair, at a dinner party in London, Ballin sat next to Winston Churchill, who had just become First Lord of the Admiralty. In his diary Churchill wrote that Ballin opened the conversation by saying prophetically: "I remember [...] old Bismark [Otto von Bismark 1815–1898, Chancellor of the German Empire] telling me the year before he died that one day the great European War would come out of some damned foolish thing in the Balkans."[89]

Ballin was worried that an incident in Serbia would force Germany to go to war against Russia and, if so, France as well. He had already discussed the possibility with the Kaiser, who had requested that he informally ask the British, should there be war with France and Russia, and should Germany defeat France and promise in advance that she would seek no French territory as reparations— only perhaps French colonies—whether England would remain neutral. Churchill was, of course, unable to answer the question.

When they parted that evening Churchill, almost with tears in his eyes, said to Ballin: "My dear friend, don't let us go to war."[90]

Ballin[91] believed that if the world's two most highly armed powers, Germany and Great Britain, would just begin talking to each other, the other European countries would be forced to participate. He was joined in his peace efforts by his friend Sir Ernest Cassel (1852–1921), a German-born naturalized British citizen, who was one of the richest men of his day. Whereas Ballin had the ear of the Kaiser, Cassel was in close touch with the leading political figures in London. Both men were true internationalists, who strongly believed that the economies of the Great Powers had become so interrelated that any war between them would be self-destructive. Both Cassel and Ballin were ahead of their time, proto–Europeans who saw themselves and their well-being fused to the destinies of many countries. According to one historian: "There was no more pro–German 'emotion' in Cassel than there was pro–British 'emotion' in his opposite number, Albert Ballin."[92]

Through men like Ballin, Cassel and later the new German Ambassador to the Court of St. James, Prince Lichnowsky (1860–1928), the Kaiser's government sent clear signals that it was ready to negotiate or at least discuss the arms race. Ballin reported back to the German government that the mood in England was ripe for an agreement. He wrote in his report: "At present the Kaiser is actually one of the most popular persons in England, and the suggestion of bringing about an Anglo-German understanding is meeting with a great deal of approval from all sections of the population."[93]

Cassel was also optimistic that the two countries could reach a naval agreement, especially after Winston Churchill became the First Lord of the Admiralty. Cassel wrote in a letter to Ballin: "His [Winston Churchill's] friendly sentiments toward Germany are known to you. I have been acquainted with him since he was quite a young man, and he has never made a secret of his admiration of the Kaiser and of the German people. He looks upon the estrangement existing between the two countries as senseless, and I am quite sure he would do anything in his power to establish friendly relations."[94]

In 1912 the British cabinet sent Cassel as an official representative to Berlin. He took with him a proposal, which, in essence, stated that if Germany would recognize British naval superiority and agree to limit its shipbuilding program, in return, Great Britain would not interfere with German colonial expansion.

In a few days Cassel was back in London with a friendly message from the German government, a clear but firm opening that could have been the beginning of military détente. In Winston Churchill's words, "the spirit may be good but the facts are grim."[95]

The British cabinet decided to put their faith in "the spirit" and hold out an olive branch to Germany. Instead of an "interested party" such as Cassel, this time a government minister would go to Berlin. When the Germans were notified they announced that they wanted the Prime Minister, H. H. Asquith (1852–1928), to come. Had he gone to Berlin, perhaps the Germans would have reacted differently. Nonetheless, to prove they were serious the British cabinet sent the Secretary of State for War, Lord Haldane (1856–1928), to lay the groundwork for further negotiations. Although not the man the Germans had asked for, Haldane was nonetheless a good choice for a friendly mission. He spoke German fluently and had translated one of Schopenhauer's works into English.[96] He had also entertained William II at his home when the Kaiser visited England in 1911.

During that visit the two Kings, William II and Edward VII (1841–1910), met several times and discussed the possibility of war, and specifically England's role, should there be a Continental conflict. At one of the meetings a British diplomat present noted down the exchange:

> The Kaiser asked: "You really mean that if there was a war in Europe tomorrow, you'd have to look for your allies?"
> Edward replied: "I do."
> The Kaiser: "*Gott im Himmel!* [God in heaven!]"

Edward: "But I want peace. One does not require military allies to ensure peace."
The Kaiser: "Ha! That's stupid! That's ridiculous! In these affairs, uncle, you are a child."
Edward: "Perhaps."
The Kaiser: "But of course. I tell you it's foolish. We are your natural allies."[97]

Later the Kaiser told the British diplomat privately: "Your future lies with ours, ours with yours [...]. I am telling you what to expect if you choose France instead of Germany. You will ally yourselves with the past and turn your backs upon the rising sun."[98]

The British had every reason to expect the Haldane Mission to be successful or at least start the process of negotiation. Sir Edward Grey, the British Foreign Secretary, had prepared the way with the German ambassador in London, Baron Marschall von Bieberstein (1842–1912),[99] who had assured the British that "the thing was to create a thoroughly good and healthy atmosphere between the two countries and then they would see that it was perfectly absurd to continue this competitive race in defense arms."[100]

Ambassador von Bieberstein may have been playing ingenuous diplomatic games, for on the day Lord Haldane arrived in Berlin, Admiral von Tirpitz (1849–1930),[101] supported by the Kaiser, publicly announced an increase in German naval spending.[102] Von Tirpitz wrote in his memoirs that he thought the Haldane Mission was just a bit of English trickery to "disconcert us in the building of a fleet."[103]

Lord Haldane traveled to Berlin under the guise of doing business for the London University Commission, and when questioned in the House of Commons about Haldane's "mysterious misson" the Prime Minster said: "It was, in fact, a real holiday, free from any taint of politics."[104] The German press was led to believe that Lord Haldane had come to Berlin to discuss African affairs.

He did of course meet with the Kaiser, and many high officials in the German government, and the encounters were more than courtesy calls. Many were a frank exchange of views. Lord Haldane had made it clear from the beginning that his remarks and suggestions were *ad referendum*,[105] that is, "for reference," a kind of fact-finding mission that would set the agenda for formal treaty discussions. He told the Germans he "was not there to make a bargain, but only to explore the ground."[106]

One of the facts that emerged was that the Germans were far more interested in obtaining a British commitment to neutrality in case of war than one to arms reduction formulas.

Lord Haldane tried to explain the British position, saying that "there was not the least prospect that we could accept the draft formula that he [the German Chancellor] had proposed [complete neutrality in case of war] [...]. We should find ourselves [...] precluded from coming to the assistance of France should

Germany attack her and aim at getting possession of such ports as Dunkirk, Calais, and Boulogne."[107]

After staying in Berlin only three days, Lord Haldane returned to London. Most observers of the time, and historians of later date, have labeled his trip "a complete failure."[108] Some British politicians couldn't understand why Lord Haldane didn't return with something more tangible. Harold Nicolson (1886–1968), for example, a British diplomat and politician, later wrote: "It seems incredible that the German Government, realizing as they did that the Haldane Mission was an absolutely serious gesture, should have responded to it in so negative a manner. Of all the problems of German prewar diplomacy this is the one which it is most difficult to understand or to explain."[109]

The Germans, however, had different view of the Haldane Mission. In a letter to Albert Ballin the Kaiser wrote: "I have made no end of concessions. But this must be the limit. He [Lord Haldane] was very nice and very reasonable, and he perfectly understood my position as commander-in-chief, and that of Tirpitz [...]. I really think I have done all I could."[110]

In fact, Lord Haldane did return to England with something vital, that, at least as a matter of principle, the German government, for example Chancellor Bethmann-Hollweg, contrary to the military, was committed to seeking a peaceful solution. Lord Haldane's trip to Berlin had not been in vain. He later wrote in his autobiography: "My impression, and I still retain it, was that Bethmann-Hollweg was then as sincerely desirous of avoiding war as I was myself [...]. I left the Chancellor with the sense that I had been talking with an honest man struggling somewhat with adversity."[111]

The German military took a very different view. For them, the price of peace was high, nothing less than a total rearrangement of European alliances, one that would completely isolate France.

Admiral von Tirpitz recorded in his diary: "We ask from England a new orientation of her general policy in the sense that she should give up her existing *ententes*, and that we should take the place of France."[112]

Despite the military hard line, the door to negotiations was not closed. Lord Haldane returned with an understanding that the talks should continue, and they did for some months as the two governments searched for the proper wording of an agreement. Prime Minister Grey proposed an open exchange of information about shipbuilding, and even an inspection program, possibly to be carried out by neutral nations, in the dockyards of Great Britain and Germany. But the Germans were not interested.

Great Britain made a serious attempt to end the armaments race and by doing so perhaps avoid war, while Germany sought to link any disarmament scheme with a non-aggression pact that would guarantee British neutrality should Germany go to war with "any other country," a euphemism for France. After a number of notes were exchanged the inherent contradiction between the two different objectives became fully apparent. In Sir Edward Grey's language: "[T]he hope of a mutual reduction in the expenditure on armaments of the two countries failed."[113]

A few months after Lord Haldane returned to London, Winston Churchill (1874–1965), then First Lord of the Admiralty, tried again. Addressing the House of Commons, he proposed a "naval holiday" from shipbuilding as a first step toward arms control. It was an audacious and radical proposition, especially from someone like Churchill, who at the time was head of the largest navy in the world. In addition to trying to halt the shipbuilding programs of the two greatest maritime powers it was also a way to counter domestic critics in his own party who thought that Britain should take the lead in arms reduction and control.

In fact, the idea went beyond England and Germany. If those two rivals could agree to a "naval holiday," then certainly the other naval powers, such as France, Japan and the United States, could be persuaded to join. Churchill's "naval holiday" was meant to be nothing less than an initial step toward world disarmament. He explained his plan:

> Take as an instance [...] the year 1913. In that year [...] Germany will build three capital ships, and it will be necessary for us to build five in consequence. Supposing we were both to take a holiday for that year [...]. The three ships that she did not build would therefore automatically wipe out no fewer than five British potential super-dreadnoughts, and that is more than I expect them to hope to do in a brilliant naval action.[114]

In fact, Churchill made the proposal twice.[115] He offered to cease naval construction immediately on the most expensive items in the naval budget, what he called "big ships." This would save Germany approximately 3 billion pounds (in contemporary pounds), and the British, 6 billion.[116] While the British were perhaps genuinely trying to curtail the arms race, save money, and start a process of disarmament, the Germans saw the concept of a "naval holiday" in a very different light. For them, a freeze on the construction of new ships, especially "big ships," that is, dreadnoughts and super-dreadnoughts, meant putting a limit on their High Seas Fleet, preventing Germany from growing and becoming a world power.[117] The Germans argued that, should they agree, German shipyards would be forced to lay off skilled workers, thereby crippling their ability to build warships in the future. Also, stopping naval construction without a firm political commitment did not make sense to the Kaiser and his admirals. To them, the "naval holiday" was simply a clever political warfare gambit.

Given this context, the German government, who basically distrusted the British, easily rejected the proposal.[118] In support, there was almost universal disapproval of the scheme in the German press.[119] One German newspaper, the *Deutsche Tageszeitung*, concluded its critical reply by suggesting that Mr. Churchill take a one-year holiday from making speeches that were likely to damage Anglo-German relations.[120]

Churchill may have known, or guessed, that Germany would reject his "naval holiday" plan, and that may have been what he wanted from the start. In any case, the German rejection gave him a clear public relations and political victory. The blame for the arms race fell on Prussian shoulders. Churchill wrote: "With every rivet that von Tirpitz drove into his ships of war, he united British opinion throughout wide circles of the most powerful people in every walk of life and in every part of the Empire."[121]

In fact, the "naval holiday" may well have been just a very clever plan where the British could not lose. If the Germans accepted it, then the British could reduce the size of their naval expenditures and the size of their fleet while maintaining their superiority. If the Germans rejected it, as they did, then that enabled Great Britain to take the moral high ground. Having publicly put forward a serious proposal for peace and disarmament, twice within the space of a year, the British could claim that they were forced to arm by necessity, for defense, not offense.[122]

In Germany the press echoed loudly with the same rhetoric, arms for defense and security, and by large majorities the Reichstag voted the army and navy more and more money for "the protection" of the fatherland.

* * *

The French were also not pleased with the proposed "British naval holiday." *Le Temps* called it an "electoral device."[123] Other Parisian newspapers pointed out that should Germany save millions by not building capital ships, that money could be spent on land fortifications or increasing the weaponry of the army. Some critics focused on the details of "a naval holiday." What was to stop a country from preparing the construction of ships, essentially pre-fabricating them, so that when the "holiday" ended they could be quickly assembled, or building ships for other countries, then transferring their ownership just before they were launched?

The only place where Churchill's "naval holiday" proposal was enthusiastically received was in the United States. The American Secretary of the Navy, Josephus Daniels (1862–1948), declared: "It is not a vacation we need, but a permanent policy to guard against extravagant and needless expansions. I venture to recommend that the navy and war officials and other representatives of all the nations be invited to hold a conference to discuss whether they cannot agree upon a plan for lessening the cost of preparation for war."[124]

A resolution proposing a worldwide "naval holiday" was introduced in the House of Representatives and directed President Wilson (1856–1924) to "use his influence to consummate the agreement suggested by Mr. Churchill."[125] The idea generated a great deal of oratory, where during a heated debate one Congressman told his fellow legislators to stop "sharpening swords for a while and do some hoeing and plowing."[126] Another representative announced that "a naval holiday [...] will sound the death knell to reckless, wanton, nonsensical and almost criminal waste of the peoples' money in naval appropriations."[127]

But when all the posturing and bombast ended, the resolution passed in the House of Representatives by a large majority, 317 to 11, but failed in the Senate. President Wilson chose to ignore it. Having only just been elected to office, and on a thin mandate, 41 percent of the popular vote, he was not ready to host a major international conference for naval disarmament.[128] On the tortuous path that led to World War One a chance to bring the Great Powers together to discuss ways to reduce their military might had been lost.

* * *

Churchill, however, was undeterred by the lack of enthusiasm in Europe and America for his "naval holiday" plan. He eagerly sought a way to reopen the arms control negotiations. In the spring of 1914, a few months before the war began, he expected to receive an invitation to visit Germany, and he intended to use it as an opportunity to talk to the admirals and the Kaiser on a face-to-face basis. Churchill produced a four-point program for discussion and the first item on the agenda was his "naval holiday" proposal, which he was convinced the Germans had misunderstood. Another of his points involved exploring ways "of reducing the unwholesome concentration of [the British and German] fleets in Home Waters."[129] Churchill believed that if the size of the fleets in the North Sea, for example, could be reduced, then the likelihood of a surprise attack, or any attack, would also be reduced. In addition, Churchill wanted to move ahead with other confidence-building measures that would lead to the "abandonment of secrecy in regard to the number and general characteristics [...] of the ships, built and building, in British and German dockyards."[130]

Churchill was even prepared to open negotiations about the upper limit on the displacement of warships, that is, how large a battleship could be. It was probably the most comprehensive proposal made by any senior member of government at the time, and even more surprising as it came from the world's dominant naval power.

But Churchill's enthusiasm for arms control was not shared by other members of the British government, in particular Sir Edward Grey, head of the Foreign Office, who had previously advocated similar plans. However, this time he and the Foreign Office favored a more cautious, step-by-step approach, one that would begin with the naval attachés, then gradually work its way up, building support, until it reached a conference negotiating table. As a result, the "naval holiday" proposal quietly disappeared from the agenda.

* * *

In South America peace also made strides in the years before the war. Mimicking those in Europe, an Asociacion Americana la Paz was founded in Buenos

Aires and quickly spread throughout the continent. At the Pan-American Conference in Mexico in 1901, 16 of the 19 American states attending signed "a protocol of adhesion" to The Hague Convention. Only Mexico and the United States had officially been invited to The Hague.

However, despite this burst of peace, soon Argentina and Chile began to prepare for war. At stake was a huge piece of the South American continent, an area along the Andes half the size of Germany. This was a boundary dispute that had been simmering for generations. It came to the surface when it was discovered that the Patagonian section of the frontier was not continuously marked by the mountain crests. Several rivers were sending their waters through the hills to the sea on the Chilean side and this led to Chile making unexpected claims on the region.[131]

As both countries mobilized their armies, public opinion rose against war. Meetings, petitions, delegations, most led by women and women's organizations, announced their opposition to the war that was clearly on the horizon.

The British embassy was enlisted to act as a go-between to search for a peaceful settlement of the dispute. At the last moment, both countries agreed to arbitration, that is, to letting a third country decide where the frontier should lie. In this case, the third country was England and the King, Edward VII, agreed to serve as the arbitrator. He, in turn, appointed Sir Thomas Holdich (1843–1929), who had settled numerous frontier disputes in Asia.[132]

An intrepid outdoorsman, Holdich spent months walking the entire length of the border, down the long, jagged crown of the Andes. He hiked over huge glaciers and crossed rivers, passing in many places where no one had gone before. His journey was more than a survey of the mountains; it was an expedition of exploration.

As he traveled, Holdich tried to study the Latin Americans' cultures and reached the conclusion that "love of nature's beauty seems to be inherent in the Chilean. Trees and flowers, clouds and sunsets—these things appeal to him just as imposing buildings, magnificent streets, miles of wharfage, and acres of wool-sheds appeal to the Argentine imagination."[133] Hence, he adopted this as his criterion. When there was a choice, scenic landscapes and uplands were given to the Chileans and the more fertile arable land went to the Argentines.[134]

When Edward VII announced the results, both Chile and Argentina cheerfully accepted his decision.[135] Both declared that they had been fairly treated. Reason had triumphed. A war had been averted. Peace had prevailed.

It was a unique moment, not only for Chile and Argentina but also for the world. Señora Angela Oliviera Cezar de Costa, president of the largest women's organization in Argentina, decided that it needed a symbol so that it would never be forgotten. She solicited funds for a dramatic statue that would be placed on the border between the two countries.[136] Describing herself as "persistent and tenacious," she waged a one-woman crusade traveling the length and breadth of Argentina until the project was fully subscribed.

Cast from old cannons left by the Spanish at the time of Argentine independence, a statue of Christ was placed three miles above the sea, on the crest of the mountainous frontier. It became known as the Christ of the Andes. The plaque at the base reads: "Sooner shall these mountains crumble into dust than Chileans and Argentines break the peace which they have sworn to maintain at the feet of Christ."[137]

Eventually Señora Angela Oliviera Cezar de Costa was nominated for the Nobel Peace Prize. Her message was clear: "The two most southern republics of this hemisphere, Chile and Argentina, are the first in the history of nations to have, at the beginning of this great century, stood for universal peace, and given a tangible example to the whole world of what can be avoided by arbitration, even though two nations may be on the verge of a bloody war."[138]

However, when the statue was unveiled, instead of pointing south, the outstretched arms faced east toward Argentina. The workers had made an error. Chileans protested that they had been slighted. The Christ figure had its back turned to Chile. Once again tempers flared and sabers rattled.[139]

A Chilean newspaperman calmed passions when he wrote in an editorial: "The statue is placed as it should be. The people of Argentina need more watching over than the Chileans."

Urged on by popular support for the arbitrated settlement, Chile and Argentina went even further. They pledged themselves to submit all controversies that should arise between them to arbitration for the next ten years and immediately reduced the size of their armed forces.[140] Battleships that were being built were sold or converted to commercial use. Several arsenals became schools, and many roads were built with monies saved from military budgets.[141]

Argentina and Chile signed a treaty of arbitration, a so-called all-in document that included three unique features: first, the reservations were negligible, that is, virtually any dispute between the two countries would be subject to arbitration; second, provision was made for the strict limitation of armaments; and third, a permanent arbitrator, the British government, was appointed to settle all disputes.[142] This marks the high point in the history of arbitration, perhaps the most inclusive pacifistic agreement signed by any state in the sanguine days before World War One.

News of the settlement rippled through the world's press. A historic example had been set. Frédéric Passy, the "apostle of peace," had been right. Arbitration worked. Men were talking, not fighting. The battlefield had been replaced by a conference table. And, as he predicted, the immediate result had been a drastic reduction in arms budgets. Passy wrote: "Arbitration is on its way to becoming the custom of the world, either in the form of permanent and general treaties

[...] or as limited specific treaties for particular cases."[143] Clearly a lesson had been learned.

When a similar boundary dispute threatened to explode between Peru and Bolivia a few years later, instead of resorting to force of arms, both parties went to the British Royal Geographical Society and asked them to act as an arbitrator.[144] The dispute was settled amicably.

* * *

The peace societies of Europe, from Portugal to Russia, were slowly accumulating proof that mankind was finally marching on the road upward. Many people believed that civilization was advancing toward perfection and, with the judicious use of arbitration to settle international disputes, sooner or later war would be abolished either by a national decision in one country after another or by mutual agreement in some sort of worldwide pact or commonwealth of nations. Nowhere were the voices for the abolition of warfare louder than in Scandinavia, where they agitated for a threefold Scandinavian Treaty of Arbitration. Lecturers toured the countries speaking in churches, schools and town halls. Petitions in favor of the accord gathered more than a quarter of million signatures in each of the three countries. (Finland at that point in time was still an integral part of Russia.) For support, Sweden boasted more than 30 newspapers that pledged themselves to the principle of arbitration and they said so again and again in their editorials. The Scandinavians sought to set an example for the world. The Nordic countries began to sign "all-in" treaties. The Danes were the first and they eventually created six such treaties: with the other Scandinavian countries, then with the Netherlands, Italy and Great Britain.

While those treaties were being negotiated, in 1905, after 90 years of union with Sweden, Norway went through a cultural revolution, a sudden awakening of national identity. As a result, Norway decided to withdraw and form their own independent state. For a short time there was talk of war. Forts were built along the border and Norwegians secretly trained and gathered arms, preparing themselves for a bloody war of independence.[145] However, both sides realized that a war would be a disaster. The Swedes had a larger military, but they knew that even if they did overcome the Norwegians, it might just be the beginning of a long guerrilla war. Fortunately, the politicians in charge, especially those in Sweden, realized this and were ready to compromise. Part of the credit for the smooth separation can be attributed to the relatively strong peace societies in both Norway and Sweden, where the leaders of the movements were also active members of the dominant political parties. In fact, the Swedish Association for Peace and Arbitration is the oldest peace organization still active in the world today.

One of the strongest advocates for Norwegian separation was the pacifist Klas Pontus Arnoldson (1844–1916). A member of the Swedish parliament, he saw the conflict with Norway coming and traveled back and forth across both countries for years, tirelessly giving lectures and participating in debates as he tried to shape public opinion in favor of a peaceful solution. A war between Sweden and Norway, he believed, had to be prevented, and he dedicated himself to that cause. An impassioned and persuasive speaker, Arnoldson urged his audience: "You are all of one blood. Love one another. People can. Nations can. All this is eminently possible because love is as natural as national hatred is the most unnatural of all human feelings."[146] He wrote extensively[147] and, like most pacifists of his day, he was also a staunch advocate of arbitration. He argued that with the appearance of heavily armed states in Europe, Germany, France and England, maintaining a strong military in Scandinavia was meaningless. The future security of the Nordic states, he predicted prophetically, lay in their neutrality and the creation of a web of treaties guaranteeing their independence.

The issue of Norwegian separation from Sweden was finally settled in 1905 at the ballot box. A referendum was held, and 85 percent of the eligible Norwegian voters participated. While 368,392 Norwegians voted to end the union, only 184 voted to preserve it.[148] Sweden had no choice but to bow to the will of the overwhelming majority. A new country was born without a single drop of blood being shed. Many people called it the velvet divorce. Probably more than anyone else, Arnoldson was responsible for the peaceful transition. In 1908 he was awarded the Nobel Peace Prize for his efforts.

For Arnoldson, the Norwegian vote had also been a vote for peace, a dramatic ballot for pacifistic populism as a means of conflict resolution. He soon carried this idea to the next stage and proposed holding a worldwide referendum for peace, letting everyone, everywhere on the planet, vote for peace or war. He was confident, of course, that few people would vote for the latter. The outcome would never be in doubt. The referendum, he hoped, would be an object lesson to politicians and generals everywhere, a statistical reminder that if their constituents were given a choice, they would certainly choose the path to peace.

The creation of an independent Norway was a milestone in the history of peace, the celebration of a war that never happened. The following year all frontier forts were razed and the long boundary between the two countries was left open and undefended, a demilitarized border, part of a pledge from both nations to create a "no-war" community.[149] Norway joined the family of nations, and not a shot had been fired.

In 1907, the new Norway set another example for the world by declaring itself perpetually neutral and formally withdrew from all international conflicts, present or future. At the same time it obtained a guarantee of its neutral status from the four most important powers of the era, Great Britain, France, Germany and Russia.[150]

* * *

In the calm and hopeful days that preceded the First World War Andrew Carnegie was one of the most enthusiastic supporters of world peace. For him, it was not some distant goal but a near reality, just over the horizon, almost within grasp. He was a believer in what has been called business pacifism, a concept that rejected all things military as out-of-date and useless in an industrial world designed to produce and sell goods. This idea sprang from two roots: the Puritan version of Protestant morality, according to which war was equated with evil, and economic liberalism, whose fundamental tenet was free trade.

Carnegie also accepted a variant of Herbert Spencer's (1820–1903) theory of evolution, which argued that the world was rapidly evolving away from primitive violence. Thus, as interpreted by Carnegie, what Spencer really meant by the phrase "the survival of the fittest" was "the survival of the most peaceful." Just as dueling and religious hatred had largely disappeared in the Western world, so too, Carnegie believed, would national rivalries and wars. His confident credo became "The world grows better."[151] He wrote in his *Autobiography* that "the abolition of war grew in importance with me until it finally overshadowed all other issues."[152]

Carnegie had a fortune at his disposal to support his almost boundless optimism in the future. In fact, Andrew Carnegie gave away more money to the cause of world peace than any other person in recorded history, including Albert Nobel.[153]

In 1903, Carnegie donated $1.5 million (approximately $35 million in today's U.S. dollars) to create a home for arbitration, the Peace Palace in The Hague. The first stone was laid during the Second Peace Conference, and it was finally completed in 1913, just one year before the European war began.[154] The building now houses the International Court of Justice, better known as the World Court, the Permanent Court of Arbitration and The Hague Academy of International Law.

At the close of the Second Hague Conference, Carnegie told a journalist, "The time is coming, much more rapidly than we dream, when war will be a thing of the past." And he added, speaking about the conference, "In spite of all that may have been said, [it] accomplished much for the cause of peace [...]. It is to meet again. It will be permanent." And when Carnegie spoke, people listened. His comments were published the next day on the front pages of the *Times* in London and the *New York Times*.[155]

As he advanced in life Carnegie became increasingly pacifistic and ignored the fact that he had made a large part of his hundreds of millions of dollars selling steel to the war industry. Perhaps his volte-face was an act of atonement, a way of compensating for his previous jingoistic support of America's wars. In his final years he spoke out clearly and became the voice of an unbounded optimism, a convert to the perfectibility of man and civilization: "I believe that in the twentieth century the earth will be purged of its foulest stain, the killing of men by men in battle under the name of war and that the profession of arms [...] will be held unworthy of any being in human form. To kill a man in that day will be considered as disgusting as we in this day consider it disgusting to eat one."[156]

Carnegie sought to use his millions to rebuild society, to create, among other things, a culture that drew its heroes not from the ranks of the ribboned military, but from those men and women who brought out the noble, altruistic side of mankind, for example, those who had undertaken to save another's life with no motive of reward.

Thus Carnegie created the Hero Fund to honor Americans or Canadians whom he called "heroes of civilization," whose lifesaving actions put them in stark contrast to "heroes of barbarism who maimed or killed" their fellow man. Carnegie was especially proud of the fund and consistently took part in its deliberations. As he explained, "I cherish a fatherly regard for it [the Hero Fund] since no one suggested it to me, and as far as I know, it has never been thought of."[157]

In fact, many people had thought of it. In one form or another, the idea had been circulating in the peace movement for a long time. Edwin D. Mead (1849–1937), for example, director for many years of the World Peace Foundation, had written several essays on the subject:

> The streets and squares of Washington swarm with statues; but it is no exaggeration to say that three quarters of them are of generals and admirals [...]. There is next to nothing among them to remind the visitor from Mars or from Maryland that the nation of Washington and Jefferson and Franklin [...] ever produced a poet or historian, a scholar or teacher, a painter or sculptor, a philosopher or philanthropist, a statesman or a man of science worthy of notice, or that up to date it really honors enough to spend any money to show it any vocation save the warrior's. It is the measure of our barbarism.[158]

Carnegie's Hero Fund is still in existence. To date it has awarded more than 9,000 medals selected from more than 80,000 nominees and has paid out a total of $29.4 million in benefits. A candidate for the award must be a civilian who voluntarily risks his or her life to an extraordinary degree while attempting to save the life of another person.[159] Carnegie was trying to create a new class of heroes, men and women who didn't lead a charge or slay others in battle but who, at the risk of their own lives, had tried to save others, in other words, exhibited the most altruistic form of heroism, each one "a rescuer who leaves a place of safety and knowingly risks death to save the life of another, without an obligation to do so."[160]

The first award went to Louis A. Baumann, Jr. (1890–1925), who jumped into a river and saved a friend from drowning. Eight more awards were made at the same time, including one to Ernestine F. Atwood (1887–?), who became the first female awardee. She saved a man from drowning by diving under a float where he had become lodged and pulled him to safety. A student of fine arts in Boston, she was also the first to benefit from the Fund's scholarship program.

In over a hundred years thousands of heroic acts have been recorded, verified, and rewarded, among them more than 3,000 rescues from water, nearly a thousand from burning vehicles, another thousand from burning buildings, hundreds from ships, and others from exposure to the elements, electrocutions, explosions, avalanches, just about every life-threatening situation conceivably possible.[161]

Rewarding acts of civil bravery was only one part of Carnegie's goal. The other was publicizing those acts so that gradually they would supplant those of the military. The initial reactions of the press were favorable, for example: "Every time that Mr. Carnegie's Commission can hold up before us […] acts of a fine, fearless sort, worthy of thought and memory […] they have done us a service. The sight may not make heroes of us, but at least it will melt off something of the crust of cynicism and selfishness which has been blinding our eyes."[162] Or another, from a popular periodical of the day: "In a time when every possible crime, every form of meanness and selfishness, is exploited at great length by the newspapers, it is well that the story of good deeds should be told as often and as completely as possible."[163]

Of course, there were the skeptics and detractors. Some columnists asked if Carnegie was promoting heroes for hire, or did a heroic person have to dive in the water headfirst or would jumping in be enough? One humorist quipped, could a man qualify as a hero if he had lived with his wife's relations for five years?

But by and large the press accepted the Carnegie heroes as welcome good news and gave their accounts the prominence they deserved. Eventually articles about the Hero Fund appeared in such magazines as *Reader's Digest, Saturday Evening Post, Esquire, Harper's Weekly, McCall's, Redbook, Family Circle, Life*, and many more.

Carnegie expanded the hero concept in 1908 with the establishment of the British Carnegie Hero Fund Trust, then in 1909 with a French Fund, and in 1910 with one in Germany with the Kaiser as the supreme patron.

Carnegie wrote to the Kaiser: "I consider this in harmony with my work for the abolition of war. Peace has its heroes much more renowned than those of war. Industrialism is producing heroes in every country. There is no accident where volunteers are called for that the number responding does not exceed that required. It is of good omen that the Hero Fund begins in Germany on New Year's Day."[164]

In 1911, Hero Funds were also established in Norway, Holland, Switzerland, Belgium, Italy, Denmark and Sweden, and all of them are still in existence, still making awards for acts of noble and unselfish bravery.[165]

Carnegie placed his confidence in the belief that man possesses an inherent rationality, thus if belligerents could meet and communicate with one another they would easily solve their differences. Men, any man, no matter where he lived and what he believed, would prefer words to weapons. But to do that they had to speak the same language. Carnegie was convinced that English should be, and would be, the lingua franca for the world. However, before this could occur, he had concluded, there was "a chief obstacle" to be overcome. He believed that a foreigner found it difficult to learn English because of its spelling. The solution was obvious: modify the spelling. Hence, Carnegie sponsored the American Simplified Spelling Board, working with Melvil Dewey (1851–1931), of Dewey decimal library classification fame. Carnegie endowed the group with $170,000 (equal to over $3 million today) and an additional $25,000 per year.[166]

Examples of "corrected" spelling proposed by the Board were: "bizness" for "business," "enuf" for "enough," "fether" for "feather," "mesure" for "measure," "plesure" for "pleasure," "red" for "read" (past tense), "ruf" for "rough," "thru" for "through," "tung" for "tongue," "yung" for "young," and so on. It was not intended to be a panacea, but Carnegie hoped it would ease the learning process.

Once the proposal went public it unleashed a firestorm of rhetoric, a few voices supporting the proposed changes; most, bitterly against.

On the one hand, the British poet Charles Swinburne (1837–1909) railed that the whole idea was "a barbarous, monstrous absurdity," while Conan Doyle (1859–1930) stormed that "reformed spelling might become universal but it would cease to be the English language."[167] On the other hand, President Roosevelt initially ordered all government printing offices to use the new spellings, and for a short period a number of newspapers used them as well. Nonetheless, a virulent campaign of English-language purists soon drowned out the reformists. After a great deal of money, many years of effort, and volumes of verbiage, the American Simplified Spelling Board withered into a footnote.[168]

Carnegie was not the only person to realize the necessity for men to be able to speak a common language if they ever hoped to live together peacefully. Ludoviko Zamenhof (1859–1917), a native of Bialystok in what is today Belarus, addressed the same problem, but he arrived at a rather different conclusion. What the world needed, Zamenhof decided, was a common second language, a simple one, straightforward, and without irrational irregularities or arbitrary idioms. Zamenhof's idea was that everyone should continue to speak their own language but use another one, available to all, to speak with anyone outside their language community. Since such a language did not exist, he set out to create what he called a *lingvo internacia*, a simple, logical verbal stew of the common European languages that would be easy to learn and easy to use. He published it under the pseudonym of Dr. Esperanto, which means "one who hopes" in the new language. Thus Esperanto was born. It immediately attracted attention, and soon enough people could speak the language to justify holding world congresses. The syncretic language reached its height at roughly the same time that

Carnegie was trying to simplify English spelling, and it still stutters on today. But it has fallen far short of its goal. No country has adopted Esperanto officially as a second language.[169]

Carnegie was an acute observer of the international scene and in the opening years of the century he correctly surmised that the German Kaiser was the major obstacle to European peace. Carnegie had met the Kaiser in 1907 and put forward a proposal for a League for Peace, which would be composed of the United States, Great Britain, France, Russia and Germany. If these great powers could agree to refer international disputes to the Permanent Court of Arbitration that had been established by the First Hague Peace Conference, Carnegie was certain a war could be averted. And should one of the powers refuse to agree to a decision of the court, then economic sanctions would be used. Force of arms would only be considered as a last resort.[170]

On the one hand, the Kaiser was not easily convinced. On the other hand, Carnegie was not easily dissuaded. Displaying his characteristic optimism and determination, he set out to somehow persuade the Kaiser to join the League for Peace. Carnegie wrote to the German ambassador to the United States that "something tells me that sooner or later he [the Kaiser] will fulfill his destiny and become the world's peace-maker."[171]

With this objective squarely in mind, in early 1910 Carnegie persuaded Theodore Roosevelt, then an ex–President, to meet with the Kaiser and present the case for arbitration. Roosevelt was extremely popular in Germany, and Carnegie knew that the Kaiser admired him.[172]

Like Carnegie, Roosevelt was a believer in arbitration, but with qualifications. When President, he had encouraged the Great Powers to arbitrate their disputes at The Hague and limit their armaments. However, his own experience with the lawlessness of frontier life had taught him that it was "both foolish and wicked to persuade [a man] to surrender his arms while the men who are dangerous to the community retain theirs."[173] For Roosevelt, a lasting peace required a police power to enforce the decrees of the court, any court, and especially an international one. In his Nobel acceptance speech Roosevelt committed himself to the creation of some kind of league of peace, the nucleus of a world government with the power to settle international disputes and enforce their decisions: "It would be a master stroke if those great powers honestly bent on peace would form a League of Peace, not only to keep the peace among themselves, but to prevent, by force if necessary, its being broken by others. [...] the ruler or statesman who should bring about such a combination would have earned his place in history for all time and his title to the gratitude of all mankind."[174] It seems Carnegie had chosen the right man to carry a message of arbitration and arms limitations to the Kaiser.

Roosevelt and the Kaiser met and spent an entire day on horseback watching a display of Prussian military might, 12,000 soldiers engaging in a mock combat. The Kaiser and Roosevelt spoke continuously in English. The Kaiser had spent much of his youth in England, as the two royal families were linked by blood. Edward VII, King of England at the time, was, in fact, the Kaiser's uncle.

According to Roosevelt, the Kaiser raised the subject of disarmament, then quickly dismissed it by saying, "The German people [...] would never consent to Germany's failing to keep herself able to enforce her rights either on land or at sea." When the talk turned to relations between England and Germany, Roosevelt ventured the opinion that a war between them would be "an unspeakable calamity."

"Next to Germany," the Kaiser is reported to have replied, "I care more for England than for any other country. I feel myself partly an Englishman." Then, with such force that Roosevelt wrote it in his notes in capital letters, Wilhelm exclaimed, "I ADORE ENGLAND!"[175]

Roosevelt continued writing in his diary: "I said that this was a stronger statement than I myself would be willing quite to make, but that I was very glad he felt so, because I believed that the English, Germans and Americans ought to be fundamentally in accord; and that nothing would so make for the peace and progress of the world. He answered that he entirely agreed with me."[176]

Roosevelt left Germany entirely convinced that Kaiser Wilhelm II could be an annoyance from time to time but only a minor threat to world peace. He was also convinced that the Kaiser would never join Carnegie's League for Peace.

* * *

Eliminating the martial template that had traditionally stamped the educational system had always been a principal aim of the Western world's peace groups. Abolish the study of nationalism, the worship of military heroes, the glory of the battlefield, and the past could be totally redefined. The school system needed a new model, a pacifist one that would bring out the best in man and not his barbaric worst. If there was any hope that the next generation would not repeat the mistakes of the previous ones, it lay in a total reform of the educational system, its subject matter, its teaching methods and its textbooks.

In the United States more than 5,000 delegates from public and private schools attended the First National Peace Congress in 1907, and immediately after that the American School Peace League was organized. A former teacher, Fannie Fern Andrews (1867–1950), became the executive director, and she devoted herself to the cause. With an optimism that was characteristic of the moment she declared that "it seemed to me, the day of better things was dawning, and I coveted the opportunity to enter the field."[177]

The League's goal was to "promote through the schools and the educational public of America, the interests of international justice and fraternity."[178] In other words, children should focus on events like the great victories of arbitration and the speeches and deliberations of the First Hague Peace Conference, and not on the nation's military history and prowess.

But even without the efforts of the American School Peace League during the first decade of the century the nation's school system was gradually becoming less bellicose. A study revealed that textbooks published between 1843 and 1885 devoted almost 40 percent of their entire content to the details of war, while those published between 1890 and 1904 averaged less than 27 percent.[179]

One of the first things that Andrews did was create an official "Peace Day," May 18th, the day the First Peace Conference opened at The Hague in 1899. Andrews launched a massive nationwide campaign to observe it, and to a large extent she was successful. By 1914 the League's guide detailing how to celebrate "Peace Day" sold more than 65,000 copies despite the fact that at the time there were only 15,000 high schools in the United States. Andrews traveled back and forth across the country tirelessly speaking to educators and educational organizations, journalists and publishers.

The American School Peace League also tried to involve teachers in other countries and thereby lay a solid pacifistic foundation for the future. Education, Andrews believed, based on the principles of peace, could span continents and even language differences. If the next generation, no matter where they might be in the world, studied the same concepts of international relations and justice, then there was a good possibility that they might behave according to these concepts. In other words, build a common history and you build a common future. With this firmly in mind, Andrews and the American organizers of the School Peace League set out to reform not only the American educational system but that of the entire world. And they were greatly encouraged by the fact that whereas in America there were hundreds, if not thousands, of independent school districts, in Europe, with its centralized systems of education, there was only one organization per country. A branch of the School Peace League was quickly established in France, another in Great Britain,[180] and even German teachers and ministers of education promised their cooperation.

The League's most ambitious endeavor was its attempt to transform the American school curriculum from a war orientation to a peace perspective. The goal was to provide a 400-page, comprehensive program of study for grades 1–8 with lesson plans for moral, social, and intellectual development. In first grade, for example, the curriculum proposed a unit titled "Avoiding Quarrels and Making Peace," which was essentially a conflict resolution program designed to teach children how to manage their anger. Second grade contained a section called "Peace Among Children" and another about "The Golden Rule." Students also studied the "Childhood of Great Men," with examples taken from the lives of Moses, Horace Mann and Ben Franklin. Women such as Louisa May Alcott and Joan of Arc were also included, and the equality of the sexes was a recurrent theme. Third grade addressed a broader perspective, "Peace Among Neighbors," and in the eighth grade respect and tolerance were extended to international relations, the message being that other nations are not barbarians, other races not inferior, nor other faiths godless. A section on the "World Family" posed the question: "Can war achieve any positive results among the world's civilized peoples?"[181]

A leitmotif running through all grade levels was the study of "peace heroes" modeled on the idea proposed by Andrew Carnegie. Children were also taught respect for animals, natural resources, and the earth, but above all the objective was to create a universal mind, a responsible, informed global citizen with a respect for international law. Andrews wrote in one of the organization's pamphlets: "The opening of the First Hague Peace Conference was [...] the beginning of a new epoch for international law [...]. The hope of civilization lies in the progressive effort which has given the family of nations [...] an international lawmaking body. Law is the only substitute for war."[182]

Using this perspective as a foundation, in the curriculum peace was defined for perhaps the first time in a strictly educational context. That definition has stood the test of times and continues to be a basis for current peace study programs: "Peace through justice implies that peace may be attained by eliminating social oppression and economic exploitation. Peace through justice is concerned with the elimination of poverty, disease, starvation, human misery, and with the preservation of human rights."[183]

At the same time, the curriculum tried to emphasize the values deemed essential for fostering a spirit of internationalism and becoming a world citizen: "responsibility," "faithfulness," "obedience," "fair play," "cheerfulness," "service," and "self-control."

At the height of the movement thousands of teachers in 40 states were involved, either directly or through teachers' organizations that participated. The American School Peace League channeled books, pamphlets and study guides to the schools, all designed to create a rational structure for peace. There were also annual peace prize contests, both local and national. But despite an avalanche of printed materials, contests and touring speakers, in the end the American School Peace League found it difficult to superimpose the principles of peace upon a system of 19th-century nationalism that fused patriotism with military prowess and accepted international warfare as an honorable means of settling international disputes. For most schools, peace became at best just one more item added to the curriculum.

Andrews had not expected an easy victory and was not dissuaded. When she realized that peace was becoming an addendum to war and not a substitute, she raised more money and even expanded her goals. With the blessing of the American President and the aid of the State Department, the League contacted European teachers' organizations asking them if they would participate in an international summit that would unify the teaching of peace, a kind of Hague conference focused on education. Most countries were receptive and 16 agreed to send official representatives. The date of the conference was postponed several times and finally set for 1915. However, the guns of August 1914 effectively canceled it and for a time also silenced the League.[184]

* * *

One of the major backers of the American School Peace League was Edwin Ginn, a publisher of textbooks and one of the wealthiest men of his day. In his late fifties he became a convert to the peace movement and with vigor and an open pocketbook he quite literally set out to change the world. "War," he declared, was "the foulest fiend ever vomited forth from the mouth of Hell."[185] Very prophetically he predicted: "If war expenses are to continue to increase in the next hundred years as they have in the last century, the accumulations of civilization are in danger of being destroyed and the nations made insolvent."[186]

Why Ginn suddenly made this transformation from a rather staid, slightly blind publisher to a dynamic and passionate crusader for peace is not clear. He didn't keep a diary and seemed to confide in no one. But obviously something, some person, event or book, changed him from one day to the next, and before he was finished he had spent over a third of his fortune trying to educate Americans and Europeans about the waste of war, the power of reason, and the perfectibility of man. He set out to attack the culture of war, the glorification of battles, the so-called fighting spirit that is learned in the classroom at a young age. Ginn knew it would take generations to change the nation's mentality and therefore attacked the base of the learning pyramid. Schools, he believed, should encourage students to realize that war is cruel and crippling: "Every book put into the hands of [...] children should be carefully examined and everything [...] that would tend to encourage [...] a martial spirit should be carefully weeded out."[187]

Like many men of his day Ginn believed in an inherent rationality of man, in the power of words, in the process of education. For him, the solution was simple. Provide people with enough knowledge and they will act on it and treat others fairly and honestly.

In 1910 Ginn founded the International School of Peace, which was not exactly a school but a mechanism to acquaint students and teachers with the literature of peace. The name was soon changed to the World Peace Foundation. Its aim was "to educate people about the evil and wastefulness of war, to encourage international justice and generally by every practical means to promote peace and good will among all mankind."[188]

In fact, Ginn was more interested in the teachers than the students. The teachers, he believed, were part of an elite, opinion-making class, a literate intelligentsia that, once convinced by the power of reason, would help him literally change the world. Wars, Ginn believed, are the result of not malice but simply misguided thinking and a primitive impulse that human beings could overcome. Thus words, logic, rationality and just common sense would be enough to change people's minds, and these could all be packaged into books. He believed that when nations have to explain and justify their actions to an active, informed public "the end of war will be in sight; for no man living can remember a war whose inauguration would have been able to abide the world's critical discussion."[189]

Ginn produced the International Library of Peace, an impressive collection of peace literature that was published at or below cost and sold to the public for a pittance. The first year it circulated over 300,000 pamphlets, which included tracts from works such as Jean de Bloch's *The Future of War*, Leo Tolstoy's *Bethink Yourselves*, Immanuel Kant's *Eternal Peace*, and Bertha von Süttner's *Memoirs*. It was a noble and ambitious endeavor, a humanistic attempt to implement democratic theory.[190]

The Foundation also sponsored a broad peace education program of speeches and lectures in the United States and overseas. Representatives were recruited to act as ambassadors who were trained to influence school curricula in order to reduce the glorification of militarism and war.

These "ambassadors" came from a wide range of peace activists and did not necessarily mirror Ginn's thinking. David Starr Jordan (1851–1931), the president of Stanford University, for example, delivered more than 100 lectures across the United States and 64 in Japan and Korea. His anti-war position, however, was based on eugenics, the belief in selective breeding applied to humans. The theory was quite popular at the time. Jordan was opposed to war because he believed it removed the strongest members of the species from the gene pool. After finishing a tour of lectures in Japan he wrote to Ginn: "I do not find in Japan any of the spirit of war for war's sake, which has been the bane of European politics, nor any desire [...] for international aggression."[191]

In 1913 Norman Angell delivered a number of lectures sponsored by the Foundation in the United States. His best-selling book was then in its fourth edition and had made Angell into a celebrity whose movements and speeches were front-page news.

Ginn was delighted by Angell's message that war between "civilized" nations was unproductive and unprofitable and that growing international trade and credit was gradually binding the nations of Europe together. Ginn wrote: "I am deeply impressed with [...] Angell's grasp of the needs of our foundation. He is by all odds the most far-seeing man that I have yet met."[192]

On the eve of the First World War Angell was assuring his American audiences that no matter how bellicose the European powers became, no matter how many battleships they built or how large their armies, war was still an impossibility.

* * *

Vrede door Recht (Peace Through Justice), the Dutch Peace Society, also made a serious effort to change the educational system by revising textbooks. The lesson was obvious—to eradicate war one must first change the way people think about both themselves and others beyond their frontiers. Thus the Dutch Peace Society sought to eliminate passages that contained a national bias and in their place weave in principles of equality and social justice. They also tried to de-emphasize so-called war heroes, those whose swords were steeped in blood. As an initial effort, they produced 25,000 copies of a highly illustrated children's book about the life of Hugo Grotius (1583–1645),[193] the father of international law. The book was distributed to elementary schools and, to make it more appealing to a young audience, the authors highlighted Grotius's dramatic escape concealed in a book chest from the castle where he was imprisoned.[194]

The Dutch Peace Society became well-known for its advocacy of an international police force, which would become a guarantee for justice as well as a means to enforce the decisions made by the courts of arbitration at The Hague.[195] As this international police force assumed more and more responsibility for the maintenance of peace it was hoped that it would dramatically lessen the need for states to arm themselves.

The idea of some kind of internationalized force was an obvious solution, a way to use existing military might for a positive purpose. In the decade before the war it was a popular theme, a recurrent topic on the literature and lecture circuits, a cascade of words devoted to its legality, moral rights, and practicality.[196]

In the United States the first person of international prominence to support the idea of "peace coercion" was Theodore Roosevelt (1858–1919), who spoke about the need to create an "international sheriff." Roosevelt mentioned the concept again when he received the Nobel Peace Prize in 1910 but didn't provide any details.[197] The same year a bill was submitted to Congress and subsequently received the consent of both Houses, proposing a worldwide limitation on armaments. The bill also invited other countries "to consider the expediency [...] of constituting the combined navies of the world in an international force for the preservation of universal peace."[198]

The congressional resolution did not spark an international conference, but it did represent the mood of America, a feeling that something positive should or must be done to preserve the peace. One journalist wrote: "The establishment of an overwhelming international force, before which the forces of any single nation, however powerful, would find themselves overmatched, seems to prudent men, who try to base their reasoning about the future on past and present facts, the most promising method of protecting Europe from the recurrence of such a catastrophe as it is now experiencing."[199]

Many people thought the problem was just to find the right formula, filling in the details that would make a peace plan feasible. Hendrik Dunlop (1867–

1944), for example, from the Dutch Peace Party, suggested the formation of an "international *gendarmerie*," that is, a police, whose strength would be 1 percent of the population, with contingents in every country. Twenty-five percent of each contingent would consist of police troops native to the territory where the contingents were located. This opened up a battle of numbers that filled lecture halls and journals for a short time but produced no concrete results.

Edwin Ginn proposed what he called an "international army," rather than police force, to be composed of 10 percent of each nation's military. This new army would "take up stations" in those localities where friction was likely to occur and thus become a deterrent. As the international army gradually assumed the responsibility for maintaining peace, the need for national armies would decrease. That at least was the principle. But Ginn was a realist and knew that it could not possibly happen soon. He remarked: "The war system has been so long in the building, it has taken hold of the lives of men so firmly, that it cannot be shaken off suddenly."[200]

* * *

In the years before the First World War peace societies bloomed in Japan. Following their European counterparts, they did their best to educate the masses, especially the working class, and introduce the concept of arbitration as a means to settle international disputes. With the outbreak of hostilities between Russia and Japan in 1904, the small Japanese Socialist Party took up the crusade for peace.

The presses of the *Heimin Shimbun*, the organ of Japanese socialism, launched a continuous tirade against the militaristic state, a stream of articles depicting the horrors of war in the most graphic terms possible, the agony of the soldiers who would be butchered on the battlefield, the grieving children soon to become orphans, and the rampant avarice of war contractors.[201] The Japanese government did nothing to stop it, for they knew that few people listened. And they were right. The beginning of the Russo-Japanese War was greeted by a wave of intense nationalism.

As long as the Japanese armies continued to advance and every headline heralded another conquest, the socialist press was largely ignored. According to one critic, its fervent appeals had as much effect as "Buddhist prayers in a horse's ear."[202]

However, when the war slowed to stalemate at the gates of Port Arthur and the casualties mounted, people started to listen to the anti-war appeals and the government acted to curtail criticism. The *Heimin Shimbun* was closed down and its editors thrown in jail. The decision was quickly appealed, and two months later, to the surprise of many, the ban on the newspaper was lifted and the editors freed. The *Heimin Shimbun* immediately returned to its anti-war campaign. But now all subscribers received visits from the police and were told to buy other newspapers. Newsstands selling the newspaper were also intimidated. Initially circulation dipped, then it slowly began to rise. The newspaper editorialized:

> If Socialists were reckless enough to resort to violent actions, it would be quite proper for the Government to use police force for the sake of social peace, but not one accusation of this kind can be brought against them. Are they not denouncing war all the time, because they believe that no violent action is justifiable at any time? We may say, without much exaggeration, that all Japanese socialists are peace-lovers in the extreme sense and that they are exactly the people for whom no police authority is required.[203]

The Japanese socialists were the only organized anti-war movement, but there were individuals who also struggled to make themselves heard. Just six weeks after the war began, Kinoshita Naoe (1869–1937) wrote in the *Mainichi Shimbun*, then one of the largest newspapers in Japan, that "the loyalty and patriotism that reporters now extol are nothing but cheap demagoguery and cannot be called true love of country."[204] His book, *Pillar of Fire*, published during the war, is perhaps Japan's foremost anti-war novel. At one point the protagonist says: "Those who clamor for war with Russia say that it will be a fight between freedom and tyranny, between civilization and barbarism. In my opinion they are utterly mistaken. It will merely be a war between two governments each as tyrannical, as barbarous as the other."[205] Kinoshita was cut off from the main thrust of the Japanese anti-war movement by his belief that war originated in the minds of people and therefore an individual, "human revolution" rather than a social revolution was essential for world peace.[206]

Unchimura Kanzo (1861–1930), was another voice of pacifism, but hardly one in the wilderness. At the beginning of the Russo-Japanese War he was the editor of the *Yorozo Choho*, which would soon become the largest daily newspaper in Japan. Previously he had denounced the way the Japanese had slaughtered the Chinese in the Sino-Japanese war (1894–1895) as "a wild boar hunt." Four months after the Russo-Japanese war began he published an article titled "For the Abolition of War." In it he condemned armed conflict as "nothing but an enormous crime"[207]: "War is diabolical [...], an insatiable beast which increasingly craves human blood as it drinks it. Modern war has replaced the love of money as the mother of all evils."[208] To protest the continuation of the war, Unchimura resigned his post as editor but continued to wage his anti-military crusade. For him, a deeply religious man, pacifism was "the single touchstone" of any faith.[209]

Another journalist who resigned from the *Yorozo Choho* was Kotoku Shusui (1871–1911), who argued that patriotism was an integral part of militarism since it had its origin in a hatred of the enemy rather than a true love of one's country. In a series of articles published in the *Heimin Shinbun*, he criticized the government for trying to indoctrinate schoolchildren and teach them to love war. He also attacked the economic arguments supporting the war with Russia, pointing out that the wars with China, 1894–1895, and the Boxer Rebellion had been of no benefit to the nation as a whole. Even the huge indemnity paid by China was spent on the military instead of being used for the benefit of those who had sacrificed their health, their limbs or their sons to the cause of a greater Japan. And he correctly predicted that ultimately the war against Russia would be far more costly than that against China. Where would the money come from? Increased taxes and borrowing from abroad were the only sources and that was precisely what occurred.[210] Kotoku advocated radical change, overthrowing the present government of "slaughter, hardship and corruption" and replacing it with one dedicated to "peace, welfare and progress."[211]

Did these men have any effect on the course of the Russo-Japanese War? Probably not, which is why the Japanese government tolerated their dissent. But they did mirror the thoughts of thousands of anti-war Japanese who subscribed to the *Heimin Shinbun*. Kinoshita Naoe, Unchimura Kanzo and Kotoku Shusui became markers of moral courage, samurai of peace, whose impassioned arguments undoubtedly encouraged other Japanese to follow their lead.

At the same time that Japanese socialists tried to influence their countrymen, they also attempted to speak to the world, and especially to their adversary. They published an open letter addressed to the people of Russia and, via neutral countries, sent it there, where it was reprinted and circulated: "We cannot foresee which of the two countries [Japan or Russia] will win, but the result of the war will be the same—general poverty, new and heavy taxes, the undermining of morality, and the extension of militarism."[212]

A few months later a Russian replied. Leo Tolstoy (1828–1910) published an appeal in the *London Times* attacking war in general and the Russo-Japanese war in particular.[213] "Bethink Yourselves" could not be published in Russia but was reprinted extensively all over the world, including Japan, where the *Heimin Shimbun* republished it in Japanese as a pamphlet.

Tolstoy was well-known in Japan thanks to Tokutomi Roka[214] (1868–1927), a popular novelist, who published translations of some of Tolstoy's works as well as a biography and analyses of his essays. He acknowledged that his own novels were modeled on scenes from Tolstoy's most famous stories. After reading a copy in English of Tokutomi's first best-selling novel, *The Cuckoo*, Tolstoy told a friend that it was "an imitation of Western literature, particularly my own."[215]

More than 8,000 copies of *Bethink Yourselves* were handed out freely at Japanese public anti-war meetings and scores of students used their vacations to distribute the leaflet in the countryside. Tolstoy's opening paragraphs are perhaps the most well-known:

> Again war. Again sufferings, necessary to nobody, utterly uncalled for: again fraud, again universal stupefaction and brutalization of men.
> Men who are separated from each other by thousands of miles, hundreds of

thousands of such men (on the one hand Buddhists, whose law forbids the killing, not only of men but of animals; on the other hand Christians, professing the law of brotherhood and love) like wild beasts on land and on sea are seeking out each other, in order to kill, torture, and mutilate each other in the most cruel way. What can this be? Is it a dream or a reality? Something is taking place which should not, cannot be; one longs to believe that it is a dream and to awake from it.

But no, it is not a dream, it is a dreadful reality![216]

Not everyone in the Japanese anti-war movement was in agreement with *Bethink Yourselves*. Tolstoy's passionate appeal revealed a division within the ranks. Christian pacifists and socialists may have had the same immediate objective, stop the killing and end the war as quickly as possible, but their motivations and ultimate goals were very different. One of the socialists wrote: "Tolstoy ascribes the causes of war to the debasement of man and, accordingly, desires to save man by teaching repentance. We socialists attribute the cause of war to economic competition and, thus, we seek to prevent war by abolishing economic competition."[217]

According to police reports at that time there were about 25,000 socialists in the country, although quite likely this number was inflated.[218] After a little more than a year of publication the Japanese government was finally goaded into action by the military and shut down the socialist presses and threw the editors into jail. This time there was no appeal. Without leaders and a public voice, the Japanese anti-war movement was effectively crushed.

When the Treaty of Portsmouth put an end to the fighting, the editors of the Japanese socialist anti-war press were let out of jail. The printing presses began to roll once again, but the war of words had ended; the rhetoric sounded hollow and blunted. Looking back at their wartime efforts, one of the editors wrote: "It is perhaps the first time in the history of Japan that the cry, 'Down with war' has been raised in the land of the samurai."[219]

The socialists hailed the Treaty of Portsmouth as proof that the process of mediation worked and that there was, in fact, a nascent international system that could stop a war and bring the belligerents to the peace table. While the world basically agreed with them, public opinion in both Russia and Japan fundamentally disagreed. In both countries people felt that their sacrifices had been in vain. Their biggest defeat had been at the conference table. Everything had been lost in the negotiation.

When the Japanese Foreign Minister, Marquis Komura Jutarō (1855–1911), left for the United States, crowds at the port of Yokohama shouted, *"Bonzai!"* Reportedly Komura turned to an aide and said, "Now they cheer. When I return they will shout '*Bakayaro!*'" (stupid fool). And so they did. When the results of the Treaty of Portsmouth were announced, the Japanese public felt they had been betrayed by their diplomats and the American mediators. They had won the war but lost the peace. With only one exception all the nearly 2,000 newspapers in Japan denounced the treaty as a national disgrace.[220]

In Tokyo a riotous crowd of 30,000 marched across the city and clashed with the police. The riots lasted for two days. When order was finally restored, angry mobs had destroyed or damaged more than 350 buildings, seventeen people had been killed and over 450 policemen injured. Hundreds were arrested.

A Tokyo newspaper fanned the flames:

> Come! Come! Come! A national assembly to protest the treaty is going to be held today at Hibiya. Come, those who have blood. Come, those who have tears. Come, those who have backbones. Come, those who have wills. Come, those who know justice. Come, those who know shame. Come, and all together raise a voice of opposition to the humiliating and shameful peace. His Majesty will surely appreciate the sincerity of his subjects.[221]

The violence quickly spread to Kobe and Yokahama and hundreds of other rallies and protests. Nonetheless, the Japanese government quickly ratified the treaty, as did the Russian government. Mediation succeeded. Reason had prevailed. The war was over.

* * *

As Europe spiraled toward war, in the German 1912 general elections the Social Democrats (the SPD, Sozialdemokratische Partei Deutschlands) obtained 34 percent of the vote. With 110 members in the Reichstag, they became Germany's strongest single party, by definition a party of peace.

The SPD had often been called men without a fatherland (*vaterlandlose Gesellen*) and for decades they waged a "war on war." According to socialist theory the workingman had no home, no flag, no nationality, and should in times of war refuse to participate in both the army and the manufacture of weapons. This anti-war unity of purpose, shared by all the socialists of Europe, was to have been their antidote to war. The logic was simple and irrefutable. No matter how bellicose the generals and politicians became, without men willing to fight and workers willing to manufacture arms and ammunition war would not be possible. There was no need for treaties or alliances or secret covenants. If threatened, the politicized workers of Europe would act in their own collective interest.

In 1912 the SPD attended a meeting of all Europe's socialist parties at Basel, Switzerland. The noted French socialist Jean Jaurès (1859–1914) set the tone: "We will leave this hall committed to the salvation of peace and civilization."[222]

Victor Adler (1852–1918), leader of the Austrian Social Democratic Party, spoke for the Germanic peoples:

> We come from a country whose ruling classes are at this very moment engaged in fateful decisions and the thought oppresses us that while we assemble here for

peace, the decision hangs in the balance, not only in Petersburg, but also in Berlin and Vienna, whether we should march or not [...]. The hour is coming when the proletariat will use its voice to indict, and the hour is coming when the proletariat will also have the sword to execute judgment.[223]

To prepare for that "hour" a resolution against war was introduced, then enthusiastically adopted by all the major socialist parties of Europe, including the Germans. It declared:

> This congress [...] calls upon the workers of all countries to oppose capitalist imperialism with the power of the international solidarity of the working class [...]. It would be insane should governments not realise that the mere thought of the monstrosity of a world war would evoke the outrage and anger of the working class. The proletariat regards it as criminal should they be forced to shoot at one another in order to further the profits of capitalists, the ambitions of dynasties or in order to honour secret diplomatic treaties.[224]

Immediately after the Basel Congress, when it appeared that hostilities might break out as a result of the Balkan wars, the SPD, true to it credo, organized protests all over Germany, culminating with an anti-war mass rally in Berlin that drew a crowd of more than a quarter of a million people.

However, at the same time the SPD began to gradually advocate what they euphemistically called tactical nationalism, support for Prussian militarism. The uncompromising stand that the party had taken against war for nearly 50 years slowly began to crumble. The SPD was no longer preaching that the working class knew no frontiers, that international conflict could be stopped by proletarian action, that nationalism was a tool of the ruling class.

In 1914, with war clearly on the horizon, the SPD had shifted their position radically to become in favor of *ein wehrhaftes Volk* (a strong nation), thus supporting Germany's "defensive" posture. The SPD had performed an almost incredible volte-face and when the fighting started at an SPD meeting 78 of the 92 members present voted in favor of granting the government the "war credits" it needed to pursue military action.[225]

Bertram Wolfe (1896–1977), a chronicler of the political left, summarized the socialist collapse in Europe at the beginning of the war:

> [T]he German socialists voted the war credits and a *Burgfrieden* [civil peace] for the duration. The French socialists, given to the more poetic phrase, formed a *sacred union*, and entered into the government of their country. The Belgian leaders declared that they would never meet with a German socialist as long as there were German troops on Belgian soil. In land after land, the socialists showed that they were Frenchmen, Germans, Englishmen, Belgians, before they were socialists. With red cards in their pockets, uniforms on their backs, and guns in their hands, stunned or stirred up workingmen of France and Germany faced each other on the frontier. The leaders were as much taken by surprise, as much swept off their feet, as much stunned and grief-stricken as their

followers—many more so, for their whole lives had been lived under the sign and the pledge of international socialist solidarity.[226]

Only the small, but very vocal, left wing of the German SPD continued to advocate the militant idea of "class war" and a general strike should hostilities break out,[227] but their voices were nearly drowned out by spirited choruses of the anthem "Deutschland, Deutschland über Alles" (Germany, Germany above all).

The initial wave of patriotism engulfed even the hardened pacifists. Ludwig Quidde (1858–1941), president of the German Peace Society, for example, who strangely enough would later be awarded the Nobel Peace Prize, heard the call to arms and raised his own. In a pamphlet written just after the war began he asserted that Germany did not bear the sole responsibility for the war and that

> since the question of war or peace has now been removed from the realm of what we want, and our nation, threatened in the East, North and West, is engaged in a fateful struggle, every German friend of peace will have to fulfill his duty toward the fatherland as any other German. He will not be outdone in patriotic devotion by those who had nothing but derision and scorn for the idea of peace when it was still time. We share the general duties with all our compatriots.[228]

* * *

As the SPD shed its mantle of peace a new organization was created in 1910 that tried to pick it up, the Verband für internationale Verständigung (Society for international communication). Its goal was more focused than that of a political party: the promotion of "an era of international political understanding."[229] The road to permanent peace lay through the creation of an informed, cosmopolitan body politic and the arbitration of any international disputes. A number of German newspapers printed its first appeal for support:

> We must strive for a new political system of international relations, by seeking to extend international arbitration and especially to promote treaties with other nations to proliferate guarantees of world peace. [...] [Germans] must come to the realization that in the final analysis the common interests of competing states are larger than their rivalries and, therefore, that international understanding is possible.[230]

From the beginning the Verband was an elite organization, made up of lawyers, scholars, clergy, newspaper editors and members of the Reichstag. Two of its charter members, for example, were Friedrich Naumann (1860–1919)[231] and Max Weber (1864–1920).[232] The Verband hoped to defuse the international arms race and its potentially explosive outcome by focusing on public opinion. This was possible, they believed, because after examining recent history in detail a number of their members had concluded that the evolution of man clearly pointed in the direction of free states united in a world federation. At the time that was hardly an astounding or radical conclusion. The two Hague Conventions,[233] for instance, were ample evidence of this trend toward *Völkerrechtswis-*

senschaft, that is, toward civil liberties. The Verband and organizations like it would be just the midwives of history, aiding the inevitable progress of man. Its president, Otfried Nippold (1864–1938), declared: "We desperately need a public opinion that is not vulnerable to the power of suggestion [...]. So long as mistrust persists, nations must be armed, but the *Verband* hopes that the education of public opinion [...] will gradually make this mistrust disappear."[234] Given considerable backing from the Carnegie Endowment for International Peace, the Verband sponsored a number of international congresses, such as the Anglo-German Understanding Conference in 1912 and a meeting of French and German parliamentarians in Berne in 1913.[235]

The Anglo-German Understanding Conference was held in London and well attended by newspaper editors, politicians, ambassadors and public officials. It was a confidence-building event, designed to assure Germans and British that their two countries were natural allies who were year by year becoming closer. Speakers made the most of the fact that the trade between the UK and Germany was more than that of France and Russia combined. Peace was the essential ingredient that made it flourish. The mayor of London told his audience: "This city is great in times of peace, and it is peace which makes it great; it is peace which makes any nation great."[236]

Conferences in Germany garnered even more media attention and the most successful were the Verband's national congresses, in 1912 and 1913, which were attended by over 300 opinion leaders. The speeches and events were closely followed by most of the German press.

Writing after the First World War, and looking back on the accomplishments of the Verband, Nippold, its president, optimistically concluded that "had it had a few more years in which to make its impact, it would in all probability have been able to overcome a great many of the obstacles that it faced."[237]

* * *

Nippold's optimism was not unfounded. During the years leading up to the First World War relations between the two major antagonists, Germany and England, actually improved. There was substantial evidence that England and Germany were learning how to manage a very volatile international environment. A good example was the Balkan wars of 1912–1913. Greece, Montenegro, Bulgaria and Serbia took advantage of Turkey's weakening position and after a series of victories on the battlefield quickly reduced Turkish territories in Europe to merely a toehold. Afraid that the Bulgarian army might take Constantinople and thus be able to block access to the Mediterranean, Russia mobilized its troops. In reaction, Austria-Hungary also mobilized its army to prevent Serbia from gaining a seaport on the Adriatic. Prince Karl Max Lichnowsky, the Kaiser's Ambassador to the Court of St. James, cabled Berlin: "The disposal of the Turkish heritage raised the spectre of a European war."[238]

One • A Prelude for Peace 53

World War One appeared to be ready to begin. Two of Europe's major powers, Russia and Austria-Hungary, were already preparing their armies for war. But with caution and restraint England and Germany refused to mobilize. Instead, the British Foreign Secretary, Sir Edward Grey, quickly convened a conference of the London ambassadors of Austria-Hungary, Germany, France, Italy and Russia to negotiate the division of the former Turkish territory in an equitable manner.

The British took a certain pride in the fact that the peace conference took place in London. One of the mass-circulation weeklies produced the doggerel:

> Not in Berlin, where night by night the Kaiser
>   Sleeps in his "shining armor" *pie-a cap* [head to toe];
> Not in Vienna, where the mobilizer
>   Calls up his levies to the war-drum's tap;
> Not in St. Petersburg, where, should he need 'em,
>   Each for his *Czar* knows how to hold the gate;
> Nor yet in Paris, city of light and freedom,
>   Where all men serve the State;
> But here in England's capital, which tenders
>   Every attraction as a Peace resort.[239]

The road to peace was a twisted, bumpy one. Drawing boundary lines through the complicated ethnic mosaic of the Balkans was not an easy task. At one point, for example, the success or failure of the conference, the decision of whether or not to return to the battlefield, hinged on the nationality of the small town of Djakova (population today about 30,000). The parties squabbled for weeks, trading hilltops and swamps, before the Austro-Hungarians finally agreed. After eight months of negotiation, much of it over the boundaries of the new state of Albania, the participants produced a peace agreement that was signed by all parties.[240]

Although not all of the Balkan boundaries had been decided, a major European, if not world, conflict had been avoided, thanks mainly to the cooperation between England and Germany. Sir Edward Grey was able to declare that "the Germans seem to me to desire peace and not to be making mischief."[241] While an aide to the German Prime Minister wrote just after the conclusion of the London Conference: "Now above all we may have an opportunity of entering into normal and even friendly relations with our English cousins; in fact we seem to be well on the way towards this and this is what we should continue to develop."[242]

The London Conference did not prevent the Second Balkan War, as the former Balkan allies fought during the summer of 1913 to define their boundaries. But there was no danger that the fighting would escalate. The London Conference had been a unique event, more of a meeting of Great Powers than a meeting to create a treaty of accord. Sir Edward Grey, who had been the chairman of the conference, wrote a fitting epitaph:

There was no formal finish; the ambassadors were not photographed in a group; there were no votes of thanks; no valedictory speeches; they just stopped meeting. The conference had not settled anything, not even the details of the Albanian boundaries; but it had served a useful purpose. It had been something to which point after point could be referred; it had been a means of keeping all the six powers in direct and friendly touch. The mere fact that it was in existence, and that it would have to be broken up before peace was broken, was in itself an appreciable barrier against war. It was a means of gaining time, and the longer it remained in being, the more reluctance there was for it to disperse. The governments concerned got used to it, and to the habit of making it useful. When the conference ceased to meet, the danger to the peace of Europe was over; the things that it did not settle were not threatening that peace; the things that had threatened the relations between the great powers in 1912–1913 it had deprived of their dangerous features.[243]

Germany and England had pulled back from the brink of war. As they did so, it seemed that a method had been created for dealing with international disputes that could easily escalate into a Continental armed conflict. Once again, words had been victorious over warfare. And perhaps most important of all, the value of an international forum where the Great Powers could meet and discuss issues of war and peace had been proved to all. German Chancellor Bethmann-Hollweg wrote that Anglo-German cooperation was "worth more than any Naval Agreement or political understanding as a starting point for future good relations."[244]

The naval rivalry that had sparked a jingoistic battle for headlines on both sides of the North Sea suddenly ceased to be a dominant issue even though no formal agreement had been signed. The two countries focused on other potential flashpoints, for example, the fate of the Portuguese colonies in Africa and the Baghdad railway, relatively minor matters but clearly exercises in cooperation. Both countries regarded those negotiations as peace pawns, the first moves in a much larger and more important gambit that would eventually bring their countries closer together. Secretary for Foreign Affairs Grey noted: "The most important motive had been the improvement of relations with Germany,"[245] while the German Foreign Secretary wrote in a dispatch that "we intend, to begin with, to start with agreements in the colonial sphere."[246]

The Portuguese colonies in Africa bordered both German and British possessions, and should Portugal suffer a financial collapse, which looked very likely at the time, the British and the Germans intended to purchase them and absorb the pieces into their colonial empires. After lengthy discussions, the two countries amicably agreed on the division of the potential spoils.[247]

The Baghdad–Basra railway, which was to be constructed by the Germans, involved the delineation of spheres of interest, removing a long-standing source of Anglo-German tension. The negotiation was carried on in a polite, cooperative atmosphere although it took nearly a year to arrive at a relatively simple formula. The British received a monopoly on river transportation in Mesopotamia, while the Germans would control the Baghdad railway. Both countries promised not to discriminate against the goods of the other. The final agreement was initialed in the summer of 1914, during an unusual moment of calm and goodwill between the two nations, only one month before the debacle of World War One began.

Winston Churchill summarized the mood at the time: "The spring and summer of 1914 were marked in Europe by an exceptional tranquility."[248] And Arthur Nicolson (1849–1928), Under-Secretary for Foreign Affairs, who was usually very critical of the Germans, wrote that "since I have been at the Foreign Office, I have not seen such calm waters."[249] Taking advantage of the peaceful times, the band of the Coldstream guards was planning a tour of Germany and the British Foreign Minister, Sir Edward Grey, intended to go there himself to consult a famous oculist.[250] Even a week after the assassination of Archduke Franz Ferdinand and his wife in Sarajevo on June 28, 1914, Sir Edward Grey wrote: "We are on good terms with Germany and we wish to avoid a revival of friction with her."[251]

The desire of the British to arrive at a détente with the Germans may have worked too well. In fact, the spirit of cooperation may have backfired and given the Germans a completely false idea of the British position with respect to the Continent. The Germans may have become convinced that their relations with the British were on such good terms that should there be a European war, England would remain neutral. In any case, that is exactly what the Germans wanted to believe.

There was plenty of corroborating evidence. Nearly a month after the shooting in Sarajevo, Prince Henry, the Kaiser's brother, had breakfast with King George V and afterwards reported, perhaps erroneously, that the King had said that Britain would, as the Germans hoped, remain neutral in any Continental war. What King George V probably said was something like "We shall *try all we can* to keep out of this and remain neutral."[252] Meanwhile, at roughly the same time the Belgian ambassador to Berlin, who certainly had no real interest in British neutrality, wired the following message, which was picked up by the Germans: "It is by no means certain that Britain will take France's side in any war with Germany. [...] it is less likely as relations between Germany and Britain have visibly improved."[253]

Had the reverse position been true, that is, had the Germans known with certainty that should they attack France England would immediately come to the aid of her ally, they might not have been so eager to launch the war. In that case, although this is purely speculation, the First World War would not have occurred. Kaiser Wilhelm at one point lamented: "If only someone had told me beforehand that England would take up arms against us."[254]

* * *

In the spring of 1914 the United States almost went to war. A party of unarmed American Marines landed at Tampico, Mexico, to buy some gasoline and were promptly arrested by Mexican Federal troops. They were freed a few hours later, but the admiral in charge of the American fleet in the harbor, Henry T. Mayo (1856–1937), demanded a formal apology, for example, a 21-gun salute to the American flag. General Huerta (1854–1916), a dictator involved in a civil war, was willing to fire a salute of 21 guns but insisted that the United States should fire a similar salute and that the guns of the respective countries should be fired alternately. Since the United States did not recognize Huerta as the legal head of the Mexican government,[255] the American admiral refused and as a riposte sent 3,000 marines to occupy Veracruz, thereby blocking the flow of arms to General Huerta.

The dispute at Veracruz threatened to boil over into a full-scale war. The Mexicans were outraged and mobilized their troops. With the exception of Pancho Villa (1878–1923), who was receiving arms from the United States, nearly all Mexicans vehemently opposed the mini-"invasion." Venustiano Carranza (1859–1920), who would later become the President of Mexico after Huerta was overthrown, wrote to President Wilson: "Your invasion of our territory and the permanency of your forces in the port of Veracruz and the violation of the rights that constitute our existence as a free and independent sovereign entity will drag us into an unequal war, which we desire to avoid."[256]

Meanwhile, the Americans were still insulted and ready to use the excuse to invade Mexico and topple the tyrant Huerta. They openly prepared for war. Ordinary citizens wrote to President Wilson and asked to serve in the military. Even a number of Congressmen volunteered for action. Governors offered their state militias. The press ratcheted up the rhetoric. For example, the *New York Evening Post* headlined that "the drumming of the guns is now the only oratory that counts."[257]

At the same time, the peace movement, suffragettes, organized labor and socialists all shouted for peace. Telegrams by the hundreds requesting peace, moderation and sagacity poured into the White House. Bill Haywood (1869–1928) of the IWW (the Industrial Workers of the World) declared at a Carnegie Hall rally that a war would signal a general strike by the nation's mine workers, "who will simply fold their arms and when they fold their arms there will be no war."[258] One socialist wrote in the *New York Call*: "War mania has hypnotized the people. Members of the working class are storming the recruiting offices clamoring for the right to be shot."[259]

While a war of words was raging in the United States, the American consulate in Monterrey was sacked and burned, American flags disgraced and American residences all over Mexico stoned and torched, each act more violent and insulting than the original indignity.

In America the cries for war clearly outshouted those for peace. Yet President Wilson hesitated, well aware that he was walking the tightrope between war and peace.

At this point, the ABC countries, as they were called, Argentina, Brazil and Chile, stepped in and offered to mediate the dispute. For President Wilson, it was an act of "Providence," for the Mexicans a face-saving way to avoid a conflict they could not hope to win.

Both countries accepted almost immediately. Niagara Falls, Canada, was chosen as a neutral location, and within a few weeks a mediation conference began.

Mexico, however, was in the middle of a revolution, as the Huerta government fought with peasant armies led by Pancho Villa (1878–1923) for control of the country. Only Villa and his allies agreed to send representatives to the Niagara Falls conference.

For months, the mediators and the delegations negotiated and compromised in secret, but with only the Mexican delegates sent by Pancho Villa and Venustiano Carranza (1859–1920) present, nothing definitive could be decided. Finally just before the fighting started in Europe, the Niagara Falls conference issued a protocol, which, in essence, admitted that it had failed in its original purpose, although it did succeed in creating "a cooling off period" during which the United States dropped its insistence that the Mexicans salute the American flag.

Despite the secrecy of the proceedings, a number of "leaks" fed an army of reporters, and as a result the Niagara Falls conference was well covered by the press, in both Latin America and the United States. The *San Francisco Chronicle*, for example, concluded: "The mediation has been a most excellent thing for us, for Mexico and for the Americas." The *New York Times* called it, "a triumph for President Wilson" and the *Christian Science Monitor* noted that "if the mediation between two North American republics is compassed by three South American republics' tactful interposition and use of moral authority, a new era of Pan-Americanism will have dawned."[260]

The three South American mediators had performed so well together that there was talk of forming an "ABC bloc." A year later, in May 1915, the three countries were to sign an "ABC Peace Treaty," in which they pledged to preserve peace and refrain from war until all disputes had been submitted to an impartial commission for mediation.

Most of the participants of the Niagara Falls conference left with a song on their lips, a satirical piece of doggerel created by the reporters that they and apparently everyone else sung with delight:

> *When it's Mediation Time in Canada,*
> *In Canada, in Canada*
> *By the good old Falls, we'll watch and wait,*
> *And Mediate.*

> *When it's Mediation Time in Canada,*
> *We'll come here for a rest;*
> *And we'll pay ten cents to cross the Bridge*
> *Whether going East or West.*[261]

Undoubtedly the most important contribution of the Niagara Conference was that it provided both Mexico and the United States with some time and distance to evaluate the possible consequences of their actions. In doing so, it clearly prevented a war. A month after the conference closed the Huerta regime collapsed, and shortly afterwards the American marines were withdrawn from Veracruz.[262] There were no casualties. Thousands, probably tens of thousands, of lives had been saved. A method of conflict resolution had worked. A major power had pulled back from the brink of a war that it surely could have won. For the international community who had been watching closely an important example had been set, more proof that man had finally entered the age of reason.

* * *

With war looming large in Europe, Norman Angell changed tactics and launched the Neutrality League. It was a desperate effort to mobilize the masses, generate a wave of protest and thus keep Great Britain out of any Continental conflict. Backed by a number of wealthy businessmen, he spent over 2,000 pounds (over a million in 2012 U.S. dollars) on direct publicity. One of his handbills co-opted the popular army recruiting phrase of the moment "ENGLISHMEN DO YOUR DUTY" by adding to it, "KEEP YOUR COUNTRY OUT OF A WICKED AND STUPID WAR."

Hundreds of meetings were held and half a million handbills distributed, most of them in London. Two hundred sandwich men patrolled the main streets, carrying their postered message to thousands of Londoners. In addition, Angell took full-page ads in some of the major newspapers. He sought to convince public opinion that if Britain joined the war on the side of France and Russia, far from maintaining the balance of power in Europe, this would upset the status quo and Russia, not Germany, would become the dominant power in Europe.[263] His efforts proved to be fruitless.

* * *

In France, during the years leading up to the First World War, the number of peace societies continued to multiply. In 1910 36 separate organizations belonged to the International Peace Bureau in Berne, which attempted to keep track of the European peace movement and become a kind of clearinghouse. It has been estimated that on the eve of the First World War perhaps 300,000 Frenchmen and women belonged to peace societies of one kind or another.[264] The organizations produced public lectures, regular journals and a long list of books, and attracted endowments, legacies and prizes.

* * *

In 1910 with French insistence the Universal Peace Congress in Stockholm, the 18th such congress, attended by most of the world's peace organizations, adopted the *Code de la paix* (the code of peace), 145 articles that set forth the fundamental principles of the movement. Among other things, the Code followed the Kantian argument that the moral precepts of nations should not differ from those of individuals in a civil society. Hence, as individuals cannot make war on one another, neither can governments. War was wrong not because it violated religious principles, but because it ignored the basic rights of man.

If these rights applied to European and American peoples, then logically they applied to colonial peoples as well. French peace advocates began to develop a universal social consciousness that transcended race and religion. Hence, they denounced the excesses of colonialism, pointing to atrocities in the Congo, brutal repression in Annam (later Vietnam), or the punishment of tribal peoples in Morocco.

In the Far East the combination of the Japanese victory in the Russo-Japanese War and the end of the Manchu dynasty in China encouraged nationalist movements throughout Asia, and the French peace movement was ready to support them. Some of the peace advocates' proposals were exceedingly modern, for example, the creation of a special section of the Colonial Office with personnel trained in Moslem culture to help bridge the gap between the French and the Arabs and reduce the possibilities for conflict.

One of the most dynamic French peace societies was the Société d'éducation pacifique, which focused on changing the school curriculum and eliminating its militaristic bias and with it the establishment of role models based on war heroes. Their perspective was straightforward. Change the attitudes of the young, change their heroes and their definition of glory and honor, and eventually you would change the entire society. Hatred, cruelty, violence and brutality bred in the dark corners of our minds, atavisms we no longer needed or wanted. Sweep them away, let them become relics of history, and war could be prevented.

The Société d'éducation pacifique claimed to have 10,000 members, the majority of them teachers. Its journal, *L'Emancipation*, boldly stated its purpose: "It is not in the name of government, not even the Republican government that the teacher imparts knowledge, nor is it in the name of the French people. It is in the name of truth."[265]

The Société provided lecturers and classroom materials that stressed cross-cultural similarities and the benefits of arbitration and pacifism. At the university level, intellectuals such as Anatole France (1844–1924),[266] David Émile Durkheim (1858–1917)[267] and Marcel Sembat (1862–1922)[268] gave lectures and held symposia.[269]

As the clouds of war began to gather, many French pacifists, among them Théodore Ruyssen (1868–1967), president of La Paix par le droit, the most prominent French peace organization, realized that one major cause of the coming conflict was the German possession of the so-called lost provinces of Alsace-Lorraine. Ruyssen advocated granting them the right of national autonomy. This, he hoped, would form a bridge between the two cultures and help diffuse hostilities. Ruyssen also proposed creating an international university at Strasbourg (Alsace) that would promote student exchanges. In essence, he proposed a de facto sharing of the provinces by establishing international organizations there. Ruyssen and many other pacifists believed that another war over Alsace-Lorraine would be too high a price for France to pay.

After the assassination of Archduke Franz Ferdinand, the French peace movement sent telegrams to all the heads of state in Europe reminding them that as signatories to the Hague Conferences of 1899 and 1907 they had promised to engage in a "cooling off" period before resorting to military operations. But events moved too quickly. When the French army began to mobilize, La Paix par le droit covered the walls of Paris with posters pleading for the government to respect the agreement it had signed at The Hague. Ruyssen complained: "Why do governments not accord the commitments made at The Hague with the same seriousness that they give to the military alliances?"[270] But it was too late for rhetoric. The black clouds of war had already begun to cover the sky.

* * *

Before that fateful August of 1914 when all Europe went to war, strangely enough, relations between Germany and England were better than they had been in many years. Rivalry seemed to be giving way to acceptance, affability and even friendship.

Two Royal British Navy squadrons, four of the latest dreadnoughts and their supporting craft attended the Kiel Yachting Week and rode at anchor beside the warships of the Kaiser's High Seas Fleet.

The Kaiser arrived on his yacht *Meteor*. At a reception for British and German officers he appeared dressed as a British admiral and told everyone that he was "proud to wear the uniform worn by Lord Nelson."[271]

The Kaiser's brother, Henry, who was also at the reception, proclaimed: "This is what I have long hoped for, to see a portion of the British and German fleets lying side by side in friendship in Kiel harbor."[272]

The British and German warships exchanged visits, receptions, dinners, dances and endless speeches and toasts of friendship. A boxing match was held on board the HMS *Ajax*, British sailors were treated to free beer in the portside bars, and all British mariners were given free railway passes to visit Bremen and Berlin.

The presence of British warships at Kiel provided the indefatigable Ballin with another opportunity to bring Churchill, First Lord of the Admiralty, and Admiral von Tirpitz together for a personal exchange of views. It was perhaps the last possibility for a British-German naval understanding. Churchill let it be known that he was ready for such a meeting and would travel to Germany if necessary. However, the German government stipulated that first the British government should make an official inquiry as to whether or not Churchill's visit would be welcome. The British government refused, preferring to begin with a more informal meeting. Once again the two governments were at an impasse. Before another attempt could be constructed, events in the Balkans dictated their own course of action.

The assassination of Archduke Ferdinand at Sarajevo cut short the festivities at Kiel. After receiving the news, the Kaiser and his retinue left almost immediately and hurried to Potsdam. A few days later the British squadrons sailed. The German ships flew the signal "Pleasant Journey." As the warships put out to sea, the British admiral sent a farewell message to the German fleet by wireless: "Friends in past and friends for ever."[273]

* * *

Just before the war began, May 14, 1914, the first anti-war film was released, *Maudite soit la guerre (War Be Damned,* also called *War Is Hell)*, produced in Belgium and hand-colored, frame by frame. Written and directed by Alfred Machin (1877–1929),[274] the film is a classic melodrama but filmed on a grand scale, using airplanes, dirigibles and hundreds of Belgian soldiers dressed in fantastic uniforms.

The plot is simple and contrived. A young Belgian girl falls in love with a foreign officer. War suddenly breaks out and separates them. During the fighting he is killed by his friend from pre-war times. Meanwhile, the Belgian girl is courted by a number of officers, one of whom presents her with a locket he has found on the field of battle. It is of course the one she had given to the foreign officer with whom she was in love. Distraught and in tears, she wanders through a forest until she finds a convent. She asks for acceptance, then joins the cloistered life. She retreats from the world, thus closing the door to earthly love. The final title appears—"*chagrin d'amour dure toute la vie*" (the sorrow of love lasts a lifetime)[275]—and the film ends with a close-up of the grieving woman.[276]

The film played in Brussels for three weeks, which was then considered to be a reasonable success, and then went on to be shown in Paris, Marseille, New York and Berlin. In some places the title was changed to *Mourir pour la patrie* (To die for your country). The intertitles, which were then a necessary part of any silent film, were also rewritten, and that could have easily changed the message of the film.

A few months later, on August 14, 1914, six weeks after Archduke Ferdinand was assassinated at Sarajevo, the Danish film *Lay Down Your Arms*,[277] based on the novel by Bertha von Süttner, had its first public screening. The book had gone through more than 40 editions, sold millions of copies, and was published in 16 languages. Contemporaries compared it to Harriet Beecher Stowe's *Uncle Tom's Cabin*.

Largely forgotten today, *Lay Down Your Arms*[278] tells the story of a young woman, Martha von Tilling, whose happiness is destroyed by a series of wars. She loses both of her husbands, one at the battle of Magenta and the other at the siege of Paris. The very realistic horrors of the battlefield become the backdrop for much of the dialogue. Millions of people had read the novel and discussed its simple, central theme, that war is the descent of man to a more primitive state:

> [I]n the game of war manslaughter is no longer to count as manslaughter; robbery counts no longer as robbery; theft is not thieving but requisition, villages burnt represent [...] positions taken [...]. It is a kind of magic. Immediately on the declaration of war one says [...] of any horror [...], Oh, that's not important! [...]. Strange how blind people are! They are horrified by the torture chambers of the Middle Ages, but their arsenal fills them with pride.[279]

Bertha von Süttner became one of the five most famous women in Europe, according to a Berlin newspaper poll.[280] She was awarded the Nobel Peace Prize in 1905, the first woman to receive it. Hanna Kvanmo, a longtime member of the Norwegian Nobel Committee, wrote: "It is possible to say that without Bertha von Süttner there would have been no peace prize."[281]

Bertha von Süttner's relationship with Alfred Nobel had begun years before with an advertisement in a Paris newspaper: "A very wealthy, highly educated older gentleman living in Paris seeks a lady well-versed in languages, also elderly, as secretary." The "older gentleman" was Alfred Nobel, and when she answered the ad he immediately fell in love with her. She was 32; he, 42. She quickly became his secretary and hostess. Nine days later Nobel left for Stockholm. Shortly afterwards Bertha von Süttner received two telegrams: one from Nobel saying that he was returning soon, the other from the man she loved, an Austrian baron, announcing that he was coming to Paris. She followed her heart and eloped with the baron. Rejected by her husband's family, the couple sought refuge in the Caucasus (Tbilisi in today's Georgia), where they remained for 12 years.

During that period Bertha von Süttner continued to correspond regularly with Nobel, and her friendship with him endured until his death in 1896. He sent her money regularly for years and his financial support permitted her to start peace societies in Vienna, Berlin and Budapest. She, in turn, wrote him long letters describing the progress of the peace movement. When she was afraid that he would create the Nobel prizes after his death without one for peace, she wrote to him, saying that "this is what I beg of you, my hands joined in supplication, never withdraw your support from us—never, not even from beyond the grave, which awaits us all."[282]

Despite the stark and dark reality of *Lay Down Your Arms*, Bertha von Süttner remained an optimist. She believed that just as science was advancing, making one astounding discovery after another, man too was advancing, shedding

One • A Prelude for Peace

his primitive past and gradually becoming more civilized, more noble, more peace loving. Mankind was moving toward perfection. The mistakes that had been made before would not be made again.

Bertha von Süttner became the peripatetic doyenne of the international peace movement and campaigned under the slogan "Europe is one!" But her optimism had been unfounded, a wish detached from reality, and she had realized it. Europe was not one. Far from it. It was many, divided by squabbles over borders, colonies, and, above all, prestige and power. Two years earlier, before the First World War began, she wrote:

> We have been mistaken—not as to our principles but in our estimate of the level of civilization to which the world in general had attained. We thought there was a far more widespread desire for justice [...] and a far deeper abhorrence of despotism than appears to be the case [...]. [This] does not prove the falsity of beliefs held by the peace party. It merely proves [...] that the peace movement is not yet powerful enough.[283]

Bertha von Süttner never saw the film made from her famous book. She died just one week before the fateful shots at Sarajevo. At the time of her death she was planning an international peace conference that was to be held in Vienna. One of the major events would have been the screening of the Danish film. The conference never happened. The call to "lay down your arms" was drowned out by the guns of August.[284]

* * *

Shortly before the war began, President Wilson sent his closest confidant, Colonel House (1858–1938),[285] to Europe to try to defuse the coming crisis. Colonel House was an enigmatic figure who preferred to remain out of sight behind events rather than lead them.[286] He held no government or diplomatic post and when asked what official position he filled called himself the "eyes and ears of the President."[287]

Acting informally on President Wilson's behalf, Colonel House had sought to create an "understanding" among what he called the three "Anglo-Saxon powers," the United States, Great Britain and Germany, in order to avoid a war that he was certain was looming on the horizon. He set out for Germany, his object nothing less than to put himself in the middle of the European maelstrom. He knew that the odds were against him. In his diary he called his mission "The Great Adventure."

In Germany, he visited the Kaiser at Potsdam when he attended the *Schrippenfest*,[288] a presentation of Prussian militarism. Colonel House was not impressed by the display, nor by the cult of war. He called it "militarism run stark mad." When the ceremony was finished the two men spoke alone for some time in English. Afterwards Colonel House noted that he found the Kaiser to be "surprisingly receptive." He had told Colonel House that Germany, Britain and America "were kindred peoples and should draw closer together," since they are "the only hope of advancing Christian civilization."[289] Colonel House replied as follows: "I told him [the Kaiser] that the President [Wilson] and I thought perhaps an American might be able to better compose the difficulties here and bring about an understanding with a view to peace than any European, because of their distrust and dislike for one another."[290] The Kaiser fully agreed and asked to be kept regularly informed as to Colonel House's progress.

Next, Colonel House went to Paris, where he found the French in the middle of a cabinet crisis, as René Viviani (1863–1925) became the Prime Minister. House wrote to President Wilson that "he did not find the war spirit dominant in France,"[291] then traveled to London. After meeting with several government officials there, he realized that the chief obstacle to his plan would be the British. In his private notes he wrote: "If England were less intolerant of Germany's aspirations for expansion good feeling could be brought about between them. I thought we could encourage Germany to exploit South America in a legitimate way, that is by development of its resources and by sending her surplus population there."[292]

A banker by profession, Colonel House wanted to create a plan for a combined British-German-American investment at low rates of interest to develop what he called "the waste places of the earth."[293] At the same time he proposed that Germany would have a free hand commercially in South America as well as in Asia Minor and Persia.

Colonel House tried to persuade the British to be more pragmatic and perhaps less suspicious. He wanted to return to Germany and arrange a meeting between the British Foreign Minister, Edward Grey, and the Kaiser as soon as possible in Kiel.

On the seventh of July 1914, while he was waiting for the British to agree and devise a way of negotiating with the Germans without offending their allies, the French and the Russians, Colonel House wrote a long letter to the Kaiser in which he said: "I have met the Prime Minister and practically every important member of the British Government, and I am convinced that they desire such an undertaking as will lay the foundation for permanent peace and security."[294] But before the letter could be delivered the Kaiser had left on his annual summer cruise to Norway, and he didn't return until after the fatal shots at Sarajevo and the delivery of the Austro-Hungarian ultimatum to Serbia. World War One had begun.

Colonel House's call for a conference of the Great Powers was drowned out by the cadence of marching men. His "Great Adventure" has become one of the "what-ifs" of the era, a near miss that, had it been given more time, might well have matured into a history-changing event, a moment that could have been a marker for peace instead of a summons to the battlefield.

Much later, after World War One was over, the Kaiser, who was in exile in

Holland, told a journalist[295] that "the visit of Colonel House to Berlin and London in the spring of 1914 almost prevented the World War."[296]

* * *

In the summer of 1914 the signs of war had already become unmistakable. To diffuse the coming crisis, the spread of an Austro-Serbian war to a Continental one, the British government proposed a four-power conference composed of Britain, France, Italy and Germany "for the purpose of discovering an issue which would prevent complications." Almost immediately the Kaiser replied that such a meeting would be "not practicable." By this time Serbia and Austro-Hungary were already at war.

Czar Nicholas II tried to keep Russia out of what could be, and would soon be, a widening war. He wrote to the Kaiser and suggested that the whole Austro-Hungarian–Serbian question should be turned over to the International Court at The Hague, something the Serbs had previously attempted to do.

One German observer has pointed out that before England declared war on Germany on August 4, Germany, having already declared war on Russia on August 1 and on France on August 3, the Entente, i.e., England, France and Russia,

> made one attempt at mediation after another. Between July 24 and 31, Grey [British Foreign Secretary] put forward no fewer than eight proposals for mediation. Cambon [French ambassador to Germany] three, and Sasonow [Russian Foreign Minister] three. It was in vain. Then they began to beg for peace. The Czar telegraphed to William [the Kaiser]: "In this anxious moment I implore you to help me [...] to avoid such a disaster as a European war. I beg you in the name of our old friendship to do everything in your power to prevent your ally going too far."[297]

There is no lack of proof that the Czar wished to avoid a war if at all possible. A strong peace party in St. Petersburg lobbied constantly, including among others Count Witte (1849–1915), the former Minister of Finance who had led the Russian delegation to Portsmouth, where the Russo-Japanese War was concluded. Witte thought that the war in 1914 was "suicidal" and the consequences "impossible to imagine." A friend of his wrote shortly after his death in 1915: "Witte considered that war (*sic*) as one does the plague; it did not matter who was responsible."[298]

After the war the French ambassador to Vienna wrote in his memoirs with the acuity of hindsight that he had been told by his Russian counterpart, Nikolai N. Schebeko (1863–?): "I cannot tell Count Berchtold [1863–1942, the Austrian Foreign Minister] how far I would go to secure peace, for he would abuse the knowledge."[299]

In addition, the Russian Foreign Minister, Sergey Sazonov (1860–1927), sent a telegram to the Russian ambassadors in Paris and London that stated that if direct negotiations with Austria-Hungary proved a failure the Czar was ready "to accept the English proposal, or any other calculated to bring about a favorable solution of the conflict."[300] The "English proposal" had been instigated by the French ambassador in London, Paul Cambon (1843–1924), who suggested that the British propose a conference of the four powers not directly interested in the crisis "in order to endeavour to find an issue to prevent complications."[301] Specifically, it asked Austria-Hungary, Russia and Serbia that "pending results of the conference all active military operations should be suspended."[302] Prince Lichnowsky, the German ambassador in London, provides further details:

> His [Britain's Foreign Secretary Sir Edward Grey's] proposal was that a committee, consisting of M. Cambon, the Marquis Imperiali [1858–1944, the Italian ambassador in London] and myself, should assemble under his presidency, and it would have been an easy matter for us to find an acceptable formula for the points at issue [...]. Given goodwill, everything could have been settled at one or two sittings [...]. I therefore strongly backed the proposal on that ground that otherwise there was danger of the world-war, through which we stood to gain nothing and lose all; but in vain.[303]

This proposal was immediately accepted by Italy and France. However, Germany labeled the proposal "extremely inopportune" and went on to say that "we cannot summon Austria before a European court of justice in its business with Serbia."[304] However, the German refusal destroyed what was probably the last and the best chance of preventing a European war.

Like the Czar, the Kaiser had also realized that Europe was poised on the threshold of war, and he telegraphed to the Czar that Russia should "remain a spectator to the Austro-Serbian conflict" and by doing so prevent Europe from enduring "the most horrible war she has ever witnessed." The Kaiser was clearly being duplicitous, because at the same time he had met with his advisors and privately "it was decided to fight through the affair or issue [*die Sache durchzufechten*], cost what it might."[305]

The Czar responded positively to the Kaiser's telegram and canceled Russia's order for general mobilization. This was not without precedent. In 1909 and 1912 mobilization had begun and was stopped by the Czar's order. But this time he waited too long. When the Kaiser tried to reply in kind by stopping the German mobilization the General Staff refused to countenance the order.

Germany continued to mobilize and Russia did the same. Suddenly Europe seemed to be poised on the point of no return. The Czar telegraphed the Kaiser: "I received your telegram. Understand you are obliged to mobilize but wish to have some guarantee from you as I gave you, that the measures do not mean war and that we shall continue negotiating for the benefit of our countries and universal peace dear to all our hearts. Our long proved friendship must succeed, with God's help, in avoiding bloodshed. Anxiously, full of confidence, await your answer."[306]

The two monarchs thought they had the power to stop the war at the very last moment. They had a long friendship, corresponded in English,[307] and often addressed each other as "Willy" and "Nicky."[308] In 1904, for example, after dozens of telegrams they anchored their yachts next to each other in the Bay of Viborg near Björkö Sound and signed a secret treaty of alliance, the so-called Treaty of Björkö.[309] It was meant to include France, which was an odd attempt at geopolitical maneuvering, since France had just signed the *Entente Cordiale* with Great Britain. At one point the Czar told the Kaiser that he put faith in a "loyal friendship which I trust beyond anything."[310] The Kaiser reciprocated: "Our treaty is a very good base to build upon. We joined hands and signed before God, who heard our vows. I therefore think that the treaty can well come into existence [...]. What is signed is signed and God is our testator."[311] Despite its intentions, ultimately the Treaty of Björkö fell into one of history's footnotes.

While all of Europe was poised on the edge of the sword, at the last minute in 1914, the monarchs were no longer in control. In both Russia and Germany the generals, and not the sovereigns, were in command, and once they had begun to assemble their troops and weapons and prepare public opinion for a patriotic war, there was no turning back. For example, General Nikolai Yanushkevich (1868–1918), the Russian Chief of the General Staff, reportedly told Sazonov, the Foreign Minister: "After that [the order by the Czar to fully mobilize], I shall go away, smash my telephone and generally adopt measures which will prevent anyone from finding me for the purpose of giving contrary orders which would again stop our general mobilization."[312]

The Czar had no choice but to agree to full mobilization. Soon millions of men had received their marching orders, gotten a day or two to settle their private affairs, then had a rendezvous with a train that would take them to the border. Within days soldiers in Russia were marching to cries of "To Berlin," while those in Germany were chanting "To Moscow." A European war, one that would soon involve all the Great Powers, was only moments away.

* * *

A minority of Europeans, albeit a small one, put their faith in their own convictions. Should the army call them, no matter what the penalty, they would refuse to take up arms, and that act of defiance would serve as an example encouraging others to do the same. Pacifists such as Romain Rolland (1866–1944) and Leo Tolstoy provided the inspiration and set the example.

Tolstoy had stated quite clearly that peace was the responsibility of the individual and armed forces, always and everywhere, were an instrument for evil. If one wanted to abolish warfare, he argued, each man, each woman, must, of his or her own free will, make the decision not to bear arms. Tolstoy defined the solution to war in very simple terms. Let every man refuse to enter military service or, as Tolstoy put it, let every man "refuse to hire himself out as a murderer."[313] In one stroke, armies and warfare would cease to exist.

Few (less than 1 percent of those inducted) were willing to take the Tolstoyan pledge and suffer the dire consequences—jail, hard labor, or solitary confinement—although many more were opposed to war. How many it is difficult to say. Accurate public-opinion polling did not appear until the 1930s. However, an indication of the popular mood might be gleaned from the efforts of the German peace activist Anna B. Eckstein (1868–1947). In the years before the war, she collected signatures from all over Europe for "The World Petition to Prevent War Between Nations" or "a world referendum," as she called it.

Eckstein spoke fluent English, French and German and traveled extensively in Germany, Denmark, Austria-Hungary, Holland, Sweden, Switzerland, France and England. She lectured wherever she could find an audience; peace societies, workers groups, women's clubs, church gatherings and social events.[314] And whenever she spoke, she passed out her peace petition and collected more signatures. The lengthy document with its 2 million signatures[315] was intended to serve as a recommendation to the 44 nations attending the Second Peace Conference in 1907. It asked them to mutually pledge to solve all international disputes by peaceful means, that is, by treaty and arbitration, and by doing so reduce the necessity of maintaining armies and expensive armaments. Any country that violated the pact would be punished by an economic boycott. Eckstein's petition anticipated the Kellogg-Briand Pact[316] by more than 20 years.

Encouraged by the attention she received at the Second Hague Conference, Eckstein prepared another petition for the Third Hague Conference, which was due to be convened in 1915.

> We, the undersigned, citizens of the different nations, believing that the adjustment of all international interests by conventions and treaties containing arbitral clause, will lead to the abolition of war, minimize the necessity of armaments, and effect their gradual reduction, hereby voice our gratitude for the official steps already taken toward this end, and, desiring to support further concerted action, respectfully petition that at the Third Hague Conference a convention be agreed upon, by which the nations shall mutually pledge themselves, guaranteeing each other's integrity and just development, to refer to arbitration all differences not settled by diplomatic negotiations.[317]

Eckstein set herself a goal of 10 million signatures and had more than 6 million recorded when her efforts were ended by the advent of World War I.

It was a monumental accomplishment. If one woman working virtually single-handed could record 6 million European votes for peace and arbitration, then it was certainly an indication of a groundswell, a significant predisposition on the part of the masses and, in any case, proof that the peace societies of Europe did not exist in a popular vacuum. For her efforts, Eckstein was nominated for the Nobel Peace Prize.

* * *

In the days just before the war a number of women produced a novel means to eliminate war, a "birth strike," a refusal to bear children, thus eventually denying society the soldiers with whom to fight a war. It was widely debated in France and Germany. It is unknown, however, how many women used birth control methods to put it into practice.

In France the movement began with the emergence of neo–Malthusianism, which saw the cause of social and economic problems in overpopulation. However, contrary to Malthus (1766–1834), who favored celibacy as the means to eliminate war and poverty, the new Malthusians advocated strict birth control.

One of the leading advocates was Nelly Roussel (1878–1922), an ardent feminist and freethinker, who made speaking tours in France, Belgium, Switzerland and Eastern Europe. Many newspapers and journals were sympathetic to the cause and gave her substantial coverage. It is not an exaggeration to say that, one way or another, her message reached hundreds of thousands of people.

But not all liberal/socialist women were in favor of it. Klara Zetkin (née Eissner, 1857–1933), for example, the editor of *Equality*, the German Social Democratic Party's national women's newspaper, was opposed. At a speech in Berlin she said: "It is further said that people should provide the fewest possible soldiers for the present capitalistic state. Only they forget that if the proletariat supplies fewer soldiers, it also decreases the numbers of revolutionaries. The proletariat must consider the need for having as many fighters as possible."[318]

Rosa Luxemburg (1871–1919), the fiery voice of the Spartacus League (Spartakusbund),[319] also joined in the fray: "As a weapon for the proletariat, child limitation [*Kinderbeschränkung*] must be rejected categorically. We will never achieve our final goal through child limitation."

In any case, it was too late for polemics. The "birth strike" was obviously a long-term solution, one that would require a generation to take effect, and at that moment the world war was only a few short years away.

* * *

Those who still believed in peace, and there were many, saw the growing flames of conflict yet could still find ample confidence in the fact that just a few years previously the Great Powers of Europe had gone to the brink of war (as in the Agadir Crisis), then pulled back at the last minute and settled their differences by negotiation. Only by confronting a possible military maelstrom that could consume millions and might also mean the demise of Western civilization had the politicians and generals been able to realize that they had gone too far. A continental war could easily destroy them all.

A month before the war began in July 1914, Sir Edward Grey, the British Foreign Secretary, wrote down his thoughts: "A great European war under modern conditions would be a catastrophe for which previous wars afforded no precedent [...]. I thought this must be obvious to everyone else, as it seemed obvious to me; and that, if once it became apparent that we were on the edge, all the Great Powers would call a halt and recoil from the abyss."[320] And if they didn't, or couldn't, stop the military before they marched to the frontiers and loaded their weapons, if the conflict became so bitter and entrenched that direct negotiation was not an option, then they could resort to arbitration, a mechanism that had been established at The Hague and had already proved its value in the settlement of numerous international disputes. It would not perhaps solve the root cause of the conflict, but it might provide, at a minimum, a compromise solution that could grow into permanence. In the words of Frédéric Passy: "You cannot humanize war. You get rid of war by becoming more human."[321]

But being "human" required time, time to reason and rationalize, time to communicate with leaders and the public, and time to search for acceptable solutions. For that, both sides would have to agree to a "cooling off period" as the United States and Mexico had done.

However, should neither side blink, then step back from the brink, or accept arbitration in The Hague or a "cooling off period," third parties, such as the United States, the Netherlands and the Scandinavian countries were always ready to offer their services as mediators or hosts of a peace conference. That, for example, had proved to be the successful way to end the Russo-Japanese War of 1904–1905, which to date had been the largest land war in half a century.

* * *

Jean Jaurès, the French socialist leader and visionary, took another tack, which he believed was a way to avoid war. He supported the concept of the nation-state, which would be the basis for a network of international arbitration that would eventually lead to the creation of a pacifistic European federation.

This approach overlapped with a very optimistic liberal view that was popular at the time and regarded the European alliance systems as the building blocks of a future federated system, a kind of United States of Europe. The logic began with the notion that the individual nation state of the early 1900s was essentially insecure and could thus engage in reckless international behavior, for example, wars of conquest. However, once a country entered into an alliance with others it lost some of its sovereignty and freedom of action, but gained in security, making adventuristic wars less likely. In other words, with alliances came increased rationality and responsibility. From that should follow more cultural, trade and arbitration agreements. These, in turn, would eventually become the foundation of a federation that would of course preclude any war between the various partners.

There was of course an inherent contradiction in this perspective. On the one hand, the socialists condemned the militarism of the nation-state, and on the other, they put their faith in the state as a necessary element in a new federation.

One way around this glaring contradiction was to reform the army. And that Jaurès set out to do. After years of study he wrote *L'Armée nouvelle* (1910), which detailed his proposals. The new army was to be a civilian force, mostly in reserve, very much like the Swiss army. Each man would keep his weapon at home and could respond to a call for mobilization immediately. The object, of course, was to get rid of a large standing, and potentially anti-democratic, army, especially the professional officer corps, the generals whom Jaurès called "the inner sanctum of the rue Saint-Dominique."[322] He introduced his proposals at the Assemblée Nationale, but they were scarcely examined. With few exceptions he failed to persuade army officers, the party rank and file, or newspaper editors. Most regarded his militia scheme as a naïve fantasy. The socialists of Europe also saw it as an object of ridicule. One German Social Democrat wrote sarcastically: "You can't put a cannon in the bed of every former gunner and give each old sea dog a little warship to put in the farmyard trough or wash tub."[323]

Jaurès and the French socialists' leadership had other means of attacking militarism. Using what was called the *sou du soldat* (a penny for a soldier), labor organizations would send soldiers a small sum of money accompanied by anti-militarist propaganda, for example, denouncing military service as "an apprenticeship of brutality and baseness [...], a school of crime, vice laziness, hypocrisy, and cowardice."[324]

The purpose of course was to urge soldiers to desert, and the campaign seems to have had the desired effect. During the years preceding the war the number of *insoumis* (draft dodgers) and deserters increased annually. By 1911 a total of nearly 80,000 individuals were being sought by the army and police for not fulfilling their military obligations.

Jaurès also put his faith in political parties, particularly the Social Democrats of Europe. He believed that the internationalist convictions of "four million courageous Germans, that is, the four million socialist Germans, will shape the destinies of the world."[325] Like most socialists, Jaurès put his trust in the Second International, an organization that included not only the European socialist and labor parties but also the nascent socialist parties from Asia and the Ottoman Empire.

Since by socialist logic the workingman had no home and followed no flag except the red banner, a general strike by all parties of the International would deprive governments of manpower for factories and soldiers for the army, thereby making a war impossible. This precept was reaffirmed, again and again, at every international congress.

In 1904 in Amsterdam, representatives of the socialist parties from 24 countries on four continents had met while the Russo-Japanese War was raging. In front of the general assembly, the delegate of the small Japanese Socialist Party, Sen Katayama (1859–1933), walked across the stage and embraced Georgi Valentinovich Plekhanov (1856–1918), the Russian delegate. As the parties they represented were small, and almost insignificant, the gesture was at best symbolic. But once again it underscored the principle—workingmen of the world are united, welded into one against the forces of militarism.

In the same year the German Social Democratic Party received 3 million votes (it would receive 4 million by 1914) and occupied 81 seats in the Reichstag. Should the working class go on strike, it would bring the German economy to its knees. That was clearly enough power to stop a war.

Men like Jaurés and Hardie had a right to feel strengthened and secure. The socialist parties were growing stronger every day and creating a formidable barrier against the military adventures of the ruling class. Subsequent congresses of the Second International in Stuttgart (1907), Copenhagen (1911) and Basel (1912) all upheld the principle of collective class action against militarism. The socialists could boast control of more than 90 newspapers and in some countries they had begun welfare programs that constituted a socialist system with the capitalist state. Should the generals and the industrialists decide to start a war, then the workers of the countries involved had pledged themselves to go on strike and wage "war on war."

In the United States Eugene V. Debs (1865–1926) campaigned for President in a Special Red Train, with red banners flying, and won 400,000 votes in 1908, 900,000 in 1912. Debs delivered perhaps the most succinct statement of the socialist position,stating that

> there can be no compromise and no misunderstanding as to my position. I have no country to fight for; my country is the earth; I am a citizen of the world. I would not violate my principles for God, much less for a crazy kaiser, a savage czar, a degenerate king, or a gang of pot-bellied parasites [...]. There is where I stand and where I believe the Socialist Party stands, or ought to stand, on the question of war.[326]

* * *

In Brussels, almost on the eve of the German invasion of Belgium, representatives of the social democratic parties of Europe—with the exception of Austria-Hungary—met for an emergency meeting of the Bureau international de la paix (International Peace Bureau). All reaffirmed their opposition to war.

The German delegate immediately assured the group that Germany neither expected nor wanted war. "Every sane person opposes the idea of a war with France," he said with confidence.[327] But it was only rhetoric. While he spoke it was becoming clear that the majority of the German workers had already deserted international solidarity to rally to the flag. What was to have been the bastion against militarism evaporated almost overnight.

Nonetheless, a request was sent to every head of state asking them to find a peaceful solution to end the crisis. Each telegram was composed to appeal to the peaceful intentions and accomplishments of the ruler, for example: "The

Emperor of Russia was reminded of the work of The Hague, due to his initiative; Emperor William II of the 25 peaceful years of his reign, and his unusually religious feeling with regard to his responsibilities; to the Emperor of Austria there was pointed out the risk that he would see his reign of a half century end in blood; President Wilson was requested, in the name of all the previous record of his country, to propose mediation."[328]

In a mass rally Jean Jaurès addressed thousands of Belgian workers and intellectuals and declared: "For us, the French Socialists, the task is simple. We don't have to force a policy of peace on our government. It already practices it. I have never hesitated to invite the bitter hatred of the chauvinists by my relentless, unhesitating campaign for a Franco-German understanding; but I can say that now the French government wants peace and is working to save it."[329] Jaurès went on, painting a vivid picture of what could happen should Europe go to war:

> When typhus finishes the work begun by bullets, disillusioned men will turn on their rulers, whether German, French, Russian, or Italian, and demand their explanation for all those corpses. And then, the unchained Revolution will cry out to them: "Begone, and ask pardon of God and men!" But if we avoid the storm, then I hope that the masses will not forget and will say: "We must prevent this spectre from rising out of its grave every six months to terrify the world." Men of all countries, we must reach our goal of peace and justice.[330]

It was Jaurès's last speech. He was assassinated the following day in a Parisian café by a demented nationalist, Raoul Villain (1885–1936).[331]

After the meeting was over the German delegate caught the Northern Express, the last train to Germany from Brussels before the lines were cut. The next day a white poster went up on Parisian walls announcing the mobilization of the army. Beside it a yellow poster of the Association de la paix par le droit proclaimed: "*GUERRE À LA GUERRE!*" (WAR ON WAR!)[332]

A few days later Germany declared war on France. Following the example of the German workers, the vast majority of French socialists also abandoned the International and joined *l'union sacrée*, which supported the war. Almost overnight the Second International collapsed.

In England, when war was declared most socialists also immediately rallied to the flag, an unexpected about-face that took many labor leaders by surprise and left them marching to the international red standard with many, if not most, of the rank and file going in another direction.

When Keir Hardie (1856–1915), one of the leaders of the Independent Labour Party, addressed a meeting at his constituency shortly after the war began, his voice was drowned out by a chorus of "Rule, Britannia." Someone stood up and taunted Hardie about why his sons had not enlisted. He shouted back: "I would rather see my two boys put up against a wall and shot than see them go to the war."[333] The response was hoots and jeers. Later that evening a hostile crowd gathered in front of the house where Hardie was staying and shouted, "Turn the German out!"[334]

An outspoken pacifist, Hardie pleaded in the House of Commons for early peace negotiations, but in return he received shouts of, "Coward!" The national anthem was softly sung from the Labour benches behind him.

Nonetheless, Hardie remained steadfast to his pacifist principles. He wrote: "The cause of International Social Democracy must be proclaimed as the one and only hope for the world. Keep the red flag flying!"[335]

A minority of the working class followed him. The Independent Labour Party (ILP), which he helped found, not only opposed the war but also was opposed to any of its members attending pro-war rallies, especially those that encouraged men to join the military. The ILP was anti-war and also anti-military. For Hardie, a standing army was proof that the state was founded on force. Militarism and freedom, he declared, could not exist side by side, as "the means to do ill deeds makes ill done [...]. Militarism and all that pertains to it is inimical to the cause of progress."[336]

The ILP was the only party to stand apart and openly and loudly condemn the war. And it continued to do so throughout the conflict.

Several times Hardie's former colleagues in the Labour Party tried to censor him, but he kept writing. He was one of the few people to fully report on the signification of the strange truce that occurred on the Western Front at Christmastime 1914 when Allied and German troops sang carols to one another and exchanged presents.

Hardie advocated total disarmament. He wanted a country, preferably Great Britain, to set an example for the world by abolishing its army and scrapping its weapons. No country, he contended, would dare to attack a nation that had the faith and courage to disarm itself.

For Hardie, unilateral disarmament was a goal, a dream he tried to force upon reality, but at the same time he knew it was not immediately attainable. The viable means to prevent, or stop, a war was concerted industrial action with the other socialist parties of Europe, especially the German one, the most powerful. A general strike would paralyze the Continent and deprive any war of manpower, leaving the politicians threatening each other with empty rhetoric. That at least was the theory. Hardie did his best to put it into practice. While England and Germany were engaged in a desperate arms race that eventually led to the war, he tried numerous times to closely collaborate with the German socialists. In one letter to them he wrote: "The Labour Party stands for peace. We are prepared to cooperate with our German friends in thwarting the malignant designs of the small group of interested scaremongers, who in both countries would like to see war break out."[337]

August Bebel (1840–1813), one of the founders of the German Social Democratic Party, wrote back:

A war between England and Germany would lead to a European—that is a world—conflagration such as never before taken place. The German Social Democratic Party will do its utmost to prevent such, but should it happen in spite of all their efforts those who light this fire would also have to bear the consequences that await them. The vast majority of Germans are not thinking of war with England, and indeed do not do so for very sober, selfish reasons. We have nothing to gain, but much to lose.[338]

But when war was declared the German Social Democrats almost overnight shed their international solidarity and became shrill patriots. However, the first flush of nationalism did not dampen the pacifist ardor of the Independent Labour Party. Nearly a month after Great Britain declared war on Germany, Keir Hardie was still waging war against the war. In London, at Trafalgar Square, he addressed thousands of British workers: "You have no quarrel with Germany! [...] German workmen have no quarrel with their French comrades [...]. We are told international treaties compel us [but] who made those? The people had no voice in them!"[339]

The cheers and applause he received were proof that not everyone supported "the patriotic war." Hardie continued at that moment convinced that he knew what had to be done: "The working class of the two nations [Great Britain and Germany] will take the issues of war and peace out of the hands of bankrupt statesmen, and instead of shooting each other in a quarrel which is not theirs, will join hands and hearts, and upon a given day make war forever impossible by means—if nothing else suffices—of the weapon of the general strike."[340]

But the general strike that would have united Europe and possibly brought an end to the conflict never occurred. Hardie died in 1915 still agitating against the war. His parliamentary seat was lost to an opponent who advocated "annihilating the Huns" (10,286 votes to 6,080).

Where did that leave the individual British pacifist who watched the men march to war and in good conscience could not join them yet felt that he or she should stand up and be counted, alone if need be, visible for all to see, an example of how to put an end to war? The London *Herald of Peace* published an answer in 1915:

> Is personal neutrality possible if your country is at war? Certainly. Why not? You are a separate entity by no means identical with your country, a moral being with responsibilities and an immortal destiny [...]. Strict personal neutrality becomes imperative. He cannot side *with* his country, for being patriotic, he cannot assist her (or, rather, the political party which has temporarily the control of things) in destroying herself as well as her opponent, as a humanitarian he cannot join in the slaughter of human beings; and being a pacifist he dare not be an accomplice in the war. He cannot side *against* her, for the same reasons accentuated a thousandfold [...]. A child is not filially bound to share in a parent's crime [...] judging such ethical questions each is answerable at the bar of his own conscience, and there only.[341]

In July 1914, just before the war began, women began to lead the way and in large numbers. The International Women's Suffrage Alliance presented a peace petition to the British government on behalf of 12 million women from 26 countries.

* * *

In the capitals of Europe even those who held the reins of power lost hope of taming the wild dogs of war. A few months before hostilities began, the German Chancellor Theobald von Bethmann-Hollweg (1856–1921) told the Reichstag, "Statesmen in every country have begun to despair of averting the final crisis."

Albert de Mun (1841–1914) editorialized pessimistically in *L'Écho de Paris* in 1913: "Europe, uncertain and troubled, prepares for an inevitable war, whose beginning and cause are as yet unknown, but which is coming with the merciless certainty of fate."[342]

No one was more pessimistic than the German Chief of Staff, Helmuth von Moltke (1848–1916), or "sad Julius," as the Kaiser liked to call him. Von Moltke harbored few romantic illusions about war. In 1913 he told the Austro-Hungarian Chief of Staff, Count Franz Conrad von Hötzendorf (1852–1925), that "as ever, I am of the persuasion that a European war must come sooner or later."[343]

Nonetheless, one month after the assassination of Archduke Franz Ferdinand, only days before the war began, von Moltke sent a memorandum to the Imperial Chancellor saying that "the mutual butchery of the civilized nations of Europe will begin [...] unless [...] a miracle happens to prevent at the last moment a war which will annihilate for decades the civilization of almost all Europe."[344]

There was no miracle.

On the morning of August 4, 1914, the day after Germany declared war on Great Britain, Sir Edward Grey gazed out his window at the Foreign Office and watched the streetlights winking off. He commented: "The lamps are going out all over Europe; we shall not see them lit again in our lifetime."[345]

TWO

"Peace Before Christmas..."

Soon after the fighting began in Europe, the American President, Woodrow Wilson (1856–1924), dispatched telegrams to all the belligerents, Germany, France, Austro-Hungary and Great Britain. Acting in the name of The Hague Convention,[1] he formally offered to mediate the conflict "either now or at any other time that might be thought more suitable."[2]

The replies came back quickly. The American Secretary of State, William Jennings Bryan (1860–1925), summarized them: "If you will examine the five answers received, you will be reminded of that passage in the Scripture which says 'that they all with one accord began to make excuses.'[3] Each one declares he is opposed to war and is anxious to avoid it and then lays the blame upon someone else."[4]

The American President's offer of mediation was fully in keeping with the times. In fact, it was more or less expected of him. The war and the ways to end it were a popular theme, a constant topic of debate in bars, schools, churches and social clubs. America had lost much of its isolation and entered what many called "the golden age of internationalism."[5] Peace and peace activists enjoyed a level of financial support, respectability and popularity that they have yet to achieve again.

It was commonly believed that one major reason why there had been no major European war in the previous 40 years was that rulers, parliamentarians, diplomats and even generals were talking to one another as they never had before. Decisions were being made thoughtfully, based on rational principles, not wanton desire or instinct. Mankind was finally emerging from its primitive past. In 1913 the *Peace Forum* declared war to be "obsolete," as statesmen now "realize how ruinous it could be for them to fight."[6]

When President Wilson tried to step between the European belligerents, his action was merely an expression of the popular will. Just after the war began he set forth the American policy in a public address: "Every man who really loves America will act and speak in the true spirit of neutrality, which is the spirit of impartiality and fairness and friendliness to all concerned."[7]

* * *

The Spanish tried to open up another avenue for mediation. The King, Alfonso XIII (1886–1941), was related to both sides. His mother was Maria Christina of Austria (1858–1929), an archduchess, and he had married Princess Victoria Eugenie of Battenberg (1887–1969), Queen Victoria's granddaughter. A firm believer in the concept of European monarchical solidarity, Alfonso XIII was convinced that its rupture had been one of the root causes of the war. He corresponded extensively with William II of Germany and through diplomatic channels let the French know that, should the right moment arrive, he would be willing to mediate the conflict. Spain remained neutral for the duration of the war.[8]

However, in 1916 when Alfonso XIII gave a German submarine permission to enter the port of Cartegena to deliver a letter from William II the Allies threatened to blockade the Spanish ports. After that the King was more careful and, perhaps to demonstrate his strict neutrality, engaged in extensive humanitarian actions that included prisoner exchanges, having Spain serve as a neutral destination for correspondence and guaranteeing the free passage of hospital ships. Quite likely he hoped to take President Wilson's place when the United States declared war, but he was never called upon for mediation. Spanish neutrality was rewarded after the war when Spain was invited as the sole neutral nation alongside the Allies and Associates to become a member of the League of Nations Council.

* * *

At roughly the same time the Danish Foreign Minister, Erik Scavenius (1877–1962), entrusted a wealthy businessman, Hans Niels Andersen (1852–1937),[9] an intimate friend of the Danish royal family, with the task of finding an end to the war. Like many others, Scavenius believed that the principal cause of the war was a breakdown in communication. If the heads of state could speak to one another, either directly or through an intermediary, the dispute could be quickly settled. However, it is quite likely that the plan originated in Berlin, as the Germans were interested in obtaining a separate peace with the Russians or at least finding out what terms the Russians would accept for an armistice. If the Allies could be broken up and Russia taken out of the war, then all of the German troops and material on the Eastern Front could be transferred to the west to fight the French and English.

Andersen was the founder of the East Asiatic Company, the largest company in Denmark, and accustomed to dealing with royalty. He intended to make use of the close family relationship among the three sovereigns, since Christian X (1870–1947) of Denmark, George V (1865–1936) of Great Britain, and Nicolas II (1868–1918) of Russia were all first cousins.

Flattered by the task given to him, that is, being the peacemaker for the world, Andersen was probably not aware of the German motives behind his mission. Had he known them, it is doubtful he would have accepted, for his sympathies were clearly with the Allies. Throughout the war he provided the British King, George V, with firsthand information regarding the internal conditions in Germany.

Andersen consulted with German diplomats in Copenhagen, then went to Berlin, where he saw both the Kaiser and the Chancellor, Theobald von Bethmann-Hollweg (1856–1921), who told him that "Germany sorely needed peace."[10] Via neutral Scandinavia, Andersen traveled to St. Petersburg, where he tried to obtain terms for a Russo-German peace, but the Russian Foreign Minister, Sergey Dmitrievich Sazonov (1860–1927), refused to see him. Undeterred, Andersen made a second tour of the two capital cities before he gave up. If nothing else, he may have indicated to the Russians a willingness of the Germans to compromise in order to achieve peace.[11]

At roughly the same moment, Prince Gottfried von Hohenlohe (1867–1932), the ambassador of the Dual Monarchy to Berlin, wrote to Sergey Dmitrievich Sazonov, Russia's Foreign Minister, whom he knew personally. Quite likely von Hohenlohe was encouraged by Andersen to do so. Von Hohenlohe suggested that the Czar send an envoy to Switzerland to meet with a representative of Franz Josef I (1830–1916), the Emperor of the Austro-Hungarian Empire. Von Hohenlohe hoped that he could begin a process leading to an honorable peace. Sazonov, however, interpreted the letter as an indication of the low morale of the Austro-Hungarian troops army and did not reply. Shortly afterwards an article appeared in the Saint Petersburg newspaper, *Birzhheviya Vyedomost*, which declared that a separate peace with the Dual Monarchy was an impossibility since it was clear that the Allies intended to dismember it.

The Germans tried several times to obtain a separate peace with Russia. Although these were genuine attempts to stop the fighting, their real purpose was of course to release troops to fight on the Western Front. Acting on instructions from the German Foreign Office, H. Monkevitz, the director of the Deutsche Bank, for example, went to Stockholm, where he spoke with a Russian businessman, a financier who was a leading member of the pro-peace camarilla in St. Petersburg. Apparently the two men met several times in Stockholm and discussed the terms of a possible peace, without compromising the official diplomacy of either Germany or Russia.[12] However, the discussion went no further.

At precisely the same moment, Gottlieb von Jagow (1863–1935), the German Secretary of Foreign Affairs, got in touch with Marie Alexandrovna Vassiltchikov, a Russian lady-in-waiting who had been caught in Austria when the war began and was interned at Gloggnitz, a mountain resort in Lower Austria. She had already written two letters to the Czar on the subject of a Russo-German peace, neither of which was answered. Von Jagow had her brought to Berlin, where he asked her to use her connections to Nicolas II to transmit certain "unofficial information." Von Jagow's message was that the major monarchies of Europe, Germany, Austria-Hungary and Russia, should be supporting one another, not fighting. Furthermore, no matter what happened, he believed the British would never let the Russians take control of the Dardanelles or Constantinople, whereas the Germans promised to create a Russo-German condominium in Turkey that would guarantee the Russians free passage. Ultimately, von Jagow was convinced that France would join them, but never the British.

Marie Alexandrovna passed through the front lines on the Eastern Front into Russian territory, then delivered her message. When she received no response from the Czarist government, she apparently passed through the front lines once more and returned to Germany.

A few months later von Jagow decided to try again. This time, acting through the Grand Duke of Hesse, he entrusted Madame Vassiltchikov with several documents. The most important was a letter to the Czar indicating explicitly that the Kaiser, William II, would be willing to make a very generous peace and also insinuating that England had already made overtures for a separate understanding with Berlin. The letter ended by saying that a reconciliation between Russia and Germany was necessary to maintain the dynastic principle in Europe.

In addition, there were two personal letters, one to the Czar, the other to the Czarina. The latter was written in an affectionate tone and appealed to the Czarina's memories of her family and youth. The last sentence read: "I know what a thorough Russian you have become, but I cannot think that every trace of Germany has been effaced from your heart."[13] The Czarina (1872–1918) had in fact been born in Germany as Alix of Hesse. In Russia, she was known as Alexandra Feodorovna Romanova. She was also the granddaughter of Queen Victoria (1819–1901).

This time Madame Vassiltchikov was given a German passport and she took a safer route, traveling by way of neutral Copenhagen and Stockholm. When she arrived in St. Petersburg she personally handed the letters, which were unsealed, to Sergey Sazanov, the Russian Foreign Minister, who, in turn, gave them to the Czar. But the Czar was in no mood to make peace. In fact, he was incensed. The French ambassador, Maurice Paléologue (1859–1944), was present to record Nicholas II's rage: "What an insult to make such proposals to me! How could this silly *intrigante* dare to bring them! [...]. All this stuff is just a tissue of lies and treachery [...]. England preparing to betray Russia! How absurd!"[14]

The Czar was also furious with Madame Vassiltchikov, insulted that a lady-in-waiting should be entrusted with what could be an important document: "To accept such a commission from an enemy sovereign! This woman is either wicked or a fool. How could she fail to realize that in carrying these letters she ran the risk of seriously compromising the Empress and myself?"

The letters that Madame Vassiltchikov carried were returned to Germany via the Spanish diplomatic service. Instead of shooting the messenger, the Czarist government confiscated Madame Vassiltchikov's German passport, banished her from the capital, then sent her to Tchernigov, a city in the northern Ukraine, where she was interned in a convent.[15]

The Germans made other attempts to contact the Russians and negotiate a separate peace, the last one after the revolution and the installation of the Provisional Government. The Bulgarian Minister to Berlin, M. Rizov, traveled to Christiana (the name was changed to Olso in 1925) using a false passport, then presented himself at the Russian embassy. When he could speak privately with Ambassador Gulkevitch, Rizov explained that he had come to Norway to offer Russia a separate peace with Germany on favorable terms including a right of passage through the Bosporus and the Dardanelles. He asked Gulkevitch to submit these proposals to the Russian government as soon as possible. Rizov went on to say that it was urgent to start the negotiations at once, as Germany was planning a new offensive for the spring that he was certain would destroy the Russian armies.

Gulkevitch immediately sent a cable to Petrograd, detailing the conversation and adding that he was certain that Rizov was acting under orders from Berlin. However, the Russian Provisional Government renewed their commitment to the Allies and vowed to continue the war.

It is tempting to speculate what might have happened if the Provisional Government had acted on the offer and concluded a separate peace with Germany. Lenin and the communists might well have remained a fringe party in a democratic Russia, and the world would have been spared the excesses of a paranoid totalitarian state.

* * *

In December 1914 Raymond Gram Swing (1887–1967), an American reporter in Berlin, obtained an interview with Theobald von Bethmann-Hollweg (1856–1921), the Chancellor of the German Empire. During the course of the interview Swing asked the all-important question: what it would take to make peace. The Chancellor replied that Berlin would not consider a cease-fire and a truce unless Belgium was completely restored and Germany was paid an indemnity for being forced into the war. Swing took the message to England and presented it to Sir Edward Grey (1862–1933), the British Foreign Secretary. According to Swing, upon hearing the word "indemnity" Grey became nearly apoplectic and let loose a stream of very undiplomatic language. In effect, the Germans were asking that England pay for the restoration of Belgium. Unfortunately, Grey chose to regard the offer as an ultimatum rather than just a first step in the process of negotiation, the opening gambit in the game of compromise.[16]

* * *

Benedict XV (1854–1922) was elected Pope only a few weeks after the war started. One of his first acts was to declare the Vatican to be neutral.[17] At the same time he publicly took an unequivocal stand against the war, which he called "the suicide of civilized Europe, the darkest tragedy of human hatred and human madness."[18]

In the new Pope's first encyclical, *Ad Beatissimi*, he associated war with Satan's envy of the Kingdom of Peace. He argued: "Surely there are other ways and means whereby violated rights can be rectified?"[19]

Small, lame, bashful, hard of hearing, and afflicted with a harsh, rasping voice, Benedict XV was an unlikely spokesman for peace. One observer described him as follows: "[I]n person, he was undersized, of a sallow, bilious complexion [...], everything about him was crooked, nose, mouth, eyes and shoulders."[20]

The Pope may have appeared to be misshapen, but his ideas were fully formed, especially his uncompromising universally pacifist beliefs. These immediately put him at odds with most of the European clergy, who had accepted a patriotic, nationalist—*Gott mit uns* (God is with us), *l'union sacrée* (the sacred union)—point of view.[21] For Benedict XV, there was no such thing as a just war. All war was wrong and contrary to scripture.

Benedict XV refused to bless the Austrian armies and thus quickly earned the title of "the Pontiff of Peace,"[22] although both sides, the Allies and the Central Powers, accused him of being partial. The French Prime Minister, Georges Clemenceau (1841–1929), for example, condemned Benedict XV as *"le pape boche,"* while the German General Ludendorff (1865–1937) referred to him disparagingly as *"der französische Papst."*[23]

After the first few months of intense warfare left nearly a million casualties on the battlefield, the Pope asked all belligerents to observe a Christmas cease-fire, saying "in the name of the Divinity [...] cease the clang of arms while Christendom celebrates the Fest of the World's Redemption."[24] Benedict XV conveniently ignored the fact that some of the countries at war, notably Japan and Turkey, were not part of "Christendom" and that Russia, although certainly Christian, was Orthodox. For them, Christmas occurred on the seventh of January, not the twenty-fifth of December.

In any case, only the German government accepted the Pope's proposal, with the clear condition that all other countries at war make a similar commitment.

The British generals paid no attention to the Pope's appeal. When they did bother to express an opinion, it was strident and bellicose. A staff officer wrote home to his wife from the trenches in Flanders: "What truth is there in the Pope proposing an armistice for Christmas? If true and accepted I don't think hostilities will be resumed—I don't think it ought to be accepted— We are out here for war and this cannot be mixed up with "Peace on Earth [...], good will towards men."[25]

Often called the most pacifist Pope in modern history,[26] Benedict XV made several other unsuccessful attempts to negotiate a peace, notably for Christmas 1915. These pleas for an end to hostilities accomplished little except to make him unpopular in Catholic countries such as Italy and France, which were committed to total victory and refused to accept the Pope's "stalemate peace." But the Pope was undeterred and, if nothing else, continued to speak out in the name of peace, referring to the war as "an unparalleled scourge [...], a carnage which is without example [...], this monstrous spectacle [...], a horrible plague."[27] He declared: "They want to silence me [...], but they shall not succeed in sealing my lips; nobody shall prevent me from calling to my own children, peace, peace, peace."[28]

Benedict XV also created a day of prayer, February 7, Sexagesima Sunday, the second Sunday before Ash Wednesday, and wrote a lengthy prayer, which was translated into the languages of the various belligerents, then printed on prayer cards. Reaction to the wording of the prayer was generally unfavorable. The French, for example, changed the line "O King of Peace, we humbly implore the peace for which we long [...]," so that the prayer cards read, "O King of Peace we humbly implore peace on conditions honorable for our fatherland."[29] Cardinal Léon-Adolphe Amette (1850–1920) of Paris mounted the pulpit of Notre Dame and explained to the faithful that what the Holy Father really meant to say was that he wished to see the war ended by a victorious peace for France.

* * *

After the failure of the Pope and the American President to mediate the conflict, a less well-known attempt took place. James Speyer (1861–1941), a pacifist who had been decorated by the Kaiser and was the head of the New York branch of a German bank, gave a dinner party that brought together Oscar S. Straus (1850–1926), formerly Secretary of Commerce and Labor, and the German ambassador, Count von Bernstorff (1862–1939). During the conversation the ambassador made it clear that his government would willingly entertain a proposal for mediation. When Straus asked if he could take that proposal to the American government, the ambassador agreed. According to von Bernstdorff: "He [Straus] turned particularly to me because the German Government were [sic] regarded as opponents of pacifist ideas. I said that we had not desired the war and would certainly be ready at the first suitable opportunity for a peace by understanding."[30]

Von Bernstorff had made it known from the moment he arrived in Washington that he was opposed to war and willing to do whatever he could to avoid it. Much later he wrote in his memoirs: "I pursued the policy of Peace with undeviating consistency, and to this day I still believe it to have been the only right policy [...]. My policy might best be described as that of 'a silent resolve to obtain Peace.'"[31]

That evening Straus got on a train for Washington, and the next day he met with the Secretary of State, William Jennings Bryan (1860–1925). Bryan, who had been an unsuccessful candidate for the Presidency three times, was a well-known pacifist, one of the few American Secretaries of State to hold such strong convictions. When the war began he had written to President Wilson: "It is not likely that either side will win so complete a victory as to be able to dictate terms, and if either side does win such a victory it will probably mean preparation for another war. It would seem better to look for a more rational basis for peace"[32]

Bryan welcomed the opportunity to search for a peaceful solution and asked Straus to take the proposal to the British and French ambassadors. Both agreed that it was an opportunity worth pursuing. But when Straus asked if the French would be willing to return to the *status quo ante*, the French ambassador replied: "*mais que ce soit le vrai statu quo; que les Allemands, qui ont envahi notre pays et tué nos gens, rendent la vie à nos morts, sans quoi il n'en saurait être question*," (but let it be the real status quo; let the Germans, who invaded our country and killed our people, bring our dead back to life, without that, it is out of the question).[33]

Straus and Bryan decided to use diplomatic channels and involve the American ambassadors in London and Paris, but no sooner had they sent off coded cables than, through an unexplained leak, news of the entire affair was published in a Chicago newspaper. It was of course impossible to negotiate with the public, both in America and in Europe, following every move. That immediately put an end to the experiment in "quiet diplomacy."

However, Colonel House (1858–1938), President Wilson's friend and advisor, had been following the affair secretly and picked up the threads.

Colonel House was no pacifist, nor was he a real humanist. Instead, he could probably be best labeled a politician's politician, a kind of backroom, behind-the-scenes pragmatist, a subtle sycophant, but shrewd and talented, taking obvious pleasure from pushing "his man" forward until he stood in the rarified air high above all others.

When the war began in Europe Colonel House was not repelled by the carnage and human suffering. He saw in the conflict an opportunity that he quickly defined as making peace. For him, peace was not a means to the obvious end, rather a way to thrust Woodrow Wilson and the United States to the forefront and center of the world stage. For example, almost nowhere in the hundreds of pages of Colonel House's notes and letters did he mention that he was appalled by the human costs or that he had used his influence and position to ameliorate the condition of the wounded or refugees. It was the machinations and maneuverings of diplomats and politicians that interested him.

Colonel House approached both the German and British ambassadors, whom he knew quite well. He inquired if they would be willing to meet privately somewhere in Washington and discuss possible terms for a peace.

The German ambassador, von Bernstorff, agreed almost immediately. But the British were suspicious, and afraid that should a secret meeting take place, the "unreliable and unmoral Germans," as the British ambassador called them, might make the discussions public, then use them as a wedge to try to divide the Allies. The French were even less trusting and flexible, thus unlikely to be willing to talk even in secret. When the French Prime Minister, Georges Clemenceau, was asked to state his war aims, he replied categorically, "My war aim is to be the victor!"[34] Colonel House was forced to abandon the project.

However, Colonel House soon renewed his peace efforts. The war in Europe confirmed his belief in the necessity for an international organization, an idea that would eventually take form as a league of nations. Colonel House recalled a long discussion he had with President Wilson: "I believed if we had had an opportunity to put this (a meeting of the Great Powers) into effect, in all human probability such a war as this would not have occurred—because with the Powers meeting at regular intervals, and with such a concrete example of the good that might be accomplished by concerted action, a conflagration as was now going on would have been impossible." This was to be the ultimate goal, the future beyond the end of the war, a permanent meeting of the Great Powers that would make sure that a world war was never repeated.

Six months after the war began, Colonel House set out once again to try to mediate the conflict. He went to first England, then France, and finally by way of neutral Switzerland to Germany, but everywhere he went he received the same message. It was the wrong moment to speak about peace. Both sides were convinced they had victory almost within their reach, and despite the staggering human cost they were determined to keep fighting.

Colonel House was not discouraged. If he couldn't have a full agreement on peace, then he was determined to get a partial one, to attack the terms piecemeal, one by one. His next idea was to obtain an accord on the freedom of the seas from the British and the Germans. It could be an advantage to both of them: the British could cease worrying about German submarines, and the Germans would be free of the British blockade. The United States would also profit of course, since it was trading with both sides and making more money from foreign trade than ever before. Should such an agreement be reached, Colonel House thought the next step might be a truce, a cease-fire, followed by an international conference hosted by the United States. President Wilson could then step in and become the decisive peace giver.

The British agreed, provided that outlawing poison gas also became part of the bargain, and for a short time Colonel House was enthused. He thought he might have found the beginning of the end of the war. But the Germans rejected the idea completely, refusing even to discuss it in principle. Colonel House returned to the United States empty-handed.

* * *

After the first two weeks of war produced more than 20,000 British casualties, it was clear that sooner or later the British government would turn to conscription. A young socialist journalist, Fenner Brockway (1888–1988), editor of the *Labour Leader*, published an appeal asking for the names of men between 18 and 38 who would refuse to be combatants if conscription was introduced. The response was immediate and substantial and thus the No-Conscription Fellowship (NCF) was founded. Members stated that they "consider human life to be sacred and cannot, therefore, assume the responsibility of inflicting death. They deny the right of governments to say 'you shall bear arms.'"[35]

The idea behind the NCF was simple. Peace began with a single moral act, one draftee looking into his conscience and deciding that he would not kill another or be a part of any organization created for the purpose of killing others. Each man's act of defiance became an example to all others. If enough men refused to fight, there would be no war. The conflict would be solved by other means, more rational and more humane.

Financed largely by wealthy Quakers, the NCF became a haven for non-religious conscientious objectors (COs). Two basic types belonged to the NCF. The first were those who for moral or religious reasons would not have anything to do with the war effort in any capacity however remote, the so-called absolutists. Most refused to wear a uniform or to submit to military discipline. The second category was composed of those who would serve in the army but only if they were not required to carry a weapon. This included socialists who opposed the war, Christian pacifists who opposed all wars, and men who were prepared to serve but only in non-combatant roles, for example, anarchists and syndicalists.

These distinctions became critical when voluntary enlistments in the army began to decline drastically and the government instituted conscription in January 1916. By the summer of that year over 1,200 men had refused to serve, and by the war's end 16,500[36] had become COs, 0.33 percent of all men recruited or conscripted. Of this number nearly 6,000 either refused to appear before a tribunal or, having appeared, refused to accept its decision.

Ultimately the NCF became the largest and most active anti-war/anti-conscription movement in modern British history.[37] Its membership exceeded 15,000. The NCF did what it could to get the conscription legislation repealed and published more than a million pamphlets and leaflets as well as a weekly newsletter, the *Tribunal*, which at one point reached a circulation in excess of 10,000.[38] The NCF also tried to assist COs when they had to appear before tribunals, providing them with sample text and arguments they could use to prevent conscription.

The tribunals were composed of local tradesmen, retired military officers, civic leaders and at least one member of the army whose sole purpose was to fill the thinning ranks in the trenches. Most of the tribunals were intensely patriotic and had little sympathy for those they suspected of lesser motives. They were also grossly overworked and unpaid. Between January and July 1916, for example, thousands of men applied for four different types of exception. Given the press of work, as the tribunals ruled on perhaps 40 to 60 cases a day, it is difficult to believe that an individual received adequate time to present his point of view. As a result, very few pacifists obtained an exception from military service. Many cases before the tribunals were turned down completely, which meant the men could be drafted as ordinary soldiers. Once handed over to the military, if they refused orders they could be court-martialed and sent to jail. George Bernard Shaw (1856–1950) attacked the "pompous insolence" and "honest barbarism" of the tribunal members, and G. K. Chesterton (1874–1936) called their procedures "moral anarchy," which could only produce tyranny.[39]

There were numerous instances of abuse, ill-treatment and injustice. One CO was told he was fit only "to be on the point of a German bayonet," another that he was not only a coward and a cad but also "a shivering mass of unwholesome fat."[40] In one infamous case a group of COs were sentenced to be shot, then at the last minute had their sentences commuted to ten years in prison. Other COs were beaten, given short rations and thrown into dank and unhealthy medieval dungeons.

Roughly 3,400 COs accepted a call-up into the Non-Combatant Corps (NCC) or the Royal Army Medical Corps (RAMC) as non-combatants. The NCC (the "No-Courage Corps," as the press rudely labeled it) became part of the army. The COs wore uniforms and were subject to military discipline, but they didn't carry arms or engage in warfare. Most worked as medical orderlies, stretcher bearers, ambulance drivers, cooks or laborers.

Many "absolutists" were forcibly inducted and when they refused to wear a uniform they were court-martialed and sent to prison. During the war 6,312 COs were arrested; 5,970 were court-martialed, then sent to jail, where most of them were badly treated, both physically and mentally.

By February 1917 3,025 COs were in prison, and ultimately over 5,000 went to jail. Five hundred and twenty-eight were sentenced to severe penalties. This included 17 who were sentenced to death (afterwards commuted to ten years in prison),[41] 142 to life imprisonment, 3 to 50 years' imprisonment, 4 to 40 years, and 57 to 25 years. By the time the war was over 819 had spent over two years in prison. At least 73 died, most due to the harsh treatment they received, nearly all from treatment that today we would call torture. Kept in solitary confinement or forced to sew mailbags or weave mats for the navy 12 hours a day, they were not allowed to speak to other prisoners and were fed starvation rations of bread and water.

Outside of jail the COs were ostracized. Mirroring public sentiment, the press called them "coddled conscience men," "disloyal," "hordes of cowards," one newspaper going as far as to say that the COs were "not worth the powder and shot," but in view of the extreme circumstances "perhaps a few rounds might be spared."[42] The *Daily Express* insinuated that the COs were receiving German financing, and the tabloid *John Bull* ranted: "The conscientious objector is a fungus growth [...], a human toadstool [...], which should be uprooted without further delay."[43]

This kind of attitude led to extremely harsh treatment for some. For example, the case of the three Walker brothers may not be atypical. They were called up in 1916 and adopted an "absolutist" position; that is, they refused to support the war effort or the military in any manner whatsoever. They were confined for two years to a detention barracks where each day they were forcibly dressed in a military uniform and fed. Unwilling to take part in drills and exercises, they were continually beaten and harassed. The price for dissent came high. One sergeant in the military police wrote in his memoirs:

> I remember one man in particular, who absolutely refused to have anything to do with the Army at all, and refused to put on khaki. Well, we were instructed to take measures to remedy this state of affairs, which included taking him to the baths, stripping him and forcing a suit of khaki on him. We took him to the open compound, and as it was very cold at night we thought he would be forced to wear this khaki to keep himself warm, but he had other ideas. During the night he stripped himself of this khaki and shredded the whole of the suit up and hung it around the barbed wire, and that man walked about all night long without a shred of clothing on him. That was the type of treatment we had to mete out, and I am bitterly ashamed that I was forced to take part in it [...], they had far more guts than we did who were doing those things to them.[44]

One group of 17 COs were forcibly enlisted in the Non-Combatant Corps, then confined to punishment cells in a Napoleonic-era prison in Harwich. One of the COs described the conditions in which they were detained as follows: "[The cells are] completely dark, dripping with water and overrun with rats [...], for three days without food. It was impossible to sleep. Our guards kept telling us we'd soon be pushing up daisies, so we weren't surprised to hear we were going to France—in irons. We were asked to make our wills, but all 17 of us refused."[45]

As the train where they were confined passed through London, one of the COs managed to throw a note out the window. It was picked up by a sympathetic railway man who alerted the NCF. The group became known as the "Harwich Frenchmen" and were sent to punishment camps. Every day some of them had their arms tied to a kind of crucifix. Later they were roped face forward into a barbed-wire fence. Then all of them were handcuffed and locked in a small wooden cage for a month. Eventually they were brought before a military court-martial and when they were in front of thousands of soldiers in formation death sentences were pronounced. At the last moment their sentences were commuted. The men were sent to work camps. The last CO was finally released in August 1919, more than a half year after the end of hostilities.

After the war was over George Bernard Shaw commented that "as far as the question was one solely of conscience, the Conchy (CO) was the hero of the war."[46]

Within the NCF there had been a great deal of squabbling. In general, the Quakers regarded the objectors as "silent witnesses" for peace, each man passively accepting whatever hardship he was forced to endure. The underlying logic contended that as the ranks of the COs swelled their collective suffering would be a beacon to illuminate man's cruelty to man. Thus the Quakers resented the NCF's attempts to obtain better treatment for the objectors in jail, while the socialists whose attention was drawn to the Russian Revolution began to question the total rejection of force. The leadership of the NCF advocated no participation in the war economy. Most of the COs, however, agreed to work at jobs of "national importance" as long as they did not involve carrying a weapon.

Despite the internal differences the NCF managed to function effectively. Detailed records were kept in duplicate so that should the offices be raided by the police, the organization would not cease to exist. One member wrote that "in various secret places, buried in an orchard in Surrey, or locked in an unsuspecting city merchant's safe, or at the back of a bookshelf in the house of a remote sympathizer [...], were duplicates of every document likely to be seized."[47] The NCF also established a "shadow structure" so that if any officer was arrested, someone else, designated in advance, would automatically take his or her place.

Clifford Allen (1889–1939), one of the founders of the NCF, was one of the first to go to jail. He thus addressed the tribunal:

> I wish to make it clear that I cannot take a share in military work in this war, because I believe there is no substantial reason to prevent peace negotiations being entered upon at once. I believe that you sitting here and the peoples of all nations on both sides are yearning for peace. I believe that the governments of all nations are too afraid of releasing their peoples to make peace [...]. Such being my attitude to all war, and to this war, I can, of course, in no way acquiesce in conscription, which is designed to equip the nation for war.[48]

When most COs appeared in front of a tribunal, they were asked the question "Are you doing work of national importance?" One militant socialist replied, "No, but I am engaged on work of international importance."[49] Another CO was asked by a woman on the tribunal why he was not in France fighting for civilization like other men his age. The CO replied, "Madam, I am the civilization they are fighting for."[50]

The British government also found other ways to discourage pacifist or anti-war activities. Newsprint, for example, dropped to a quarter of what was available before the war and was tightly rationed based on pre-war circulation.

Since most of the anti-war press came into existence after the war began, they were excluded from access to stocks of paper. Food was also strictly rationed. Overt opposition to the war, or industrial action as a protest, could mean the cancellation of ration cards. It was simple and effective. No work, no food.

The only dissenters who were able to openly oppose the war without fear of reprisal were Members of Parliament, who were protected by a parliamentary immunity. MPs such as Charles P. Trevelyan,[51] Phillip Snowden (1864–1937),[52] and Ramsay MacDonald,[53] after the war began continued their anti-war activities, mainly speaking and writing, without harassment. Watched closely by the police, they were allowed to dissent, a fact that was used extensively in propaganda, proof that domestically the war was a contest of ideas and not simply a contest of strength.

The NCF ultimately failed in its objectives: conscription was never repealed, peace propaganda never aroused the public into a mass movement, and the organization never produced the spark to ignite an international movement. It did, however, give aid, comfort and camaraderie to its members and "almost by default became Britain's most prominent defender of the principle of freedom of conscience during the First World War."[54]

At the same time, the NCF tested the limits of dissent in a liberal society at war. In the words of one historian: "There was no equivalent organization in any other belligerent country from 1914 to 1918, and there has been none since."[55]

For their small numbers, the NCF did what it could and, in doing so, stood out as an example, each conscientious objector "driving a nail in the coffin of the war."[56] The blame for their lack of success should perhaps be placed, not on them, but, as Bertrand Russell succinctly put it, on those who did "follow a multitude to do evil."[57]

* * *

Few people spoke louder for the NCF and the pacifists in Great Britain than Bertrand Russell (1872–1970). He took over a caretaker administration for the NCF and, despite harassment by the authorities, the organization continued to function and indeed grow. He wrote and lectured extensively against the war, his message clear and uncompromising: under no circumstances could war ever be justified. For example, he declared in a letter to *The Nation* just after hostilities began:

> Against the vast majority of countrymen, even at this moment, in the name of humanity and civilization, I protest against our share in the destruction of Germany. A month ago, Europe was a peaceful comity of nations; if an Englishman killed a German, he was hanged. Now, if an Englishman kills a German, or if a German kills an Englishman, he is a patriot, who has deserved well of his country. We scan the newspapers with greedy eyes for news of slaughter, and rejoice when we read of innocent young men, blindly obedient to the word of command, mown down in thousands [...].[58]

Patriots always talk about dying for their country, and never about killing for their country.[59]

Russell did more than just protest. He set forth a positive plan that enlarged on the Platonic thesis that the man who inflicted justice was more to be pitied than the man who suffered it.

Russell posed the argument for passive resistance first as a question:

> Let us imagine that England were to disband its army and navy, after a generation of instruction in the principles of passive resistance as a better defense than war. Let us suppose that England at the time publicly announced that no armed opposition would be offered to an invader, that all might come freely, but that no obedience would be yielded to any commands that a foreign authority might issue. What would happen in this case?[60]

He then answered his own question by analyzing what would occur if a German army came to England and found, instead of an opposing military force, a population steeped in passive resistance:

> If England had no army and no navy, the Germans would be hard put to find a pretext for invasion. [...] suppose the invading army arrived in London [...]. All existing officials would refuse to cooperate with the Germans [...]. Whatever edicts they (the Germans) might issue would be quietly ignored by the population [...]. The same courage and idealism which are now put into war could easily be directed by education into the channel of passive resistance [...] [and] would prove to any invading army that the task of subjecting England to alien domination was an impossible one.[61]

Neither England, nor any other country in the world was ready to prove the value of passive resistance. Russell knew this. He was sufficiently a realist to accept the fact that that day, if it ever came, was far into the future saying that "war will end only after a great labor has been preformed in altering men's moral ideals, directing them to the good of all mankind, and not only of the separate nations into which men happen to have been born."[62]

Nonetheless, Russell continued to do what he could, encouraging others to follow the dictates of their conscience no matter what the cost. He documented the resistance, the punishment, the suffering, case by case, in handbills and brochures often ending with the question: "Can you remain silent whilst this goes on?"[63]

When six men were sent to prison for distributing a leaflet he authored, Russell wrote to the *Times*: "Six men have been condemned to varying terms of imprisonment with hard labour for distributing this leaflet. I wish to make it known that I am the author of this leaflet and that if anyone is to be prosecuted, I am the person primarily responsible."[64] Russell was held responsible and charged with making "statements likely to prejudice the recruiting and discipline of His Majesty's forces." He was found guilty and fined 100 pounds. When he refused to pay the fine, he hoped he would be sent to prison. Instead, the belongings in his rooms at Trinity College, Cambridge, were seized. When they were sold at auction many of Russell's friends tried to buy them back for him. Russell was dismissed from his post at Cambridge and prevented from speaking in so-called prohibited areas, which meant anywhere along the British coast and cities like Glasgow, Edinburgh and Newcastle. Eventually in 1918 he was sentenced to six months in prison.

* * *

At the outbreak of hostilities, in 1914, the German peace movement numbered perhaps 10,000 active members. Though not a mass movement, it was certainly a vocal one which could count on thousands of sympathizers and just under a hundred local groups. It was a secular organization and undoubtedly the weakest in Europe.[65] One of the founders of the German Peace Society declared that "it would be a distortion of the facts to credit the German peace movement with any perceptible influence whatsoever on the fate of the German people in the sixteen years before the war."[66]

Whereas most peace movements cut across social and economic lines, the German one was largely confined to the lower middles classes, small shopkeepers, clerks, and primary school teachers. There was a noticeable absence of blue-collar workers, university students, professors and clergymen. German universities bred nationalism, not internationalism, and student organizations from abroad garnered little or no support. Pacifists were commonly portrayed as utopians or visionaries totally out of touch with the realities of international politics.

The overwhelming majority of religious leaders supported Germany's military establishment. The alliance of *Thron und Altar* (state and church) produced a vociferous nationalism that stood behind the country's most belligerent goals.

There were few exceptions, for the state made it difficult to be a pacifist. Peace publications were frequently banned, and it was forbidden to hold pacifist meetings even in private homes. European Catholics, for example, had created the Gratry Society[67] in 1907 with the blessings of Pope Pius X (1835–1914).[68] By 1910 it had become the International Catholic Peace League, with active branches in France, Spain, Switzerland and Belgium, but not in Germany.

The position of the Evangelical Church was even stronger in its support of the Kaiser's war aims. The churches were state supported; therefore, those who worked for them were technically civil servants and formed a highly nationalistic bureaucracy that regarded as suspect any organization with international ties. This was reinforced by Evangelical logic, which postulated that if wars occurred, it was proof of God's will. Even Martin Luther (1483–1546) had justified war.[69] Thus to advocate peace on earth placed an individual in opposition to God's plan. One annoyed pastor wrote: "We must protest again the peace movement in the name of Christianity, for it does not present the truth, but a lie, which is all the more captivating since it is covered with a froth of Christian-sounding phrases."[70]

The German Peace Society made numerous attempts to influence the church, but few of them were successful. Even such a benign proposition as the creation of a "Peace Sunday" once a month was rejected. Clergymen of all sorts consistently refused invitations to pacifist meetings, lectures and discussions. When, for example, a local peace organization sent an appeal to the priests and pastors of Königsberg, it did not receive a single answer. At the outbreak of the First World War the German Peace Society could count on only 117 clergymen among its adherents.

Even groups like the Mennonites, who traditionally took an unequivocal stand toward violence, willingly served in the Kaiser's military. Approximately 2,000 of them joined the army and 400 died on the battlefield.[71] During the entire war, from 1914 to 1918, in all of Germany, only 47 men were sentenced to death as war resisters.[72]

More than any of the other European peace parties, the German Peace Society had stood for what was called scientific pacifism,[73] the idea that the cultural and commercial interdependence of the advanced nations was both making warfare impossible and at the same time creating the basis for a new international order in which all disputes would be peacefully adjudicated. The man most identified with this perspective was Alfred H. Fried (1864–1921), one of the original founders of the society.[74]

Fried succeeded in raising many of the tenets of the peace movement, such as arbitration and arms limitation, to the level of academic respectability. Discarding the vestiges of moralism and idealism, he called pacifism "the science of peace" (*pazifistisch Wissenschaft*) and the person who practices it a *Friedenstechniker*, a peace technician. This scientific basis appealed broadly to pacifists in both Austria and Germany. Although it never attained the popularity and support of the movement in France or the Anglo-Saxon countries, nonetheless at one point the German Peace Society had over 50 branches.[75]

According to Fried, if "a peace technician" examined the international situation dispassionately, that is, scientifically, with an exacting, surgical logic, he would come to the conclusion that there is only one cause of war, international anarchy. Thus the motto of the German pacifist campaign became "*Organisiert die Welt!*" (Organize—or unite—the world!) Put simply, world peace could only come through world government, the creation of an *Übernation,* a superstate, which had the means, military if necessary, to enforce its will. This giant collective, Fried firmly believed, could never be evil or be used for evil purposes. He wrote: "We can say with confidence that the state, with its scientific academics, its parliaments and its universities, cannot assume the role of a criminal or highwayman."[76]

Fried's contribution was almost purely intellectual, an analysis of the forces of history at work. This left the individual, the man on the street, more or less impotent. He could do little more than sit on the sidelines, discuss the path and progress of peace, and then celebrate its inevitable success.

"Scientific pacifism" was modern, compelling and optimistic: man was moving inexorably on the path to a higher civilization and the non-violent resolution of conflict through economic interdependence. There was an empirical base for the theory. In 1910, for example, four years before the war began, approximately 45 percent of the British gross domestic product, 35 percent of the French and nearly 40 percent of the German came from foreign trade.[77] And every year those percentages grew larger. The facts were right but the conclusion wrong.

The moment the war began, "scientific pacifism" collapsed into reams of meaningless statistics. Suddenly the German Peace Party appeared to be impotent and irrelevant. All its conferences, pamphlets, books, debates and discussions had achieved nothing, millions of words of arguments, dreams and prayers instantly deadened by the roar of the guns. History appeared to be marching backwards. Reason had failed. Science had been enslaved by generals. The military parades were a funeral march for the German Peace Party.

However, as soon as the first wave of casualties arrived home and another set of realities, those of modern warfare, became evident, the ranks of the party began to swell again. But even at its peak the movement never became a threat to Germany's industrial mobilization and did little to interfere with the country's ability to wage war.

Nonetheless, the German government cracked down. In their eyes advocacy of peace meant weakness, internal discontent, and a lack of confidence that would give the wrong impression to the outside world. Rather than focus on individuals and perhaps turn them into martyrs, the government stilled the movement's voice. All public meetings and speeches were forbidden, as was all communication with foreigners. The publications from the Peace Party were banned from the post office and the authorities made it difficult, if not impossible, for them to obtain paper. Their bookstores were closed and their personal mail was intercepted and read. They were treated like a secretive fifth column, an underground ready to seize power at any moment.

Had they had any conspiratorial secrets to hide, pacifists certainly would not have published them or confided them to the post office. Most referred to the annoying censorship as "a landmark in the history of stupidity."[78]

The party continued to circulate handbills and pamphlets as best they could. But instead of confronting war, the senseless waste of men and material, hoping to escape the ire of the authorities, they focused on the peace that they hoped would soon arrive and how the world should be organized after the war. The German Peace Party blunted its own spear.

In 1916, from exile in Switzerland, Alfred H. Fried tried to provide an explanation for the failure of the German peace movement:

When, then, the war broke out [...], superficial and infatuated thinkers held but one opinion: that pacifism had failed and was proven an illusion [...]. The war has brought no collapse of pacifism [...]. They are bankrupt [...], they who lived in the belief that peace could be secured by preparing for war and only by preparing for war; they who thought that a sharp sword and dry powder outweighed all the instruments of reconciliation and peaceful settlement [...]. Pacifists never indulged in the dream that they who fed the fires of national hatred would escape without war [...]. No, the war was no surprise to us. We knew that it might have been avoided, and we struggled loyally for that end [...]. But the forces of international anarchy were too strong. The war came before our ideas had won full sway.

In millions of minds the world over the thought arises, and the fearful question is put: Was it inevitable? Must it be thus eternally? And the answer swells to an iron echo, awakening and sweeping the world: NO![79]

But the Peace Party was moribund and remained so, just another casualty of the war.

* * *

When Germany declared war, Karl Liebknecht (1871–1919),[80] a member of the Social Democratic Party (SPD), was the first to cast his vote against military credits for the war. In a hostile Reichstag, bursting with patriotic, pro-war rhetoric, Liebknecht stood up and, very much alone, addressed the deputies: "A speedy peace, a peace without conquests, this is what we must demand [...]. But as a protest against the war, against those who are responsible for it and have caused it, against those who direct it [...], against plans of annexation, against the violation of neutrality, against unlimited rule of martial law [...], I vote against the war credits demanded."[81]

Liebknecht's voice was an almost solitary and ineffective cry of protest. Few heard it. After decades of anti-war rallies, conferences and demonstrations, the German socialists, that is, the Social Democrats, suddenly forgot their pacifism and performed a volte-face, enthusiastically marching to the nationalistic drums of war.[82]

Liebknecht's break with his party did not come easily. The party (the SPD) had been his life, his raison d'être, and casting it off, in effect saying, "I know better than the party, and everyone in it," did not come easily. He had previously written: "I have, so to speak, grown up in the life of the party [...]. I imbibed it with my mother's milk and it rang in my ears from my earliest childhood, from my father's lips. One thing is necessary: discipline."[83]

However, a few years earlier Liebknecht had written a lengthy treatise titled *Militarism and Anti-Militarism*, where he had assembled a studied, logical assault on the hallowed German institution of the army:

> The struggle against the standing army and the jingoist militaristic spirit is a fight against the danger threatening the peace of the nations.[84]

He who believes that the progress of humanity is inevitable must see in the existence of militarism the most important obstacle in the way of a peaceful and continuous evolution.[85]

The moment the book was published the authorities took him to court and charged him with treason, trying to destroy the morale of the army, the first step in the destruction of the state. After deliberating for a mere half hour the German judges handed down the sentence: "The accused is found guilty of having set foot on a treasonable undertaking and is condemned to incarceration in a fortress for eighteen months [...]. All copies of the work *Militarism and Anti-Militarism* [...] in the possession of the author, printer, publisher, wholesale booksellers and booksellers [...], as well as the plates and forms for their production, are to be destroyed."[86]

But as the books were being destroyed and Liebknecht escorted to jail, in other European countries the book was being translated and published. By the time he was released from prison Liebknecht had become a well-known spokesman for anti-militarism, a virulent opponent of the Prussian war machine. He has been described as a man who "lived in a gallop, in eternal haste."[87]

Leon Trotsky once characterized Liebknecht as "a man of direct action. Impulsive and passionate by nature, he possessed an exceptional intuition [...], an unrivalled courage and revolutionary initiative."[88] In 1912 he was elected by the citizens of Potsdam-Spandau, most workers in government ammunition factories, to be their representative in the Reichstag. Once the war began he hurriedly wrote a pamphlet against it that he circulated among his fellow legislators. In it he made his perspective clear: "For capitalism, war and peace are business and nothing but business," he wrote, then added an impassioned, stirring indictment of war: "This madness will not stop, and this bloody nightmare of hell will not cease until the workers of Germany, of France, of Russia, and of England will wake up out of their drunken sleep, will clasp each others' hands in brotherhood and will drown the bestial chorus of capitalist hyenas with the mighty cry of labor, 'Proletarians of all countries, unite!'"[89]

When the government suppressed the *Internationale*, the weekly journal Liebknecht created at the beginning of the war, he and a small group of others formed the so-called Spartacus League (Spartakusbund) and published a newspaper titled *Spartakusbriefe* (Spartacus letters), which was soon declared illegal. However, the leaflets continued to circulate throughout the country. The tone was direct and accusatory: the real enemy was in Germany, not abroad, and it was German imperialism, German militarism, German secret diplomacy....

Despite his immunity as a Member of Parliament, Liebknecht was soon arrested again, drafted into the army, then sent to the Eastern Front. When he refused to fight, he was forced to work burying the dead, a task made deliberately disgusting and onerous. His health slowly deteriorated and finally, after more than a year of living and working in the worst of conditions, he was sent back to Germany.

No sooner was he a free man, when walking down a Berlin street he passed a group of soldiers. Impetuously Liebknecht shouted at them, "Down with war!" Back to prison he went, this time for 30 months.

By May 1916 Karl Liebknecht was out of jail and back on the streets of Berlin. For May Day 1916 his organization, Spartakusbund, called a mass meeting in the Potsdamer Platz and circulated a leaflet titled *On to May Day*:

> Let not this second May Day of the world war pass by without a protest of international socialists against the imperialist slaughter [...]. On the first of May we reach out a brotherly hand to the people in France, in Belgium, in Russia, in England, in Serbia, in the entire world. Our enemies are not the French, Russian or English people. They are the German *junkers*, German capitalists, and the German regime.[90]
>
> We Germans in Prussia have three cardinal rights: the right to be soldiers, to pay taxes, to keep our tongues between our teeth.[91]

Nearly 10,000 Berliners had the courage to come to the square to hear Liebknecht speak for peace. It was an illegal assembly, the first sizable German anti-war protest.

"Down with the war! Down with the government!" Liebknecht yelled to the applauding crowd.

The police dragged him from the speakers' platform. He was summarily tried for "attempted treason" and "contumacy to the authority of the state," found guilty and immediately sent back to prison. German workers in Bremen, Dresden, Leipzig, Stuttgart, Weimar and other cities joined the protest against the war. The day Liebknecht was sentenced, 55,000 workers in munitions factories put down their tools, the first political protest strike in wartime Germany.

* * *

After only a few months of fighting the carnage could be measured in hundreds of thousands of casualties. Among those deeply troubled by this waste of life was a Canadian teacher of English at the University of Wisconsin, Julia Grace Wales (1881–1957). The question she posed to herself was: "Can a means be found by which a conference of the neutral powers may bring the moral forces of the world to bear upon the present war situation and offer to the belligerents some opportunity, involving neither committal to an arbitrary programme nor humiliation on the part of any one of them, to consider the possibility of peace?"[92]

She mediated about the problem at great length, and as a practicing spiritualist she attended séances where she identified herself with Joan of Arc, who reportedly had visions of her own. Wales wrote that in "the spiritual suffering of the multitudes of the warring countries [...], there are currents of hidden energy that need in some way to be liberated, liberated and combined, and made active."[93]

In one of these visions, either Joan's or Julia's, she saw the neutrals meeting in Switzerland, where they debated solutions to end the war. Hence, with the aid of some kind of ethereal "heavenly guidance"[94] she reached a novel conclusion and formulated a plan that became summarized in the phrase "continuous mediation without armistice." In essence, Miss Wales urged that the United States call a conference of the neutral countries of the world, at that time about 35 nations.[95] The conference would then constitute a "world thinking organ," a commission of inquiry that would mediate the conflict and would sit as long as the war continued. It would invite suggestions from all the warring countries and submit to them "reasonable" proposals to end the conflict. Each proposal would be based on two principles: first, peace must not mean humiliation to any nation, and second, it must not involve a compromise that might later restart the conflict. She concluded her argument by saying: "Shall we wait until these blind and futile forces have spent themselves? The time to make a resolute effort to save our world is *now* [emphasis hers], before the destruction has gone any further."[96]

It was an ingenious plan, unusual in that apparently no one had thought of it before. Miss Wales produced a small pamphlet outlining the details,[97] then presented it to numerous peace organizations: "At present each side is resolved to fight practically to extermination rather than yield. Our proposal would hold before each one a hope of escape from indefinitely continuing a self-destructive struggle."[98]

Nearly everyone who took the time to study the plan came to the conclusion that it was inherently feasible. The idea immediately won enthusiastic converts and soon it was known as "the Wisconsin Plan." A number of prominent politicians and peace advocates presented it to President Wilson, who apparently read it seriously and discussed it with his cabinet. Critics called the plan "a visionary's tea party."[99]

Miss Wales became a minor celebrity and was invited to be a part of the American delegation to the International Congress of Women at The Hague. The conference had been called by Dutch suffragists to demonstrate women's solidarity against war.

Among the peace societies of the neutral nations during the war the Dutch Peace Society was probably the most dynamic group attacking the problem from a number of directions. Immediately after war was declared they created the Anti-Oorlog Raad (Anti-War Council), which began looking for peace proposals "that should not contain the germ of future wars."[100] They examined various socialist, Christian and economic schemes and in November 1914 issued what they called the Minimum Program. This became one of the most widely discussed plans, partially because it harbored no "stop the war immediately" delusion. It undoubtedly influenced U.S. President Wilson when he formulated the Fourteen Points. Among other things, the Minimum Program postulated that plebiscites were to be held in all regions transferred by the peace treaties, there was to be freedom of commerce in all colonies and protectorates, secret treaties were to be replaced by parliamentary control, and a World League of Peace, when it would be created, would have the full power to impose economic sanctions.

In perhaps a more pragmatic day-to-day attempt to establish communication between the two sides the Anti-Oorlog Raad tried to keep the belligerents informed of each other's official statements in a monthly review published in three languages, German, French and English. This journal, which attempted to be impartial, was widely circulated and read by both sides for the duration of the war.

In the spring of 1915 the Central Organization for a Durable Peace was founded in The Hague. Forty nations were represented, including all the belligerents, though not officially of course, and the major neutral nations. For obvious reasons all names remained confidential and the sessions were not open to the press.

The Organization recognized the unfortunate fact that when the war finally ended a limited number of states would draw up the settlement, probably the same group of men who failed to prevent the disastrous conflict. The purpose of the Organization was to deal with the peace whenever and however the war was concluded. Basically they endorsed "the Minimum Program" formulated by the Anti-Oorlog Raad and tried to create study groups in each country to deal with the details and at the same time prepare world public opinion for the moment when the fighting would cease and the process of creating a durable peace would begin.

The Dutch Peace Party also sponsored the International Congress of Women at the Hague. If men could not seem to find a way to settle differences other than fighting over them, then women should step in and settle the conflict. All belligerent countries, with the exception of France, which refused to grant a delegation passports, were represented at the Congress. A total of 1,200 delegates from 12 countries discussed various proposals to end the war through negotiation. It was a "business congress with no festivities."[101]

Aletta Jacobs (1854–1929),[102] the Dutch suffragette who was one of the major sponsors, stated that the Congress had been called because "the mother-heart of woman" had too long "suffered in silence." All participants had to adhere to two principles:

That international disputes should be settled by pacific means;
That the parliamentary franchise should be extended to women.[103]

After four days of deliberations, meetings, and speeches, most of which reiterated the same obvious point, that the war must be ended, the congress unanimously approved Julia Grace Wales's Wisconsin Plan. Also, two delegations were elected, one to travel to the belligerent countries and the other to neutral states to try to persuade the heads of state to make peace.[104] Jane Addams (1860–1935), the leader of the group sent to belligerent countries, wrote:

> Our message was a simple one [...], that the 1,500 women who met in The Hague, coming in smaller or larger numbers from twelve different countries, urge that whatever the causes of the war and however necessary it may have been to carry it on for the past ten months, that the time has come for beginning some sort of negotiations which must in the end take place unless the war shall continue year after year and at last be terminated through sheer exhaustion.[105]

Almost without exception the women's delegations were received with unusual warmth and encouragement. Sir Edward Grey, the British Foreign Secretary, told them that no belligerent could offer mediation without admitting defeat and the neutrals must act instead. When one of the women remarked that the neutrals were waiting for the right moment, Sir Edward Grey asked them when they thought that might come. A week later the German Secretary of State for Foreign Affairs, von Jagow, essentially repeated the British position, namely, that the neutral countries must begin the process. The German Chancellor, von Bethmann-Hollweg, told the women that at least "someone had begun to talk negotiation." A few days later in Vienna the Austrian Prime Minister declared that their remarks were "the first sensible words that have been uttered in this room for ten months." The French and the Russians were less enthusiastic.[106] After having been received by 21 ministers of state, a King, a President and the Pope, the delegations sailed for the United States.

The neutral countries, especially the Scandinavian ones, had been supportive, and the Swedes had agreed that they would host a conference of neutrals provided it had the support of the most powerful of the neutral countries, the United States. The delegations went straight to see President Wilson, who was non-committal and apparently unwilling to take part in mediation unless he was directly asked to do so. In fact, President Wilson was afraid that if he called a conference of neutrals the United States might be outvoted. That was one of the deficiencies of the "continuous mediation" plan. All countries, small and large—for example, Switzerland and the United States—would have an equal vote.

The plan was perhaps too passive, offering the American public little that was substantively positive or material. Julia Grace Wales realized this when she perceptively commented: "That is the funny part of peace work: it is harmless. We seem to be like the Salvation Army or the Society of Friends. Nobody molests us. I hope, however, that we shall soon be taken seriously as well as kindly."[107]

In addition, the timing was bad. A few weeks before the women's delegation arrived in the Oval Office, the Cunard liner *Lusitania* had been sunk by a German U-boat. The more than 1,000 civilians who drowned included 128 of the

139 U.S. citizens on board. A wave of anti-German, pro-war feeling swept through the country. As the peace delegation left the Oval Office, President Wilson replied directly to their question: "Would he act?" "No," the President replied, "that is for me to say when the right moment, in my judgment, arrives."[108]

Even the participants themselves realized that the world saw them as irrelevant and even a little ridiculous. In the words of Emily Hobhouse (1860–1926): "The Women's Congress unfurled the white flag of Peace and—despite ridicule, disdain, opposition and disbelief—held it aloft before a bloodstained world."[109]

* * *

When the Great Powers of Europe went to war, for a brief moment almost everywhere there was a burst of patriotism. Young men volunteered for service, enthusiastic crowds threw flowers at the departing soldiers, and politicians trumpeted that the war would be over by Christmas.

In England, when war was declared two members of the House of Commons who were serving in the government, Charles P. Trevelyan (1870–1958) and John Burns (1858–1943), resigned their posts in opposition to the war.[110] Burns refused to account for his action to the House and never took an active role in the peace movement, making it clear that his decision had been a very personal one. Trevelyan, however, sent a letter of explanation to his constituents in which he wrote: "We ought to have no side in this quarrel except the one overwhelming interest of our people. That interest is peace."[111]

Trevelyan had seen the war coming and done his best to organize and encourage neutralist opinion. He had financed the British Neutrality Committee, which publicly argued that England was not bound by her engagements to give armed support to France and Russia and that to do so would be disastrous to both domestic and imperial interests. But it was too little and too late to have an effect. Trevelyan later wrote:

> I was as lonely as ever could be in opposition to the first war and my criticisms for not trying for a settlement.[112]
> All one can do is preach peace and appeal to the general sense of men.[113]

Although opposed to the war, Trevelyan could not really be called a pacifist. He did share, however, many of the pacifists' beliefs and often spoke at their meetings. He extolled the virtues of arbitration, was a founding member of the National Peace Council,[114] and argued that armaments expenditures should be limited so there would be sufficient funds to improve the conditions of the poor. Privately he thought pacifists were "a funny crowd. [...] There were even people who thought we ought to disarm altogether."[115]

Trevelyan joined Ramsay MacDonald (1866–1937), who resigned as chairman of the Labour Party when it supported the war, Norman Angell (1872–1967),[116] E. D. Morel (1873–1924)[117] and others to form the Union of Democratic

Control—the UDC,[118] as it became known—in the belief that the war resulted from international treaties, made in secret by the government elite, which were not subject to democratic review. Thus the choice of the name. The Union of Democratic Control did not call for an immediate end to the war but for an immediate public review of the war, which at that time was very close to the same thing.[119] Speaking wherever he could, Trevelyan attacked the upper class and appealed to the collective wisdom of the people. "I tell you straight that I do not trust statesmen and diplomats unaided by public opinion to pursue a policy which will make peace a permanence. Everything in history leads me to distrust them."[120]

But no matter how many speeches he or the other UDC spokesmen made, most people in England unquestioningly accepted the government's definition of a just and righteous war, a fight to the finish, a war to end war. It was like trying to swim against a flooding tide of patriotism. As he often admitted, "the right thinkers are a sad minority."[121] Perhaps the proof of this precept arrived when Trevelyan returned to his constituency to stand for re-election to the House of Commons in 1918. Out of 23,154 votes cast, he came in fourth with just 1,286.

In all fairness, it is highly doubtful that the British public at the time could have made informed, rational decisions concerning foreign policy. The few statistical glimpses we have of their knowledge of the wider world are appalling. In 1902, for example, 12 years before the war began, Moberly Bell (1847–1911), editor of the *Times*, asked all the regular subscribers to make suggestions as to what they liked best in the paper. Of the 17,000 answers received only one[122] mentioned the foreign news. During the war, in August 1918, a monthly magazine, *War and Peace*,[123] one of the few journals devoted to international affairs, had to remind its readers that the Czechoslovakians were neither Siberians nor Russians.

The UDC also opposed conscription and censorship and favored disarmament and collective security. Most of its financial backing came from wealthy Quakers. The UDC quickly became more than just a fringe group trying to shout above the drums of war. By 1915, it had over 300,000 members.

The UDC continued to grow throughout the war, and by 1917 it had over 100 branches in Great Britain. Through it, or associated with it, ultimately more than half a million people in the UK—at least one in ten Britons—publicly announced that they were opposed to the war and ready to negotiate a peace.

The UDC refused to succumb to the wave of hatred for Germany that consumed the country. One professor wrote: "I will not [...] disown the intellectual debt which I owe to Germany and its great universities, which in happier times have also afforded me a home and a welcome."[124]

Charles Trevelyan, one of the founders, put it more simply: "It takes two to make a quarrel, even if one of the two is most quarrelsome."[125] E. D. Morel, who was responsible for the day-to-day operations of the UDC, was less prosaic, more impassioned and perhaps bitter: "Europe totters to ruin amid the bones of her dead, to the imbecile patter of her statesmen, proclaiming the purity of their motives while the peoples perish. And for what? What conceivable military success on either side can compensate for the havoc which has been wrought and for the further havoc which lies ahead if this thing is to go on? What is the value of ideals when preached in a graveyard?"[126]

The UDC became the spearhead for a reform in foreign policy, and to a lesser or greater degree its views were represented in and accepted by the readers of the *Manchester Guardian*, the *Westminster Gazette*, the *Daily News*, *The Nation*, the *Herald* and the *Labour Leader*. But perhaps the most influential journal that aired its proposals was the *Cambridge Magazine*. At one time it had a circulation of more than 25,000, which is surprising for a university magazine.

An unusual feature of the *Cambridge Magazine* was its "Notes from the Foreign Press" drawn from over 100 European periodicals, which filled half of each issue. Using a large team of translators, the articles provided an English-language digest of the European press, favoring those accounts that advocated moderate, not military, solutions to the conflict. The magazine was read by many in influential government circles, even by Members of Parliament usually not associated with "left-wing" politics. Its influence could not be exaggerated, and at the same time it couldn't be measured. For example, its articles are credited with helping Lord Lansdowne (1845–1927), a member of the cabinet, formulate a restatement of the government's war aims in very moderate terms to create a basis for a negotiated peace in 1916. (See Chapter Three.)

At first there was little the government could do to combat the UDC other than refuse police protection for their meetings and lectures, thereby encouraging violence with so-called patriotic organizations.

In Manchester, for example, in March 1916 a UDC meeting was packed with soldiers and patriotic civilians who smashed the electric lights and sang "Rule, Britannia" and "The Maple Leaf" again and again to prevent anyone from speaking. The following day the Manchester City Council took an advertisement in the local papers to the effect that in the future no halls would be let to the UDC.

With the introduction of conscription for single men in the spring of 1916 and married men in the winter of the same year, the government suddenly had a mechanism to use against individuals who refused to fight.[127] They could be tried in both civil and military courts. The entire leadership of the UDC quickly found themselves behind bars. Nonetheless, the UDC continued to be the leading anti-war organization in Great Britain.

* * *

In France, the opposition to conscription took a very different form. Rarely did someone refuse to serve in the army, for universal military service went to the heart of the republican tradition. Opposition tended to coalesce toward exceptions for students and the clergy, the length of service, and the need for an *armée de métier*, that is, a standing professional army. Opposed to this was the republican theory of *la nation armée*, the "nation in arms," which posited that a standing army was only useful for wars of aggression and/or crushing political opposition, both, it was hoped unnecessary in a democratic system. The peace movement took a stand as early as 1900 in favor of the militia system, more or less patterned after the one in Switzerland, and this was often reaffirmed. In short, pacifism dovetailed with patriotism, which had certain very legal and acceptable demands. One observer summed up the French attitude:

> In France, the concept of the citizen soldier and the obligation of male citizens for military service through universal conscription have been vital parts of the nation's tradition since the French Revolution linked democracy and universal service. In the French view, conscription contributes to the republican tradition and national unity as well as to national defense. Those who refuse to serve are seen as directly challenging a unifying and primary principle that underlies the nation and the state itself.[128]

When the first shots were fired in 1914 a spirit of patriotism suddenly consumed the country. Most members of the peace societies put principles behind them and joined the *union sacrée*, the truce that united all the various factions within the Third Republic. The Socialist René Viviani (1863–1925), a man who once called himself "a patriotic pacifist," became Prime Minister and rallied the country behind the phrase "*la paix par la victoire*" (peace through victory), in other words, join the army and defeat the Germans on the field of battle. And Emile Arnaud (1864–1921), who takes credit for coining the word "pacifism," entered the army at the age of 50 and earned a Croix de Guerre fighting in the trenches.[129] He wrote: "We believe the state has the right to demand sacrifices from its subjects. It can and must assure its defense [...]. Our lesson is two-fold: to offer *la patrie* what it requires for its defense and to work to demonstrate that war is an anachronism that must disappear. We are patriots in the good sense. We will do nothing that might diminish *la patrie*."[130]

Addressing the French Senate, General Gallieni (1849–1916), Minister of War, expressed the common thought, when he said: "Sixteen months ago France wanted peace; today she wants war (*long-continued applause*). She wants it with all her energy; she employs all her children in it; she devotes all her thought to it. And if, in some workshop, some badly inspired individual happens to pronounce the word peace, he is immediately looked upon as a bad citizen (*Hear! Hear! Applause*)."[131]

Despite the general agreement on the goals of pacifism and the duties of citizens to the state, a number of Christian fundamentalists, absolute pacifists and internationalists staunchly refused to bear arms. It was a minority, a small one, who ignored the call to arms, stood fast and refused to compromise. Romain Rolland (1866–1944), the French novelist, for example, went into a self-imposed exile in Switzerland. Roughly six weeks after war was declared, on September 22, 1914, his essay "Au-dessus de la mêlée" (Above the battle) was published in *Le Journal de Genève*:

> O young men that shed your blood with so generous a joy for the starving earth! O heroism of the world! What a harvest for destruction to reap under this splendid summer sun! Young men of all nations, brought into conflict by a common ideal, making enemies of those who should be brothers; all of you, marching to your death, are dear to me. Slavs, hastening to the aid of your race; Englishmen fighting for honor and right; intrepid Belgians who dared to oppose the Teutonic colossus, and defend against him the Thermopylæ of the West; Germans fighting to defend the philosophy and the birthplace of Kant against the Cossack avalanche; and you, above all, my young compatriots, in whom the generation of heroes of the Revolution lives again; you, who for years have confided your dreams to me, and now, on the verge of battle, bid me a sublime farewell.[132]

For many of those, mainly socialists, who chose to change their pacifism for firearms, Rolland's plea for peace and Franco-German reconciliation turned him into an intellectual traitor or enemy sympathizer. Suddenly he fell out of favor. Some parents even forbade their children to read his books, and for the cultivated, but patriotic, public he became a pariah.

The storm of criticism also came from Germany. In a *Letter to Gerhart Hauptmann*,[133] Romain Rolland accused German youth: "Are you the sons of Goethe or of Attila?" This and similar charges produced angry echoes. A dozen or more German professors and writers quickly hastened to "chastise" what they called French arrogance.

Romain Rolland knew that he was hurling words to the wind, that few would read what he wrote and even fewer would act on it. Yet "Au-dessus de la mêlée" was translated into many languages and distributed in pamphlet form. His stand was clearly humanitarian, apolitical, internationalist, charitable and fervently anti-war.

> I know that such thoughts have little chance of being heard today. Young Europe, burning with the fever of battle, will smile with disdain and show its fangs like a young wolf. But when the access of fever has spent itself, wounded and less proud of its voracious heroism, it will come to itself again.
>
> Moreover, I do not speak to convince it. I speak but to solace my conscience [...] and I know that at the same time I shall solace the hearts of thousands of others who, in all countries, cannot or dare not speak themselves.[134]

Soon Romain Rolland became known as the "conscience of Europe."[135] Many years earlier, while still a student in Paris, Romain Rolland had written to Leo Tolstoy (1828–1910) asking for spiritual advice. Tolstoy replied with a letter of 38 pages. Later Romain Rolland called Tolstoy "the conscience of the world."[136]

For those men who refused to take any part in the conflict, either directly by bearing arms or indirectly by supporting the war effort, Romain Rolland became a pillar of pacifism, one that grew stronger and more uncompromising as the war became more bitter and entrenched:

> It would seem then, that love of our country can flourish only through the hatred of other countries and the massacre of those who sacrifice themselves in the defense of them. There is in this theory a ferocious absurdity [...] which repels me to the very depths of my being. No! Love of my country does not demand that I shall hate and slay those noble and faithful souls who also love theirs, but rather that I should honor them and seek to unite with them for our common good.[137]

In scathing prose Rolland scolded the socialists, not just the French but all the socialists of Europe, for neglecting their moral duty, for choosing patriotism over principles. He believed that the responsibility for the war lay squarely on the powers of autocracy and militarism. Public opinion, he was convinced, had the power to stop the slaughter, but to do so intellectuals, who were, in fact, the leaders of public opinion, had to separate themselves from the nationalist hatreds and quarrels and place themselves *au-dessus de la mêlée* (above the battle). In 1915 he was awarded the Nobel Prize for Literature.

"The spirit is light," Romain Rolland wrote: "it is our duty to lift it above tempests, and thrust aside the clouds which threaten to obscure it; to build higher and stronger, dominating the injustice and hatred of nations, the walls of that city wherein the souls of the world may assemble."[138]

Stefan Zweig (1881–1942), the Austrian novelist and playwright, called *Au-dessus de la mêlée* a "declaration of war against hatred, this foundation stone of the invisible European church."[139] But for Romain Rolland it was just the beginning, "the first stroke of the woodman's axe in the overgrown forest of hatred"[140]:

> Let us be bold and proclaim the truth to the elders of these young men, to their moral guides, to their religious and secular leaders, to the Churches, the great thinkers, the leaders of socialism; these living riches, these treasures of heroism you held in your hands; for what are you squandering them? What ideal have you held up to the devotion of these youths so eager to sacrifice themselves? Their mutual slaughter! A European war! A sacrilegious conflict which shows a maddened Europe ascending its funeral pyre, and, like Hercules, destroying itself with its own hands![141]

> Let us help the victims! It is true that we cannot do very much. In the everlasting struggle between good and evil, the balance is unequal. We require a century for the upbuilding of that which a day destroys.[142]

* * *

Leo Tolstoy was an equally intractable voice of non-violence. Even though he died in 1910, four years before the war began, he was considered to be the most influential pacifist in the world.

At the heart of Tolstoy's pacifism lay the idea of individual action in the face of violence: no complicated ideology, no party to join, no leaders to follow, just a simple, rigorous personal decision not to bear arms or participate in warfare. At its source was the Christian anarchist principle of non-resistance, and with it a rejection of all violence, including that of governments, law courts, police, prisons, and armies:

> Every man, by refusing to take part personally in military service, either as a recruit or as a payer of taxes to the government, which uses these taxes for military matters, by this refusal in the most efficacious manner does a great service to God and men, because by this refusal he in the most efficacious manner contributes to the forward movement of humanity toward that better social structure, towards which humanity is striving and at which it must arrive.[143]

Tolstoy was a prophet in the Old Testament tradition, fearlessly speaking what he believed to be the truth. He was often called "the Saint of Yasnaya Polyana."[144] Excommunicated from the Orthodox Church, he advocated an urgent human need to connect the way we live to a more fulfilling conception of the meaning of life. The ideas were simple, enticing and contagious: non-violence, selflessness and simple living. Tolstoy reduced his creed to five basic imperatives: Love your enemies, do not be angry, return evil with good, do not lust, and do not take oaths. He also condemned private property and money, advocated living by one's own physical labor and became a believer in vegetarianism,[145] complete chastity and abstinence from tobacco and alcohol:

> The question is not whether it will be good or bad for human society to follow the law of love and the resulting law of non-resistance, but whether you—a being that lives today and is dying by degrees tomorrow and every moment—will now, this very minute, fully do the will of Him who sent you [...]. As soon as the question is put in this form, there will be but one answer: I want at once, this very minute, without any delay, without waiting for anyone, and without considering the seeming consequences, with all my strength to fulfill what alone I am indubitably commanded to do by Him who sent me into this world, and in no case, under no condition, will I, can I, do what is contrary to it, because in this lies the only possibility of my rational, unwretched life.[146]

Tolstoy argued and wrote with such an intensity, such force, and such conviction that he alone was right that there is inherent in his prose a certain unmistakable aggression, a constant assault to the reader's ethical code. And undoubtedly that was Tolstoy's intention. He stepped away from human selfishness and violence to deliver a moral slap in the face, a rude challenge to pit the readers' principles against his. Romain Rolland certainly felt this when he wrote: "With Tolstoy, everything is proud revolt against pride, hatred against hatred, passion against passion. Everything in Tolstoy is violence, even his doctrine of non-violence."[147]

Tolstoy always spoke to the individual, man-to-man, one anguished soul to another. He thought it a mistake to create an organized movement and instead he urged individuals to listen to their own consciences. Answering a letter he received from a would-be disciple, he wrote:

> To speak of "Tolstoyism," to seek guidance, to inquire about my solution of questions, is a great and gross error. There has not been, nor is there any "teaching" of mine. There exists only the one eternal universal teaching of the Truth, which for me, for us, is especially clearly expressed in the Gospels [...]. I advised this young lady to live not by my conscience, as she wished, but by her own.[148]

People from all over the world read Tolstoy's works and many tried to live by his principles. Occasionally they formed groups, often to demonstrate their collective opposition to war. Tolstoyan communities were started in England,[149] the United States,[150] Chile,[151] South Africa,[152] and other countries. Most grew larger after his death.

In Russia before the war, thousands of young people left the cities and created self-sufficient agricultural communities across the Russian Empire where they tried to live according to the dictates of Christian anarchy/pacifism as laid down by Tolstoy.[153] They also published periodicals and editions of his works for mass circulation.

Tolstoy emphatically rejected the role of a prophet, a saint on earth, and often spoke about his faults and weaknesses:

> It makes me feel bad, or rather, awkward, when frequently men well disposed to me take me seriously, seeking and demanding a complete correspondence between my words and my acts.
> "But how is it that you say one thing, and do another?"
> I am no saint, and I have never given myself out for a saint; I am a man who am carried away, and sometimes, or, more correctly, always, say, not fully what I think and feel, not because I do not want to say it, but because I cannot, frequently exaggerate, and simply err.
> This is so as regards words. As regards acts, it is even worse.
> I am an absolutely weak man, with vicious habits, who wishes to serve the God of truth, but who keeps constantly getting off the road.[154]

* * *

In his later years Tolstoy found himself as the de facto spokesman for several sects, for example, the Doukhobors, a fundamentalist Christian group that adamantly refused to serve in the Czar's army.

The word "Doukhobor" emerged at the end of the 18th century and means literally "spirit wrestler," since the Doukhobors believe they are constantly fighting with the spirit of God, which dwells within each man.[155] In what is perhaps the definitive study of Doukhobors, authors George Woodcock and Ivan Avakumovic state that

> the Doukhobors stand on the extreme left of the theological spectrum. From the traditional churches [Greek Orthodox] they differ in having no liturgy and no ikons, no fasts and no festivals, no churches and no priests [...]. They believe heaven and hell to be states of the mind [...], each man is his own priest in the direct contact with the divine. The only visible symbols of their faith are the loaf of bread, the cellar of salt and the jug of water that stand on the table in the middle of the meeting-house symbolizing the basic elements of existence.[156]

For Tolstoy, the Doukhobors were Christian anarchists like himself, pacifists and peasants who, without study, or even literacy, had arrived at a system of thought very similar to his own. They were, he wrote, "the germinating of that seed sown by Christ 1,800 years ago: the resurrection of Christ himself, [and he added that the main condition for the realization of Christian life] [...] is the existence and the gathering together of people who even now realize that towards which we are all striving. And behold, these people exist."[157]

Tolstoy was also attracted to the Doukhobors by their fierce and unrelenting pacifism. On St. Peter's Day, the 29th of June, 1895, for example, Doukhobor communities collected all the weapons they possessed, for either hunting or their own self-defense, including their knives and daggers, and burned them in huge pyres to symbolize the purity of their belief. It was also a clear statement to the Russian government that the Doukhobors did not intend to be conscripted into the army. For this act, their lands were confiscated, their leaders imprisoned and 4,000 of them exiled to the mountains.

In the years before the First World War, the Doukhobors attracted a certain amount of international sympathy, being portrayed as an idealistic group of farmers who, as simple communists, in the pure sense of the word, and vegetarians, who neither smoked nor drank alcohol, clung to the strict principles of non-violence and were willing to sacrifice even their own lives if necessary to follow what they believed to be God's path. They appeared to be ideal pacifists, each Doukhobor an unflinching, unerring example, a philosopher's conception of how men should think and act. Without formal education, using only the depths of their own consciences as guides, they had realized that non-violence was the only way to a good and meaningful life.

There was, and for that matter still is, another side to the Doukhobors, the fact that they obeyed the dictates of an autocratic leader, Peter the Lordly Verigin, whom they believed to be their spiritual guide. Many people, including Tolstoy, tended to overlook this trait. However, when the two men, Tolstoy and Peter the Lordly Verigin, did finally meet it was a stormy encounter. Tolstoy was slowly becoming enlightened about the real nature of the Doukhobor theocracy and accused Verigin: "How it is that you have changed from a martyr for the truth into a despot?"[158] Verigin of course denied the charge, and that ended the meeting.

When a Czarist general reportedly accused the Doukhobors of not being prepared to lay down their lives for the Czar, they replied: "You say wrong. We are ready to lay down our life for every man, as well as the Tsar; if we saw him being tortured, we would lay our life down for his sake as well as for any other man, but we cannot murder for any man, because it is forbidden by God."[159]

At first the Czarist government systematically tried to destroy the Doukhobors by exiling them to the extremities of the Russian Empire, the Kola Peninsula in the north, the Caucasus in the south, and the frozen wilds of Siberia. But wherever they went the Doukhobors made converts, so instead of the sect being eradicated by the government's splintering it into pieces, each piece grew into a new whole as strong if not stronger than the original one.

Rather than fill Russian jails with pacifists, the Czarist government finally gave the Doukhobors permission to emigrate. The anarchist Peter Kropotkin (1842–1921), who lived in England, proposed that the Doukhobors move to Canada. After a delegation found a promising home in the plains provinces, the Canadian government granted the Doukhobors a permanent military exception. To pay for their voyage, Tolstoy donated the royalties from his novel *Resurrection* and also solicited funds from wealthy friends and Quakers. Kropotkin and the anarchists also contributed to the Doukhobors' cause. Over 7,000 Doukhobors migrated to Canada, where they settled and prospered mainly in Saskatchewan and Alberta.[160] Perhaps 20,000 of the less dedicated remained in Russia, where most of them were eventually consumed by the Soviet state.[161]

Tolstoy and the Canadian Doukhobors eventually came into conflict. The issue was not their theocratic beliefs but land registration. The Canadian government asked all Doukhobors to register their farms in their own names. Tolstoy wrote to them urging them not to do so. He counseled that "if you acknowledge property, which is only maintainable by soldiers and police, there was no need for you to refuse military or police service."[162]

The community split on the issue. Those who refused to register their land eventually lost most of it. Others gave up the principle of communal property and registered their farms in their own names. Disenchanted, Tolstoy broke off contact with the community. Tolstoy was, after all, a totalist. His spiritual world could not be subdivided. Lose a piece and you lose the whole: "If it is not accepted in its entirety, it may as well not be accepted at all. Some single feature, for example equality, brotherhood, humility or non-violence, is disregarded, and the whole teaching loses its meaning."[163]

* * *

Perhaps the most renowned follower of Tolstoy was Mohandas Gandhi (1869–1948), who corresponded with him shortly before his death. Although it took Gandhi a long time to fully develop his theory of non-violence, he did not hesitate to acknowledge his debt to Tolstoy: "Russia gave me in Tolstoy a teacher who furnished a reasoned basis for my non-violence."[164] Gandhi also wrote: "It was Tolstoy who helped me to realize the infinite possibilities of universal love. Of all the utterances of modern ethical doctrine, it was his writings which most strongly confirmed me in my ideas of the positive power of non-resistance, and of the renunciation of all types of violence."[165]

In fact, Tolstoy sought much more than just the elimination of arms and armies and the mentality that would produce and use them. He wanted to redesign the world and in the process eliminate, among other evils, the injustices of colonialism: "It will be impossible to reduce armaments which not only persist in acquiring new possessions, like the Philippines, Port Arthur and the rest, but also keeping what they have acquired, like Poland, India, Alsace-Lorraine and the rest."[166]

Gandhi of course completely agreed with Tolstoy's anti-colonialism, but Tolstoy, on the other hand, had reservations about Gandhi. They corresponded for years, in English, and it was quite clear that Tolstoy admired Gandhi greatly "except for his Hindu patriotism, which spoils everything."[167] That comment highlights a fundamental difference between the two men. For Tolstoy non-violence was little more than an uncompromising religious stance. It was Gandhi who made non-violent resistance into a social and political strategy. Tolstoy rejected politics. Gandhi almost welcomed it, and wrote that "politics today encircles us like the coils of a snake from which one cannot get out no matter how one tries."[168] Gandhi could accept compromise in that it represented one of perhaps many steps on the way to his end.[169] But Tolstoy was an ideologue who accepted no concessions, no transitions, no shortcuts. Principles could not be tested by reality, or modified, or invalidated. "It is impossible to admit the slightest compromise over an idea,"[170] he wrote. A Tolstoyan scholar commented that "Tolstoy needed no help to discover the truth, as he already possessed it. Other people were to be beneficiaries of his sacrifice and nothing else. There was no truth that he could learn from them, and no vital work to undertake, that required their collaboration. He had no interest in other people's view of the truth or their opinion of the meaning of life."[171]

Tolstoy's total rejection of compromise and incrementalism has led many observers to wonder what would have happened had Tolstoy been more open to change, had he been willing to lend his name and his force to some sort of reformist movement. Theodore Roosevelt, for example, as American President at the time, wrote that the Tolstoyans could have accomplished a great deal in Russia and "instead of insisting upon doing nothing unless they could immediately introduce the millennium and reform all the abuses of society out of hand with one jump."[172]

A typical "lost chance" occurred when Tolstoy and Czar Nicholas II met a few months before the opening of the Second Hague Peace Conference. The meeting took place at a railway station in Siberia. According to those present the Czar "kissed Tolstoy on the mouth and both cheeks [...]. Tolstoy readily responded."[173] The two men discussed the peace conference at length, with Tolstoy taking his customary absolutist position by asking the Czar to disarm totally and immediately and thus set an example for other countries in the world.

The Czar replied that such a dramatic step required an agreement that would unite the Great Powers. The Czar asked Tolstoy for his cooperation in seeking such an agreement, but Tolstoy refused to sanction the conference. Tolstoy later published his caustic opinion of the Czar: "This unfortunate, entangled young man, recognized as the leader of 130,000,000 people, continually deceived and compelled to contradict himself, confidently thanks and blesses the troops whom he calls his own for murder in defense of lands which with yet less right he also calls his own."[174]

Tolstoy remained steadfast to his principles, above all those of non-violence. He went beyond just anti-militarism and preached a "law of love," civil disobedience on the widest possible scale. He wanted to cleanse the world of organized bodies, governments in any form, leading to a tabula rasa and a kind of Christian anarchism. Tolstoy believed that "there is not one war in all history that was not provoked by the governments, and by the governments alone, independently of the advantages to their respective nations, to which war, even if it is successful, is always harmful."[175]

* * *

At the beginning of the First World War, virtually from the moment the mobilization was declared, a small number of militant French teachers took a firm stand against the conflict. Their numbers were never large—perhaps only 4 or 5 percent of France's 120,000 teachers[176]—but almost all of them were young, determined and vocal. The task in front of them was clear. They intended to slay the Goliath of war with an onslaught of words.[177] A young teacher in Nantes, for example, composed these lines for his civics course: "War is a horrible crime: entire regions given over to pillage and fires, thousands of young and strong men killed by bullets and shrapnel, millions of women and old people without bread, thousands of children without fathers, frightful misery everywhere, that is war: it is a disgrace for all humanity."[178]

When the war began, elementary school teachers distributed pacifist flyers called *papillons* (butterflies), which circulated widely throughout France and even found their way into the trenches at the front. The messages were brief, for example: "Peace without annexation, without conquest, without indemnity," "Women want their rights and peace," and "Enough men killed. Peace!"[179] Some of these *papillons* encouraged other teachers to send pacifist messages of their own and, if they were poor, to take advantage of the military franchise by putting the name of an imaginary soldier on the envelope in place of a stamp.

The government censors labeled these *papillons* "forbidden thoughts" and cracked down on the teachers. One of the first to be arrested was a teacher from the Vosges, Julia Bertrand (1877–1960). Only 18 days after Germany declared war on France she was sent to a detention camp for German prisoners of war and informed that "her ideas are an insult to the fatherland."[180] Julia Bertrand wrote back: "This anti-militarism is [...] perhaps the most sincere expression of patriotism in its purist form [...], a true and disinterested love for one's country, a country where one would like all inhabitants to be complete human beings, living a sane life."[181]

L'Affaire Bertrand soon became a cause célèbre in pacifist circles and teachers all over France contributed francs to support their "comrade fallen in the battle of ideas."[182] She was released a year later, but not permitted to teach again until 1925.

One group of teachers, led by Marie (1878–1969) and François (1882–1967) Mayoux, issued a manifesto whose first words were: "*Assez de sang versé*" (Enough spilled blood). "It was time," the statement continued, "for the Allies to end the butchery, to initiate peace talks."[183] The husband and wife wrote their messages on little pieces of paper, which they glued on objects destined for the front, food, clothing and even military supplies. They were quickly caught, taken to court, and tried for disseminating "defeatist" propaganda. Found guilty after a short trial, they were sentenced to six months in prison. On appeal, the sentence was increased to two years. The husband and wife were finally reunited when they were released in the general amnesty of 1919. However, they were forbidden to teach again until 1924.

In the Dordogne an elementary school teacher was sentenced to six months in prison for telling his class not to "confuse hatred for the German people with hatred for their leaders."[184] And another teacher in Paris drew the attention of the military police when her students reported that she was a "German sympathizer." In fact, she had told her class that the crown prince of Germany was not as ugly as the caricatures portrayed him in French newspapers.

Another Frenchwoman who refused to compromise her principles was Louise Saumoneau (1875–1949), who later became a well-known figure in the French socialist movement. Coming from a working-class background, she believed that the war was the result of the rapacious ruling classes in Europe. No matter how it was packaged, as a defensive conflict or a patriotic one, she was convinced the people of France had nothing to gain and much to lose. She issued a series of pamphlets under the title of *Les Femmes socialistes contre la Guerre* (Socialist women Against the war) and distributed them as widely as she could. In 1915 she was imprisoned for seven weeks, then released without a trial only because the government did not want to let the pacifist cause be argued in court.[185]

The French policy of refusing to let pacifists find a forum in the courts probably protected another anti-war activist, Madeleine Vernet (1878–1949). The moment war was declared she made a personal decision to do what she could to halt it. For days, she walked the Parisian streets and whenever she encountered a soldier she stopped him and tried to persuade him to desert.[186] It is amazing that she was not arrested. Later she avoided the wartime rules of censorship and clandestinely circulated the poem *Pour les venger* (To avenge them), which she dedicated to "all our missing comrades" who had fallen "victims of error." When some of her pacifist poems were finally censored in France, she had them printed on postcards, then mailed to the soldiers fighting in the trenches. Still the authorities did not detain her, knowing that she was ready for a public debate.

When the war ended, Madeleine Vernet continued to work toward what she considered to be a "true peace," a peace between peoples that could only begin once the fighting ended. As a feminist, she addressed Frenchwomen and asked them to reach out to the Germans and end the emotional war that lingered long after the physical one had ended. The notion that their former enemy was a barbaric horde ready to sack and pillage Europe had to be extinguished and replaced by the realization that it was a people very much like any other. This rational, constructive image had to be methodically inculcated. The place to begin, Madeleine Vernet believed, was in the schools, For her, like many others in the French pacifist movement, the key to a pacifist future lay in the power of education.

Marie Lenéru (1875–1918), a dramatist, took a different approach. Women, she believed, had the pre-eminent role as guardians of the collective memory. She became the first woman since George Sand (1804–1876) to have her plays produced by the Comédie Française. Her last play, *La Paix* (The peace),[187] focused on the role of women in changing the perceptions of war and peace. For her, millions of soldiers had died on the battlefield in order to create a lasting peace. To fail to support that goal would be to debase their memory.

* * *

Lenéru took many of her ideas about how the world after the war could or should look from the British author H. G. Wells (1866–1946), who at the time was one of the most popular writers in the English language.[188] He was also one of the most scandalous, openly endorsing such causes as "free love" and women's rights. In addition, he was an outspoken pacifist, that is, until the First World War began. Then, suddenly, he changed his mind and switched sides.

Becoming convinced that there would never be peace in Europe, or the world, until Germany was defeated militarily and democratized, Wells supported British involvement in the war while at the same time never giving up his pacifist beliefs. It was a difficult duality, one that no one could be comfortable with:

I avow myself an extreme Pacifist. I am against the man who first takes up the weapon. [...] I do not merely want to stop this war. I want to nail down war in its coffin. Modern war is an intolerable thing [...]. I have always hated it [...]. I hate it more than ever.
It is my unshakeable belief that essentially the Allies fight for a permanent world peace, that primarily they do not make war but resist war [...]. This war is tragedy and sacrifice for most of the world, for the Germans it is simply the catastrophic outcome of 50 years of elaborate intellectual foolery [...]. It is a disaster. It may be a necessary disaster; it may teach a lesson that could be learnt in no other way; but for all that, I insist, it remains waste, disorder, disaster.[189]

Wells came as close as any man to having the proverbial crystal ball. He looked at the horrors of the battlefield and saw in them either a return to the "agricultural barbarism" from which mankind had just emerged or the creation of a new world order, one that would put an end to warfare. The world war, Wells declared, must be the last, the final series of battles before man puts an end to the evils of the sovereign state. It was H. G. Wells who coined the phrase "the war that will end war."[190]

* * *

A few months after the war began, 93 German intellectuals and artists issued "An Appeal to the World of Culture" ("Aufruf an die Kulturwelt!"), also known as the "Manifesto of the 93," which declared that they supported the war. The document proclaimed an inseparable link between German culture and German militarism. All blame for the war was laid on France, England and Russia. The list of signatories read like a who's who of the arts and sciences in Germany and included 58 university professors, among others Walter Nernst (1864–1941), a chemist who later won the Nobel Prize, Max Planck (1858–1947), who also won a Nobel Prize, and Wilhelm Roentgen (1845–1923), winner of the first Nobel Prize in Physics. The "Appeal" was translated into 14 languages and sent out to the world.[191]

At about the same time the "Declaration of University Teachers" appeared, which was also provocatively pro-war. Written by a classic professor, Ulrich von Willamowitz Moellendorff (1848–1931), it was signed by over 3,600 professors, a large majority. Among the non-signers were Albert Einstein (1879–1955) and Friedrich Wilhelm Foerster (1832–1921). Although Einstein lived and taught in Berlin at the time, he was partially excused from not signing either document as he was technically a Swiss citizen.

To counter these pro-war documents, Georg Friedrich Nicolai, né Georg Lewinstein, (1874–1964), a physiologist and heart specialist, wrote an "Appeal to the Europeans" ("Aufruf an die Europäer") which was co-signed by Albert Einstein, F. W. Foerster and Otto Buek (1873–1966), a philosopher.

The anti-war "Appeal" urged scholars to support "a common world culture" and labeled the war "a catastrophic disruption of cultural ties between kindred nations."[192] It also predicted that the war would produce no victors, only losers, and called for a peace that would not become the source of new wars. Professor Nicolai circulated his "Appeal" among the German intelligentsia, but acquired no more signatures than the original three, plus his own. It was a quixotic gesture, symbolic at best, a pinprick that enraged the Prussian war machine. However, Professor Nicolai stood firm. For him, his "Appeal" was a way of demonstrating to the world that some men in the land of Goethe, Beethoven and Kant had not given up their principles.

Later the *New York Times* called Professor Nicolai "a moral hero": "a man who from the beginning of the war risked his whole career, indeed his entire existence, for the sake of what he believed to be right and true."[193]

The German government reacted to this pacifist "Appeal" by seizing Professor Nicolai's property and immediately drafting him into the army. He was deprived of his chair at the University of Berlin, and, despite the fact that he had previously attended to the Empress, he was sent as an assistant doctor to a hospital for infectious diseases, obviously in the hope that he would contract one.

According to articles in the world press, Professor Nicolai was punished for "refusal of military service [...]. Professor Nicolai refused energetically to have anything to do with the making of bombshells to contain the germs of cholera or plague bacilli, and to inoculate Russian prisoners with bacteria."[194] He was also punished for speaking his mind over meals in the officers' mess. Reportedly at one point he said "that the violation of Belgian neutrality, the use of poison gases, and the torpedoing of merchant ships were at one and the same time moral delinquencies and inexpressible stupidities. Sooner or later they would cause the downfall of Germany."[195] He stood trial in Danzig, where a German courts-martial summarily sentenced him to five months in jail for refusing to salute the military colors.

Professor Nicolai was sent into exile at an old Prussian fortress in Graudenz, East Prussia. However, he was allowed to write and study and even go hunting with the commandant.

While confined to Graudenz Nicolai wrote *Die Biologie des Krieges* (The biology of war) and he used his anti-war "Appeal," written at the outset of the conflict, as an introduction. The rest of the book is a well-organized account of the causes of war, an indictment of war itself, then a study of how war may be abolished. It has often been called "unquestionably the most potent antiwar book of its time."[196] It draws on almost every field of human knowledge, both historically and contemporaneously, and has intimidated most who have tried to recapitulate its arguments. One critic commented that "most reviewers who tried to summarize the contents ... were torn between admiration and despair."[197] Nonetheless, the same critic offered his own summation: "He (Nicolai) wished to examine it (war) from every angle, as a natural phenomenon and evolutionary cul-de-sac and as a moral and political problem, as an example of misdirected technology and faulty utilization of energy and other resources, and as a social disease, as both cause and result of aberrations in national and individual behavior."[198]

The title, *The Biology of War*, is obviously a misnomer, for only 5 of the 15 chapters are devoted to the biological aspects of war. The rest are a tour de force through practically the whole of human knowledge, beginning with Confucius and Heraclitus and ending with Bismarck and Woodrow Wilson. On the way, Nicolai digresses in many directions, into military history, social statistics, pacifist thinkers in Germany, the Slavic countries and the Far East, as well as religious thinkers of all stripes and hues. As for God, like Auguste Comte (1798–1857), Nicolai saw the brotherhood of mankind as the only possible substitute for the absolutes of religion, and any future morality, a social code for man, must be compatible with the realities of human nature. Nicolai wrote: "To be human means nothing less than to have understood the evolutionary history of mankind, to know whence we have come, to sense whither we are headed, and to try to adapt ourselves accordingly to the general process of nature which, for us, unfolds in the development of the human race."[199]

For Professor Nicolai, there was no biological justification for war. It was not the result of a pseudo–Darwinian struggle, that is, a means of natural selection. Instead, he argued that war is an atavism, an aggressive instinct that had ceased to be useful to the species and needed to be subdued and controlled so that the social instincts of mankind can thrive: "Universal brotherhood among men is older and more primitive than all combat, which was not introduced among men until later [...]. Wars and combat between animals of the same kind should be of such extreme rarity that it may almost be said that war, like so much else, is a human invention [...] propertyless [sic] animals live in peace with one another."[200]

Chauvinism and nationalism were, Nicolai believed, one and the same and should be abolished as well as national sovereignties. Civilizations, not the nation-state, should be the essential units of history, the building blocks of progress. In passionate tones he appealed to his readers, arguing that if they, and indeed all men and women, would only follow their best instincts, there would be no need for war: "Truly our tools are weapons, but to be used against nature and not against man. For in the end all civilization is based on respect for life."[201]

A German government courier, a sympathetic pacifist, smuggled the manuscript of *The Biology of War* in the diplomatic pouch to Switzerland. It was published there in 1917, then in every major European language except French, where the censorship during the war was just as rigid as in Germany. Even though it was an obvious attack on German militarism, the French censor was taking no chances. The French had just passed through what was called *le buveur de sang*, a horrible bloodletting in the trenches, and pacifist ideas would certainly not help revive the country's will to fight.[202]

Two thousand copies of the German edition of *The Biology of War* with specially printed jackets bearing the title *The Grain Economy of Switzerland* passed German customs with ease, then were distributed throughout the country.

Romain Rolland called the book "the noblest work that has appeared in these terrible war years,"[203] and he went on to write to his fellow pacifist Albert Einstein: "I have read Professor Nicolai's book with passionate interest. I believe he is a friend of yours. Please let him know how much I liked his book.... It is a wonderful thing in these terrible times to come upon such a great, free, and serene soul." And the *Neue Zürcher Zeitung,* German-speaking Switzerland's foremost newspaper at the time, devoted almost the entire front page to a review that praised *The Biology of War* as "[a] good book, strong, pitiless, spacious, spiritual, and demanding, a work that belongs to the future and to those who believe in the human being of the future because they themselves carry a piece of that human being in their breast."

An American journalist at the time wondered why Nicolai was "not hanged" and went on to state: "Such a book, written and published in the United States in a time of war by a citizen who believed and taught that the war was infamous and that our government deliberately and infamously began it, would have been held treasonable, beyond a doubt."[204]

Obviously the German government thought they had Professor Nicolai well isolated in East Prussia. But he kept writing and during the winter of 1917–1918 he produced a pamphlet that he mimeographed and distributed by post. It was titled *Six Facts as a Basis for Judging Today's Power Politics.* The six facts were:

1. The German people did know their true situation.
2. The nationalist notion of the German fatherland is false.
3. The war has been a fruitless waste of lives.
4. A real fatherland, Europe, already exists.
5. One's duty is to follow his beliefs.
6. The longing for peace is the most widespread phenomenon in Europe.

Professor Nicolai concluded his pamphlet with a solution for the end of the war: "We must demand that our government offer peace under one single condition: the formation of a general congress of all civilized states with complete sovereignty, in which each state is represented according to its number of inhabitants."[205] This congress would then decide and arbitrate all the issues raised by the war, following the principle of self-determination of peoples. It was, in essence Wilson's League of Nations before he proposed it.

Needless to say, in wartime Germany this sort of message was highly subversive, and certainly would not be tolerated. Professor Nicolai knew that once he distributed the pamphlet his days in East Prussia were numbered.

Not far from his place of exile was a major aerodrome of the German air force. He visited it many times and became acquainted with several of the pilots, a few of whom were sympathetic and offered to help him[206]: "[I]t occurred to me that the youngest child of our modern technology, the airplane, had been originally intended by its optimistic inventors to fly over those frontiers which one could not step over. I was intrigued by the thought of restoring this nation-uniting device, so shamefully misused in the war, to its true purpose, at least somewhat—to use this blood-stained instrument at least once for peaceful purposes."[207]

At dawn one morning two biplanes took off and flew northwards, an Albatross with Professor Nicolai on board, the other, a Fokker 16, as an escort. When they arrived at the North Sea they threw their weapons overboard. Soon Professor Nicolai was safe in neutral Denmark.

An exile for the rest of his life,[208] Professor Nicolai tried to live what he believed, simply, humanely, altruistically. Non-violence and self-sacrifice were essential parts of his philosophy, fundamental elements, he was convinced, that allow a society, any society, to prosper and endure. After he arrived in Denmark he was given a large sum of money for his living expenses. He refused to accept it. Instead, he immediately donated it to the Red Cross.

* * *

F. W. Foerster,[209] another signatory of the anti-war "Appeal," was a professor of astronomy and philosophy at the University of Munich. He told his classes: "We must abandon national egoism and join a new European cultural order."[210] The Faculty of Philosophy protested, declaring that Foerster's opinions should "make every German blush."[211]

Undeterred and knowing that he was provoking the wrath of German officialdom, in 1916 Foerster published an article in which he proposed a New Europe to be organized on a pacifist basis. It was a total rejection of Bismarckian principles. Foerster claimed to have received many letters from soldiers at the front who agreed with him. He was also supported by most of his students, but, as a group, the staff and faculty of the university did not approve. Neither of course did the government and police. One step ahead of them, Foerster fled to Switzerland, where he remained for the duration of the war.

At the end of the war, while still in exile, Foerster wrote:

> I have not lost faith in Germany. But [...] the German people will have to pass through much suffering before they will turn away from their idols [...]. Now everything will depend on whether the Germans recognize in the peace treaty the natural consequence of what we have done for the last 50 years or will see it only as the shameful vileness of the Allies [...]. I shall do my share that the correct interpretation of recent history not be forgotten.[212]

Foerster tried to do his share; for example, after the end of the war he proposed to the Chancellor of the Reich that several hundred German volunteers be sent to help rebuild the areas of Belgium and northern France devastated by the war. The proposal was ignored.

* * *

Like many other German intellectuals and academics who were opposed to the war, Hermann Fernau (1884–?), a writer and a politician, joined the colony of exiles in Switzerland. Soon after he arrived he wrote: "The German people were made enthusiastic for the war because their ruler deceived them into thinking that it was a war for defense."[213]

Fernau went further than Foerster, taking the short logical step from being opposed to Prussian militarism to wishing to see Germany defeated on the field of battle. He accepted the idea that the only way that Germany would ever have a peaceful and democratic state would be if it lost the war. In his book *Das Königtum is der Krieg* (The kingdom of war), he argued that Germany was solely responsible for the war and that the only way to get rid of the Kaiser was to suffer a military defeat. He willingly took the title of an "authentic defeatist."[214] But a defeat on the field of battle would not be enough. Germany should pay for what it had done to Europe: "War in the modern world is a crime, and its instigators are criminals in the legal sense of the word."[215]

When the war was over Fernau[216] wanted to conduct a trial into its causes, an inquiry not in the name of several nations, the victorious ones, but in the "name of all Europe." He wrote in the conclusion to his book *Because I Am a German*: "In the name of millions who have already fallen in this gigantic war, in the name of the millions perchance yet to fall, in the name of public peace and security of Europe, in the name of the culture and civilization of our earth, in the name of the inviolable, unwritten, and eternal right of the nations, I demand this trial and this punishment, and I demand them Just Because I Am a German."[217]

Richard Grelling (1853–1929), another German pacifist in the refugee community in Switzerland, was one of the founders of the Deutsche Friedensgesellschaft (German Peace Society). As soon as the war began he delved into its causes and became convinced that Imperial Germany was waging a deliberate, offensive war of conquest. To enlighten the German people, and the world, he wrote *J'accuse!* to prove the war had been avoidable and was a calculated act of the German government and the Prussian-German general staff. Although originally "A German" was the only identification of the author, it soon became evident that Grelling was the author. The 445-page indictment of German militarism quickly became a world success and was translated into 16 languages, proof that not all Germans had rallied to the flag. The book was of course forbidden in Germany; however, copies were smuggled in and circulated widely. Each reader was asked to keep the book no more than 48 hours before he or she passed it on. The German government labeled Grelling "a paid mercenary writer for the enemy" and declared him to be guilty of "high treason."[218]

In a chapter titled "Guilt" Grelling does not mince his words:

[T]he plans and the preparations for this war have long been made by Germany and Austria not only from a military but also from a political point of view;
[...] for long it had been resolved to represent this offensive war to the German people as a war of liberation, because it was known that only thus could the necessary popular enthusiasm be awakened;
[...] the object of this war is an attempt to establish a hegemony on the continent and, as a later sequel, the acquisition of England's position of power in the world according to the principle *ôte-toi de là que je m'y mette (remove yourself so that I can take your place)*.[219]

In May 1918 Grelling was tried in absentia for "treason to the nation." He was found guilty, his property was confiscated and he lost more than a million marks (approximately 3 million 2012 U.S. dollars).

* * *

Albert Einstein, probably the most famous signatory of the German anti-war "Appeal," took part in the peace movement from the beginning of the war. But he was never an active member at the forefront, where, given his international reputation, one would expect to find him.

From the perspective of other theoretical physicists, Einstein was certainly "a fearless fighter for the mutual understanding of nations and world peace,"[220] as one biographer has called him. Most scientists at the time believed in the strict separation of science and politics, the maintenance of a rigid objectivity that produced political neutrality. But for Einstein, there was no question but that "noncooperation in military matters should be an essential moral principle for all true scientists."[221] In fact, non-compliance should be a part of any pacifist's behavior. According to one of Einstein's biographers: "[E]xcept for his devotion to science, no cause was more important or closer to his heart than the determination that the institution of war be forever abolished."[222]

However, if one looks at Einstein's pacifism from the point of view of the German anti-war movement as a whole, he is at best a marginal figure who was never in the streets waving a banner or on the podium haranguing a crowd. In any case, the German government never considered Einstein to be a threat to the war effort. Although they monitored his activities from time to time, they never censored him or interfered with his movements. During the war Einstein often traveled to neutral countries, usually Holland and Switzerland.

Pacifism for Einstein was apparently very individual and cerebral, an attitude created by the interaction of intuition and reflection. According to Konrad Wachsmann (1901–1980), the architect of Einstein's summerhouse in Caputh: "Einstein's pacifism was rooted in a deep disdain of brutality, cruelty, hatred, and every form of destruction. He considered it perverse to honor humans for killing other humans [...] and give them medals. He considered the admiration of heroes as an invitation to murder and manslaughter [...]. Einstein's pacifism came from logical thinking as well as from a warm human feeling."[223]

Einstein put his name on other appeals for peace and reason, for example, the Delbrück-Dernburg Petition. Hans Delbrück (1848–1929) was a historian at the University of Berlin; and Bernhart Dernburg (1865–1937), a banker and liberal politician. Their petition, which was presented to Chancellor von Bethmann-Hollweg, was against the "incorporation or annexation of politically independent peoples" in other words, it argued that it was unwise for Germany to attempt the absorption of bitterly hostile groups from other countries.

The petition did not have a wide circulation and soon became a forgotten footnote to the war. Only 141 people, mostly academics, signed it and it is rather surprising to find Einstein's name on the list, as the document also contained militant sentences like "We all are firmly convinced, together with the whole people, that this war will end with a full victory for Germany."[224]

Only eight weeks later Einstein appears to have changed his position. In Geneva he met Romain Rolland, who later wrote that "he [Einstein] hoped for a victory of the Allies that would destroy the might of Prussia and its dynasty."[225]

Lamenting the fact that the European intellectuals had not organized themselves into a cohesive and vocal anti-war movement, Einstein told Romain Rolland that

> three centuries of painstaking cultural effort have carried us no further than from religious fanaticism to the insanity of nationalism.[226]
> Even the learned men of the different countries are behaving as if their cerebrum had been amputated eight months ago.[227]

However, this was a period in his life when Einstein was working out the details of his theories and, apart from his visceral hatred for war and his ethic of non-violence, he apparently paid little attention to the daily news from the front. Lise Meitner (1879–1968), a physicist who often came in contact with him, commented after spending an evening with Einstein: "The very fact that an educated human being exists who, during this time, does not consult a single newspaper is surely a curiosity."[228]

Virtually all of Einstein's statements about the war were made in the relative privacy of conversations or correspondence that had a limited circulation. Only once during the conflict did he speak to a wider public. In the fall of 1915 the Berlin chapter of the Goethebund[229] invited Einstein to express, "without any restriction as to form or content," his opinion concerning the war. Einstein did not hesitate to put down his thoughts revealing an optimistic view about the nature of man: "The fine spirits of all times were united in their belief that war belongs to the worst enemies of human evolution, and that everything possible has to be done to prevent it. Despite the unspeakably sad conditions of the present, I am convinced that, in a future not far away, a political organization of European states can be reached that will exclude European wars."²³⁰

* * *

On the other side of the trenches, in France, there were many who reflected roughly the same point of view, namely stop the fighting immediately then negotiate a peace. Sébastien Faure (1858–1942), for example, in 1915 wrote *Vers la paix* (*Towards Peace*) which was one of the first proscriptive anti-war tracts to appear. Faure had a solution to the conflict: an immediate ceasefire followed by a conference of neutral states which would negotiate the terms of the final peace.

Although it was addressed to "socialists [...], revolutionaries [...], and anarchists,"²³¹ those who were most likely to take action, *Vers la paix* was read throughout the country as well as in the trenches where it was passed, hand to hand, unit to unit. It was one of the first anti-war tracts to reach the French front lines. In passionate tones Faure pleads for peace: "Even though we have not been able to prevent this calamity—and that will be the regret and the shame of our generation—let us at least put an end as soon as possible to the disastrous aftermath for that will be our joy and rehabilitation."²³²

Certainly a measure of the substantial success of *Vers la Paix* was the fact that early in 1915 the minister of the interior, Louis-Jean Malvy (1875–1949), summoned Faure in his office.

The minister politely asked Faure to cease distributing anti-war tracts at the front. In almost the next sentence he made it clear that army intelligence had the names and dossiers of most of the soldiers who had read it. If Faure did not cease sending tracts to the trenches, the minister threatened, those soldiers would be arrested and severely punished. Faure felt he had no choice, and agreed "for the moment" to stop sending anti-war tracts to the trenches.

The minister was true to his word. Faure did indeed save many, probably thousands, of soldiers from being sent to disciplinary battalions,²³³ but others went to prison for their pacifist convictions, often caught handing out antimilitarist tracts or trying to persuade soldiers to desert. Most went to solitary cells unheralded, their names lost, their suffering not even awarded a footnote.

Louis Lecoin (1888–1971), for example, spent more than 12 years of his life in jail for his beliefs. An absolutist, his spirit permitted no compromises: "If it were proved to me that in making war my ideal had a chance of being realized, I would still say "No" to war. For one does not create a human society on mounds of corpses."²³⁴

In 1913, a year before the war began, he helped found an organization that called upon young conscripts to refuse to serve in the army and soldiers to shed their uniforms and desert. It was a principle that united virtually all the pacifist parties. Abolish the army, by fiat or more likely by the simple addition of individual decisions, each man refusing to bear arms, and in one stroke armies disintegrated and war became impossible. In large bold type Lecoin's leaflet proclaimed:

> We want to see weapons done away with and militarism [...]. We do not desert out of fear of the fighting or out of cowardice. If our brethren will but some day stand up at last to the Authorities in all their guises, we will be at the ready!
> DO NOT REPORT TO BARRACKS!
> DO NOT, BY YOUR PASSIVITY, CONTRIBUTE TO THE PERPETUATION OF THIS SCOURGE, MILITARISM!
> DESERT![235]

Arrested while he was trying to persuade soldiers to desert, Lecoin was brought to trial and sentenced to five years in jail, the maximum sentence. When it was announced, he defiantly yelled, "Down with war!"

While behind bars with a fellow prisoner, Pierre Ruff (1877–1942),[236] Lecoin wrote a pamphlet that declared: "Enough barbarism! Enough blood! Let us demand peace. Let us impose peace."[237] Ruff had been sent to prison for "*provocation au meurtre, à l'incendie et au pillage*" (incitement to murder, arson and plunder); in fact, he was guilty of quite the opposite, trying to persuade men of conscription age not to kill anyone and to respect the rights and property of others. He was released in November 1916, then arrested a month later when he was caught distributing the pacifist leaflet *Imposons la paix!* (Let us impose peace). He was immediately sent back to prison.

Meanwhile, for the French left Louis Lecoin had become a martyr, and *Le Libertaire*, the anarchist publication, waged a campaign in his behalf. Lecoin was set free in 1917, then quickly rearrested when he refused to report for military service. Spending a total of eight years in prison, he was finally released in 1920.

* * *

As Americans watched the war clouds settle over Europe their initial reaction was a blend of horror and relief. The *New York Times* editorialized that "[the European nations] have reverted to the condition of savage tribes roaming the forests and falling upon each other in a fury of blood and carnage to achieve the ambitious designs of chieftains clad in skins and drunk on mead."[238] And most Americans seemed to agree. One midwestern editor wrote: "We have never appreciated so keenly as now the foresight exercised our forefathers in emigrating from Europe."

Hamilton Holt (1872–1951),[239] a peace activist and editor of the influential American magazine *The Independent*, came to the conclusion that instead of eliminating weapons and armed forces from one minute to the next, as most pacifists advocated, people should put military might at the service of the forces of peace and use it as a guarantee. In his "The Way to Disarm: A Practical Proposal," Holt suggested the establishment of a League for Peace[240] based on the original American Articles of Confederation, which would be ready to enforce its mandate against nations that refused to peacefully settle their disputes. Force was good, Holt maintained, if it supported a legal and worthwhile goal. His neo–Kantian ideas[241] seemed to make good sense, and the League to Enforce Peace was born, coming into existence as the first shots of war were being fired in Europe. It would become perhaps the most famous of all organizations that heralded the postwar League of Nations.

The organization was headed by an ex–U.S. President, William Howard Taft. Despite the war in Europe, he remained optimistic and determined to find a way to stop the bloodshed. Ex-President Theodore Roosevelt, Andrew Carnegie, A. L. Lowell (1856–1943), president of Harvard University, and 120 like-minded leaders in education, law, business and politics immediately joined.

The American Peace Society was split and ultimately refused to sanction the League, as it "tied around the neck [...] the millstone of physical force."[242]

The League to Enforce Peace was not shy about its willingness to use bullets and bayonets. The word "Enforce" on its letterhead was printed in bright red ink. The League defined its objective as "a world organization which will tend to prevent war by forcing its members to try peaceable means first [...] and to make immediate and certain war upon any nation which goes to war without a previous hearing of the dispute."[243]

Ex-President Taft refined the use of force still further: "The force is to be applied in securing the due process under the agreements of the League [...]. The essence of the plan is the delay and deliberation involved in orderly procedure for the hearing and decision of the controversy. It is thought that most wars can be avoided by such a procedure."[244]

Holt reduced the purpose of the League to a facile syllogism, a logical jingle that was easy to remember: "Peace follows justice, justice follows law, and law follows political organization."[245]

The inaugural ceremony was held in Independence Hall in Philadelphia (where the American Declaration of Independence had been signed in 1776). The choice of venue was obvious, a return to the place where the American republic had been born. Taft fervently hoped that he would be taking the first step in founding the peaceful union of the world.[246]

The League was to be based on four principles:

1. A nation that joins the League agrees to settle in a court all justiciable disputes.

2. All non-justiciable questions will be referred to a council of conciliation for investigation.

3. The signatory powers shall use their economic and military forces against any member that goes to war before taking their case to either the council or the court.

4. All member nations shall meet at stated intervals to make international law for themselves.[247]

In general, the propositions were so airy that it was difficult to disagree with them, and most people, especially those in the peace movement, didn't. The third article was the most contentious. But as one of original framers of the document was quick to point out: "Observe that we do not say that we shall enforce the judgment of the court or council of conciliation, but only that we shall enforce a reference to that council before a nation goes to war."[248]

The vagueness of the "four principles" was both the strength and the weakness of the League. It could only force a country to submit its dispute to a court or council. And should a war already exist, as it did in 1914 when Europe burst into flames, or should a country refuse to abide by the decision of the court, ignore the League and go to war, what then? The League was based on the precepts of pre–World War One jurisprudence, a belief in the moral force of the law. One of its leaders, Harvard president A. Lawrence Lowell (1856–1943), stated the problem succinctly: no international organization could be effective once war erupted; it had to succeed in preventing war, not ending war. In other words, the League to Enforce Peace was totally irrelevant for the world as it existed in 1915.

Nonetheless, ex–President Taft clearly had the support and respect of millions of Americans. The proposal received wide media coverage, caught the public imagination and soon made a tremendous impression on American public opinion.

Holt's strongest argument in favor of the League to Enforce Peace was that it did not necessitate a fundamental change in human nature. This marked a radical departure from most pacifist solutions, which typically required human beings, from one moment to the next, to become kinder, more caring, more socially conscious, and more moral, to somehow depart from the traditional egoism and collectively emerge as new "socialist men." The "how" for this transformation had always been the weak link in the theory, usually provided by one of three options: by example, by persuasion, i.e., the written word, or by religious conversion. All of them had been tried many times and in many forms and none had proved to be efficacious.[249]

For Holt, "force is the universal fact on earth."[250] The only thing that he wanted to change was who commanded the army and navy. Lucia Ames Mead (1856–1936), an activist for peace and one of the founders of the Woman's Peace Party, put the argument quite simply: "The reign of law has come in families, in cities, in the States, in the nations. It is coming between the nations. There is no new principle to be invented, simply the extension of an old and tried principle."[251]

Within a short time the League had nearly two dozen full-time employees in a national office and more than 4,000 branches in every state except Minnesota, Nebraska and Nevada. At its peak it had a budget of nearly $300,000 (the equivalent of approximately $7 million in 2012), employed 23 full-time staff workers and sent out dozens of speakers to address clubs, labor unions, schools and churches. The League quickly became the most powerful wartime pressure group on behalf of the ideal of a postwar League of Nations, thereby helping to lay the foundation for the international organization that would be one result of the end of the war.

At the League's first National Assembly President Wilson was the keynote speaker. He delivered a very carefully prepared speech, his first formal commitment to the League of Nations idea. It was also the first time the head of a world power had proposed to lead his country into a commonwealth of nations. It was more than just a string of political platitudes. Wilson was candid and prophetic: "We are participants, whether we would or not, in the life of the world. The interests of all nations are our own also. We are partners with the rest. What affects mankind is inevitably our affair as well as the affair of the nations of Europe and Asia [...]. The nations of the world have become each other's neighbors."[252]

The President went on to detail what he believed to be the three fundamental rights of nations: the right of people to choose the sovereignty under which they live, the right of small nations to enjoy the same respect for their sovereignty that great nations insist on, and the right of all nations to be free from aggression and the disregard of peoples and nations. Then, to an enthusiastic and cheering crowd, President Wilson stated categorically that the United States should become "a partner in any feasible association of nations formed to realize these objectives and make them secure against violation."[253]

The President continued and made it clear that he favored the use of force, moral, economic, and, in certain circumstances, physical, on the part of this association, which should also formulate the international rights of nations. Wilson called it a "new diplomacy," the end of American isolation. The speech set the tone for American foreign policy for the rest of the war.

In America the immediate reaction was overwhelmingly positive and the speech received bipartisan support. *The Independent* went so far as to declare that President Wilson's speech was a "Declaration of Independence" that should be added to the original Declaration of Independence.[254]

Wilson went on to use the issue as a plank in his 1916 re-election campaign, and after frequent mentions in his speeches his "new diplomacy" became refined and more precise. While he was elected under the slogan "He kept us out of war," and increased his share of the popular vote by several million from the previous election, at the same time he told the people of the United States that he intended to involve them in world affairs, both in peace and in war: "The nations of the world must get together and say, 'Nobody can hereafter be neutral as respects the disturbance of the world's peace for an object which the world's opinion cannot sanction.' The world's peace ought to be disturbed if the fundamental rights of humanity are invaded, but it ought not to be disturbed for any other thing that I can think of."[255]

In addition, President Wilson asked the Allies and the Central Powers if they would be willing to join in such a League after the war and they all agreed. Chancellor von Bethmann-Hollweg said: "We not only believe in this movement, but we should like to lead."[256]

In London, the Prime Minister, Lloyd George, also agreed in principle: "[When this war is over ...] [t]he peace and security for peace will be that the nations will band themselves together to punish the first peacebreaker who comes out. As to the armies of Europe, every weapon will be a sword of justice in the Government of men; every arm will be a constabulary of peace."[257]

The other Allied countries, as well as Switzerland, Spain and the Scandinavian countries, also agreed to participate.[258]

Meanwhile a well-known spokesman for the League, Theodore Marburg (1862–1946), constantly underscored the fact that the new plan rested squarely on the traditional values and for that reason it was practical, down-to-earth and immediately employable: "Altruism is a factor in its operations, but the plan [that of the League] still recognizes self-interest as the governing motive of States, as of individuals."[259] Marburg was a former diplomat (U.S. ambassador to Belgium), who took the title of Chairman of the Committee on Foreign Organization of the League to Enforce Peace and sought to have the warring nations agree to the principles of peace, that is, the principles of the League to Enforce Peace, before the fighting ended. It was a novel approach: a signed and binding peace agreement before the war had ended, a way to guarantee that the peace would not be creating the seeds of revanche for the next conflict.

Marburg spent most of 1916 shuttling from one European capital to the next enlisting support for the League. He believed that a time of intense crisis, like a war, offers a unique opportunity for change: "while the nerves of the world are exposed, while the minds of men are fully alive to the evils of existing conditions, while men's souls are, in fact, on fire with horror."[260] Marburg was convinced that when men looked at their world through the lens of war and barbarism they began to question the institutions that brought them to this primitive condition. At that moment, more than any other, they would be open to something with a different perspective, something perhaps better, perhaps more peaceful, something that could prevent the next war. Afterwards it would be too late. Marburg knew that history was clear on that point. When a war was over nations tried to return to the *status quo ante bellum*, the way things used to be, the comfortable and familiar.

Marburg went first to London, where he found that Edward Grey, the British Foreign Secretary, was an enthusiastic supporter. Grey told the foreign press: "I would like to say that if we seem to have little time to give to such ideas ourselves while we are engaged in this struggle, such a work in neutral countries is one to which we would all look with favor and with hope."[261]

In France, Aristide Briand (1862–1932), the Prime Minister, publicly approved of the plan. In Germany, von Bethmann-Hollweg, the Chancellor, stated that if as a condition of the future peace "no more aggressive coalitions are formed [...], Germany will at all times be ready to enter a league for the purpose of restraining the disturbers of peace."[262]

While this was not the binding agreement for the peace that Marburg had hoped for, it was a step in the right direction. The real disappointment came from the neutral countries. Switzerland and Spain, for example, were prepared to make definite commitments, but the Danes and other Scandinavians were not.

Despite Marburg's efforts, the backing of three American Presidents, Roosevelt, Taft and Wilson, and the financial support of Edwin Ginn, the League failed to accomplish its major objective.

Speaking before a meeting of the League presided by ex–President Taft in 1916, after more than a year of warfare in Europe, Jacob H. Schiff (1847–1920), the noted banker, made an impassioned plea for the United States to step in by whatever means available and become a peacemaker. Schiff argued that by doing so the United States would gain the friendship of all nations and would be fulfilling its role as "the trustee of the interests of humanity."[263]

When America declared war in 1917, the League immediately supported it, arguing that the war must be fought and won in order to obtain peace in Europe. "Peace through Victory" became the popular slogan and the League mobilized its considerable resources, sending out speakers, printing pamphlets, and lobbying Congressmen.[264] In 1917 more than 2 million pieces of League literature were distributed. And they seemed to be having an effect. During one six-week period there were 152 editorials about the League, 149 of them favorable.

Ex-President Taft suddenly found himself backing a war he had tried so hard to prevent. The League to Enforce Peace disintegrated after the armistice. But it had served an important purpose. Without a doubt, ex–President Taft and the League to Enforce Peace became the real parents of the League of Nations.[265]

* * *

When the war broke out in Europe the Carnegie Endowment for Peace cut off their support for European peace societies. Nicholas Murray Butler (1862–1947), the head of international education and communication for the Endowment[266] and president of Columbia University, declared that Europe's large-scale armaments had led directly to the war: "In modern democracies the functions of the army and navy are police, philanthropic, and sanitary. [He urged the American people] [...] to put behind us forever the notion that we must arm in peace as a preventive of war [...]. No people will be hostile to us unless we, by our conduct, make them so [...]. It must not be forgotten that militarism has its origin in a state of mind."[267]

Butler became one of the leading supporter of the anti-preparedness campaign, to keep America out of the war and neutral. However, he soon switched sides: "I believe that a victory for the German Imperial Government would plunge all of us into the black night of military barbarism."[268] And Butler took the Carnegie Endowment for Peace with him. Suddenly he became virulently opposed to all dissent. There was only one road to take, his. Speaking about pacifism and pacifists, he said candidly: "No one has less sympathy with these morally half-witted people than I have."[269]

It is often said that the shock of World War One killed Andrew Carnegie. If so, then undoubtedly the use of the Endowment for Peace to rally the forces of war, rather than those of peace, hastened his demise. Butler even permitted George Creel's (1876–1953) dogmatic Committee on Public Information, America's wartime propaganda machine, to use the Carnegie Endowment's offices.

* * *

While nearly all of Europe went to war, the Italians, including the socialists and pacifists, initially voted against Italy's entry into the conflict and Italy did, in fact, remain neutral.

Ernesto Teodoro Moneta (1833–1918), Italy's most eminent peace activist and the winner of the Nobel Peace Prize in 1907,[270] wrote with pride: "As Italians we may congratulate ourselves with confidence that neutrality will be preserved to the very end and whatever may be the direction that the war will take."[271]

Most Italians agreed with him. By treaty, the country was not obliged to follow its Triple Alliance partners unless it had been attacked first. Addressing a large, applauding crowd, Eduardo Giretti (1864–1940), a pacifist Deputy to the Italian Assembly, declared: "The Italian people want war with no one [...]. In the present crisis [we] do not wish the state to undertake any action that is not one of peaceful mediation among the peoples being sucked into the whirlwind of a struggle which is the utter negation of civilization and humanity."[272]

However, during the following months of neutrality, the peace and pacifist parties slowly shifted from neutrality to intervention, from an abhorrence of violence to a readiness to bear arms, their rhetoric increasingly laced with fierce, jingoistic anti–German barbs. Some of the peace societies went so far as to request the government to "intervene at the opportune moment [...] employing its moral as well as material forces" to hasten a just and rapid end to the war.[273]

The swell of nationalism conquered even the most convinced anti-militarist and pacifist. For example, Professor Regina Terruzzi (1862–1951) of the National

Council of Italian Socialist Women wrote: "[D]o you want Pan-Germanism to triumph everywhere? [...] I do not want to become German. If by chance your [German] soldiers will trample upon Italian soil, even I—I who have a total horror of all violence—even I will help defend my country."[274]

The dramatic change from peace to war in Italy can perhaps be partially explained by the tales of horror that emerged from the German invasion of neutral Belgium and Luxembourg, stories of Belgian children whose hands were cut off, Canadian soldiers crucified to doors, nurses whose breasts were cut off, and Germans distilling glycerin from the dead in order to obtain lubricants. Many of these atrocities were the invention of the British propaganda machine, but they were given wide circulation by inflammatory speakers such as Dr. Charles Richet (1850–1935), a leading spokesman for French pacifists, who toured Italy painting vivid portraits of German cruelty. Fleeing the invading army, which destroyed thousands of homes, over 20 percent of the Belgian population had become refugees. The Italians were easily persuaded that they could be next.

One after another many of the Italian peace societies and socialist parties dropped the standard of peace and international solidarity and began to militantly march behind the flag. Even Moneta, who had been granted the Nobel Peace Prize[275] for his decades of devotion to the cause of peace, suddenly joined the linguistic violence. He predicted that a kind of new Dark Ages would result if Germany won the war. It would "realize its dream of hegemony over Europe [...] all the peoples of this continent, ours among the first, would become serfs and this ancient center of civilization would [...] relapse under a new Teutonic military barbarism."[276]

Not everyone joined the ranks of the militants. Italy was largely divided on the issue of war or peace. According to one observer, there was "widespread recognition that the majority of Italians remained neutralists."[277]

The strongly Catholic south was "interventionist," that is, in favor of declaring war on Austria-Hungary, while the more industrialized north remained vehemently opposed. With a declaration of war clearly on the horizon, over 80,000 workers in Turin went on strike. Barricades went up, and for three days workers and troops battled in the streets, leaving one dead and dozens wounded. Order was restored a few days before Italy entered the war.

After nearly ten months of neutrality and many voices still advocating peace, sanity and neutrality, Italy declared war against Austria-Hungary in May of 1915.

* * *

While the soldiers in the trenches were receiving their parcels from home for the first Christmas of the war, a group of 101 British suffragists sent an open letter addressed to "The women of Germany and Austria":

Sisters:

Some of us wish to send you a word at this sad Christmastide. [...] those of us who wished and still wish for peace may surely offer a solemn greeting to such of you who feel as we do. [...] the brunt of modern war falls upon non-combatants, and the conscience of the world cannot bear the sight.

Is it not our mission to preserve life? Do not humanity and common sense alike prompt us to join hands with the women of neutral countries, and urge our rulers to stay further bloodshed? [...] Even through the clash of arms, we treasure our poet's vision, and already seem to hear

A hundred nations swear that there shall be Pity and Peace and Love among the good and free.

May Christmas hasten that day.[278]

The letter was written by Emily Hobhouse, who had become famous over a decade earlier for bringing to the attention of the public the appalling conditions in the British concentration camps built for women and children during the Boer War (1899–1902). Most of the letter's signatories were women's suffrage activists, but also on the list were Mrs. M. K. Gandhi (1869–1944), wife of Mohandas Gandhi, and a single American, Florence Edgar Hobson, a dramatist and wife of the economist John A. Hobson (1858–1940).

Since there was no direct contact between England and Germany, the open letter was sent via America, which at the time was a neutral nation. The letter of course did not stop a single bullet or propose a viable means to end the fighting. However, for women, for perhaps the first time, it fused two issues, pacifism and the suffragette movement, and thus became one of a number of stepping-stones that led to the Women's Peace Congress that was held the following year at The Hague.

Not all women supported the drive for peace. At roughly the same time a pamphlet signed by "A Little Mother" appeared which declared that "we women [...] will tolerate no such cry as "Peace! Peace! [...] There is only one temperature for the women of the British race, and that is white heat [...]. We women pass on the human ammunition of only sons to fill up the gaps."[279]

The pamphlet sold 75,000 copies in a few days.

* * *

If the politicians, diplomats, generals and women couldn't, or wouldn't, make peace, the men on the front lines realized they would have to do it themselves, and in fact they briefly did. On Christmas Day, 1914, after almost five months of warfare on the Western Front, thousands of soldiers stepped out of the trenches, walked toward one another and realized the enemy were men very much like themselves.

This one real moment of peace on the Western Front arrived not as the result of diplomacy or the intervention of Kings or Popes or Presidents but as a spontaneous initiative by the soldiers themselves, the men in the trenches, who on Christmas Day decided that the spirit of "peace on earth" also included the battlefield. The main participants were the British and the Germans, but some French and the Belgian units took part as well.

All governments concerned tended to suppress information about the Christmas truce. Most histories, and certainly official histories of the First World War, dismiss it as an aberration, an oddity that could be easily omitted and forgotten. But this is a mistake. The facts speak for themselves. On Christmas Eve, 1914, at least 100,000 front-line troops, climbed out of the trenches and voted for peace with their feet and their hearts. No other modern war has witnessed such a poignant demonstration in favor of ending a conflict. Suddenly, from one moment to the next, thousands of soldiers stopped fighting, put down their weapons, then greeted one another in the middle of no-man's-land.

It has been called the populism of the battlefield, a uniquely modern mass movement that could have easily created a revolution and changed the course of history. Two armies, coming from radically different military traditions, proved that peace could be both spontaneous and infectious. Each act of fraternization, each meeting on no-man's-land, each exchange of gifts, could have been the spark that ignited a firestorm of mass desertions and effectively ended the war.

In fact, peace had already made its appearance, albeit a very short one, well before Christmas. In many places along the 700-kilometer Western Front pragmatic, informal cease-fires had been occurring almost since the beginning of the conflict.[280] A British soldier described one in his letter home:

> The trenches are only 60 yards apart in one place, and every morning about breakfast time one of the soldiers sticks a board in the air. As soon as this board goes up all firing ceases, and men from either side draw their water and rations. All through the breakfast hour, and so long as this board is up, silence reigns supreme, but whenever the board comes down the first unlucky devil who shows even so much as a hand gets a bullet through it.[281]

Often these mini-truces were approved, if not initiated, by the officers on both sides and were reported as "war news" in the national press. A month before Christmas, for example, the *London Times* printed the story of one of these cease-fires of convenience:

> A sort of tacit understanding is sometimes reached between the two sides, each reciprocally refraining in certain circumstances from molesting the other. An instance occurred recently when the men of one of our battalions found that the only means of boiling water for their tea was to carry it in the mess-tins to the smouldering ruins of some farm buildings nearby to "hot it up." The Germans, having a like desire to drink their coffee hot, availed themselves of another smouldering building within close rifle range. Friend and foe continued peacefully to make use of the two places for some days.[282]

A week before Christmas a *Daily Express* correspondent reported that the Germans slipped a "splendid" chocolate cake into the British lines with the message:

> We propose having a concert tonight as it is our Captain's birthday, and we cordially invite you to attend—provided you will give us your word of honour as guests that you agree to cease all hostilities between 7:30 and 8:30 [...]. When you see us light the candles and footlights at the edge of our trench at 7:30 sharp you can safely put your heads above your trenches, and we shall do the same, and begin the concert.[283]

A note accepting the invitation was sent back with an offer of English tobacco.

There was noticeably less fraternization between the French and German troops. One French soldier wrote to his parents:

> Things are happening in the war that you would not believe! [...] the day before yesterday—and this lasted for two days in the trenches that the 90th are occupying now—French and German soldiers shook each other's hands; unbelievable, I can tell you [...]. They came out of their trenches, without weapons, nothing at all, with an officer in the lead; we did the same and it was a real visit from one trench to the other, exchanging cigars and cigarettes, and a hundred metres away other men were firing over our heads from both sides.[284]

By the time Christmas arrived the men on both sides of the Western Front were ready for a break. Five months of constant fighting had cost over a million casualties. To make matters worse, December had been an exceptionally wet month, more than two inches above average, with rain pouring into the muddy trenches almost every day. Where possible, the Germans had pumped excess water into the British trenches, and vice versa. Most men at the front lived in a mix of mud, mire and muck and were nearly frozen most of the time. Morale was at all-time low.

The Christmas truce actually began on the 23rd of December and was apparently initiated by the Germans. A British officer recorded the event:

> [O]ne of the men on sentry duty called my attention to the fact that the German troops opposite were clambering out into the open, waving their arms in the air and making friendly gestures in our direction [...]. Although the temporary truce that followed was apparently a purely spontaneous act of mutual friendship and goodwill, it was of so unique and surprising a nature that it was just as well to take no undue risks. The company on our left, however, allowed a couple of Germans to come across and a friendly exchange of cigars and verbal greetings took place, one of the two Germans jocularly remarking that he hoped the war would end soon, as he wanted to return to his former job as a taxi-driver in Birmingham.[285]

The two sides often communicated by signboards that were pushed above the parapet. The Germans assumed, and rightly so, that the English would not be able to read their Gothic letters, so they wrote in English. To create a cease-fire, if only for the removal of the dead and wounded from no-man's-land, they would hoist a sign that read "YOU NO FIGHT, WE NO FIGHT," then some unarmed men, usually officers, would meet in the middle of no-man's-land and discuss the terms: "As a sign of their friendliness the Germans put up a sign saying '*Gott mit uns*' which means 'God is with us' and so we put up a sign in English saying 'We got mittens too.' I don't know if they enjoyed that joke."[286]

By the time Christmas Eve arrived, the fraternization became more general, rippling contagiously up and down the front where the British and Germans faced each other.

A British rifleman in the front trenches facing the Germans wrote in his reminiscences:

> Then suddenly lights began to appear along the German parapet, which were evidently makeshift Christmas trees, adorned with lighted candles, which burnt steadily in the still, frosty air! Other sentries had, of course, seen the same thing, and quickly awoke those on duty, asleep in the shelters, to "come and see this thing, which had come to pass." Then our opponents began to sing *Stille Nacht, Heilige Nacht*. This was actually the first time I heard this carol, which was not then so popular in this country as it has since become. They finished their carol and we thought that we ought to retaliate in some way, so we sang, *The First Nowell*, and when we finished that they all began clapping; and then they struck up another favorite of theirs, *O' Tannenbaum*. And so it went on. First the Germans would sing one of their carols and then we would sing one of ours, until we started up *O Come All Ye Faithful* the Germans immediately joined in singing the same hymn to the Latin words *Adeste Fideles*. And I thought, well, this was really a most extraordinary thing—two nations both singing the same carol in the middle of a war.[287]
>
> I think I have seen one of the most extraordinary sights today that anyone has ever seen. About 10 o'clock this morning I was peeping over the parapet when I saw a German, waving his arms, and presently two of them got out of their trenches and came towards ours—we were just going to fire on them when we saw they had no rifles. So one of our men went out to meet them and in about two minutes the ground between the two lines of trenches was swarming with men and officers of both sides, shaking hands and wishing each other a happy Christmas [...]. The truce will probably go on until someone is foolish enough to let off his rifle—we nearly messed it up this afternoon, by one of our fellows letting off his rifle skywards by mistake but they did not seem to notice it so it did not matter [...]. This extraordinary truce has been quite impromptu.[288]

There was no systematic fraternization, no political or military policy designed to systematically engage the enemy; instead it was almost always a spontaneous, heartfelt, individualistic affair. More than likely one soldier, occasionally perhaps two or even three, usually German, suddenly decided that "peace and goodwill" was incompatible with the rifle they held. In plain view of the "enemy," they discarded their weapons, stepped over the parapet and signaled to their opponents to meet them in the middle of no-man's-land.

A young, British soldier—not yet 17—arrived at the front just before Christmas and wrote back to his family:

> As for me, I had a very novel, interesting, exciting and withal jovial day [Christmas]. Would you believe it—by mutual consent our battalion and the Germans opposite had a little armistice. We did not fire a shot all day. We met one another and had a chat halfway between the two lines of trenches and exchanged buttons, cigars and cigarettes. It was really funny to see the "hated antagonists" standing in groups, laughing and talking and shaking hands [...]. Talk about peace and goodwill—I never saw a friendlier sight. We tried to explain to each other that we bore no malice.[289]

The French and Belgian troops were less likely to lay down their arms to celebrate Christmas with the Germans. To allow the holiday spirit to impose a sort of "live and let live" attitude and create a momentary halt to the fighting was one thing, but to be genuinely friendly with the soldiers who had invaded their country was quite another. One Belgian soldier recorded his surprise and as well as his doubts and misgivings about being too cordial with the enemy:

> Now I am going to tell you something which you will think incredible, but I give you my word that it is true. At dawn the Germans displayed a placard over the trenches on which was written "Happy Christmas" and then, leaving their trenches, unarmed, they advanced toward us singing and shouting "Comrades!" No one fired. We also left our trenches and, separated from each other only by the half-frozen Yser, we exchanged presents. They gave us cigars, and we threw them some chocolate. Thus almost fraternizing we passed all the morning [...].
>
> They asked us to spend Christmas without firing, and the whole day passed without any fighting [...]. Was it not splendid? Think you that we were wrong? We have been criticized here; it is said we ought to have fired. But would it not have been dastardly? And then, why kill one another on such a festival day?[290]

The French also arrived at a détente with the Germans, a distant but cordial respect for their fellow soldiers that produced a lull in the fighting. Very few units actually crossed no-man's-land to meet the enemy, much less fraternize with them. Some, like the Foreign Legion, launched attacks on Christmas Day. But most French troops stopped firing and withdrew to their bunkers. One unit even celebrated mass on a makeshift altar in no-man's-land less than 50 yards from the German lines. Throughout the entire ceremony the Germans, mostly Bavarian Catholics, watched from the parapets of their trenches and did not fire a single shot.

At one place on the Somme, 300 unarmed Germans, led by an officer, suddenly climbed out of their trenches and advanced to the French positions. The Germans were apparently sick of fighting. "*À bas la guerre!*" (Down with war!) shouted the French soldiers. "*Nie wieder Krieg! Das walte Gott!*" (No more war! It's what God wants!) replied the Germans.[291] For days the war ceased. Every morning the men met in the middle of no-man's-land, between the lines of barbed wire, and soon a thriving barter market, a kind of village fair, in bread, cognac, postcards and newspapers appeared. According to a French officer present, later a well-trained German dog carried messages between the two sets of trenches to make the daily arrangements.

Farther down the front, on Christmas Eve, a German violinist climbed up on top of the parapet and, silhouetted against the evening sky, played Handel's Largo, while elsewhere the French brought in a celebrated tenor from the Paris Opera to sing, "*Minuit, Chrétiens, c'est l'heure solennelle*" (known in English as the carol "O Holy Night").

The French postal censor included the following in his report to the General Staff: "These cavalrymen hold the trenches on the extreme right of the front, right up against the Swiss frontier [...]. This particular situation gave rise to a curious incident: a Swiss military band had come to the meeting point of the three frontiers. The Germans and French came out of their trenches to listen to their concert."[292]

The French official *Journal des marches et opérations*, which recorded the war day by day, has the following entry for December 27, two days after the truce began: "Situation stationary. The Christmas truce continues and the whole front is entirely calm. Along the two opposing lines, men do not hesitate to come out of the trenches. The Germans come over to meet our men, they exchange newspapers, tobacco and cigarettes. No other activity all day long."[293]

When confronted with acts of fraternization, officers typically turned their backs or chose to ignore them, knowing that there was little they could do to stop them. Often the officers led their men across no-man's-land to meet "the enemy." But in any case, the field officers, those actually in the trenches, were not likely to mention what had happened to their superiors. For this reason, it is impossible to ascertain with any accuracy the full extent of the fraternization or how long it lasted. It is known that whole sections of the front became "quiet" for often months at a time. Presumably they each found their own very special détente.

The French writer Gabriel Chevallier (1895–1969),[294] who served with the army in the Vosges, wrote:

> One section was living in a state of good understanding with the enemy. Each side carried on with its business in the usual way, without concealment, and sent cordial greetings across to the enemy group. Everyone wandered about freely and missiles consisted of nothing more than more serious than loaves of bread and packets of tobacco. Once or twice a day a German would shout: *Offizier!* to give warning of an officer's tour of inspection in the ranks. That indicated: *Take care! We may find ourselves obliged to send over a few grenades.* They even gave us advance warning of raids, and the information always turned out to be accurate.[295]

A French officer wrote home about the first time he found his men in friendly contact with the German soldiers in the opposite trench:

One morning, I don't know why, before going to sleep, I glanced over the parapet, and I was transfixed with astonishment at what I saw: all the men in my section were on their feet on the parapet or on the canal towpath. I saw some of them making wide gestures, as if they were throwing grenades, others bending down to pick up something, and others trying to catch objects, jumping in the air. I rushed along the trench: my soldiers were throwing chunks of bread, even whole loaves, or chocolate, across to the other side of the canal! In exchange the *Boches* were sending packets of tobacco in hand-grenades, previously defused and emptied of their explosive charge.[296]

In one sector relations became so friendly and courteous that the French felt compelled to send the following message to the Germans in the trenches facing them: "Be on guard tomorrow. A general is coming to visit our position. For reasons of shame and honour, we shall have to fire."[297]

For the 30 miles of front held by the British, the truce usually began with the Germans. On Christmas Eve they waved a white flag, hoisted a board asking for a cease-fire, or sang traditional songs such as "Silent Night," well-known to both the English and the Germans. In some places the trenches were as close as 50 or 60 meters apart, so that a song from one trench would be answered by a chorus in another. Occasionally a soldier, either British or German, would suddenly stand up, cast his rifle aside, then, hands in the air, walk to the middle of no-man's-land.

The Germans also placed small Christmas trees lit by candles on the parapet of the trenches; then they shouted, often dozens of men in unison: "English soldiers, English soldiers, Happy Christmas! Where are your Christmas trees?"[298]

Once the two sides began to communicate, each section of the front seemed to find its own, often unique, way to fraternize. Within 24 hours these spontaneous outbursts of peace covered more than two-thirds of the British-held sector. Most of the German and British soldiers facing each other in the trenches were involved.

In a letter home a German soldier proudly wrote: "We achieved what the Pope himself could not do and in the middle of the war we had a merry Christmas."[299]

As soon as he returned to his own trench from no-man's-land a Scottish corporal tried to describe the event to his family:

> We were walking between the trenches. At any other time this would have been suicide; even to show your head above the parapet would have been fatal, but tonight we go unarmed [...] out to meet our enemies [...].
>
> What a sight—little groups of Germans and British extending almost the length of our front! Out of the darkness we could hear laughter and see lighted matches, a German lighting a Scotchman's cigarette and vice versa, exchanging cigarettes and souvenirs. Where they couldn't talk the language they were making themselves understood by signs, and everyone seemed to be getting along nicely.

Here we were laughing and chatting to men whom only a few hours before we were trying to kill.[300]

Afterwards, a British soldier wrote on a postcard to his parents that "while you were eating your turkey, etc., I was out talking and shaking hands with the very men I had been trying to kill a few hours before!! It was astounding!"[301]

On Christmas Eve a German officer noted in his diary: "I have ordered my troops that, if at all avoidable, no shot shall be fired from our side either today on Christmas Eve or on the pursuant Christmas holidays. Hardly have we occupied the trenches both we and the English find ourselves trying to attract the other side's attention."[302]

A Mannheim newspaper published a postcard from a German soldier that was subsequently reprinted by the *New York Herald*. Some 20 men including officers, both French and German, had gathered in no-man's-land to bury their dead:

> There was general handshaking. [...] cigars, cigarettes and newspapers were exchanged and a general celebration ensued. Then the Frenchmen suggested that we shoot no longer, promised that they themselves would not resume hostilities in that event [...]. Well, we gladly agreed to this. Again there was handshaking, arms were resumed, and everybody crawled back to his trench. It was peace in the midst of war.[303]

Expressions of fascination, astonishment and excitement surface in virtually every account of the fraternization that occurred that Christmas. "This sight I will never forget in my entire life," wrote one British infantryman. "[O]ne of the most extraordinary days of our lives," added a Scotsman.[304] In one place a German juggler performed his tricks in no-man's-land and apparently drew a large and appreciative crowd. In another location a German barber who had worked in High Holborn, London, set up shop in a shell hole and gave shaves and trims to all, including some of his former clients. A British regiment slaughtered a pig, roasted it in no-man's-land, then shared it with the Germans, while some Saxon soldiers rolled a keg of beer over the parapet. A British rifleman wrote: "I miss the sounds of the shots going over, it is like a clock that has stopped ticking."[305]

At noon on Christmas Day the men went back to their trenches when the traditional meal was served, then they returned to no-man's-land. Both armies had received parcels from their families and friends as well as from royalty, the Kaiser for the Germans and Princess Mary for the British.[306]

A British officer whose letter home was published in a national newspaper tried to describe the atmosphere during the truce: "As I walked slowly back to the trenches I thought of Mr. Asquith's sentence[307] about not sheathing the sword until the enemy be finally crushed. It is all very well for Englishmen living at home to talk in flowing periods, but when you are out here you begin to realize that sustained hatred is impossible."[308]

Armed with sweets, biscuits, chocolate, plus their own rations, the men returned to no-man's-land and instantly a lively barter market was created. The Germans, on the one hand, appear to have had a particular affection for British bully beef, which had less fat than German meats, and also for British preserves. The British, on the other hand, favored German beer and tobacco.[309]

During the truce a British rifleman met a German soldier who had lived in London and spoke English. They chatted for several hours in the desolate no-man's-land. As they parted the German said: "Today we have peace. Tomorrow you fight for your country. I fight for mine. Good luck!"[310]

However, not everyone was pleased with the fraternization. A British soldier whose unit was pulled back on Boxing Day wrote in his diary: "Going through Armentières that night some of the French women were standing in the doors and shouting at us: 'You no bon (good), you English soldiers, you boko (beaucoup—very) kamerade Allemenge (Germans).' We cursed them back until we were blue in the nose."[311]

Once the generals on both sides, British and German, had received the daily reports from the trenches, they quickly realized that they had been left out. On Christmas Eve military discipline had suddenly collapsed. Without permission, over 100,000 men, and in many cases their officers too, had turned the battlefield into a spontaneous social event. Each side was rapidly discovering that the soldiers in the opposing trenches were men very much like themselves, farmers, workers, tradesmen and shopkeepers.

The battlefield had become a general's nightmare. More than anyone else they knew that fraternization could easily destroy an army's will to fight and, should it continue unchecked, the Christmas cease-fire could even lead to the end of the war. Only one short step separated fraternization from insubordination, the refusal, en masse, to fight, and, should that have happened, the news of thousands of men discarding their weapons rippling through the trenches could easily have become the spark for a populist mutiny.

Several weeks before Christmas one of the British commanding generals noted in his diary:

> Weird stories come in from the trenches about fraternizing with the Germans. They shout to each other and offer to exchange certain articles and give certain information. In one place, by arrangement, a bottle was put out between the trenches and then they held a competition as to which could break it first. There is a danger of opposing troops becoming too friendly, but it is only too likely to happen and it happened in the Peninsula.[312] I therefore intend to issue instructions to my Corps not to fraternize in any way with the enemy for fear one day they may be lulled into such a state of confidence as to be caught off guard and rushed.[313]

It is safe to say that many officers, at least on the British side, were well aware of the pacifistic potential of fraternization. A British officer who served on the Flanders front and later rose to the rank of general wrote in his diary: "It is interesting to visualize the close of a campaign owing to the opposing armies—neither of them defeated—having become too friendly to continue the fight."[314]

One British officer, who took an active part in the Christmas truce, despite the directives of his superiors, and yet ultimately became a cabinet minister, also realized that the hands across the barbed wire could have marked the beginning of peace:

> We went over in front of the trenches, and shook hands with many of our German enemies [...]. I then came to the conclusion that I have held very firmly ever since, that if we had been left to ourselves there would never have been another shot fired. For a fortnight the truce went on. We were on the most friendly terms, and it was only the fact that we were being controlled by others that made it necessary for us to start trying to shoot one another again.[315]

The day after the Christmas truce a commanding British general, obviously reduced to almost impotence, wrote in his notes: "This is only illustrative of the apathetic state we are gradually sinking into, apart also from illustrating that any orders I issue on the subject are useless."[316]

The generals weren't the only ones to realize that once military discipline crumbled, peace was a real possibility. It was obvious to all that the more the soldiers of the two armies met on friendly terms the less likely they were to shoot at one another. A German sergeant later told a friend:

> The difficulty began on the 26th [of December] when the order to fire was given, for the men *struck* [emphasis his]. Herr Lange says that in the accumulated years [of his service] he had never heard such language as the officers indulged in, while they stormed up and down, and got, as the only result, the answer "We can't—they are good fellows, and we can't." Finally, the officers turned on the men with, "Fire, or we do—and not at the *enemy*." Not a shot had come from the other side, but at least they fired, and an answering fire came back, but not a man fell. "We spent that day and the next," said Herr Lange, "wasting ammunition in trying to shoot the stars down from the sky."[317]

Upon hearing the news of fraternization, Sir John French, commander of the British forces, wrote in his memoirs, "I issued immediate orders to prevent any recurrence of such conduct, and called the local commanders to strict account, which resulted in a good deal of trouble."[318]

"A good deal of trouble" was indeed an understatement, a euphemism for the fact that, for a short period of time the commander in chief had effectively lost control of his army. While he was "issuing orders" the overwhelming majority of his fighting men, those in the trenches, had put down their arms and were standing in the middle of no-man's-land shaking hands and singing Christmas carols with the enemy. Officers up to the rank of colonel were involved, although most of them wisely kept a low profile.

Another British general immediately sent a confidential memorandum to his field commanders:

> On my return [to the front] I was shown a report from one section of how, on Christmas Day, a friendly gathering had taken place of Germans and British on the neutral ground between the two lines, recounting that many officers had taken part in it [...]. I have issued the strictest orders that on no account is intercourse to be allowed between the opposing troops. To finish this war quickly, we must keep up the fighting spirit and do all we can to discourage friendly intercourse.[319]

Strangely enough, it took nearly a week for the generals on both sides to fully react. The Germans issued an order on the 29th of December clearly stating that all fraternization was forbidden, as were all approaches to the enemy in the trenches. All acts contrary to the order were to be punished as high treason. The British did not try to enforce a similar order until January 2, 1915.

Despite this threat of severe discipline, no one, neither German nor British, was ever punished for the Christmas truce, nor was any unit deemed unreliable and removed from the front. Perhaps the generals were afraid that the news of a court-martial for fraternization might be the spark for even more of the same. Both the British and the German high command decided to overlook the breech in discipline and, if possible, continue the war.

Yet in many places along the British-German front the truce went on. Soldiers refused to stand guard, to snipe or fire at the enemy, or, when they did, to shoot accurately. Some units did not fire a shot in anger for weeks. Men on both sides regularly sat on the parapet, repaired their trenches and dugouts, or took shortcuts across no-man's-land without fear. Rifles were put away and the enemy became the mud and the fierce Flanders winter.

After the general anti-fraternization order was issued, the commander of a German company in the trenches sent the following message to British troops facing him: "Dear Comrades, I beg to inform you that it is forbidden for us to go out to you, but we remain your comrades. If we shall be forced to fire, we will fire too high [...] offering you some cigars, I remain, yours truly [...]."[320] The officer in charge of the British troops replied by sending back his tacit agreement and a large box of chocolates.

During the lull in the fighting a British colonel wrote to his wife: "We are all very peaceful [...]. [The Germans] say they want the truce to go on till after New Year and I am sure I have no objection. A rest from bullets will be distinctly a change."[321]

Contrary to popular thought, news of the Christmas truce was not suppressed by the censors, by neither the British nor the German. In fact, the opposite was true. The British press, for example, totally overlooked the breech in military discipline and instead focused on the spirit of Christmas goodwill. The tone was clearly positive, with the *Times* endorsing the "lack of malice" felt by both sides and the *Mirror* regretting that the "absurdity and the tragedy" of the war would begin again.

The national press carried headlines like: "Extraordinary Unofficial Armistice," "Remarkable Christmas Day Incidents," and "British, Indians and Germans Shake Hands."[322] London's *Daily Telegraph* went so far as to say: "All this [the Christmas truce] seems incredible in view of the ferocity of the combatants during months past and of the authenticated tales of German atrocities and trickery. It seems to prove the assertion that the German soldier is a good-hearted peace-loving individual once he is outside the influence of the Prussian military machine."[323]

Punch had its own humoristic comment, its message unmistakable—five months of war had solved nothing.

> A scent of truce was in the air,
>   And mutual compliments were paid—
> A sausage here, a mince-pie there,
>   In lieu of bomb and hand-grenade;
> And foes forgot, that Christmastide,
>   Their business was to kill the other side.[324]

* * *

It was the custom of the time for newspapers and magazines to print letters from soldiers, and friends, girlfriends and families often forwarded what they thought the best ones on to the press. Throughout 1915 local and national newspapers in both countries published photos of the soldiers fraternizing and an endless stream of letters and postcard messages from the soldiers who took part in the Christmas truce.

The French, by contrast, muzzled all mention of fraternization. The press was forbidden to print anything about the event or reprint articles from the foreign press.[325] Even the English-language *Paris Tribune* was censored. Pro-nationalist propaganda was the rule, and no exceptions were permitted. A typical article of the time, published on *Le Figaro*'s front page just after Christmas 1914, for example, began with the line: "No German can open his mouth or take up his pen without lying!"[326]

But the ban on fraternization in the press didn't stop French soldiers from writing what they thought. Some letters managed to slide past the censors. A French officer, for example, wrote home: "All the soldiers are the same poor beggars, whether they are officially friends or enemies; they all carry the same vermin and the same misery. Well! I can bet one thing: put a hundred Boches on one side and a hundred French soldiers on the other, they would all say the same, *Vive la paix!* Let's have peace!"[327]

A popular misconception, one that has grown to achieve mythical status, is that a football match was played between British and the German soldiers in no-man's-land on Christmas Day, 1914. With this myth comes the clear object lesson that nations should settle their disputes on a football pitch rather than on the battlefield. That a simple game, well-known and played by all the nationalities involved in the war, could possibly be substituted for the murderous killing fields of Flanders is a powerful message, one that can easily be understood.

However, it is very doubtful that the legendary football match took place. Given the circumstances, the uneven, shell-pocked no-man's-land, the inclement weather, the frozen ground,[328] and the total lack of order, it is doubtful that British and Germans organized themselves into teams of 11 men, set up goals and boundaries, and played a formal game. A more likely origin to the myth is that someone produced a football and whoever felt like it gave it a kick, the British probably sending the ball to the Germans and then the Germans speeding it back. The football scrimmage was probably just a minor amusement while the soldiers traded badges, tobacco, rations, Christmas presents and spirits and tried as best they could to communicate with one another.[329]

A British soldier who took part in the game wrote in his memoirs:

> The ball appeared from somewhere, I don't know where, but it came from their side [...]. They made up some goals and one fellow went in [to score a] goal and then it was just a general kickabout. I should think there were about a couple of hundred taking part [...]. Everybody seemed to be enjoying themselves. There was no sort of ill-will between us [...]. There was no referee, and no score, no tally at all. It was simply a *mêlée*—nothing like the soccer you see [...]. The boots we wore were a menace—those great big boots we had on—and in those days the balls were made of leather and they soon got very soggy.[330]

Despite the clear orders after Christmas to suppress any kind of fraternization in some, relatively isolated places along the front, the truce lasted almost to Easter. On both sides, officers and men passively refused to engage "the enemy." Orders were quietly ignored, snipers aimed high, and soldiers spread coils of barbed wire across the no-man's-land with no fear of being shot.

But when at Easter time the Germans held up white flags above their trenches, indicating that they wanted to renew the truce and fraternization, the British reaction was firm and uncompromising. Military discipline was imposed. The war must go on.

The Christmas truce lasted at most 100 days; then it slipped into history. Sir Arthur Conan Doyle (1859–1930) in his history of 1914 called it "an amazing spectacle [...], one human episode amid all the atrocities which have stained the memory of the war."[331] And a German soldier commented wistfully, "It was a day of peace in war [...]. It is only a pity that it was not a decisive peace."[332] Another sent a message to the opposing British trench: "We don't want to kill you, and you don't want to kill us, so why shoot?"[333] A British officer who arrived at the front just in time to take part in the Boxing day scrimmage wrote that it was "probably the most extraordinary event of the whole war—a soldier's truce without any sanction by officers and generals."[334]

* * *

The following year, 1915, fearful that events might repeat themselves, the British ordered a slow artillery barrage on Christmas Eve and Christmas Day and the Germans reciprocated. But that wasn't sufficient to stop the fraternization. While it never reached the same scale as 1914, in places along the front there was still an echo of the mood and atmosphere of the previous year.

A German airplane dropped a message proposing a cease-fire and the British waved an acceptance. For a few hours, German and English stretcher bearers wandered through no-man's-land at will, carrying the wounded back to their trenches. And at several secluded locations along the long web of trenches that stretched from Switzerland to the sea, peace did arrive with Christmas. For example, at dawn on Christmas Day, 1915, according to a British soldier who witnessed the truce, "both sides poked their heads up and started to climb out of their respective trenches and we met halfway [...] a rush of men from both sides, carrying tins of meat, biscuits and other commodities for barter [...]. This was the first time I had seen No-Man's Land, and it was now Every Man's Land, or nearly so."[335]

A German infantryman relates how he had been recruited to prepare a soldiers' choir to sing carols at Christmas Eve on the front line. He had been chosen for the task because he could play the violin and thus lead the singing:

> Shortly before Christmas we were ready. In the trench it was comparatively quiet with little artillery activity and isolated rifle and machine gun fire [...]. We were only about 60–80 meters away from the English positions. We climbed out of the trench and sung our first carol, *Stille Nacht, Heilige Nacht* (Silent Night, Holy Night). When the sound had faded away, we could see in the light of some flares some English on the top of their trench breastworks listening to us. As the carols went on, more and more joined them, so that finally a large group stood listening in the open [...]. During this night no shot fell.[336]

Most troops stayed close to their own trenches and confined their fraternization to singing carols back and forth and shouting messages of Christmas goodwill. All governments, friend and foe, were united by the desire to continue the war. Staff officers had received strict instructions not to fraternize. This time the threat of severe discipline was real. On both sides of the trenches, strict orders were handed down to cease all unmilitary-like conduct. Fraternization with the enemy, even trading cigarettes by throwing them from one trench to another, was equated with treason and punishable by death. Reinforcing those orders was the fact that 1915 had been a year of bitter fighting. The casualties now totaled in the millions. The sad truth was there were few veterans of the 1914 Christmas truce left.

The Christmas truce of 1914 remains an unusual event in modern warfare, one of the few instances when tens of thousands of soldiers expressed their collective will and revealed the absurdity and the tragedy of the war they were called upon to fight. If they had had their way, once stopped the war would never have started again.

Frederick Niven (1878–1944), a Scottish poet, expressed the spirit of the 1914 Christmas truce in his poem "A Carol from Flanders":

> O ye who read this truthful rime
> From Flanders, kneel and say:
> God speed the time when every day
> Shall be as Christmas Day.[337]

THREE

The Long Road to Peace

In May 1916, President Woodrow Wilson (1856–1924) decided the right moment had arrived to try once again to end the war. In an address to the League to Enforce Peace he declared that the United States had no interest in the "causes and objects" of the war but only in "peace and its future guarantees." In a subtle yet clear fashion he stated that he wished to be asked "to initiate a movement for peace among the nations now at war." Having had his previous offers to make peace refused, this time President Wilson would only become a peacemaker if he were given assurances beforehand that he would succeed. But the belligerent countries were not ready to put down their swords and in their replies one after another they reiterated their resolve to fight onwards to a military victory.

President Wilson's intransigence to step forward should have put a damper on American peace efforts, but the contrary was true. For example, Julia Grace Wales's (1881–1957) plan for constant mediation by neutral countries seemed to flourish. It was supported and popularized by numerous organizations, among them the American Woman's Peace Party, which continued to hold demonstrations in most American large cities. It was perhaps the first American peace organization to use the tactics of direct action. Go straight to the people: speak to them on street corners, at bus stops and assembly halls, even bars and social clubs. The message was straightforward: a peace built upon national self-determination, with an international organization to guarantee it and the democratic control of foreign policy. The movement began less than a month after war was declared in Europe when, in protest, 1,500 women solemnly marched down New York's Fifth Avenue behind a white banner bearing a white dove.

A journalist, Oswald Garrison Villard (1872–1949), grandson of the abolitionist William Lloyd Garrison (1805–1879), witnessed the event and later wrote:

> There were no bands; there was dead silence and the crowds watched the parade in the spirit of the marchers, with sympathy and approval [...]; the paraders [decided] to carry no flags except the peace flag and to have no set speeches at

the conclusion of the parade [...]. The silence, the dignity, the black dresses of the marchers—those who did not have black dresses wore black arm bands—the solemnity of the crowds, all of these produced a profound effect on the beholders.[1]

The organization later became the Woman's Peace Party, and their efforts to popularize the cause of peace produced an unexpected convert, Henry Ford (1863–1947). He suddenly called a press conference and announced that he was willing to spend his fortune on peace work. Politically naïve, he saw war in very simplistic terms. Wars, he said, were basically caused by one group of men wanting what another group possessed. Give the men who went to war because they were promised rewards tractors instead of guns; then, Ford believed, war and its causes would cease. War, in his words, "was plain, ordinary murder."[2]

Once peace activists had convinced Ford that Miss Wales's plan could in fact work, he acted quickly to put it into effect. Almost immediately he chartered the liner *Oscar II* to take a delegation of distinguished publicists and leaders of opinion from New York to Scandinavia, where, he hoped, they would create a conference of neutrals for continuous mediation. The ship didn't sail until early December. Nonetheless, Ford announced he would end the war by Christmas. He had given himself less than a month to end the conflict and, when he realized that goal was unattainable, he modified his statement to "Get the boys out of the trenches by Christmas."[3]

Later a reporter asked, "Do you really expect to get the boys out by Christmas?" Ford replied, smiling, "Well, there's New Year's and Easter and the Fourth of July, isn't there?... 'Out of the trenches by Christmas' is not a boast, it's a prayer, a prayer that the world joins in."[4] Ford never expected to end the war by himself. At best he knew he would be a catalyst who might be able to create a public forum that would force the politicians to act. "Men sitting around a table, not men dying in a trench, will finally settle the differences."[5]

The Wilson administration refused to endorse the peace ship, and without some kind of government sponsorship nearly every invited official, businessman and community leader politely declined. Only the governor of North Dakota and the lieutenant governor of North Carolina accepted. A judge from the juvenile court of Denver also signed on as a delegate; however, as the press quickly pointed out, he was better known as an advocate of free love than a pacifist.

Hundreds of people petitioned Ford to sign on. A junk dealer, for example, asked to join the trip with the idea that Ford would buy up the world's battleships, then use them for scrap steel. A herbalist who was ready to treat the wounds of the world also volunteered to come on board. And to add to the grist handed to journalists, an invitation was sent to the Pope, but addressed to the wrong one, a pope who had been dead for centuries.[6]

After short initial fascination with the idea, the American press turned nasty and cynical and began calling the peace mission, among other things,

"Ford's Folly," "A Ship of Fools," "Quixotic" and "The Good Ship Nutty."[7] One New York newspaper published some doggerel as its editorial:

> I saw a little fordship
> Go chugging out to sea [...]
> And so without a quiver
> The dreadful task they are
>   Of teaching peace
>   To France and Greece
> And Teuton, Celt and Bear.
> Ho for the good ship Fliver,
> Propelled by heated air![8]

Abuse also came from the political elite. Ex-President Theodore Roosevelt (1858–1919) quipped: "Mr. Ford's visit abroad will not be mischievous only because it is ridiculous."[9]

But Ford shrugged off the barrage of words. "The best fertilizer in the world is weeds," he declared.[10] Undaunted, he kept writing checks convinced that a standing committee of distinguished private individuals, backed by worldwide publicity, might be able to formulate the terms of peace and bring useful suggestions to the attention of the belligerent countries.

Ford also had his supporters who recognized the altruistic intent of the voyage, but they were largely outside of the press and political elites. Hundreds of farmers and workers wrote to him encouraging him, praising him for his philanthropy and humanism and for his willingness to spend his fortune trying to save lives. Ford could also take consolation in the words of a Philadelphia rabbi who wrote to say that he would "rather a thousand times be branded a fool in the service of humanity than be hailed a hero for having shed rivers of blood."[11]

An optimist and believer in the good qualities inherent in man, Ford declared: "I have absolute confidence in the better side of human nature [...]. People never disappoint you if you trust them." And as an example, proof of what he said, he often cited the fact that "only three of the 600 convicts [working] in my factory have failed to make good."[12]

The *Oscar II* sailed on December 5, 1915. Ford told the press just before departure: "This is the most serious thing that has ever come into my life."[13] He called the ship "the longest gun in world."[14] And it was to make a dramatic journey through submarine-infested waters to focus the world's attention on peace.[15] On board were 55 peace delegates (most from the Woman's Peace Party), 44 members of the press, 25 students and one stowaway.[16] Twenty-three more participants, half of them students, followed on another ship, the *Frederick VIII*.[17] It was by no means a cross section of America. Almost half the delegates were writers; the next largest group were lecturers and workers for causes. There were a few government officials, ministers and teachers, but no businessmen (apart from Ford), farmers, scientists, engineers, or labor officials.[18] It was the world's first peace ship,[19] and when the ship left the harbor the mood on board was buoyant. Most of the delegates felt like pilgrims sailing on a voyage literally through minefields and from there into the uncharted waters of peacemaking. It was perhaps the first time in history that ordinary people had tried to end a war.

Ford knew exactly what he wanted from the voyage. He told one of the reporters on board that "I consider the peace ship will have been worth while if it does nothing more than what it has done already in driving [military] preparedness off the front page of the newspapers and putting peace on the front page."[20] And that it had clearly accomplished. The departure of the peace ship had been front-page news across the country.

When the *Oscar II* was mid-Atlantic, the White House issued a formal disavowal, stating that "President Wilson has neither made suggestions for peace, nor intends to do so in the near future, unless there is an unexpected turn in the belligerent situation."[21] Added to that was the news that the President had asked Congress in his State of the Union Address to expand the size of the military. This immediately produced a schism among the delegates, between those who supported the President and those who took an absolutistic pacifist position. The purpose of the voyage nearly became lost in the lengthy debates and squabbling as whatever unity they may have had when they left New York dissolved into a furious dispute. "War has broken out on board Henry Ford's peace argosy," one newspaper reporter telegraphed.[22]

The stories of the bitter internecine conflict became so graphic, in essence painting a lurid portrait of a mutiny, that reportedly two passing vessels volunteered to come to the aid of the captain of Ford's ship. As soon as the *Oscar II* docked in Norway, Henry Ford, baffled by the infighting, over which he had no control, made a hasty exit and boarded the next ship for New York. "Guess I had better go home to mother [...]," he told the delegates. "You've got this thing started now and can get along without me."[23]

The delegates traveled on to Sweden, Denmark and Holland, where they were well received, the response being far more favorable and substantial than that the Americans gave them. Several members of the Swiss and Swedish parliaments stepped forward to endorse the conference and were joined by feminists, intellectuals and Social Democrats. The lower house of the Swedish parliament unanimously approved a resolution asking the government to call an official neutral conference, but the motion was defeated in the upper house. In French the word *Fordisme* was coined to denote the act of cutting through red tape by means of direct, popular intervention.[24]

In January 1916 "A Neutral Conference for Continuous Mediation" was finally established in Stockholm. The infighting among the delegates continued and, if anything, intensified when the disunited American delegation came in contact with delegations from Scandinavia and Holland. Nonetheless, they finally issued a joint "Easter Appeal" that antedated much of the letter and spirit of Wilson's Fourteen Points. The appeal was ignored by all the warring countries.

Although the conference ultimately failed to accomplish its original purpose, it did for about a year become a kind of clearinghouse and sounding board for peace proposals from the neutral countries. It also tried to translate and circulate stories indicating a desire for peace, which appeared in the press of the belligerent countries to counter the stream of bitter, nationalist propaganda that each of them was producing.

Ford continued to pay the bills until 1917. In January of that year President Wilson delivered his so-called peace without victory speech. Standing in front of the American Senate, the President declared that any lasting peace must be "peace without victory [...]. Victory would mean peace forced upon the loser, a victor's terms imposed upon the vanquished. It would be accepted in humiliation, under duress, at an intolerable sacrifice, and would leave a sting, a resentment, a bitter memory upon which the terms of peace would rest, not permanently, but only as upon quicksand. Only a peace between equals can last."[25] This was, in essence, very similar to the goal inherent in "continuous mediation." The peace, especially its durability and justice, depended upon how the war ended. Now that President Wilson had picked up the conference's crusade, Ford declared that the delegates in Europe had accomplished their task and could go home. He immediately ceased funding the conference. It had cost him approximately half a million dollars—at least $10 million in today's currency.[26]

In later postwar years Ford became ambivalent about the peace ship, sometimes so embarrassed by it that he would not permit anyone to mention the affair in his presence.[27] At the same time he often took pride in his pacifistic venture. He once when speaking about the peace ship with hindsight remarked to a journalist: "I wanted to see peace. I at least tried to bring it about. Most men did not even try."[28]

Barbara S. Kraft, the historian who wrote *The Peace Ship*, concludes at the end of her definitive study of the voyage of Ford pacifists: "Never before had a gathering of neutral citizens, acting in the name of the people, asked warring nations to stop fighting and settle their disputes, not on the basis of military conquest, but according to the principles of justice and humanity."[29]

From the beginning the endeavor had been clearly idealistic, stemming from a genuine desire to save humanity from death and destruction. In this sense Ford was ahead of his time, and had he immediately succeeded as he planned, had the war reached a negotiated settlement in 1916 with neither the Allies nor the Central Powers defeated, the world might have been spared the horrors of an economic collapse, Communism, Fascism, and Nazism. To a large extent the spirit of Julia Grace Wales's "continuous mediation" lives on in the Charter of the United Nations.

* * *

The Spanish tried to open up another avenue for mediation. The King, Alfonso XIII (1886–1941), was related to both sides. His mother was Maria Christina of Austria (1858–1929), an archduchess, and he had married Princess Victoria Eugenie of Battenberg (1887–1969), Queen Victoria's granddaughter. A firm believer in the concept of European monarchical solidarity, Alfonso XIII was convinced that its rupture had been one of the root causes of the war. He corresponded extensively with William II of Germany and, through diplomatic channels, let the French know that, if the right moment arrived, he would to be willing to mediate the conflict. Spain remained neutral for the duration of the war.[30] However, in 1916 when Alfonso XIII gave a German submarine permission to enter the port of Cartegena to deliver a letter from William II, the Allies threatened to blockade the Spanish ports. After that the King of Spain was more careful and, perhaps to demonstrate his strict neutrality, he engaged in extensive humanitarian actions that included prisoner exchanges, serving as a neutral destination for correspondence and guaranteeing the free passage of hospital ships. Quite likely he hoped to take President Wilson's place when the United States declared war, but the King was never called upon for mediation. Spanish neutrality was rewarded after the war when Spain was invited as the sole neutral alongside the Allies and Associates to become a member of the League of Nations Council.

* * *

Meanwhile the British tried to use a similar tactic, that is, the network of dynastic relationships, to separate the Central Powers. They focused on Austria-Hungary. Although technically at war through their alliances, the two countries were not actually fighting each other on the battlefield.

The British Foreign Office secretly sent Sir Francis Hopwood (1860–1947) to Copenhagen to meet with Count Mensdorff-Pouilly (1861–1945), who had been the Ambassador of Austria-Hungary to the Court of St. James until the declaration of war in 1914.

Count Mensdorff was the right man to contact. A devoted Anglophile, he was the second cousin to King Edward VII (1841–1910) and enjoyed a close relationship with the King's successor, George V (1865–1936). Like many others in the Dual Kingdom, Count Mensdorff thought that Austria-Hungary's real enemy was Germany, not Great Britain.

But before the two men could meet in Copenhagen to start negotiations, the Germans appear to have learned about the contact and its purpose. As a result of German pressure, Count Mensdorff was suddenly forced to become diplomatically unavailable.

If nothing else, the ease with which two of the belligerents, England and Austria-Hungary, made contact and were ready to discuss peace terms was a good omen for the future.[31]

A nascent peace movement already existed in Austria, much of it spontaneous outbursts that were a clear indication of the popular mood. As early as the summer of 1915 several thousand working-class women invaded the inner courtyard of the Hofburg Palace, the Emperor's residence, to petition him for peace. A newspaper reported the incident:

> They were jammed tightly on every available square inch of ground, and there was an overflow of them at all the approaches. Many of them were dressed in deep mourning for the husbands and sons lost at the front in this terrible war, against which they had assembled to demonstrate. No sooner was the palace courtyard full than all the women began a heart-rendering wail: "We want peace. We want our men to return. We want bread and work. We want peace."[32]

At about the same time David Lloyd George (1863–1945), then the Prime Minister of the UK, sent Sir Francis Hopwood, who was still in Copenhagen, the following message: "We have no desire to negotiate with Germany and we are clear that nothing should be said directly or indirectly to the Germans and suggestions to the contrary effect [...] should receive no favour at our hands."[33] The British were afraid that any negotiations with the Germans might prevent the Austro-Hungarians from seeking a separate peace. This became more important later, after the Russian Revolution in 1917, when it became evident that the Russians would drop out of the war. Lloyd George told a cabinet meeting: "If we failed to induce Austria to make a separate peace [he, Lloyd George] could see no hope of the sort of victory in the war that we had desired."[34]

Count Mensdorff later met with General Jan Smuts (1870–1950), who was a member of the British War Cabinet, in Geneva. Despite the goodwill on both sides—General Smuts was known as a man of peace favoring conciliation and moderation—it proved to be impossible to separate Austro-Hungary from its Germanic ally.

The chances for a negotiated settlement between the Germans and the British were always slight. It would have been difficult for compromise to bridge the enormous distance between their respective war aims. When the Germans appeared to hold the military advantage, the British refused to talk to them, and later in the war the possibility of an inconclusive peace, that is, *status quo ante bellum*, was never acceptable to either side. Complicating matters further were the commitments to France and Italy that further enlarged the distance between the two blocs and encouraged a fight until a decisive military victory.

* * *

Emily Hobhouse (1860–1926) was one of the British signatories to the women's Christmas letter. She had arrived in England from South Africa shortly before the war began and had been immediately horrified by what she saw on the horizon. Still well-known for her exploits during the Boer War, she had an easy access to the press and knew personally many members of the government, including some in the cabinet. Shortly before war was declared in 1914 she wrote in the *Manchester Guardian*: "Few English people have seen war in its nakedness, hence the thoughtless cry for it. They know nothing of the poverty, destruction, disease, pain, misery and mortality which follow in its trail. I have seen all this [in the Boer War, 1899–1902] and my experience adds force to my appeal to all lovers of humanity to avert the horror that is threatened."[35]

When the war arrived, she declared it to be the result of international blundering and national stupidity. Working mainly through women's organizations, she became more firmly entrenched in her pacifist beliefs than ever. Her convictions were clear, forceful and strident: war was evil, senseless, and a wanton waste of life that had to be stopped.

While she enthusiastically backed virtually every cause she thought would promote the idea of peace, she did not fear, as one biographer put it, "to go entirely counter to public opinion in the advocacy of this unpopular cause, and continued her effort throughout the war [...] at the price of great misunderstanding and consequent suffering."[36] She traveled abroad, to France, Holland (which remained neutral), and Italy (which at the time was also neutral). In each country she addressed meetings and tried to spread the message that in one rational, pacifistic way or another, the conflict had to be brought to end. She wrote to a friend: "Think of our beloved fatherland, think of beautiful Italy, of France and of Germany, all of them working at full capacity to produce weapons of war and destruction. It seems as if we have reached the end of our civilization. It is all too hideous for words." The Foreign Office kept close track of her, despite that fact that the Prime Minister, H. H. Asquith (Prime Minister 1908–1916), had labeled the women's anti-war movement in 1915 as "the twittering of sparrows in a storm."[37]

Gradually Emily Hobhouse began to lose faith in what she called "those infernal gatherings of women." All of her speeches, letters—and there must have been hundreds—travels, and arguments were proving to be useless, clearly words to the wind. Those who listened were already believers, and those who weren't paid little or no attention. While in Italy she reached the conclusion that she needed to change and focus on a single, determined course of action. Pretentious as it may sound, she decided to become a modern-day David and single-handedly defeat the Goliath of war. She would try to stop the fighting by herself. Her mission would be "to go as a messenger of peace to the people of Germany, and to make a tour of investigation in Belgium."[38]

One rather frail Englishwoman, ensconced in the countryside, had decided that an international conflict involving millions of men should and would cease. It seems an outrageous, even farcical decision until one remembers that during the Boer War, virtually single-handed, Emily Hobhouse had brought an end to the abuses of the British concentration camps where tens of thousands of people were imprisoned. She told no one and began to act on her own instincts and initiative. Her project was independent, neither inspired nor financed by any organization. No doubt she was convinced that once she had made a spectacular gesture her friends would approve and support her.

She traveled to Berne, Switzerland. At roughly the same moment the British government decided that her anti-war behavior had become "absurd and undesirable conduct."[39] The Foreign Office instructed to the British ambassador in Switzerland to pick up her passport, and issue her with one that would be valid only for the return trip to England.

However, by this time Emily Hobhouse no longer needed a British passport. She had made arrangements to obtain German traveling papers.

For years, she spent the winter months in Italy. There she met Gottlieb von Jagow (1863–1935), then the German ambassador to Italy (1909–1913) and afterwards the German Foreign Minister. Through the German embassy in Switzerland, she contacted him in Berlin and obtained permission to visit one of the POW camps for British soldiers, then travel to Berlin for a meeting.

Near the Swiss-German frontier, in June 1916, she met a German officer, her escort for the voyage; then, using her new passport, she easily crossed the border. It was later to be called "her private invasion of Germany."[40]

She traveled to Cologne, then on to Brussels, and from there to Berlin. Emily Hobhouse was not the first woman pacifist to meet the German Foreign Minister. The American Jane Addams (1860–1935) and the Hungarian activist Rosika Schwimmer (1877–1948) had also had an audience with him. What made Emily Hobhouse's meeting unique was that she was a national of an enemy state, rather than of a neutral one, like Addams, or of an ally, like Schwimmer.

Emily Hobhouse spoke with the German Foreign Minister for over an hour, and apparently during that time von Jagow told her "she might 'take the hint' to England that Germany was willing to negotiate a peace if London would make some proper 'advances' to Berlin."[41] The Foreign Minister stressed that Germany's offer was made out of humanity, not weakness. The details of the offer, if there were any, were never made clear.

Before she left Germany, Emily Hobhouse also visited a POW camp at Ruhleben, five miles outside Berlin, where the largest number of British soldiers, four to five thousand, were being held. Her report, which was published in the British press, was considered to be pro–German propaganda. She wrote: "I can and most truthfully say that the Ruhleben Camp was not a bad one—that much was done for the amusement and occupation and instruction of the inmates, that the food was good (the bread was coarse but wholesome) and kindness shown by the enemy authorities."[42]

When she arrived back in Switzerland, the British ambassador was waiting for her and, following instructions, handed her a passport valid only for a one-way trip back to England. Once in London, she tried to see the acting Foreign Secretary, Lord Robert Cecil, but one of his assistants dismissed her as "a mischievous pacifist."[43] Scotland Yard questioned her and suggested she be arrested and tried for treason. Questions were raised in the House of Commons, for example, "Is there no means of bringing to justice a lady who goes abroad for the purpose of betraying her country?" Not all the comments were negative. Another member stood up and stated that Emily Hobhouse's trip was "very desirable" and went on to suggest that "the visits of this lady to high officials in the German Foreign Office might be of great service to this country."[44]

Speaking for the government, a Member of Parliament replied: "I do not know anything about that (the legal question of whether or not a British subject has the right to travel to a belligerent country), but I know that the general opinion of the House—and I believe of the country—is that Miss Hobhouse's activities have not been in the interests of this country."[45] In fact, the government couldn't decide what to do with her.

Finally she wrote directly to the British Foreign Secretary: "I am anxious to inform you of the truth of the matter [...]. I hoped that the act of going there [to Germany] voluntarily in the midst of a great war would have a softening influence and be a link to draw our two countries together. I believe it has helped toward this [...]. I shall always be glad I went and grateful to our opponents for their noble comprehension of my aims."[46] Her letter went unanswered. In the end, after a certain amount of debate and a lot of dithering the British government opted for the easiest solution. They simply ignored her.

Emily Hobhouse undoubtedly saw herself as a spectacular peacemaker, which was, on the one hand, perhaps portentous and arrogant, but, on the other hand, she could easily have been successful. The Germans were more than likely sincere. Otherwise, why would they have allowed her to enter the country and spend an evening with the Foreign Minister? The German government, but not necessarily the military, had been looking for a quiet, semi-secretive way to begin the negotiations to end the war. They fully realized that the war on the Western Front had reached a stalemate and the most sensible thing to do was negotiate an end to the conflict.

If the Germans were indeed serious about being ready to negotiate then the British probably missed an opportunity to end the slaughter in the trenches or at least, if nothing else, to stop it for a few months while the generals and diplomats tried to hammer out a permanent peace.

* * *

Many tens of thousands of women in Great Britain registered their rage against the war by joining organizations such as the Fellowship of Reconciliation, the Women's Social and Political Union (WSPU), the Women's Peace Crusade and the No-Conscription Fellowship.

A few women made dramatic personal statements. One of the most poignant and unheralded gestures was that of Kate Sharpley (1895–1978), a 22-

year-old munitions factory worker. Her father and her brother were killed in action and her boyfriend (an active anarchist) was listed as missing but had probably been shot for mutiny. When she was called to receive her family's medals from Queen Mary (1867–1953), wife of George V, Kate threw the medals back at her, saying, "If you like them so much you can have them." The Queen's face was scratched, as was that of one of her attendant ladies. Kate Sharpley was beaten by the police, jailed for a few days, then fired from her job. The local press said she had been influenced by anarchist tracts, which was essentially correct. Later when she was caught distributing anti-war anarchist literature in the streets, the police threatened to send her to jail "as a prostitute."[47]

Kate Sharpley was not alone. In 1915, for example, a socialist, William Holliday, was sentenced to three months in jail at hard labor for announcing at a public meeting: "Freedom's battle has not to be fought on the blood-drenched soil of France but nearer home—our enemy is within the gates."[48] Holliday was acquitted on appeal, but once freed he was soon arrested again when he spoke out more clearly against the war. He died in prison. Speaking his mind had cost him his life.

Like Holliday, John Maclean was arrested for making statements encouraging men not to enlist in the army. He was prosecuted under the Defense of the Realm Act in October 1915. During one of his speeches in Glasgow, a persistent heckler had kept shouting, "Why don't you enlist?" Maclean had shouted back: "I have been enlisted for fifteen years in the socialist army, which is the only army worth fighting for. God damn all other armies!" He went on to say that in his opinion a soldier who shot another was a murderer.

When Maclean came to trial some of the evidence provided a rare glimpse of the extent of the anti-war support that existed in the industrial area of the Clyde River, Scotland. The sheriff asked the policeman who arrested Maclean: "What was the size of the audience at the time?" "About 300," was the reply. "You mean to say," the sheriff continued, somewhat aghast, "that 300 citizens of Glasgow heard a man say, 'God damn the King's army,' and did not resent it?" "No one spoke," replied the policeman.[49]

Referring to another occasion at which Maclean was the principal speaker, a detective was asked why he did not take action while the meeting was taking place. He answered candidly: "Our interference would have resulted in a riot."

Another person who paid a price for speaking his mind was Lord Lansdowne (1845–1927). A member of the cabinet, he circulated a letter in 1916 that advocated a restatement of war aims in very moderate terms, with the hope that the Germans would reply in kind and thus lay the groundwork for immediate peace negotiations. The letter began by stating that he believed that the war's

> wanton prolongation would be a crime, differing only in degree from that of the criminals who provoked it.

Can we afford [given the 1.1 million British casualties to date ...] to go on paying the same sort of price for the same sort of gains?[50]

To this General Robertson (1860–1933), Chief of the British Imperial Staff, replied that only "cranks, cowards and philosophers" would think of peace before the enemy had been crushed.[51]

Lansdowne sought an honorable end to the war that might "prevent the same curse from falling upon our children." He correctly prophesied that if there was another war in the future, "the prostitution of science for the purpose of pure destruction" would be still more horrific. While the government's policy was to go for a "knockout blow," that is, total annihilation of the German army, Lansdowne argued for some form of collective security, "an international pact," as he called it, so that all nations would guarantee the peace.

Lansdowne's letter only became public a year later when it appeared in the British press. The *Times* immediately condemned it as "an extraordinarily foolish and mischievous letter." Arthur Bonar Law (1858–1923), the Tory leader in the House of Commons, called it a "deed of shame." Lansdowne was ostracized from London society and condemned in public whenever he appeared.

It was of course easy for spokesmen for the British government to advocate a war to the bitter end. Their lives were never at stake. Few Members of Parliament ever ventured into harm's way. What they advocated so boldly was the sacrifice of other people's lives, tens and hundreds of thousands of them, so that they, the ruling party, could never be charged with being fainthearted or lacking resolve. And since the British did in the end win the war, by a bit of twisted logic that the end justifies the means, with hindsight, they had been right to portray themselves constantly astride the moral white horse and justified in labeling Lansdowne's proposal to negotiate a solution in 1916 as "appeasement" or "defeatism."

* * *

While Emily Hobhouse was meeting with Foreign Minister von Jagow, Berlin had other peace feelers in play. Hugo Stinnes (1870–1924),[52] for example, a well-known German industrialist, attempted to have an exchange of "peace views" in Stockholm among the Germans, Russians and Japanese. However, the Japanese refused to be a part of the discussions, as they felt it would violate the terms of their alliance with the British and French. Stinnes also tried to arrange a meeting in Stockholm between the German general Ludendorff and a British general, but in the end both sides refused to take part.

Max Warburg (1867–1946), a prominent German banker, also used Stockholm as a meeting place. He had been a financial advisor to the Kaiser and met with Alexander Protopopov (1866–1918), who later became the Russian Minister of the Interior. According to observers who were present at the time Warburg was apparently no diplomat and presented the German position so strongly that he left little room for negotiation. He claimed, for example, that the military situation was so favorable to Germany that it was useless for the Russians to continue fighting. As a result, Protopopov politely withdrew and an excellent opportunity for peace was lost.

In fact, the window for peace was wider than the Germans realized. Protopopov went back to Petrograd and joined a camarilla that included the Empress, Rasputin, and a number of highly placed politicians, all of whom saw a separate, negotiated peace with Germany as the only way to preserve the Czarist regime. Had Protopopov returned with a concrete proposal, a position from which to begin serious discussions, it is conceivable that a cease-fire and perhaps a truce could have been arranged, especially since at that point the Germans were willing to grant Russia completely free access to the Bosporus and the Dardanelles, one of the major Russian war aims.

From a military point of view the ideal time for peace talks was the late fall and winter, traditionally the season when armies rest and prepare for a spring offensive. Thus in the fall of 1916 the German government, with the reluctant acquiescence of the military, was ready to discuss terms to end the conflict. They preferred that the impetus for any peace conference should come from a third party. If not, if the Germans were forced to present their own peace initiative, it might be perceived as a weakness, when in fact they saw themselves in a position of strength. If they waited too long—December was chosen as the limit—then the generals would set plans in motion for a new spring offensive.

The first large peace demonstration in Berlin took place in the summer of 1915 when more than a thousand women marched to a cemetery for those who had fallen in the 1848 revolution. They intended to lay a wreath there commemorating the first year of the war. But first, in order that their gesture would not pass unnoticed, they stopped in front of the Reichstag. According to one of the participants:

> There were only a few policemen there, and they were taken by surprise, to the extent that the thousand people were able to stand for more than half an hour unmolested in front of Portal V of the Reichstag, through which the Reichstag representatives entered the building. One after another they came, the "representatives of the people." We want peace! Give us back our husbands! Give us back our fathers and brothers! These words rang out to the bourgeois Reichstag representatives.[53]

Without the slightest incident the women turned their backs on the Reichstag, then marched gravely on to the cemetery.

They were not the only ones advocating an end to the war. Within Germany there were several small groups lobbying for peace in a gentle, restrained fashion, no street rallies or inflaming speeches or handbills urging strikes and demonstration, more like orderly meetings or social clubs that discussed the various issues involved in creating a lasting peace. For example, the Zentralstelle Völkerrecht (the ZV, or Central Unity for International Law), numbered perhaps 1,300 members at its height, a large percentage of them academics. After lengthy discussions the ZV sent a petition to the Reichstag well laced with platitudes and good intentions, for instance that "the coming peace should not force unbearable conditions upon any country, especially it should not imply annexations violating the free will of a population or infringements on the independence of states [...] lest it contain the germ for future wars."[54]

There is no record that the Reichstag ever paid any attention to the petition or even acknowledged receiving it. The government reacted by forbidding the ZV to hold public meetings or advertise in any way its discussions and goals.

Perhaps the strongest peace card that the German government had to play was in Washington, where throughout the fall and winter of 1916–1917 its ambassador, Johann von Bernstdorff (1862–1939), encouraged President Wilson to step forward as a mediator.[55] The ambassador wrote in a cable to Berlin that "the peace vote in America continues to grow and Mr. Wilson can count with certainty on re-election if he establishes a peace conference. We shall therefore daily gain ground here as long as we appear to be ready to encourage the American peace movement, while our enemies adopt an unfavorable attitude. The American people is now pacifically minded."[56]

Wilson publicly launched his plan for a League of Nations and considered many peace schemes, often discussing them with his advisor Colonel House (1858–1938), who, in turn, informed the German ambassador. But the President still refused to take the initiative and summon the belligerents to a peace conference.

Finally, on December 12 the German government handed a peace proposal to the American chargé d'affaires in Berlin and asked that it be transmitted to the French, British, Japanese, Russian and Serbian governments. No specific terms were suggested. Instead, the note read: "They [the four Central Powers] feel sure that the propositions which they would bring forward and which would aim to insure the existence, honor and free development of their peoples, would be such as to serve as a basis for the restoration of a lasting peace."[57]

President Wilson was not pleased. According to the German ambassador: "The President himself, as Colonel House told me, was very disappointed when he received the news of our peace offer. Colonel House told me that he would naturally have liked to take the first step himself. Apart from this, he had always warned us against mentioning peace, because this would be interpreted by the Entente as weakness."[58]

The French reaction arrived the following day. Aristide Briand (1862–1932), the Prime Minister, told the Chambre des Députés (French parliament): "Herr Bethmann-Hollweg [1856–1921, Chancellor of the German Empire] says: 'It is not we who wanted this horrible war. It was forced upon us.' To that I reply for the hundredth time, 'You were the aggressor and whatever you may say the facts prove it, and the bloodshed is on your heads, not ours.'"[59]

The British condemned the German offer as a maneuver, a gesture made from weakness, their "peace offensive," proof that they couldn't win on the battlefield. Lloyd George told the House of Commons: "What hope is there [...] that the arrogant spirit of the Prussian military caste will not be as dominant as ever if we patch up peace now?"[60]

Two days later the Russian Foreign Minister told the Duma: "All the innumerable sacrifices already made would be in vain if a premature peace were concluded with an enemy whose forces have been shaken but not broken, an enemy who is seeking a breathing space by making deceitful offers of a permanent peace."[61]

None of the Allies waited to find out what precisely the Germans wanted in return for peace. The Allies refused to look further than the bluster of belligerence—there obviously as a concession to the generals—to see if there were some points on which they could agree and which could be used as a basis for a cease-fire and initial discussion at a negotiating table.

The Italian *Messagero* declared: "The time has not yet come for an Allied peace."[62] And another paper, the *Secolo*, took the position that "[i]t may be that there are some among us who would accept a compromise and the consequences of an enemy victory. Were such a compromise publicly proposed all Italy would rise up and reply 'No!'"[63]

But no matter how emphatic the Italian press may have been, it did not put an end to the individual and often temporary truces that occurred at the front. For example, an Italian soldier wrote home and described an incident that occurred on Christmas of 1916:

> Someone stuck his head above the parapet, but the snipers did not react. The faces of some Hungarians appeared. Cautiously they spoke a few hesitant words in Italian, the first that came into their head. They just wanted to say something. The officers did not intervene; they were themselves surprised and disarmed by the unreal peaceful atmosphere in this second year of warfare in our front trench. We outdid each other in sending presents: a little wine, dried fruit, biscuits; little things, part of our poor Christmas, of our own poverty like the poverty of the Hungarians in this rich man's war. The truce lasted till the next evening.[64]

Eventually the *London Times* published the text of the German peace offer; however, the official text, that is, the translation sent by the Kaiser's government, did not appear until two weeks later. When it did, it corrected a number of very misleading inaccuracies; for example, the phrase "winning considerable successes at war" had previously been translated as "winning gigantic advantages over adversaries superior in number and material," and, importantly the phrase "carrying it on to a victorious end" was corrected to leave out the word "victorious."[65] But these details were unfortunately lost in the small print, which few people bothered to read. In any case, the politicians, the press and the public had already made up their minds. A real opportunity for an armistice, at a minimum a cease-fire to discuss the terms of peace, was lost.

However, acting independently, Sir William Wiseman (1885–1962), the head of British counterintelligence in America, working through the British embassy in Washington contacted the Americans and asked them to find out exactly what the German terms were. At the same time the embassy cabled London asking them to wait until the Germans provided clarification. London refused and rejected the German offer without first hearing their terms.

A month after they received the German proposal, the Allies sent their formal reply, calling the peace note "[i]llusory peace proposals" and stating that "the overtures made by the Central Powers are nothing more than a calculated attempt to influence the future course of the war, and to end it by imposing a German peace. [... The Allied governments] refuse to consider a proposal which is empty and insincere."[66]

The rebuff by the Allies had a predictable result in Germany. Viewing the rebuff as a humiliation, a slap in public to Prussian honor, the *Vossische Zeitung* stated: "After this insulting refusal there is only one answer—energetic fighting until our cold steel forces the enemies' feverish temperature down to normal."[67] "The peace dream is over for the present," added the *Tagliche Rundschau*. Another daily added a note of sadness: "Since our enemies desire to continue the war, no choice remains to the German people.[68]

The Germans may well have been sincere in sending out a public peace proposal. Both sides had long realized that the fighting in the trenches had become a stalemate. Or the proposal may well have been a feint, an attempt to draw out the enemy and find out what exactly the Allies would accept for an armistice, for neither side had ever clearly delineated their war aims and what they would accept for a negotiated settlement. However, if the peace proposal was merely a propaganda ploy, a moral horse that would carry them to the high ground, then it succeeded completely. In a statement to the neutral nations, the German Foreign Ministry concluded: "The Imperial Government takes the position that the decision as to whether the road which led to peace should be followed or not depended entirely on their opponents. The enemy Powers have refused to take this path and upon them rests the entire responsibility for further bloodshed."[69]

* * *

On the Eastern Front, where the German and the Austro-Hungarian armies fought the Russians, spontaneous truces were common. Often the soldiers on both sides spoke the same language and shared the same religion. Contact was inevitable.

The most likely moment there, because many were orthodox on both sides, was not Christmas but Easter Sunday. Generals seemed to tolerate the break in discipline and often turned a blind eye when their armies suddenly disbanded. In a burst of goodwill, often both officers and men would leave the trenches unarmed and venture out into no-man's-land to meet their foe. On one Easter Sunday, for example, four Russian regiments, several thousand men, crossed into the Austrian lines to fraternize with their fellow Christians. They talked and traded, exchanging rations and cigarettes. Some even exchanged rifles in a symbolic act that went well beyond the power of words. The days following Easter were usually quiet ones, reflecting the private arrangements soldiers had made between themselves to prolong the peace.

However, one Russian commander, General Brusilov (1853–1926), was enraged by his troops' behavior and issued a standing order: "I declare once and for all that contact with the enemy is permitted only by gun and bayonet."[70] In a desperate attempt to reinstate discipline and prevent fraternization, the Russian high command legalized flogging.

* * *

In 1916 the well-known Russian poet Maximilian Voloshin (1877–1932) was called up. He told the military authorities that it was morally preferable to be killed than to kill. "I cannot participate in [...] war undertaken for whatever purpose." Fortunately for Voloshin, he was rejected by the army for medical reasons.[71] He went on to write:

Alone among unfriendly hordes
I don't take sides,
I favour nobody.
I am a voice of springs inside me

These days no foe or brother can be found
All are in me, and I'm in everyone.
So zealots, every of its kind
Thought that a poet was to find
For them protection, and advise them too.
But then I've done all that I ever could
To prevent the brothers from ruining themselves and killing each other.[72]

In Russia most pacifists came from religious sects, groups like the Old Believers[73] or the German-speaking Mennonites, who were opposed to violence and war.

When war broke out the Mennonites patriotically declared their allegiance to the Russian motherland and offered their non-combatant services. The Czarist regime readily accepted. About 14,000 men were eventually mobilized. Half of these served in the forest service. Others worked in the Red Cross or the medical corps on both the Western Front and the Turkish front. Perhaps 100 or more died in battle or were victims of disease.[74]

* * *

International social democracy had fallen apart when the World War began in 1914. After decades of proclaiming their allegiance to unity and world peace, one after another the European socialist parties suddenly changed their collective minds and became armed and aggressive patriots. But after several years of war and millions of casualties, many socialists, particularly those in the center who had been a minority, tried to re-establish the Second International. Joined by socialists from neutral countries and led by the Belgian Camille Huysmans (1871–1968), they proposed holding an international peace conference in Stockholm in the summer of 1917.[75]

A number of "patriotic" socialists drifted back to an anti-war position and announced they would take part in the conference. Many Russian socialists (mostly Mensheviks and Social Revolutionaries) also decided to join them. It seemed that finally the Social Democrats of the world were going to live up to their principles, the belief in the brotherhood of man and universal peace.

As the first delegates began to arrive in Stockholm, mainly from the Central Powers and neutral countries, they began to prepare the terms for a truce, a peace based on the principles of no annexations and no indemnities. It was a simple formula that essentially restored France and Belgium to their pre-war borders. A supplemental item on their agenda, the conflicts on the periphery of Europe, tried to cope with topics remarkably similar to those of our times: for example, the position of Turkey within Europe, and Western intervention in Iran.

The goal was to reach an agreement in Stockholm on a rough outline of a settlement. Then the Social Democrats would return to their respective countries and appeal to the people to exert pressure on their governments to accept the agreement. The final details would be worked out by diplomats after the fighting stopped. Given the war weariness of the times, the meeting in Stockholm held a real promise of a solution to the conflict, a public forum where representatives of all sides could create a web of compromises to end the war.

However, the United States refused passports to those labor leaders and socialists who wished to travel to Stockholm, citing the Logan law of 1799,[76] which prohibits the participation of private individuals in diplomatic activities. Since the Russian and German delegations had quasi-official status the conference could be classified as a diplomatic one.

The French also refused their delegates passports, the Foreign Minister, Alexandre Ribot (1842–1923), declaring: "*La paix ne peut sortir que de la victoire*" (Peace can only come through victory).[77]

The attitude of the British Labour government—reserved at first, sympathetic later on, and uncooperative at the end—may be traced to its changing assessment of the possibilities of a separate German-Russian peace treaty. As that seemed to be more and more likely, the British took a strong stand against the conference. Bonar Law, then the Chancellor of the Exchequer, stated the official position: "The law officers of the Crown have advised the Government that it is not legal for any persons resident in His Majesty's dominions to engage in a conference with enemy subjects. Therefore, permission to attend the Stockholm Conference will not be granted."[78]

The Italians, Belgians and Japanese also refused to give their delegates passports.

Those delegates already at Stockholm issued a joint statement on the refusal of the Allied governments to issue passports:

> The Stockholm conference is the best and, perhaps, the only opportunity for the representatives of the entente peoples to make clear to the German masses the conditions upon which peace is possible. And yet President Wilson refuses to allow the delegates of American Socialist and Labor groups to come to Stockholm.
> The peoples of the world are sick of war, whatever policy their governments see fit publicly to adopt.[79]

With half of the belligerent countries, essentially all the Allies, unrepresented, the Stockholm Peace Conference quickly slipped into the past almost before it was ever convened. International socialism had perhaps waited too long to make a concerted effort to end the war.

One historian commented that the Allied conservative governments "had very neatly nipped in the bud what might have been the climax of the rising tide of leftist opposition to the war."[80]

* * *

In the spring of 1917 the huge French offensive led by General Nivelle quickly turned into a disaster. Over 200,000 casualties were left on the battlefield and the average French soldier, the *poilu*, saw himself thrown into one futile assault after another, Napoleonic-era–type charges were cut to pieces by modern machine guns. That senseless slaughter, plus poor food, the sordid life in the trenches, and the revolutionary spirit of the times led to the most widespread revolt of the war. If the generals and politicians wouldn't end the war, then, as in the Christmas truce of 1914, the soldiers themselves would impose peace in the easiest way possible. They would simply refuse to fight.[81]

The French army was suddenly wracked by mutiny, not one but many, extending nearly the entire length of the front. Nearly half the divisions were ultimately affected. Some units in the trenches put down their weapons and refused to pick them up; others in reserve positions announced to their officers that they would not return to the battlefield, or do guard duty, or do anything other than drink cheap *pinard* (wine) and write slogans like "Down with War!" and "Death to the Generals!" on the walls of their barracks and eating halls, as well as messages like:

Ah! Tu l'auras ta croix,
Si c'est pas la Croix de Guerre,
C'est qu' ça s'ra la Croix de bois!

Oh, you'll get your cross all right.
If it's not the *Croix de Guerre,*
It'll be a wooden cross![82]

Other groups broke away from their units, held meetings where they called for an immediate peace and, waving red flags, demanded to elect their officers. Military discipline disappeared. A *poilu* shouted at an officer who tried to persuade him to return to his barracks: "We've got to make peace at all costs. It's madness to go on fighting like this. The High Command is incapable! It'll never get anything done."[83] One regiment beat up its officers, burned their barracks, then sent a deputation to the commanding general with the terse message: "We are exhausted, we can't fight any more. The war must stop, we don't care how!"[84] Another defiant unit, shouting, "Long live peace!" and singing "L'Internationale" commandeered a convoy of trucks and set out for Paris, where they vowed "to throw the whole General Staff of the army into the Seine." When three military policemen tried to stop them at a crossroad, the mutineers lynched them from a tree, then drove into a railway station where they surged onto a waiting train. They forced the engineer to depart for Paris at gunpoint, but a few kilometers from the station they found the tracks blocked by boulders. Waiting for them was a detachment of loyal troops armed with machine guns and given orders to shoot if necessary. They soon encircled the train and brought the mutiny to an end.

There were many other dramatic incidents, a clear reflection of the army's will to end the war. According to French military records there were at least 110 "serious" outbreaks. Despite the large number of soldiers involved, there was little or no coordination among the various regiments or divisions in revolt. Each unit's laying down their arms was a separate incident, but since they all happened at roughly the same time it appeared as if the whole system of military discipline had suddenly broken down. In all, about half the units in the French army rebelled in one fashion or another.

A group of pacifist and anti-militarist organizations fanned the flames of revolt and desertion and did what they could to support the mutinies. Most of the soldiers going on leave—they were supposed to have seven to ten days' leave every four months—passed through one of two Paris train stations, the Gare de Nord and Gare de l'Est. There a dedicated band of pacifists, often operating from drinks or sandwich concessions, passed out leaflets and news sheets with names like *Le Bonnet Rouge* (The red cap),[85] *La Tranchée Républicaine* (The republican trench) and *Ce Qu'il Faut Dire* (What must be said). A typical tract began: "Comrades! You seek to destroy Prussian militarism, and for that you are causing the massacre of the proletariat of all the nations, while everywhere militarism gets stronger. Go on with the comedy, gentlemen of our governments! We are no longer unconscious spectators, and we reply to your hateful tirades: 'Down with war! Long live Peace!'"[86]

The train station pacifists tried to persuade the *poilus* to desert, to take off their uniforms, put on civilian clothes, then disappear into the crowd. If enough soldiers put down their weapons and left the trenches, then the generals would be forced to end the war and make peace. In the wake of the mutinies thousands of soldiers voted with their feet against the war. "A rational army," Montesquieu[87] had written, "would run away." And so they did. The army of deserters in Paris alone was destined to reach at least 27,000.

Many of the pacifist tracts found their way back to the front lines, where they were widely circulated and discussed. Tens of thousands of tracts were also mailed directly to the men in the trenches. But they had to pass through the army's postal censorship section, where many were seized and destroyed. They carried headlines such as "The soldiers of France are fighting for an unjust cause [...]. Only peace will solve our problems."[88] Postal Censorship tried to keep track of the flow, both to the front and back home, and in that way monitor morale. What had once been only whispered in the trenches was now being written in letters to the families: "We've had enough of being killed on the barbed wire!" and, "Down with war!"[89]

At the height of the mutiny crisis the Chambre des Députés met in a secret session and debated the state of the nation. One deputy, who had formerly taken a pro-war position, stood up and announced:

> Gentlemen, everywhere you go in the country, you find people clamouring for peace. At the front and in the rear a weakness has developed. It is war fatigue, let us be certain on this point, which has led to these recent events. We are not here to lie to each other, nor to compose brilliant odes on the courage of France. We must speak the truth: there is, throughout France, a war-weariness and a current opinion in favour of peace.[90]

While many deputies were delivering a message of war fatigue to the Assemblée Nationale, the Minister of War addressed the French War Cabinet: "Gentlemen, at this moment there stand between the front line and Paris only two loyal divisions."[91]

Had the Germans known this and taken advantage of the situation, it is quite possible the outcome of the First World War might have been very different. It remains one of the great "ifs" of the war. But by the time the German high command realized what had happened on the other side of no-man's-land it was too late. The French army defeated the mutinies one by one and replaced the rebellious units with disciplined forces.

There were a total of 3,427 *conseils de guerre* (courts-martial), at which 23,385 men were convicted of mutinous behavior. Since the army tried to punish only the leaders of the mutiny or, if they were unable to identify them, arbitrarily singled out one man in 10 or 20, the number of soldiers actually taking part in the mutiny was obviously in the hundreds of thousands.

Ultimately, 554 men were sentenced to death. But only 49 were actually executed, the rest had their sentences commuted by either the President of the Republic or the new commander in chief of the army, General Pétain (1856–1951). Others were given long terms of penal servitude, most at hard labor, many sent to the infamous Devil's Island.[92] One soldier escaped. As he was being led to the field of execution a German shell exploded nearby, killing the two guards escorting him. The soldier ran and disappeared into a forest nearby. He was never recaptured. Rumor has it that he spent the rest of his life in Spain.[93]

As part of the cleanup operations the drink and sandwich concessions in the Gare de Nord and Gare de l'Est were closed, as was most of the anti-war press. Approximately 1,700 pacifists, publishers and other anti-war activists were arrested, some tried and given long sentences, others just held under various charges until the end of the war.

Despite the fact that large numbers of soldiers were involved, the French authorities, both civil and military, managed to shroud the entire mutiny in a veil of secrecy, one that, to a large extent, still exists. To this day the French army is referred to as *la grande muette* (the big one that cannot speak). Called collective indiscipline, the mutinies passed totally unreported by the press. Only several well-informed Deputies knew about them, as well as the President of the Republic and the War Cabinet. But even those privileged few never had all the details.

Only those at the highest levels of the French army actually knew what was happening. And they did not share the information. The British and the Belgians who were in the trenches beside them had no idea of the real extent of the revolt.[94] Even military historians have not been able to put all the pieces together. By French law the official records of the mutiny will not be released until 2017, 100 years after the event.

At roughly the same time the British had their own mutiny problems, although on a much smaller scale. The largest occurred at Étaples, a training camp near Boulogne-sur-Mer. At most a thousand men broke military discipline, and the demonstration was quickly contained. Unlike the French mutinies, many of which were politically motivated, the British revolts appear to have been caused by harsh treatment, long working hours and lack of adequate food. The worst incidents occurred with labor companies, which were made up of Chinese or Egyptians, and they received the most severe punishment. Loyal troops did not hesitate to fire on "native" labor companies, and several dozen were killed. The mutinies lasted but a short time, a few days at most; then military discipline was re-established.

The French mutinies also failed, but perhaps not completely. They sufficiently weakened the French army so that for the rest of the year, 1917, it was unable to take any offensive action. While the mutiny may not have directly led to peace, it undoubtedly saved many lives.

* * *

At roughly the same moment Charles I (1887–1922) came to the throne of the Austro-Hungarian Dual Monarchy (Franz Josef died in December 1916).[95] The young Emperor inherited a country that was exhausted by war. Whichever way he looked, disaster loomed on the horizon, in the form of an internal collapse or the victory of either side. Should the Allies win, it would mean the dismemberment of the Austro-Hungarian Empire, whereas a victory by Germany would probably lead to domination from Berlin. Charles I reportedly said that "a striking military success by Germany would be our ruin." A journalist once remarked to him that if the Russians and Italians were defeated he would then have to free himself from the Germans. The Emperor wrote in his notebook, "*Ich möchte schon, aber wie?*" "I would if I could."[96]

In fact, Charles I's personal sympathies, and those of his wife, were clearly with the other side. A British foreign office report marked "MOST SECRET" states:

> From numerous conversations with the Princes of Bourbon-Parma (the Empress's brothers) the following points may be of interest [...]. The present Emperor and Empress are entirely pro–French and pro–English. They are strongly anti–German and hate (a) the Kaiser (b) Prince Rupprecht [1869–1955, Crown Prince of Bavaria] both on political and private grounds. The Kaiser insulted the present Empress when she was young. Prince Rupprecht is a coarse dissolute Prussianised atheist who bullies the Empress and Emperor for their religious and moral principles.[97]

A deeply religious man,[98] Charles I realized that a negotiated peace was the only alternative and he immediately began to look for a way to withdraw the Austro-Hungarian Empire from the war. "I am firmly resolved to bring the war to an end in 1917," he declared.[99] Had he been able to do so, he would undoubtedly have dramatically changed the outcome of the war, if not subsequent history. Millions of lives could have been saved.

Anatole France, the radical French novelist, who was certainly no friend of royalty, wrote: "Emperor Karl [Charles I] is the only decent man to come out of the war in a leadership position, yet he was a saint and no one listened to him. He sincerely wanted peace, and therefore was despised by the whole world. It was a wonderful chance that was lost."

Charles I may well have been one of the few heads of state who genuinely stood for peace. It can, of course, be argued that he did so because it was the only course of action that made sense, but apparently his convictions were real and not just pragmatic. Proof of this might be found in the fact that, on his order, Austro-Hungary was the only belligerent country that did not use poison gas. He was often referred to as the *"Friedenskaiser,"*[100] that is, the "Peace Emperor." Nearly a century later, in October 2004, Charles I was beatified[101] by Pope John Paul II, who told an audience in Rome: "I hope Emperor Karl [Charles I] will serve as an example, especially for those with political responsibilities in Europe today."

As soon as he was crowned, Charles I began urging his ally Germany to propose some kind of peace negotiations. This met with no immediate success, as the Germans were convinced that they would achieve peace through a military victory.

At the same time, Charles I sent his mother-in-law, the Archduchess Maria Antonia of Bourbon Parma (1862–1959), to Neuchâtel in Switzerland, where she met her two sons, Xavier and Sixtus, Bourbon princes who were serving in the Belgian army. Using a Swiss journalist, William Martin (1888–1934),[102] stationed in Paris, they managed to establish direct contact with the French President, Raymond Poincaré (1860–1934, President of France 1913–1920). It was decided that Prince Sixtus (1866–1934) should be the intermediary and handcarry messages from Paris to Switzerland. A childhood friend of the Emperor, Count Thomas Erdody, would bring the letters from Switzerland to Vienna. This connection became the most extensive Austrian contact with the Allies.

It is not clear who first proposed the terms, the French or the Austro-Hungarians. In any case, when the crucial Austro-Hungarian reply to a French offer was passed on to Prince Sixtus to deliver to Paris the Prince destroyed it, a precaution, he later claimed, should he be searched en route. He reconstituted it once he arrived in Paris and quite likely he added his own interpretation in order to please both sides. However, in addition to the formal letter, which essentially proposed a restoration of the *status quo ante bellum*, Emperor Charles I added a secret addendum written in his own hand. It softened Austro-Hungary's position even further and stated that while Germany was determined to achieve peace by military victory, Charles I was ready to make a separate peace if Germany would not be reasonable and accept "just and equitable terms."[103] In addition, in the interest of peace, the Emperor wrote to Prince Sixtus that the Austro-Hungarians were willing to consider what they called France's "just demand" for the return of Alsace-Lorraine. This was precisely what the Allies, and especially the French, wanted to hear. In the letter to Prince Sixtus, Charles I wrote that "it is a special pleasure to me to note that, although for the moment adversaries, no real divergence of views or aspirations separates many of my empire from France [...]. I beg you to convey privately and unofficially to President Poincaré that I will support by every means, and by exerting all my personal influence with my allies, France's just claim regarding Alsace-Lorraine."[104]

Later, after the war, Prince Sixtus wrote: "The young Emperor was innocent of his predecessor's faults and had come to the throne with only one desire, which was to put an end to the universal slaughter."[105]

The French reacted positively and enthusiastically. Within a few weeks Prince Sixtus had several meetings with the French President, who at one point went so far as to say that if Austro-Hungary made a separate peace with the Allies and Germany took reprisals, at the end of the war, after an Allied victory, Austro-Hungary would be compensated, that is, given territory at the expense of the Germans.

Prince Sixtus undoubtedly thought he had a formula for peace. He immediately returned to Neuchâtel, where Count Erdody was waiting for him. Then they both went straight to Vienna.

The Emperor received them at once. Prince Sixtus explained that the French also wanted Europe to return to the way it was, but with a few modifications: Alsace-Lorraine should be French again, Russia should take control of Constantinople and Serbia should have an outlet to the Adriatic. The Austro-Hungarians and the French seemed to agree on enough basic issues that the next step might well be the announcement of a peace conference.

Meanwhile, the Austrians secretly discussed the terms with the Germans, while the French consulted with the British. True to their word, the Austrians tried to "reason" with the Germans and persuade them to hand Alsace-Lorraine back to the French. As compensation the Austrians offered part of Poland and Galicia, but the Germans stubbornly refused to consider any kind of territorial swap. General Erich Ludendorff (1865–1937), one of the architects of the German war effort, for example, refused to consider any evacuation of what he called "the *Reichsland*."[106] When the two Kaisers met to discuss possible terms for a cease-fire, William II made it clear that the Germans were not going to be drawn into the Sixtus plan for peace.

William II had his own rather special view of what peace should be and how it could occur. Since he fervently believed that God had selected him as an earthly ruler, the creation of peace became a kind of self-obsessed moral gambit he was willing to play with very few, if any, others. As he declared in 1916[107]: "To propose to make peace is a moral act [...], to free the world, including the neutrals, of a heavy burden [...], such an act is the province of a ruler, who has a conscience and feels himself responsible to God, who has a heart for his own people and those of the enemy, and the will to free the world from its suffering. I have the courage for all this and I will risk it for God's sake."[108]

With whom was he planning to share this "province?" France had disposed of its King more than a hundred years before and in England the monarch had little more than ceremonial powers. That left only Russia and his cousin Czar Nicholas II. After the first Russian Revolution in 1917, he was gone. In any case, the Kaiser had made it clear: "We all pray for peace, but I will not have anything to do with it from our enemies."[109]

The Austrians continued to explore the possibilities for peace, but now they did so secretly and carefully. A single slip would reveal their duplicity and deceit. And they could not afford to betray their powerful ally. At a moment's notice Germany could ruin Austria financially, for her currency depended completely on the German Reichsbank. There was also the fact that on all fronts German and Austrian armies were mixed and, more often than not, in the hands of German officers. A separate peace might have meant a new war, a kind of internecine conflict among the armies of the Central Powers. And should that occur, Germany had already drawn up plans to invade Austria ready to be implemented whenever necessary. However, through the French the Entente was willing to give Austria-Hungary a pledge of support should Germany take reprisals against the Dual Monarchy.

Prince Sixtus shuttled quietly back and forth between Vienna, Paris and London, keeping his meetings secret, often arriving in the middle of the night and using hidden doors and secret passages. His negotiations were limited to a small number of key individuals, Presidents and Prime Ministers, who juggled provinces and cities and mountain frontiers like Monopoly properties while they searched for some almost magical blueprint that would please everyone. They came very close to succeeding. Unfortunately, just before the arrival of the last letter from Charles I the government of France changed. The new Prime Minister, Alexander Ribot (1842–1923), was committed to fighting the war to a military victory, not negotiating a settlement. According to one historian who was also on the periphery of the Sixtus affair, "Peace was lost by a fortnight."[110]

The veil of secrecy had been so complete that only a few people had known about the negotiations. Reginald Brett, Second Viscount Esher (1852–1930), a government insider who had been largely left out, later wrote:

> This Austrian business gets worse and worse [...]. Clémenceau [1841–1929, who became the French Prime Minister in 1917] probably enjoys it. But think of our unfortunate country dragged at the heels of Sonnino [1847–1922, Italian Prime Minister] and Ribot [1842–1923, French Prime Minister]. Did Curzon [1859–1925, leader of the House of Lords] or Bonar Law [1858–1923, Chancellor of the Exchequer] know what was going on for months? Not they. Thus is our democratic country governed. What a farce. Forty-five million of our own people, 200 millions of Indians, 20 million or more in the Dominions, and 100 millions in the United States, know nothing of these peace overtures that were dished because Poincaré wanted a Rhine frontier and the coal fields of the Saar. And we might [...] have split up the Central Powers [...]. What hypocrisy all this cry for a democratic victory.[111]

Ultimately, it was the Italians who refused to join the negotiations. When they were eventually brought into the discussions they proved to be obdurate. The territorial pledges given to them by the Allies in secret treaties were inconsistent with those being proposed to the Austrians. The Italian Prime Minister, Sydney Sonnino (1847–1922), insisted that Italy receive all the territory it had been previously promised as an inducement to enter the war. There would be no compromises or land swaps. As a result, the Sixtus plan was finally abandoned.

Not trusting only one avenue for peace feelers, Charles I sent Count Revertera, an Austrian nobleman who lived in Freiburg, Switzerland, to meet a "throat specialist" who had recently arrived in the country. In a typical surreptitious fashion, de rigueur for the secret diplomacy of the day, the "specialist" told the count that "an important French personality"[112] had made peace overtures to him that he would like to transmit to the Emperor. The "personality" turned out to be Major Count Abel Armand, who was the head of the Intelligence Department at the French Ministry of War.[113] He was in Switzerland to negotiate the terms of a separate peace that had already been approved by the Prime Ministers of Great Britain and France.[114]

The Austrians, through Count Revertera, who was now shuttling between Switzerland and Vienna, indicated that they would have to consult with their allies the Germans. Should the Germans agree, then talks could begin almost immediately, perhaps with the Foreign Ministers, in Vaduze, Liechtenstein.

The French count replied that the Allies were interested only in a separate peace, thus there was no need to inform the Germans. Count Revertera handcarried each exchange to Vienna, then brought the reply back to Switzerland. Negotiations seemed to stagnate, but the Austrians were reluctant to end them. The Austrian Minister in Berne complained: "If things go well for the Entente, they [the Allies] don't want to hear of peace. If things go well for us, the Germans exclaim 'Don't hurry!'"[115]

The French finally insisted that before serious discussions could begin the Austrians had to agree to the return of Alsace-Lorraine. At that point the Austrians broke off the contact, unsure as to whether the Allies really wanted peace or just to drive a wedge between the Germans and the Austro-Hungarians. And that the Allies almost did. When William II found out that Charles I had been negotiating about Alsace-Lorraine behind his back, Charles I was summoned to the German Emperor's headquarters at Spa to explain and apologize. As a result, Austria-Hungary became bound even tighter to the German Empire.

Nonetheless, in a subsequent letter to William II just after the Russian Revolution of 1917, Charles I wrote: "We are fighting against a new enemy which is more dangerous than the Entente: international revolution, which finds its strongest ally in general starvation. I beseech you not to overlook this portentous aspect of the matter and to reflect that a quick finish to the war even at the cost of heavy sacrifice give us a chance of confronting the coming upheaval with success."[116] The letter was unanswered.

Charles I's next attempt for a separate peace was to send his former tutor, Professor Lammasch (1853–1920), to Bern, Switzerland, to meet George D. Herron (1862–1925), a clergyman and an American agent.

Professor Lammasch was a good choice. He had been an early advocate of a league of nations as well as an international arbitrator at The Hague who had taken part in the settlement of the Newfoundland dispute between Great Britain and the United States (1910) and the Orinoco dispute between the United States and Venezuela in the same year.

Herron was an internationalist, a member of the American Socialist Party and one of the early supporters of Eugene Debs. In Europe Herron filed regular intelligence reports on German public opinion that were given to the American embassy, then immediately passed on to the British governments and the other Allies.

The two men met at a hotel near the Austrian embassy. Herron was apparently impressed by Lammasch's offer for an immediate separate peace and asked "to sleep on it," then continue the discussions the next day. However, when they met the following morning Herron was decidedly cool and disinterested. He had obviously been in touch with Washington, and perhaps London, during the night. By this time the Allies had collectively decided that they would accept only an unconditional surrender.

Professor Lammasch returned to Vienna empty-handed and reported to the Emperor that a separate peace was no longer possible. Lammasch later became the last Minister-President of Austria. In office only a few months, he is credited with being the person who finally persuaded Charles I to give up his right to exercise sovereign authority and end the Habsburgs' seven-century rule over Austria.

Charles I made a last and final attempt at peace. In 1918 he appointed Baron von Burián (1851–1922) as Foreign Minister and instructed him to send a message to the Allied governments calling for an immediate meeting on neutral soil to discuss an end to the war. Baron von Burián had been Foreign Minister two years earlier, in 1916, and had proposed a peace plan that called for the re-establishment of a free Belgium and the return of all captured French territory in exchange for recognition of German and Austro-Hungarian rights in Eastern Europe. The Germans had vigorously protested, and as a result the plan had been dropped and Baron von Burián had been dismissed from his post.

The 1918 peace proposal was ignored by the Germans and by the Allies, who had realized that a military victory was finally within their grasp. Charles I lost both the peace and his country. He and his family went into exile, first in Switzerland, then finally in Madeira.

* * *

There were those in Germany who posed the question "why?" Why was the fighting continuing, especially after the Kaiser, the Reichstag and the Pope had all proposed a peace without success?

F. W. Foerster (1869–1966), for example, a professor of philosophy at the University in Munich, wrestled with the conundrum:

Did not the majority resolution of the German Reichstag, as well as the answers of the Central Powers to the Pope's Note, express unequivocally our readiness to cooperate in the realization of such plans for the future? What more could be asked? The answer is very simple: the Entente find no convincing moral guarantee behind all these declarations [...]. A nation's genuine desire for peace must manifest itself more concretely than in general and ambiguous declarations.[117]

In a professorial style Foerster endeavors to answer his own question, being slightly elliptical, not naming names but leaving no doubt as to who he thinks is to blame. Since this was written during wartime he had to be circumspect:

It is inconceivable that so large a proportion of the German people should talk continually about the enemy's determination to go on with the war and the Germans' wish for peace, without asking themselves if that determination to continue the war does not arise from the fact that our offers of peace are made worthless by the military pride and the spirit of conquest which dominates our interviews and speeches.[118]

The unspoken conclusion was a pessimistic one. In Professor Foerster's opinion it didn't matter who issued the call for peace; it would be rendered void by the military, who at this point controlled the country and who were determined to pursue the war to the bitter end.

* * *

In 1916, Colonel House was back in Europe again. This time the peace plan he carried was more elaborate and potentially persuasive. The President of the United States intended to call all belligerents to a conference that would not only end the war but also plan the postwar period as well. Freedom of the seas would be just one part of it; another would be a League of Nations to govern the future peace of the world.

To force both the Allies and the Central Powers to attend such a conference the President was ready to announce that if one side refused to attend, the United States would give its support to the other. It was an aggressive, audacious plan but did not fully take into account all the realities of the war, especially the mood and expectations of the man in the street.

For over two years the propaganda machines of the belligerent countries had been promising their citizens victory with honor, a glorious success on the battlefield that would justify all the sacrifices they were being asked to make. A sudden switch from clear military objectives to a secretive negotiated settlement that would certainly entail compromises could easily be portrayed as a stalemate or even a defeat. For the politicians at the helm of the state that could mean political suicide. The jingoistic press would undoubtedly be outraged, patriotic organizations would stage mass demonstrations, and morale in the armed forces would sag.

Colonel House made a tour of the capitals London, Berlin and Paris. No one would agree, even when faced with the threat of American support or lack of it. Colonel House settled in London and began to work on the British Foreign Secretary, Sir Edward Grey (1862–1933), whom he knew well socially. Finally, the day before Colonel House sailed for New York he and the Foreign Secretary signed a confidential memorandum, which in effect embodied the essence of Colonel House's proposal, namely, that America would go to war against whichever side did not agree. When Colonel House arrived in Washington, President Wilson read the document and accepted it in toto, with one reservation. He added the word "probably" to the central clause, changing it to that the United States would "probably" go to war. To the British, this had the effect of nullifying the entire agreement, and they immediately backed off. It is quite likely that Colonel House, who was a dedicated Anglophile, went beyond his mandate and tried to force the United States to enter the war on the side of the Allies. If so, he was clearly trying to deceive both sides, President Wilson and Foreign Secretary Grey. One historian summed up Colonel House's mission: "He dangled war before one (British Foreign Secretary Grey), peace before the other (President Wilson), and in reality achieved neither."[119]

The Germans made it clear that they also were not interested in the agreement. They did so by action and not word. They widened the war and declared unrestricted submarine warfare in the waters around the British Isles; that is, they announced that they would sink any ship, neutral or belligerent, that attempted to trade with Great Britain. They intended to slowly force England to negotiate through starvation.

Even if both sides agreed to meet at a negotiating table, there were fundamental differences between what the Allies and the Central Powers would accept as the pre-conditions for a lasting ceasefire.

The Germans insisted that any proposal Wilson might make must not include territorial issues, "since questions of that kind must be one of the objects of peace negotiations."[120] At the same time, the Germans publicly endorsed the formation of a league of nations, so that it should be impossible to build great hostile coalitions again. "Germany is always ready to enter into a league of nations," one of the leading newspapers editorialized, "even to head such a league, for the purpose of holding in restraint the destroyer of peace."[121]

However, the French, and their ally England, made it clear that they would not go to the peace table without a prior agreement that Belgium be restored to a sovereign state and Alsace-Lorraine be returned to France. The gap between the belligerents appeared to be impossible to bridge.

One of the more imaginative ways that was proposed to deal with the Alsace-Lorraine issue and thus bring about a meeting of antagonistic minds was to let Russia pay the price; that is, Germany would surrender Alsace-Lorraine to France and in turn be compensated by a sizable piece of the Russian Empire.

The Russians were of course not consulted, and the British generals were predictably opposed to the plan. Field Marshal Douglas Haig (1861–1928) callously wrote: "It would be better for the future of our race to fail in next year's offensive than to accept the enemy's terms now when after more than three years of splendid efforts we have brought the German resistance so near the breaking point."[122] The general's optimism proved to be thoroughly unfounded.[123] There were several years and millions of casualties ahead before the war could be brought to a conclusion.

* * *

The Germans had their own ideas as to how to end the war. Before they launched their policy of "unrestricted submarine warfare," they put forward a peace plan of their own. Theobald von Bethmann-Hollweg, the German Chancellor, called together the envoys of Spain, Switzerland and the United States and handed them each a note, asking them to pass it on to the Allied nations.

At the heart of the note was the following statement: "Conscious of their military and economic strength and ready to carry on to the end, if they must, the struggle that is forced upon them, but animated at the same time by the desire to stem the flood of blood and to bring the horrors of war to an end, the four allied powers [Germany, Austria-Hungary, Bulgaria and Turkey] propose to enter even now into peace negotiations."[124]

Two days later, partially as a result of the German note, President Wilson invited all belligerents to state concretely their war aims. He made it clear that he was neither proposing peace nor offering mediation but "merely proposing that soundings be taken in order that we may learn [...] how near the haven of peace may be."[125] The President hoped that the belligerents would announce moderate terms so that they would not appear to be too intransigent or aggressive. Thus once they were committed to moderate, more or less reasonable, terms negotiations could begin.

It was a clever maneuver. President Wilson could on the one hand, launch a peace proposal while, on the other, quite ingenuously denying that he was trying to mediate or demand peace. Unfortunately, he misjudged the situation. He had been waiting for the right moment to try to step between the antagonists and when he received the German peace note he thought he had found it. He wrote to Colonel House: "It may be that peace is nearer than we know; that the terms which the belligerents on the one side and on the other would deem it necessary to insist upon are not so irreconcilable as some have feared; that an interchange of views would clear the way at least for a conference and make the permanent concord of the nations a hope of the immediate future, a concert of nations immediately practicable."[126]

The Allied response to President Wilson's proposal was cautious and lacking in enthusiasm. As the proposal came right on the heels of the German note, the Allies thought it was a little too much "made in Germany" for their taste. And the Central Powers had always considered President Wilson and the United States to be a lackey of the English, so they too were immediately suspicious. In fact, Colonel House, President Wilson's close friend and advisor, had counseled him to show the text to the English before he sent it, but he had refused to do so. In any case, the Germans, who were convinced that at the moment they were in a superior military position, had no intention of revealing their terms for peace until their were face-to-face with their enemies across the peace table. President Wilson's proposal elicited polite replies from both sides, who simply restated their positions, then promptly ignored it.

In fact, the Central Powers already had compiled a detailed list of their war aims. In 1915 Stephan Burián von Rajecz (1851–1922), the Austro-Hungarian Foreign Minister, had reached the conclusion that neither side would ever achieve a decisive victory. Sooner or later there would be a negotiated peace. The Emperor Franz Joseph (1830–1916) agreed with him and gave von Burián permission to consult with their allies. Burián drew up a list of conditions.[127] The Kaiser agreed, and with certain minor modifications[128] so did the German military. The only major disagreement was whether or not to announce them publicly. On the one hand, von Burián favored an open declaration signed by all the Central Powers. On the other hand, Bethmann-Hollweg, the German Chancellor, was afraid of public opinion. Should the people know exactly what the Central Powers were bringing to the negotiating table they might be dissatisfied with the result. After much discussion Foreign Minister von Burián agreed with the German position and thus the conditions for peace—what President Wilson and others called "the war aims"—were to be kept a secret until a peace conference was convened.

The German government thought that America, including its President, was firmly committed to the Allied cause, but this was probably not the case. Certainly President Wilson, who had just won re-election on the campaign slogan "He kept us out of war," had become more pacifistic than ever. He was convinced that the aspirations of the Allies were just as inflexible, unrealistic and selfish as those of the Central Powers.

The closest that the Allies came to a statement of their war aims was Lloyd George's terse summation: "complete restitution, full reparation, and effectual guarantees for the future."[129] In the same speech the Prime Minister made it clear that the Allies placed the entire blame for the war on the Central Powers, which was hardly a first step toward the negotiating table. In addition, while addressing the House of Commons, Lloyd George quoted Abraham Lincoln, who had faced "similar circumstances" during the American Civil War and declared: "We accepted this war for an object, and a worthy object, and the war will end when that object is attained. Under God I hope it will never end until that time."[130]

Three • The Long Road to Peace

The Lincoln quote was undoubtedly cited for President Wilson's ears, but it was well chosen. Lincoln had been running for re-election faced with an opponent who advocated a negotiated peace. Like Lincoln, Lloyd George was not anxious to end the war, not until the other side received a crushing defeat. With millions already dead in the trenches of France, Lloyd George callously turned his back on a negotiated peace, and he did so before the House of Commons, a chamber elected by the people, among them hundreds of thousands who would certainly perish if the war continued:

> Are we likely to achieve that object [peace] by accepting the invitation of the German Chancellor? That is the only question we have to put to ourselves. There has been some talk about proposals of peace. What are the proposals? There are none. To enter at the invitation of Germany, proclaiming herself victorious, without any knowledge of the proposals she proposes to make, into a conference, is to put our head into a noose with the rope end in the hands of Germany.[131]

* * *

In January 1917 President Wilson used the U.S. Senate as a forum to make yet one more attempt at peace. He addressed the peoples of the belligerent nations. "Speaking for the silent mass of mankind everywhere," the American President called for "peace without victory" because "only peace between equals can last."[132]

President Wilson went on to declare that no security for the future could be expected from a settlement that left one side crushed and revengeful. He did his best to lay out the basis for the future, one that rejected the old system of European alliances. The President pledged America's involvement in a postwar league that would be "not a balance of power but a community of power": "There is no entangling alliance in a concert of power. When all unite to act in the same sense and with the same purpose, all act in the common interest and are free to live their own lives under a common protection."[133]

The press on both sides of the Atlantic immediately picked up the phrase "peace without victory" and used it for headlines. Others called the speech "a brilliant piece of statecraft," and an influential international banker, Jacob Schriff (1847–1920), went so far as to publicly label it as "one of the greatest state papers in the history of nations."[134]

Strangely enough, Wilson later regretted his choice of words. What he really wanted to say, he realized afterwards, was "a peace of reconciliation."[135]

Working quietly through the German ambassador to the United States, Johann von Bernstorff,[136] Colonel House tried to convince the Germans that this was the moment to take the moral high ground, to say, in effect, that it no longer mattered how the war began or how many battles had been won or lost, the human toll had been so staggering and enormous that the time had come to end the slaughter and to make sure that such a tragic debacle did not occur again. Ambassador von Bernstorff was in complete agreement and did what he could to persuade the German government to adopt that position. He wrote in his memoirs: "I pursued a policy of peace with undeviating consistency, and to this day I still believe it to have been the only right policy."[137]

The British Foreign Secretary, Sir Edward Grey, writing much later, also thought that the Germans had let the peace initiative fall from their grasp:

> In the light of after events, it is clear that Germany missed a great opportunity of peace. If she had accepted the Wilson policy, and was ready to agree to the Conference, the Allies could not have refused [...].
> Germans have only to reflect upon the peace they might have had in 1916 as compared with the Peace of 1919.[138]

However, Berlin was blind to the opportunity. They had obviously decided that there was little or nothing to be gained by negotiation and the war would be settled on the battlefield or at sea. For some time there had been within the German government substantial disagreement and debate over the use of submarines. The German Admiralty promised that the unrestricted use of their submarines would compel England "to turn to thoughts of peace within a few months."[139]

The reply to President Wilson's Senate speech and the declaration of the resumption of unrestricted submarine warfare were blended into one.

The United States immediately broke off diplomatic relations. A declaration of war was not far away.

Ambassador von Bernstorff had done his best to avoid war with America. For three years he had consistently taken an internationalist, almost pacifistic point of view. Although it was in Germany's interest to keep the United States out of the war, he often chided the German government for its belligerence and truculence. Colonel House added a note in his daily journal, stating that "in my opinion, there is no German of today who deserves better of his country than Bernstorff [...]. If it had not been for his patience, good sense, and untiring effort, we would now be at war with Germany [...]. We all feel that Bernstorff deserves great credit—just how much may never be known until after this terrible war is over."[140]

When Ambassador von Bernstorff was forced to leave after the United States broke relations with Germany, he sent a message to Colonel House that he "deeply regretted" the action taken by his government and "believed that peace would have come soon through [President Wilson's] efforts if they had not been interrupted [by the German resumption of unrestricted submarine warfare]."[141]

In a warm farewell letter Colonel House wrote to Ambassador von Bernstorff: "The day will come when people in Germany will see how much you have done for your country in America."[142]

* * *

For the German government, the American declaration of war was almost a self-fulfilling prophecy, proving that President Wilson had never been an honest broker. They had always suspected that he had favored the Allies (Colonel House certainly did) and had constantly tried to maneuver the Central Powers into a disadvantageous position both diplomatically and militarily. Now they had manipulated events to confirm it.

Suddenly the possibility for peace became remote and yet it had been close, probably closer than most people realized. After more than three years of exhausting warfare President Wilson had in fact honorably and impartially tried to bring the two sides together at a negotiating table. Ambassador von Bernstorff wrote after the rupture of relations with Germany: "My conviction that we could in the year 1917 have obtained a peace which would have been acceptable to ourselves, is based not so much on Wilson's good will, as upon the fact that, without American help, the Entente could not possibly have achieved a victory."[143]

However, peace was still possible even after the United States declared war, albeit on a fading, distant horizon. The United States did not immediately sever relations with Germany's close ally Austria-Hungary. Instead the Americans attempted to use the Dual Monarchy as a channel for peace negotiations. A new ambassador, Count Tarnowski von Tarnów (1866–1946), arrived in Washington on almost the same day as the German ambassador left. Count Tarnowski was not allowed to formally present his credentials, but he made it clear that privately Austria-Hungary did not agree with Germany's unrestricted submarine warfare. Count Tarnowski was quite at home in America, having been a diplomat there before.[144] Through him, and with the consent of the Allies, for two months President Wilson tried to negotiate a separate peace with Austria-Hungary. When this failed, the United States finally broke relations with the Dual Monarchy.

* * *

After the Vatican's offer to mediate a peace in 1914 was turned down by all the belligerents, Pope Benedict XV was determined to try again. All the belligerents were convinced they could win on the battlefield; hence none of them would take the first step toward a negotiated peace. The Vatican, however, did not give up hope of finding a way to end the conflict.

After one year of warfare, in July 1915, the Vatican published the *Apostolic Exhortation* addressed "To the Belligerent Peoples and their Rulers," containing an apocalyptic and very prophetic warning of the dangers ahead if a negotiated peace was not achieved: "Abandon the mutual threat of destruction. Remember, Nations do not die; humiliated and oppressed, they bear the weight of the yoke imposed upon them, preparing themselves for their comeback and transmitting from one generation to the next a sad legacy of hatred and vendetta."[145]

But spiritual words and dire predictions for the future had little or no impact on the course of the war. Realizing this, the Vatican changed tactics and switched to quiet diplomacy, engaging in several secret attempts to bring the two warring sides together.

In 1917, for example, papal emissaries contacted Werner de Mérode (1881–1930),[146] a Belgian nobleman who had previously worked for the Vatican, and informed him that Baron von der Lancken (1865–1933), head of the Kaiser's secret service in occupied Belgium,[147] wished to meet with someone "at a high level" from the French government. The baron had indicated that the Germans were apparently ready to make concessions for peace, for instance, on the annexation of Alsace-Lorraine and the status of postwar Belgium. According to von der Lancken, the German government and the military were at this point ready to trade the French-speaking region of Lorraine and the southwestern tip of Alsace for peace. This is indeed surprising, as the German government had consistently and publicly stated that Alsace-Lorraine would always remain German. Von der Lancken may have been hoping to somehow arrive at a compromise that would satisfy both Berlin and Paris or at least get them to the negotiating table.

Aristide Briand (1862–1932) was selected as the right French negotiator, as he had previously served as Prime Minister and was well-known for his pacifistic views.[148] Respected as a man willing to make compromises, he was not an advocate of the French hard line *"la paix par la victoire"* (peace through military victory). In a speech that was well reported in the international press, he had told a Parisian audience: "Just one step toward peace means a great success if one is determined to take another step the next day."[149] Without hesitation, Briand agreed to meet with von der Lancken.

A meeting was scheduled to take place at a villa in Lausanne, Switzerland. The Vatican's representative was to be Eugenio Pacelli (176–1958), the future Pope Pius XII (1939–1958), who was then working for the Vatican's counterespionage group Sodalitium Pianum. Briand contacted Charles de Brocqueville (1860–1940), the Prime Minister of Belgium, who agreed to go with him, but first Briand had to inform Raymond Poincaré (1860–1934), the President of the French Republic. The President called a meeting of Ministers, who were highly suspicious of the démarche. The Foreign Minister, Alexandre Ribot (1842–1923), for example, called it "a snare." In any case, before any peace negotiations could take place, by treaty, the French were obliged to inform their partners in the alliance, the British and the Italians. Both countries turned out to be less than enthusiastic and neither was willing to entrust a lone Frenchman to speak for them. The British had not forgotten that von der Lancken was responsible for the execution of the celebrated nurse Edith Cavell[150] and the Italians had their own intelligence, which had labeled him *"triste et louche"* (sad and fishy).[151]

At literally the last minute, just before Briand was due to leave Paris by train for Switzerland, Charles de Brocqueville, the Belgian Prime Minister, announced that he had changed his mind. Like the Italians and the British, he didn't trust von der Lancken and had decided not to take part in any negotiations with him. Briand had no choice but to abandon the talks and give his word to Foreign Minister Ribot that he would break off all contact with von der Lancken.

A few days later, Richard von Kühlmann (1873–1948), the German Secretary of State for Foreign Affairs, ended a speech to the Reichstag with the words: "Alsace and Lorraire—no never!"[152]

In fact, a number of plans to deal with Alsace-Lorriane had been proposed, some imaginative and viable, for example, a simple referendum to determine the boundaries or the creation of an international zone belonging to no one.

Afterwards the French Foreign Minister, Ribot, had the candor to write in his memoirs: "If France had renounced Alsace-Lorraine and Italy Trieste, then Germany without a doubt would have made concessions in Lorraine and Austria would have ceded the Trentino for colonial compensation [...]. A peace on this basis was the plan of both Emperors."[153]

If von der Lancken had been telling the truth and if von Kühlmann's remark had been only spite, then the posturing, nationalism and intransigence of politicians and diplomats far from the killing fields had let peace slip past and millions of casualties paid the price.

* * *

In addition to his secret peace initiatives, Pope Benedict XV also focused the Vatican's attention on humanitarian issues, such as the fate of POWs and refugees. Using the Vatican's diplomatic offices, the Pope negotiated with the warring parties for an exchange of tens of thousands of wounded POWs as well as more than 20,000 civilians from occupied zones who were sent to southern France. In 1916 nearly 30,000 prisoners with lung diseases from gas attacks were sent to neutral Switzerland to convalesce. The Vatican also handled over 600,000 items of correspondence for POWs, including 170,000 inquiries about missing persons and 40,000 appeals for help in the repatriation of sick POWs. In addition, the Vatican set up funds to feed the starving children in German-occupied Belgium as well as in Lithuania, Poland, Lebanon, Montenegro, Syria and Russia.[154]

On the first of August 1917, after almost exactly three years of fighting, Pope Benedict XV thought the right psychological moment had arrived to initiate a formal peace conference. Although motivated by humanitarian concerns, he was also worried about the possible demise of Austro-Hungary, which was a bastion of Catholicism, and also the distinct possibility that if the war did not end soon revolution might engulf all of Europe.

Addressing the rulers of the belligerent countries, Benedict XV asked them "to arrive at an agreement on the following points which seem to offer the basis of a just and lasting peace."[155] The Pope put forward a seven-point plan, which was undoubtedly the most detailed peace proposal yet to be made:

1. "[T]he moral force of right [...] should be substituted for the material force of arms."
2. There must be "simultaneous and reciprocal diminution of armaments," that is, a controlled and definitive disarmament of the belligerent nations.
3. A mechanism for "international arbitration must be established," i.e., a permanent international organization to deal with international conflicts must be created.
4. "[T]rue liberty and common rights over the sea" should exist; that is, freedom of the seas should be guaranteed to all.
5. There should be a "renunciation of war indemnities."
6. The occupied territories, e.g., those in France, should be evacuated, including Belgium.
7. There should be a rational "examination [...] of rival claims" (a direct reference to Alsace-Lorraine).[156]

The German government saw the proposal before anyone else. The papal nuncio to Germany, Eugenio Pacelli, brought a draft of the document to Berlin and discussed it at length with State Secretary Arthur Zimmermann (1854–1940), who had numerous objections. According to one historian: "Detailed peace preparations after a massive victory [...] had been most impressive, preparations for a negotiated peace of understanding simply did not exist. It was easier to plan for victory than for a state of affairs somewhere between victory and defeat."[157]

Worse, no German politician or general had had the foresight, or the ability, to prepare the public or the civil or military bureaucracy for "a peace of understanding." The German government was totally unprepared to sit down at a peace table and discuss the terms of an agreement. Undoubtedly the papacy knew this and was trying to notify the German officialdom that given the fact that on the Western Front victory on the battlefield had withered into an impasse, a negotiated peace might well be the only way to end the war. The government was well aware of this. Writing after the war, in 1920, the German Chancellor von Bethmann-Hollweg candidly summarized the situation in 1917:

> Whatever happened, for 1917 we could not hope for a victory, either on land or at sea which would mean a final decision. In addition, the gradual depletion of all our reserve of manpower and material continued remorsefully [...]. The material and moral resources of Austria-Hungary were vanishing even faster [...]. Time was against us [...] the Kaiser was prepared in principle to consider concessions if they promised to lead to peace.[158]

The German people were also war weary and appeared to be ready to accept a peace process. But the Kaiser was apparently in no mood to let the papacy become the mediator to end the war. According to Admiral Georg Alexander von Müller (1854–1940), Chief of the Naval Cabinet, who was present when the papal nuncio at Munich, Pacelli, spoke with the Kaiser: "His Majesty, as he admitted later, said that the Catholic Church had given him no support in his peace feelers. Now he would continue the war until his enemies had bitten the dust."[159]

The Kaiser was either being rancorous or sending mixed signals to his government. At roughly the same moment he told Richard von Kühlmann, the Secretary of State for Foreign Affairs: "Now you have a free hand. Show what you can do and get peace for us by Christmas."[160]

In any case, the Kaiser could also be quite diplomatic when he wished to be so. Apparently he told the papal nuncio exactly what he wanted to hear. In his memoirs the Kaiser wrote:

> Nothing could be more glorious for him [the Pope], I went on, than to devote himself unreservedly, body and soul, to the great cause of peace [...]. With shining eyes, the Nuncio grasped my hand and said deeply moved *"Vous avez parfaitement raison! C'est le devoir du Pape; il faut qu'il agisse; c'est par lui que le monde doit être regagné à la paix. Je transmettrai vos paroles à Sa Sainteté."* ("You are absolutely right! It is the duty of the Pope; he must act; it is through him that the world must be won back to peace. I shall transmit your words to His Holiness.")[161]

In the Reichstag a "Committee of Seven" was formed to consider the papal note with the new Chancellor, Georg Michaelis (1857–1936). After much discussion the result was a shrewd but inconclusive reply, a qualified "yes," coupled with many explanatory phrases, deliberately vague and lacking precise details, especially with respect to Belgium. Even with those reservations taken into account, for the German government the document would still be unacceptable as a starting point for a peace conference.

According to one German observer, "Chancellor Michaelis has been blamed with as much justice as severity for his rejection of the papal offer of mediation. In fact his refusal made no difference. No one at the time could have brought the German people, the victim of lying propaganda and in a process of passing from one illusion to another, to accept the only terms on which the Allies were prepared to make peace."[162]

Nonetheless, the Pope modified his proposal slightly before publicly presenting it to both sides. The Pope was obviously convinced that he must have a German acceptance for his plan to work. It is interesting to note that no similar preliminary consultations took place between the Vatican and either England or France.

The Central Powers led by Germany failed to make use of the diplomatic advantage that was given them. Had they replied in a strong and positive fashion, besides the obvious propaganda coup, it would have put the Allied powers under pressure from their people to begin negotiations on the basis of the Pope's proposal.

The final document prepared by the Vatican pleased no one fully. Each alliance became convinced that the Pope's proposal had been created by the opposing side and included the ideals and aims of the enemy.[163] In fact, the diplomats of Europe shied away from attempts to mediate the conflict partially in fear that a desire for peace might be seen as a sign of weakness, exactly the type of attack that no wartime leader could long endure.

Yet the initial reaction was promising. Great Britain issued a favorable but slightly ambiguous response.[164] The Bulgarians waxed positive. It has often been argued that the only country that could have accepted the Pope's proposal without reserve was Austria-Hungary, as it left the problems of the Balkans for a future peace conference where Austria-Hungary would have had a voice.[165]

The French, however, were dismissive. Clemenceau, the French Prime Minister, dubbed Benedict XV's proposal "a peace against France."[166] The American President, Woodrow Wilson, speaking for the Allies, made the only formal reply and completely rejected the proposal.[167] That put an end to the papal démarche.

Benedict XV later confessed to one of his friends that the bitterest moment of his life was when he received the rejection note by Wilson. The Pope had long believed that America held the key to peace. On numerous occasions he said that "America had it in her power to make peace within 24 hours if she wished to do so."[168]

Just six months previously, in January 1917, President Wilson had advocated a negotiated peace as the best outcome for the war; then when the Pope proposed one the American President surprised most people by refusing to accept it. President Wilson argued that the Pope's plan would not deliver a stable peace: "This agony [the war] must not be gone through again, and it must be a matter of very sober judgment that will insure us against it."[169]

Or, to put it another way, President Wilson thought that if Germany was not totally defeated in this war it would have to be done all over again in another war. In President Wilson's eyes, Benedict XV's peace plan also ignored the question of Belgium and reparations thus could easily lead to a return to the *status quo ante bellum*, something Wilson had become pledged to avoid. The object of the war, Wilson wrote to the Vatican, was now (after the American declaration of war) to "deliver the free peoples of the world from the menace and the actual power of a vast military establishment controlled by an irresponsible Government."[170]

Unfortunately, both sides thought they were riding white horses of truth and justice. The Kaiser on the 30th anniversary of his accession described the war as "[A] conflict between two approaches to the world. Either the Prussian-

German-Germanic approach—Right, Freedom, Honour, Morality—is to remain respected, or the Anglo-Saxon which would mean enthroning the worship of gold."[171]

Neither leader, it seemed, was concerned with how many more lives would be lost or maimed, certainly hundreds of thousands, while the leaders pranced on the world stage.

The American rejection effectively stopped the Pope's 1917 proposal. In fact, Benedict's XV's peace plan was moot long before that. Great Britain, Germany and the United States had always suspected that the Vatican had its own very Catholic agenda. It was virtually impossible for the Vatican to convince the Protestant world of the purity of its intentions, its impartiality and its neutrality. The final blow arrived when Leon Trotsky (1879–1940) became the People's Commissar for Foreign Affairs in November 1917 and revealed a secret clause in the Treaty of London of 1915 in which Britain, France and Russia pledged to work together with Italy to reject any Vatican peace initiative.

The only result of the Pope's peace plan was that it helped inspire anti-war strikes in Turin, which were ruthlessly suppressed by the Italian government. More than 50 people were killed, 800 wounded, and over 1,000 workers hastily sent to the front.

* * *

A month before the Pope introduced his proposal, in July 1917, the German Reichstag passed a peace resolution of its own, a spectacular act of defiance against both the military and the government. For the first time since the beginning of the war there was a major public rift between the German government and the people.

Matthias Erzberger (1875–1921), acting largely on his own initiative,[172] introduced a peace resolution in the Reichstag, "a peace of understanding," as he called it, "with no forced territorial acquisitions." He had just returned from a tour of the Eastern Front and fully realized the German navy's promise of bringing England to her knees by "unrestricted submarine warfare" was not a reality. In a graphic and forthright manner Erzberger presented the military situation to the Reichstag. He concluded by announcing that the time had come to end the war, and as soon as possible.

In the Reichstag the response to the peace resolution was immediate and overwhelmingly favorable. A leading member of the Social Democrats declared: "We Social Democrats demand a peace which leaves nobody conqueror or conquered."[173] Another Deputy said that "we can speak of peace as those who speak for the German people."[174] Yet another added: "Millions of men and women are looking to us to see if a glimmer of peace will arise from our deliberations. Sufferings are growing into inhuman proportions [...]. An agreement must be sought without delay. It is necessary to save the people from the worst."[175]

After little discussion on the floor of the Reichstag the resolution passed by 212 votes to 126 with 17 abstentions. In other words, nearly 63 percent of the members of the Reichstag voted for peace. The resolution was unfortunately non-binding, but since the members of the Reichstag were elected by the population, their votes were as close as one could come to a poll of German public opinion. The German people were obviously war weary, tired of waiting for the spectacular victory that would end war and which never arrived.

The Reichstag peace resolution essentially called for no annexations, no indemnities, freedom of the seas, and international arbitration. It was immediately reprinted in the international press, for example, the *London Times* and the *New York Times*:

> As on August 4, 1914, so also now on the threshold of the fourth year of war, the German people stand the assurance of the speech from the throne: "We are driven by no lust of conquest."
>
> Germany took up arms in defense of its liberty and independence, and for the integrity of its territories. The *Reichstag* labors for peace and a mutual understanding and lasting reconciliation among the nations. Forced acquisitions of territory, and political, economic, and financial violations are incompatible with such a peace.
>
> The *Reichstag* rejects all plans aiming at an economic blockage and the stirring up of enmity among the peoples after the war. The freedom of the seas must be assured. Only an economic peace can prepare the ground for the friendly association of peoples.
>
> The *Reichstag* will energetically promote the creation of international juridical organizations. So long, however, as the enemy Governments do not accept such a peace, so long as they threaten Germany and her allies with conquest and violation, the German people will stand together as one man, hold out unshaken, and fight until the rights of itself and its allies to life and development are secured. The German nation united is unconquerable.
>
> The *Reichstag* knows that in this announcement it is at one with the men who are defending the Fatherland. In their heroic struggles they are sure of the undying thanks of the whole people.[176]

The Reichstag peace resolution infuriated the German military high command led by Generals Paul von Hindenburg (1847–1934) and Erich Ludendorff (1865–1937) and served to hasten the downfall of the Chancellor, Theobald von Bethmann-Hollweg, who was held responsible by the military for allowing the resolution to pass.

The new Chancellor, Georg Michaelis, stood before an applauding Reichstag and approved the resolution. However, in his acceptance he appended the phrase "as I understand it." A few days later he wrote to the Kaiser: "By means of my interpretation of it [the Reichstag resolution], I robbed it of its greatest dangers. We can make any kind of peace we want with this resolution."[177]

* * *

Despite the failure of the papal peace proposal and the Reichstag proposal, the Germans continued to quietly and diplomatically search for ways to end the war through negotiation. The German Secretary of State for Foreign Affairs, Richard von Kühlmann, decided to go around the papal nuncio and to use secretly the Marquis de Villalobar (1864–1926), the Spanish Minister to Belgium, to sound out the British and find out just how far they were willing to go to have peace. Villalobar was a confidant of the King of Spain and had been attached to the Spanish embassy in London from 1904 to 1909. In addition to Villalobar's contacts within the British government, he also had close personal ties with the English royal family.

On the other side of the trenches Villalobar had known von Kühlmann, the German Secretary of State for Foreign Affairs, for years and the two had become close friends. Von Kühlmann had previously been the councilor of the German embassy in London for six years and had become an Anglophile. According to a close British friend,[178] von Kühlmann had been opposed to the German declaration of war and favored a peaceful resolution of the conflict. In 1913, less than a year before the war began, he had anonymously published a pamphlet titled *German World Policy and No War* (*Deutsche Weltpolitik und kein Krieg*). In it he argued that German expansion could continue without creating a conflict with England. "Give us ten years of peace," von Kühlmann declared, "and war will have become a thing of the past."[179]

In the interest of peace von Kühlmann was willing to go well beyond his mandate and propose concrete terms, for example, the complete restoration of sovereignty to Belgium, conditions that could have been the starting point for a peace conference. If the British did agree, von Kühlmann knew he would then have to sell the plan to the German generals, von Hindenburg and Ludendorff, and, of course, to the Kaiser. But if von Kühlmann could get an initial commitment from the British, he calculated that he might be able to persuade the Germans to agree to a cease-fire and sit down at a negotiating table.

However, before Villalobar could begin to act as a confidential mediator he needed the permission of the King of Spain and the Foreign Minister. After the coded messages left the Spanish embassy in Brussels via The Hague for Madrid they were intercepted on the first leg by the German military and on the second by the British and the French. All secrecy evaporated and with it any hope of a candid exchange of views between the Germans and the British.

Von Kühlmann had been hoping to deal with the British separately and thus build an agreement for peace while at the same time avoiding the thorny and potentially explosive issue of Alsace-Lorraine. It was the major stumbling block to any negotiated peace. The French believed that the Germans stole Alsace-Lorraine from them in 1871, and in 1917 the Germans considered it an integral part of the German *Reich*. There seemed to be no room for compromise.

Almost every peace feeler seemed to founder on the inflexible boundaries of this small piece of Europe less than half the size of Belgium.

There is every reason to believe that von Kühlmann sincerely wanted to end the war and do so by establishing a dialogue among the belligerents. He told the Reichstag that "an end of this gigantic war could hardly be expected from military decisions alone without any diplomatic negotiations."[180]

In any case, the opening for peace did not last long. Von Kühlmann's statement, a public declaration advocating negotiation, eventually cost him his job. The German generals claimed it was disastrous to army morale and that they had been "painfully surprised"[181] by the speech. Admiral Alfred von Tirpitz (1849–1930) set the tone: "Anyone who goes searching too urgently or too openly for an agreement only reduces his chances of attaining it."[182]

The only way to end the war, the generals claimed, was by an overwhelming German military victory. The Kaiser was forced to agree and as a result von Kühlmann was obliged to resign.

* * *

At roughly the same time the British Prime Minister, Lloyd George, was also seriously considering different ways to make peace. He had realized that after three years of warfare cracks had begun to appear in the so-called British iron will. Signs of war weariness were becoming more and more evident and pacifists were the first to take advantage of them.

Charlotte Despard (1844–1939), a wealthy suffragette, for example, created the Women's Peace Crusade and traveled through the country speaking to large, war-weary crowds about the need for an immediate peace. One hundred thousand people bought copies of her anti-war pamphlet. When she tried to organize a workers' and soldiers' soviet in Newcastle, patterned after those in Russia, the government reacted with force, raiding pacifist groups, seizing files, printing equipment, those printed pamphlets on hand, and letting thugs and off-duty soldiers break up pacifist meetings. Later during the 1918 General Election, Despard was selected as the Labour candidate for Battersea North and received 33 percent of the vote.

Bertrand Russell (1872–1970), who was already a well-known public figure, made a tour of Wales speaking to workers, sometimes several thousand at a time, where he proposed peace terms such as promising Germany no loss of "genuinely German territory" and suggesting that an "International Council" be established to prevent future conflicts from becoming wars. Russell delivered dozens of speeches and discovered a curious anomaly which he was at a loss to explain. "Munition workers," he reported, "oddly enough, tended to be pacifists."[183]

But while large numbers of the British working class supported the peace movement in one form or another, their numbers were never even close to a majority. When delegates representing nearly 2 million workers met in Manchester they voted by a margin of five to one to continue the war until Germany was fully defeated on the field of battle. In 1916 when the Reverend Edward Lyttelton, the headmaster of Eton, proposed some possible peace terms from his pulpit, the resulting public uproar forced him to resign. Those in favor of a war to the bitter end, no matter what it cost, clearly ruled the country.

* * *

Another fissure in the public resolve came from a rather unexpected source, poetry. Before the First World War, verse was a well-accepted and popular means of expression. Every day thousands of poems were written and sent to the world's press, and many were published.[184] Hardly a newspaper in Europe or the Americas went to press without sidebars of poetry. Slim volumes of verse often sold well, some so well that their authors could actually live from their royalties and a few poets became wealthy. Poetry was social currency, and the man on the street, the soldier, the sailor, the factory worker and student, often memorized some of the more popular verses, then recited them at the dinner table or social events or in bars and the trenches.

When the European war began, the tone of this poetry became shrill and strident as it was swept into the high tide of nationalism. Suddenly mortal combat became glorious, honorable and ennobling, a kind of sport where at the end of the game an untarnished victor emerged from the fray to receive his laurels. The British poet Julian Grenfell (1888–1915), for example, wrote from the front soon after he arrived: "I adore war. It is like a big picnic but without the objectivelessness of a picnic. I have never been more well or more happy."[185] In his most famous poem, "Into Battle," the soldier in battle assumes almost mythic proportions:

> The fighting man shall from the sun
> Take warmth, and life from the glowing earth;
> Speed with the light-foot winds to run,
> And with the trees to newer birth;
> And find, when fighting shall be done,
> Great rest, and fullness after dearth.[186]

As a general rule, this euphoric spirit continued during the first year of the war, then the mood of muse shifted radically as poets began to write about their squalid, precarious lives in the trenches. The sentimental patriotism waned, and a harsh, barbed reality took its place. Death loomed large, everywhere, not a Valhalla for heroes but, in the words of Siegfried Sassoon (1886–1967), "[t]he hell where youth and laughter go."[187] Charles Sorley (1895–1915), who survived barely a year in the trenches, wrote just before he died:

> Such, such is Death: no triumph: no defeat:
> Only an empty pail, a slate rubbed clean,
> A merciful putting away of what has been.[188]

From then on and for most of the war English-language poetry plunged into a downhill slide, further and further into a pit of naked barbarity, almost as if the poets were engaged in a breakneck race to discover who could charge his words with the most inhumanity and horror.

The British poet Isaac Rosenberg (1890–1918) spent nearly three years at the front in France before he was killed at the end of the war. His *Poems from the Trenches* paints a macabre graphic picture of the day-to-day confrontation with death and dying. In "Dead Man's Dump":

> The wheels lurched over sprawled dead
> But pained them not, though their bones crunched,
> Their shut mouths made no moan.
> They lie there huddled, friend and foeman,
> Man born of man, and born of woman,
> And shells go crying over them
> From night till night and now.
>
> Earth has waited for them,
> All the time of their growth
> Fretting for their decay:
> Now she has them at last!
> In the strength of their strength
> Suspended—stopped and held.
>
> A man's brains splattered on
> A stretcher-bearer's face;
> His shook shoulders slipped their load,
> But when they bent to look again
> The drowning soul was sunk too deep
> For human tenderness.
>
> Here is one not long dead;
> His dark hearing caught our far wheels,
> And the choked soul stretched weak hands
> To reach the living word the far wheels said,
> The blood-dazed intelligence beating for light,
> Crying through the suspense of the far torturing wheels
> Swift for the end to break
> Or the wheels to break,
> Cried as the tide of the world broke over his sight.[189]

Few poets expressed a soldier's plight and fatalism better than the American Alan Seeger. He came to France in 1915, two years before America declared war, and joined the French Foreign Legion. While serving in the trenches he wrote:

> I have a rendezvous with Death
> At some disputed barricade,
> When Spring comes back with rustling shade
> And apple-blossoms fill the air—

> I have a rendezvous with Death
> When Spring brings back blue days and fair.
> [...]
> But I've a rendezvous with Death
> At midnight in some flaming town,
> When Spring trips north again this year,
> And I to my pledged word am true,
> I shall not fail that rendezvous.[190]

Seeger kept his rendezvous. He was killed at the Battle of the Somme. "I Have a Rendezvous with Death" was published more than a year later and became one of the most widely read and memorized poems of the war.

As the fighting continued, more and more voices began to rise against it. Herbert Read (1893–1968), later Sir Herbert Read, wrote two volumes of war poetry, much of it devoted to describing the fragility of man as he came in contact with the inflexibility and unpredictability of the battlefield. In the preface of *Naked Warriors* he made his point of view clear:

> I would like to speak for a generation to following effect:
> We, who in manhood's dawn have been compelled to care not a damn for life or death, now care less still for the convention of glory and the intellectual apologies for what can never be to us other than a riot of ghastliness and horror, of inhumanity and negation.[191]

Read was one of the few English poets to survive the war. He retained his bitterness, his rancor and above all the conviction that the huge human sacrifice accomplished nothing.

Siegfried Sassoon was another survivor. He initially responded to the patriotic call to arms, but once he arrived in the trenches and witnessed the senseless slaughter he began to doubt the wisdom behind the war. He nonetheless gained a reputation for bravery and bravado under fire, earning him the epithet "Mad Jack." He was wounded, decorated, then sent back to England to recover.

When he was again fit for duty, Sassoon refused to return to the trenches. Encouraged by pacifist friends such as Bertrand Russell (1872–1970) and Lady Ottoline Morrell (1873–1938), Sassoon took a firm stand against the war. Instead of returning to France, he sent a letter to his commanding officer, titled "Finished with the War: A Soldier's Declaration." The letter was read aloud in Parliament by a sympathetic MP and published in the *Times* the following day:

> I am making this statement as an act of willful defiance of military authority, because I believe that the War is being deliberately prolonged by those who have the power to end it. I am a soldier, convinced that I am acting on behalf of soldiers. I believe that this War, on which I entered as a war of defense and liberation, has now become a war of aggression and conquest. I believe that the purpose for which I and my fellow soldiers entered upon this war should have been so clearly stated as to have made it impossible to change them, and that, had

this been done, the objects which actuated us would now be attainable by negotiation. I have seen and endured the sufferings of the troops, and I can no longer be a party to prolong these sufferings for ends which I believe to be evil and unjust. I am not protesting against the conduct of the war, but against the political errors and insincerities for which the fighting men are being sacrificed. On behalf of those who are suffering now I make this protest against the deception which is being practiced on them; also I believe that I may help to destroy the callous complacency with which the majority of those at home regard the contrivance of agonies which they do not, and which they have not sufficient imagination to realize.[192]

The letter was seen by many as treasonous or, at best, condemnatory of the war government's motives. Rather than court-martial Sassoon, the Under-Secretary of State for War, Ian Macpherson (1880–1937), decided that he was unfit for service and sent him to Craiglockhart War Hospital near Edinburgh, where he was officially treated for neurasthenia ("being shell-shocked"). As a personal act of defiance Sassoon threw the ribbon from his Military Cross into the river Mersey.

Sassoon spent several months convalescing at Craiglockhart. He called it "a gloomy cavernous place [...], a live museum of neuroses."[193] At night its wards reverberated with the screams of men who had seen too much and been pushed beyond their limits. Sassoon's poem "Dreamers" was first published in the hospital magazine. The opening lines are almost an echo of Read's pessimism and despair about the vainglorious war:

> Soldiers are citizens of death's grey land,
> Drawing no dividend from time's to-morrows.[194]

Sassoon's first anti-war poem appeared at that time. It was terse and simplistic but revealed his changed perspective.

> [E]verything but wretchedness is forgotten,
> To-night he's in the pink, but soon he'll die.
> And still the war goes on—he don't know why.[195]

While still in the hospital Sassoon wrote "Does It Matter?" He was undoubtedly thinking of other patients he encountered as well as his own fears.

> Does it matter—losing your legs?
> For people will always be kind,
> And you need not show that you mind
> When others come in after hunting
> To gobble their muffins and eggs.
>
> Does it matter?—losing your sight?
> There's such splendid work for the blind;
> And people will always be kind,
> As you sit on the terrace remembering
> And turning your face to the light.

> Do they matter?—those dreams in the pit?
> You can drink and forget and be glad,
> And people won't say that you're mad;
> For they know that you've fought for your country,
> And no one will worry a bit.[196]

The notion that the public neither knew nor cared about the hardships and sacrifices of the soldier in the trenches became a recurrent theme in Sassoon's poetry. Life in England seemed like a light-year away from the grim realities of the trenches, and no matter what he wrote he knew that no combination of words could ever link the two.

Adding to his frustration, Sassoon had nothing but contempt for the older generation of officers who lived well, even in the trenches, and thought nothing of sending thousands, even hundreds of thousands, of men "over the top" and into an almost certain death.

> "Good morning; good morning!" the General said
> When we met him last week on our way to the line.
> Now the soldiers he smiled at are most of 'em dead,
> And we're cursing his staff for incompetent swine.[197]

In Sassoon's mind the British officer corps bore the responsibility for the debacle in France, and he had no illusions about their incompetence. At best he treated them with disgust and distrust:

> If I were fierce, and bald, and short of breath,
>   I'd live with scarlet Majors at the Base,
> And speed glum heroes up the line to death.
>   You'd see me with my puffy petulant face,
> Guzzling and gulping in the best hotel,
>   Reading the Roll of Honour. "Poor young chap,"
> I'd say—"I used to know his father well;
>   Yes, we've lost heavily in this last scrap."
> And when the war is done and youth stone dead,
>   I'd toddle safely home and die—in bed.[198]

Sassoon's sarcasm became more bitter as the war dragged on. And the intent behind his words became clearer and more focused. With a heavy, harsh realism Sassoon obviously was trying to shock his public into an awareness of the sordid life on the front. "Suicide in the Trenches" is a good reflection of his thinking at that moment:

> I knew a simple soldier boy
> Who grinned at life in empty joy,
> Slept soundly through the lonesome dark,
> And whistled early with the lark.
>
> In winter trenches, cowed and glum,
> With crumps and lice and lack of rum,

> He put a bullet through his brain.
> No one spoke of him again.
>
> You smug-faced crowds with kindling eye
> Who cheer when soldier lads march by,
> Sneak home and pray you'll never know
> The hell where youth and laughter go.[199]

Sassoon's war poetry manifests a certain driven quality, constantly trying to relate more of the stark naked truth of the war and be ever more shocking, forceful, persuasive, more intimate. It was as though he were under the sentence of the last poem by Charles Sorley (1895–1915), found in his kit after he was killed by a sniper.

> When you see millions of the mouthless dead
> Across your dreams in pale battalions go,
> Say not soft things as other men have said.[200]

Despite Sassoon's firm but unpopular anti-war stance, he went on to become one of the best-known of the English war poets. It is a laurel he shares with only few others, among them his protégé and friend Wilfred Owen (1893–1918), whom many consider to be the leading English-language poet of the war.

The two met at Craiglockhart War Hospital, where Owen was also being treated for neurasthenia. He recovered and went back to active duty, being awarded the Military Cross for bravery, an award he had always sought as a way to justify himself as a war poet.

Owen's poetry changed dramatically after he met Sassoon. He adopted much of his mentor's style, his realism and his sense of satire, but Owen kept a certain romanticism that he had developed himself. The result was a unique synthesis that gave his poetry a potent, very distinctive sound.

Aside from a few poems that appeared in the Craiglockhart magazine, Owen never saw any of his work published. His fame arrived posthumously. He was killed only a week before the end of the war.

Anthem for Doomed Youth[201]

> What passing-bells for these who die as cattle?
>   Only the monstrous anger of the guns.
>   Only the stuttering rifles' rapid rattle
> Can patter out their hasty orisons.
> No mockeries now for them; no prayers nor bells,
>   Nor any voice of mourning save the choirs,—
> The shrill, demented choirs of wailing shells;
>   And bugles calling for them from sad shires.
> What candles may be held to speed them all?
>   Not in the hands of boys, but in their eyes
> Shall shine the holy glimmers of good-byes.
>   The pallor of girls' brows shall be their pall;

> Their flowers the tenderness of patient minds,
> And each slow dusk a drawing-down of blinds.

For English speakers, the anti-war poetry of Owen and Sassoon set a new paradigm, one that has stood the test of time. Their poetry is still known and studied long after the events that shaped it have become forgotten ripples in the wide flow of history. Shortly before his death in the trenches, Owen wrote:

> My subject is war, and the pity of war,
> The Poetry is in the pity.[202]

Even the alleged arch-imperialist Rudyard Kipling (1865–1936) became sufficiently disillusioned by the war to compose a fitting epitaph:

> If any question why we died,
> Tell them, because our fathers lied.[203]

* * *

Few poets had access to the trenches on the French side like René Arcos (1881–1959), a French pacifist. As the war correspondent for the *Chicago Daily News* he could come and go as he liked. His pockets were always full of poems, which he handed out to the soldiers he met, always coupling them with a request that the soldiers pass them down the line.

His poem "Les Morts" is yet another echo of the "brotherhood of the battlefield" theme. Censored many times by the military authorities, it was still published in numerous newspapers as well as circulated in the trenches:

> *Serrés les uns contre les autres*
> *Les morts sans haine et sans drapeau,*
> *Cheveux plaqués de sang caillé,*
> *Les morts sont tous d'un seul côté.*[204]
>
> (Close to each other
> The dead without hate and without flag,
> Their hair flattened by curdled blood,
> The dead are all on the same side.)

Another French poet who addressed the concept of the universal soldier was Eugène Camille Délong (1882–1954), who wrote under the pseudonym of Genold. For him, all soldiers were the same, no matter what flag they followed. Forced to kill his fellow man, a soldier died a slow but certain death.

> *Soldat, ô assassin de toi-même*
> *L'Univers n'existe qu'en toi.*
> *Chaque ennemi abattu*
> *est un peu de toi-même qui meurt,*
> *le sang du troupeau est un peu de ton sang,*
> *et chaque jour qui passe et chaque mort qui tombe*
> *te rapproche du néant.*[205]

> (Soldier, you who are your own murderer
> The universe only exists inside you.
> Every enemy killed
> is a little bit of yourself dying,
> the blood of the herd is a little bit of your blood,
> and every day that passes and every dead man that falls
> brings you closer to nothingness.)

* * *

On the other side of the barbed wire, German poets were writing much the same kind of verse, a humanistic yet equally gruesome echo that circulated widely both in the trenches and in the cities.

Georg Heym (1187–1912), for instance, prophetically saw war hovering just beyond the horizon, a demon rising from the collective unconsciousness, and was perhaps the first German poet to put a tragic label on the face of modern warfare. Just before he died he wrote:

> Now he has arisen: he, who slept so long,
> from the depth arisen, out of arches strong.
> Huge he stands and unknown in the twilight land,
> and the moon he crushes in his blackened hand.[206]

Once the fighting began, others soon followed Heym's lead. Gerrit Engelke (1890–1918), a housepainter, wrote poetry at night. He had been working in Denmark when war was declared. Following the call to the flag, he immediately returned to Germany and enlisted in the army. While in the trenches he once wrote to his father that Walt Whitman had been his muse and inspiration. "He is always in the breast pocket of my tunic."[207] After spending years at the front, Engelke wrote "To the Soldiers of the Great War." It was to be one of his final poems. He was killed only a few weeks before the war ended.

> Rise up! Out of trenches, muddy holes, bunkers, quarries!
> Up out of mud and fire, chalk dust, stench of bodies!
> Off with your steel helmets!
> Throw your rifles away!
> Enough of this murderous enmity!
> [...]
> Frenchmen,
> Whether from Bordeaux, Brest, Garonne;
> Ukrainian, Turk, Serb, Austrian;
> I appeal to all soldiers of the Great War—
> American, Russian, Britisher—
> You were brave men. Now throw away national pride.
> The green sea is rising. Just take my hand.[208]

Life—and death—in the trenches became perhaps the greatest shared experience of the war, a common hardship that every soldier at the front endured no matter what flag he fought under. Like a *peste* it spread across the no-man's-lands of the war, making the soldiers on both sides more alike than different, their mutual foe disease, mud, and the freezing winter.

Heinrich Lersch (1889–1936) addressed the spirit of man, any man, any soldier. After spending several years in the trenches he concluded that many poets, whatever their nationality, thought and felt as he did. Most, he realized, had made the trek from patriotic idealism through the horrors of the battlefield to some sort of anti-war idealism. Lersch was no different from the others. In a letter to a friend he described himself as having become *tout à fait européen* (completely European),[209] and at the same time he published "Brothers":

> Before our wire there lay for long a dead man full in view:
> The sun burned down upon him, he was cooled by wind and dew.
>
> Day after day upon his pallid face I used to stare,
> And ever grew more certain: 'twas my brother lying there.
>
> And often as I looked at him outstretched before my gaze,
> I seemed to hear his merry voice from far-off peaceful days.
>
> And in my dreams I heard him crying out and weeping sore,
> "Ah, brother, dearest brother, do you love me then no more?"
>
> At last I risked the bullets and the shrapnel-rain, and ran
> And fetched him in, and buried ... an unknown fellow man.
>
> My eyes deceived me, but my heart proclaimed the truth to me:
> In every dead man's countenance a brother's face I see.[210]

For Lersch to become "completely European" meant he had gone through a dramatic transformation, a total change of perspective. When war was declared, like Engelke, Lersch had volunteered for the army in the first flush of patriotism. His early poems reflected that sense of duty. In one, he so vividly painted a verbal portrait of a departing soldier that it became one of the most popular German poems of the war. He concluded with:

> *Denn wir gehen, das Vaterland zu schützen*
> (For we are going to protect the Fatherland).[211]

And in the refrain of a popular song at the time he wrote: "Germany must live, even if we must die."[212] But months in the trenches changed Lersch, as it did so many men. Patriotism and glory were left behind, and the new shared enemy became death, death from disease, the winter and the indiscriminate machine-gun fire. Soldiers, all soldiers, he realized, were condemned men, waiting in the mud and slime for the inevitable sentence to be delivered.

Poetry was not confined to just the trenches in France and Belgium. On the lesser fronts of the war, particularly in the Middle East, the cold and mud were replaced by thirst and scorching sands. But the meaninglessness of battle remained a common theme. The hollowness of purpose haunted them all. An anonymous British poet wrote:

> The hot red rocks of Aden
> Stand from their burnished sea;
> The bitter sands of Aden
> Lie shimmering in their lee.
>
> We have no joy of battle,
> No honour here is won;
> Our little fights are nameless,
> With Turk and sand and gun.[213]

There is no way to judge the effect this outpouring of bitter, impassioned words had upon society. Accurate public opinion polling was still decades away. But it is certain that in general the men in the trenches read poems and those that they liked, which expressed what they thought and felt, they passed on so that there was a more or less constant circulation up and down the front.

At home, in all the belligerent countries, not only was poetry published and read, but particularly popular poems were often subsequently discussed in articles and letters to the editor. One poem could easily spawn a whole debate about meaning and interpretation, subjects that could easily overlap into discussions about the purpose of the war and its conduct.

An astute observer had no choice but to conclude that a substantial segment of the population had become war weary and ready to look for ways to end the carnage other than *"La paix ne peut sortir que de la victoire."* (Peace can only come through victory.)

* * *

If the generals and politicians weren't going to make peace, then the men on the front lines would, and some in fact did even on the remote battlefields of the Middle East.

In what is now an almost forgotten theater of the war, at Gallipoli (1915), on the Dardanelles not far from Istanbul, Allied and Turkish soldiers fought each other to a standstill, and before it was over nearly half a million soldiers were casualties.[214]

With one notable exception there are no records of truces or live-and-let-live agreements here such as one finds on the Western Front. Apparently the fighting at Gallipoli was so intense and bitter that there was hardly a propitious moment for one to occur. One Australian officer wrote in his memoirs:

> We have been amusing ourselves by trying to discover the longest period of absolute quiet. We have been fighting now continuously for 22 days, all day and all night, and most of us think that the longest period during which there was absolutely no sound of gun or rifle fire throughout the whole of that time was 10 seconds. One man says he was able on one occasion to count fourteen but nobody believes him.[215]

Nonetheless, after one exceptionally terrible battle, with thousands of dead and dying lying between the lines, Colonel Aubrey Herbert (1880–1923) crept close to the Turkish trenches, weighted a note with a rock, then threw it over the barbed wire to the Turks. Herbert was an odd figure to find crawling through the mud and gore. A Member of Parliament who had turned soldier, he was also a poet and scholar of the Middle East who spoke fluent Turkish. In his diary he described the battlefield:

> The dead fill acres of ground, mostly killed in one big attack [...]. They fill the myrtle-grown gullies. One saw the result of machine-gun fire very clearly; entire companies annihilated—not wounded, but killed, their heads doubled under them with the impetus of their rush and both hands clasping their bayonets. It was as if God had breathed in their faces, as "The Assyrian came down like a wolf on the fold."[216]

Over 4,000 dead filled the no-man's-land, a huge killing field that became a nightmare for those who survived the bloodbath. Soldiers on both sides were stilled by the sight. Everyone spoke in undertones.

Herbert proposed a cease-fire that would stop the fighting long enough so that both sides could retrieve their dead and wounded. The Turks threw back their reply, suggesting a meeting of officers. A Turkish officer later whispered to Herbert, "At this spectacle even the most gentle must feel savage, and even the most savage must weep."

As a show of good faith, Herbert offered himself as a hostage. While British and Turkish officers worked out the terms of the temporary truce, Herbert was led blindfolded through the Turkish lines to a café where he was served an elegant meal. There was good faith on both sides.

The truce extended along the breadth of the front. For nine hours warfare ceased. White flags were planted on the parapets and those who entered the no-man's-land wore white armbands. Turks and Allied soldiers hurried to bury their dead, often making them share a common, nameless grave.

While those still standing were quietly covering up the fallen in the mud of shallow graves, Herbert and a Turkish captain sauntered through the stench of the dead trying to remain composed, for they realized that the success of the truce depended on their demeanor.

The Turkish captain, who had witnessed the carnage, pointed to some graves and told Herbert, "That's politics." Then he gestured to a pile of dead bodies and said, "That's diplomacy. God pity all of us poor soldiers."[217]

Herbert told the Turkish captain: "We must take care that nobody loses his head. Your men won't shoot you and my men won't shoot me, so we must walk about, otherwise a gun will go off and everybody will get shot."[218]

When the fields were cleared and the bodies interred, the troops began to fraternize, exchanging badges and cigarettes and trading Turkish grapes and sweets for British tinned milk.

Herbert and the Turkish captain strolled through the no-man's-land, stopping to translate for one group of soldiers after another, helping the Turks and Australians to communicate, and letting them arrange their own private rules of warfare after the truce was over, signals so the other side would know when they were shooting to kill and when they were shooting to miss.

As the nine hours allotted for the truce neared its end, the soldiers returned to their trenches, took off their white armbands and prepared for war.

Herbert was the last man to return to the trench. As he bid the Turks farewell, the Turkish captain left him with a proverb: "Smiling may you go and smiling may you come again."[219] Herbert replied with another Turkish proverb: "An old friend cannot be an enemy."

The truce was successful, perhaps too successful. The war was not easily restarted. The soldiers in the trenches had developed a kind of battle-hardened camaraderie that spanned the desolate no-man's-land. Both Turks and Allied troops, British, Australians and New Zealanders, had lost their image as propaganda monsters, godless fanatics, who killed for pleasure and took no prisoners. Instead, they became men who fought reluctantly, for they had all come to realize that the enemy was merely a reflection of themselves.

* * *

Feelers from the Turks seeking a separate peace began early in the war, the first arriving just after New Year's in 1915. At the close of the holiday season the Russian ambassador in London, Count Benckendorff (1846–1917), informed the British Foreign Office that some members of the Young Turk party had made contact with the official in charge of the Russian embassy in Constantinople requesting assistance. When they were refused, they asked to have their petition passed on to the British and the French. The British ignored the request. So did the French.

In August of the same year Vahan Cardishian, the Imperial Ottoman Commissioner to the San Francisco Exhibition, made contact with American officials to say that he was confident that a separate peace could be concluded if the British would initiate the process. The request was duly passed on to the British, who once again ignored it. The following month the Turkish Minister in Stockholm asked a Japanese diplomat to make inquiries if the Entente would be interested in making a separate peace with Turkey. However, before negotiations could get started, a few days later the same Minister announced that it had suddenly become too late to negotiate. A Turko-Bulgarian Convention had just been signed, giving the Germans direct land access to Turkey and thus sealing Turkey's fate as a member of the Central Powers.

At the end of 1915, the Russians, through Armenian sources, received the information that Çemal Pasha (one of the triumvirate who ruled the Ottoman Empire) was ready to lead a revolt against both the government in Constantinople and the Germans if he received support from the Allies. He presented a list of terms, the most important of which were military supplies and weapons and an agreement that after the war the Turkish Empire in the Middle East would be left intact. Since at that point the British and the French were committed to victory on the battlefield and believed that they could achieve it, they disregarded the request. More feelers arrived in 1916, one from a Turkish general in Paris, another from diplomats in Switzerland. The Turks gradually softened their position, making it clear they were willing to give up Constantinople, their last toehold in Europe. However, once again all the proposals were ignored.

Had one of these feelers been nurtured it might well have matured into serious negotiations or, at a minimum, stopped the fighting, if only for a short time. But the politicians in London and Paris were a long way from the reality of the trenches. The daily toll of lives lost or crippled seemed to have little effect on their decisions. Their gaze was fixed on the geopolitical future, their decisions veiled in wartime secrecy. They paid no penalty for letting peace slip through their fingers.

Turkish peace overtures found a more receptive audience in America. Two days before the United States entered the war in 1917 the American ambassador to the Ottoman Empire, Abraham Elkus (1867–1947), cabled Washington that although the Turkish military was pro-German, many civilian groups clearly favored peace. Even the ruling elite, he reported, "were beginning to suspect that the Germans designed to rule Turkey after the war."[220] The stumbling blocks to negotiations were two German armored cruisers, the *Goeben* and the *Breslau*, which were anchored in the Dardanelles. Should Turkey negotiate with the Allies, the warships' guns would be turned on Constantinople.

The same day this information was received in Washington, Henry Morgenthau (1856–1946), who previously had been the ambassador to Turkey (1913–1916),[221] met with the American Secretary of State, Robert Lansing (1864–1928). Morgenthau had his own plan to conclude a separate peace with Turkey.[222]

The scheme rested on Morgenthau's friendly relations with the Turkish ruling elite. Despite the fact that as ambassador he had been outraged by the Armenian genocide and had not hesitated to tell the world about it, he claimed that he had remained on friendly terms with the rulers of the Turkish state. Whether this was in fact the case is debatable. Some scholars[223] have argued that Morgenthau was indeed a persona non grata in Constaninople. Ambassador Elkus had reported that Enver Pasha, the key Ottoman on whom Morgenthau was counting, would be the least likely of the Turkish elite to defy the Germans. It was the ambassador's opinion that Enver Pasha wanted Turkey "to follow the German lead and advice not only in all military matters but even in those not of purely military character."[224]

In any case, Morgenthau proposed that he go to Switzerland and arrange a secret meeting with the Turkish leaders. He would then propose a separate peace and offer the Turks generous terms, which might include a large sum of money. In return, the Turks would quietly open the Dardanelles to Allied submarines, which would sneak up on the two German armored cruisers and torpedo them before they had a chance to take reprisals.

The plan was clever, ingenious, and sufficiently audacious that Morgenthau was convinced it just might work. Although skeptical at first—Lansing's initial reaction was "You don't really mean this, do you?"—he eventually conceded that the scheme had merit and agreed to present it to President Wilson. Much later Lansing admitted: "I did not believe there was one chance in 50 of success, [but] I thought we ought not to ignore any chance, however slight, of gaining so tremendous an advantage as would result from alienating Turkey from the Teutonic Alliance."[225]

A few days later President Wilson approved the plan. He wrote: "If it succeeds it would be a decisive factor in the war, if it failed, we would be no worse off than before."[226]

Strangely enough, the plan was not totally original. The British had turned down a similar proposal the year before whereby a group of Young Turks offered to open the Dardanelles to the British fleet in return for a substantial sum—4 million pounds (over 200 million pounds today) was mentioned—and a safe passage to New York. It is doubtful that Morgenthau knew about this.

But before Morgenthau could leave for Switzerland the British had to agree. Reversing their earlier position the Foreign Office at first favored the plan and suggested that Egypt would be a better venue given the large number of spies in Switzerland. Secretary of State Lansing agreed and announced the official cover of Morgenthau's trip, a fact-finding mission to the Levant to search for ways to ameliorate the condition of the Palestinian Jews. Since Morgenthau's anti–Zionist views were well-known, to make the mission sound more plausible it was decided to send Felix Frankfurter[227] (1882–1965), a Harvard law professor, and Eliahu Lewin-Epstein,[228] a New York businessman, with him. Both Frankfurter and Lewin-Epstein were prominent Zionists. Another member of the group was Morgenthau's trusted aide, Arshag K. Schmavonian[229] (?–1922), an Armenian.

Frankfurter reluctantly agreed to join the mission. In his judgment Morgenthau's motivations were far from altruistic. Frankfurter later wrote that the former ambassador "was incapable of continuity of thought, or effort, and I soon saw that his preoccupation was, 'who will be at the green table?'—the green table meaning the peace conference. I soon realized that his ego was enormous, insatiable."[230]

The secrecy surrounding Morgenthau's trip began to slowly evaporate. Many Zionists started to guess the real purpose of the mission and realized that a separate peace with Turkey would probably mean that much of the Ottoman

Empire would be left intact, certainly the Asian part. This was the last thing the Palestinian Jews, Arabs, Armenians and other minorities wanted. If the Ottoman Empire was dismembered there was at least a possibility they could obtain independence or, at a minimum, some form of autonomy, but to be left under Turkish rule went against everything they had fought for.

The British, French and Americans agreed to meet and join forces at Gibraltar, then travel together to Egypt. However, at roughly the same time, in fact, two weeks before Morgenthau and his party sailed from New York, the British decided to invade the Middle East and seize Jerusalem. Hence, there was no point in making a separate truce with Turkey, who would certainly want to retain much, if not all, of the region. War-weary France might welcome a separate peace, and Russia as well, since they would probably get control of the Straits of Dardanelles, but the British were now committed to the destruction of the Ottoman Empire. The Foreign Office suddenly decided that the Morgenthau peace plan was "foredoomed to failure" and ceased to actively support it.

The result was that the British and the Americans appeared to be at odds, the Americans sending out serious peace feelers and the British refusing to back them. For the British, the way out of this slightly embarrassing situation was to persuade Morgenthau the moment was not right for negotiations and to turn back. Thus the British sent Dr. Chaim Weizmann[231] (1874–1952), president of the British Zionist Federation and much later to become the first President of Israel, to Gibraltar "to talk to Mr. Morgenthau and to keep on talking"[232] until he had talked him out of his mission.

Once in Gibraltar, from the first meeting Dr. Weizmann was forceful, undiplomatic and persuasive as he did his best to demonstrate that Morgenthau's plan for a separate peace was ill timed and not based on political realities. Certainly from a Zionist perspective it wasn't. A Jewish Palestine would fare far better under Allied or British rule than under Turkish. Dr. Weizmann described the proceedings:

> It was midsummer, and very hot. We had been given one of the casements in the Rock for our sessions, and the windows were kept open. As Mr. Morgenthau did not speak French, and Colonel Weyl did not speak English, we had to fall back on German. And the Tommies on guard marched up and down outside, no doubt convinced that we were a pack of spies who had been lured into a trap, to be court-martialed the next morning and shot out of hand.[233]

After two days of constant meetings Dr. Weizmann prevailed.[234] The trip to Egypt was canceled and the participants issued a joint communiqué, a face-saving statement: "The time is not now ripe to open channels of communication with Turkish leaders. [...] attempts at negotiation now would be construed as a sign of Allied weakness."[235]

When he heard this, Colonel House, President Wilson's trusted advisor, wrote to Morgenthau: "In my opinion, they [the British emissaries] should have been seen upon your return trip rather than now [at Gibraltar]."²³⁶ Had Morgenthau taken Colonel House's advice, the outcome of his mission may well have been very different.

In essence, military expedience and minority interests had effectively canceled what might have been a real chance for a separate peace with Turkey.

* * *

At this point in time, the Turks were, according to the British Foreign Office, genuinely "nibbling"²³⁷ at a separate peace. While the preparations for Morgenthau's trip were being made, in Berne, Switzerland, Horace Rumbold (1869–1941), a British diplomat, received a statement from a Turkish opposition party, the Ottoman League for Peace, who wanted to establish contact and discuss the possible terms for a separate peace. Although nothing came of those discussions they were still a clear indication that the mood in Turkey was changing.

A few weeks later, when the Morgenthau mission was at sea on board the SS *Buenos Aires* bound for Gibraltar, Dr. Noureddin Bey, a prominent member of the Turkish elite and a personal friend of Talaat Pasha (1874–1921, one of the ruling triumvirate) arrived in Switzerland, made contact with a British agent and informed him that Talaat Pasha and Vehir Bey, the former commander of the Third Turkish Army, wished to send emissaries to Switzerland to discuss a scheme whereby Britain would let Turkey recover a portion of Macedonia as compensation for future changes in Syria, Mesopotamia and Armenia. In other words, the door was open for negotiations with one of the three leaders of the Ottoman Empire.

Almost on the same day that the British Foreign Office sent Dr. Weizmann to Gibraltar to put an end to Mongenthau's peace mission, they also sent Aubrey Herbert to Switzerland to investigate the terms of a separate peace. Thus the British were pursuing two completely different goals, war and peace, at the same time.

Once he arrived in Geneva Herbert went straight to Interlaken, where he met Dr. Noureddin Bey. The two men strolled in the garden of the Kursaal (then a spa, now a casino) and discussed the situation.

Dr. Noureddin Bey came straight to the point and reported that Talaat Pasha was definitely interested in peace, as he had reached the conclusion that there was little hope of a victory for the Central Powers. Afterwards, Herbert wrote in his journal that he believed everything that had been said had been in good faith. The Turks, he was certain, were ready to begin talks that would lead to a compromise peace. In his report to the British government Herbert noted: "Dr. Noureddin Bey should return to Turkey where he would see Talaat. Talaat would then appoint an authoritative person with credentials who would journey to Switzerland on the grounds of ill-health accompanied by Dr. Noureddin as his physician [...]. On arriving in Switzerland this envoy would enter into direct relations with the British Government."²³⁸

Herbert and Dr. Noureddin Bey had gone further and discussed at length what a negotiated peace might look like. Herbert also wrote in his report: "If [...] the Turks see a chance [...] that their country will be ringed round by a chain of semi-autonomous friendly Moslem States, half the reason that compelled them to continue fighting will have gone."²³⁹

Since it was well-known that Herbert was a Turkophile, his objectivity was immediately questioned. The British War Cabinet was reluctant to send a peace emissary to Switzerland, which, they were afraid, would be perceived as weakness, a lack of will to continue the war. This was confirmed by several other "experts" on the Middle East who also felt that before any further discussions could take place Great Britain should also consult with its allies, the French, the Russians, the Italians and the Americans.

Events, however, quickly muted the issue, slamming shut the window of opportunity on what Herbert had called "a golden moment." Before the British were ready to make a decision, Russia was consumed by a revolution and her armies disintegrated. En masse, soldiers left their weapons on the battlefield and began the long march home. Suddenly the Turks had one less war to fight. Tens of thousands of men were released to fight elsewhere. Instead of seeking a separate peace, the Pashas turned their back on negotiation and planned new military offensives in the Levant.

Although Aubrey Herbert did not succeed in creating a peace of compromise, many of his exploits were reborn into a fictional life in the spy novel *Greenmantle*²⁴⁰ by John Buchan (1875–1940). Herbert and Buchan were close friends and undoubtedly with Herbert's permission the author novelized many of the stories he must have heard. Buchan is best known for his book, and later film, *The 39 Steps*.²⁴¹

* * *

While Aubrey Herbert was in Switzerland, the British sent a third mission to explore a separate peace with Turkey.

Basil Zaharoff (1849–1936),²⁴² a prominent shareholder of Vickers, one of the largest arms manufacturers in Great Britain, had connections all over the world, including Ottoman Turkey. He moved easily through the Balkans and became known as a kind of "evil genius" who profited from the misery of war, selling arms to anyone, governments, insurrectionists, bandits, the prototype of the "merchant of death," a man whose only principle was making money. He once commented to a journalist that he helped create wars only so he could sell arms to both sides. Ruthless and unscrupulous, Zaharoff had in fact clearly sided with the Entente and did what he could, even spending some of his own fortune, to further the Allied cause. This is not to say that Zaharoff suddenly became patriotic. He was apparently immune to such passions. Coming from the gutters of Constantinople, he sought something his wealth could not buy, respectability, a formal acknowledgment of a service rendered, an award, a decoration, a title. By trying to negotiate a separate peace with the Turks, Zaharoff hoped to elevate himself to become a peer of the British mandarins. And he did not try to hide his motivation. It was clearly appended to many of his "reports" to the British government. Probably the best chance of ending the war in the Middle East through a negotiated settlement rested in the hands of a man who was not in the least interested in how many lives might be saved but only in his own, very personal aggrandizement, a silver starburst that he could pin on his chest. In the end, for services he did not render he received the Grand Cross of the British Empire and the Knight Grand Cross of the Order of the Bath.

In April 1916, over a year before Morgenthau arrived in Gibraltar, Zaharoff met in Marseille a Turkish emissary, Abdul Kerim Bey, who represented Enver Pasha, Minister of War and one of the most powerful men in the country. Zaharoff described their conversation: "He [Abdul Kerim Bey] said that all talk of a separate peace with Turkey was out of the question because the Germans held Constantinople in their iron grip, but, added he, why not open the Dardanelles to you treacherously? What is it worth to the Allies in American dollars payable in America? Would you not be delighted to take Enver and 40 or 50 of the Party straight to N.Y.?"[243]

The proposal went to the British government, who discussed it at length and even at one point considered offering 50,000 pounds (the equivalent of over a million in today's pounds), before they decided it was too risky. For one thing, if the British fleet did pass the Dardanelles into the Sea of Marmara and the Turks decided to close the straits behind them there would be very little the British could do to open them.

Abdul Kerim Bey sent a message that he wished to negotiate further in Andrianople (known today as Edirne), but when Zaharoff did not reply he sent word that the offer had been withdrawn.

In the spring of 1917, it appears that the Turks were again in the mood to negotiate and Abdul Kerim Bey contacted Zaharoff, who was then living in Paris. Zaharoff, in turn, reported to the British that Abdul Kerim was "throwing out his hooks again."[244] Lloyd George, the Prime Minister, dealt with the matter himself and wrote directly to Zaharoff telling him "it would be very worthwhile your undertaking the journey to Switzerland and finding out all you could about the possibilities."[245]

At almost the same time the British were exploring Zaharoff's contacts, they were sending Chaim Weizmann to Gibraltar to scuttle the Morgenthau mission and Herbert Aubrey to Switzerland to make his inquiries from another source about a separate peace.

Zaharoff arrived in Switzerland to find Abdul Kerim Bey waiting for him at the hotel. He had missed Enver Pasha, the Turkish Minister of War, by one day. Abdul Kerim told Zaharoff: "Things have changed [since the previous year] [...] Turkey was ruined and lost and [...] Enver & Co. were willing to throw up the sponge on "reasonable conditions" and get on with their lives."[246]

The terms were clear and incredibly precise, so many millions for the withdrawal of Turkish troops from Mesopotamia, more for evacuating Palestine, for allowing the British fleet to pass through the Dardanelles, and still more to occupy the commanding forts, et cetera. The total was approximately 10 million U.S. dollars, over 200 million in today's dollars.

Zaharoff took the message to London, where it received the immediate attention of the Prime Minister. The large sum didn't seem to be a problem. However, the British did insist that before any money was transferred there had be a direct meeting with Enver Pasha. Zaharoff agreed. He believed Abdul Kerim Bey was "a rogue" and questioned "what reliance should be placed on any of the Forty Thieves."[247]

Making it clear that he was working for a reward he had code-named "chocolate," a distinction from the British honors system, Zaharoff returned to Geneva.

Zaharoff also thoroughly enjoyed the intrigue, playing the spy and living on his wits. Once, on the request of Lloyd George, Zaharoff put on a Bulgarian army doctor's uniform and traveled through Germany to Berlin and Potsdam. It's not clear what he did or even how long he was there, but it was sufficiently important that when he returned Georges Clemenceau (1841–1929), the French Prime Minister, was waiting for him at a railway station in Paris.

In Geneva Zaharoff met Abdul Kerim Bey at the usual hotel, but this time the negotiations immediately turned sour. According to Zaharoff, after a few terse formalities the Turk delivered an ultimatum: "*C'est à prendre ou à laisser* (Take it or leave it!)."[248] Then, he refused to speak any further and abruptly, but courteously, ended the meeting. Zaharoff favored "taking it" and taking a chance, but Lloyd George refused. Perhaps one reason for Abdul Kerim Bey's truculence might have been that he had just heard that the Turks intended to launch a new offensive in the Middle East. A military victory would certainly strengthen his bargaining position. The offensive failed and the military situation returned to stagnation.

Three months later Zaharoff received word that once again Abdul Kerim Bey would be in Geneva and wished to meet. This time Zaharoff carried with him $2 million, which the British had authorized him to hand over as a down payment, in fact a bribe, a token to prove they were serious about negotiating and paying for a separate peace. Only a few people, besides Lloyd George and Zaharoff, knew about the money. Even the War Cabinet had been kept in the dark.

At first Abdul Kerim Bey refused the bribe. He appeared to be just testing the water, making sure that the British were still ready to negotiate. He announced that before he could seriously discuss the terms of a truce first he had to consult with Enver Pasha. Zaharoff returned to Paris to wait.

The answer came less than a week later. Zaharoff sent a message off to London asking for the British negotiating position and including of course a persistent request for "chocolate"; then he hurried back to Geneva to meet Abdul Kerim Bey for the fourth time.

Enver Pasha was now willing to talk and accept the bribe. Thus Zaharoff paid $500,000 to Abdul Kerim Bey and $1,500,000 into an account in the Crédit Suisse et Français for Enver Pasha. The two men dined together, according to Zaharoff, in sumptuous surroundings, and it was agreed that the meeting with Enver Pasha would take place in Lucerne, where Enver Pasha's wife had a property, in one month's time.

In January 1918 Zaharoff met Adbul Kerim Bey in Geneva. Enver Pasha arrived the next day from Lucerne but refused to meet directly with Zaharoff. As a result, Adbul Kerim Bey shuttled back and forth carrying messages for an entire afternoon; between rooms in the same hotel or between different hotels, it is not clear. Most observers agree that this was not just a ploy. Enver Pasha was really there in Geneva, however, for one reason or another, wished to keep his distance. Using this cumbersome communication, Zaharoff and Enver Pasha discussed the basic terms for a Middle East peace, who would get what territory, and what flag would fly over it. The British, for example, were prepared to accept what they called the Egyptian solution for much of the Middle East, Palestine, Syria, and Mesopotamia, that is, a British colonial administration under a Turkish flag. For a short time during the afternoon it appeared that the entire Middle East tangle would be unraveled, then re-twisted, in a couple of hotel rooms in Geneva. But, for one reason or another, Enver Pasha, the man most responsible for the German-Ottoman alliance, suddenly got cold feet and decided to back out of the deal. He offered to pay back the bribe, which he did, in fact, do. But Adbul Kerim Bey refused to do the same. Later Zaharoff wrote in his report that "he [Adbul Kerim Bey] would not part with one piaster; [he believed] he had honestly done his share, and if E [Enver Pasha] was now backing out, through fear, it was not his fault."[249]

The next morning both Enver Pasha and Adbul Kerim Bey were gone. That short afternoon when both sides seemed ready to negotiate and make compromises had probably been the best chance for a separate peace. For most of the war the British and the Turks had been completely out of sync. When the military situation favored the Central Powers the British were ready to talk, and when the tide flowed in the other direction the Turks bargained in the Oriental fashion, starting high, then slowly, under pressure, reducing the price, selling peace as if it were a threadbare rug in the bazaar.

Zaharoff and Adbul Kerim Bey did meet one last time in Geneva six months later, but it was a standoff from the beginning. Adbul Kerim Bey now wanted more than double the original bribe money, and when Zaharoff backed off the Turk tried to peddle individual documents, for example, verbatim reports of Central Powers' war councils. The two men then spent four or five days together in one of Geneva's most luxurious hotels and left behind them nothing but a wake of platitudes and a pile of dirty dishes.

* * *

The United States did not go into the European war easily. Peace had become part of the fabric of American society. Never before had the concept carried such importance. Drawing upon the 19th-century faith in human reason and inevitable progress, peace societies bloomed in the years before World War I. People joined them by the thousands. Lawyers belonged to groups such as the Inter-Parliamentary Union and the American Society of International Lawyers. Educators supported the World Peace Foundation and the Carnegie Endowment for International Peace. Pacifists formed the core of the American Union Against Militarism and the National Council for Prevention of War. Women joined the Woman's Peace Party, which was succeeded by the United States Section of the Women's International League for Peace and Freedom. And churches created the Fellowship of Reconciliation, the American Friends Service Committee, and the Church Peace Union. These were only a few. Nearly 50 new peace organizations appeared between 1901 and 1914.

The outbreak of the European war horrified America. Mirroring public sentiment, the *New York Times* called it "the least justified of all wars since man emerged from barbarism."[250]

President Wilson told the nation: "The United States must be neutral in fact as well as in name during these days that are to try men's souls." The President went on to appeal to the country to be "impartial in thought as well as in action."[251]

For the first two years of the European war, the United States tried to be an honest broker and made several attempts to mediate the conflict. In 1916 President Wilson campaigned for a second term under the slogan of "He kept us out of the war," and it rang true. His actions had matched his words. Peace groups all over the country supported him. President Wilson had been quite categorical when he stated that "so far as I can remember, this is a government of the people, and this people is not going to choose war."[252]

Wilson won the election, but only by a hair and, in fact, the final result was in doubt for several days. The election hinged on California, and Wilson won the state by only 3,800 votes. He took New Hampshire by a mere 54. However, his opponent, Charles Evans Hughes (1862–1948), while urging greater military preparedness, also wished to keep clear of the European war. It was an unusual moment in American history. Essentially two anti-war candidates had competed for the nation's highest office. A vote for either was a clear vote for peace. In 1916 the mood in America was decidedly non-interventionist and pacifist.

At the time of Wilson's inauguration for a second term, immigrants constituted one-third of the American population. Allied and German propaganda did their best to revive old-world loyalties. Opinions about U.S. intervention were sharply polarized. More than 8 million German-Americans lived in America, and many, if not most, were sympathetic to the cause of their homeland. Meanwhile, anti–German feeling was strong among the upper classes on the Atlantic coast and was particularly intense among those with social and business connections to Britain or France. This was reflected in the financial ties to the two European blocs. American investors bought over $2 billion in bonds from the Allies but only $20 million from the Central Powers. At the same time trade with the Allies soared while that with the Central Powers dropped to almost nothing.

Despite these economic realities, most Americans were not connected to the European conflict by blood or capital and had demonstrated quite clearly that they were not interested in waging war overseas.

* * *

While millions of Europeans dueled in the trenches, for the first time in history people could actually see for themselves a war that was taking place a continent away. The movie had burst into existence and quickly demonstrated a tremendous power to mold men's minds. Attitudes could be formed or changed by what they saw on the silver screen. By 1915 perhaps as much as a quarter of the American population went to a movie theater at least once a week. Suddenly they could see (but not hear, as the first "talkie" did not appear until 1927) with painful reality the horrors of modern warfare. The legendary producer/director Thomas H. Ince (1882–1924) reportedly spent $1 million (at least $20 million in today's dollars) on the epic anti-war film *Civilization*, which took over a year to make. When it was released in 1916 it became an immediate popular success, ranking on par with *The Birth of a Nation*.

Civilization's opening title cards clearly express its anti-war message:

> [I]n nineteen centuries Civilization has failed to accept honestly the teachings of Jesus Christ. This is an allegorical story of a war that has laughed at the world's flaunting boast of a higher progress. It does not concern itself as to which side is in the right or wrong, but deals with those ranks which are paying, the grim penalty—the ranks of Humanity. If the awful trail of battle stretches vividly through the scenes of the narrative, it is in the hope that a shocked and appalled world may henceforth devote itself more earnestly in the cause of peace. Let our Civilization not be a mockery of our cherished ideals, but rather a synonym of that glorious work—Humanity. Dedicated to that vast, pitiful army whose tears have girdled the universe—the mothers of the dead.

The plotline is fanciful and slightly convoluted, but audiences apparently liked it, for it was the right message at the right time. A submarine commander refuses to torpedo a passenger ship even though it is carrying munitions for his country's enemies and destroys his submarine instead. He is then rescued from damnation by the spirit of Jesus Christ and returns to life. The commander is put on trial by the King and sentenced to death. Thousands of women gather at the palace singing songs of peace and pleading with the King to end the war. The King visits the cell of the condemned commander and finds him dead. But Christ emerges from the commander's body. In the most famous scene of the film Jesus takes the King on a tour of the battlefield. It was, in fact, the first time Jesus Christ was depicted as a character in a motion picture. As they walk together through the carnage of modern war Christ asks the King: "See here thy handiwork? Under thy reign, thy domain hath become a raging hell!" The King realizes his error and ends the war. A peace treaty is signed and the soldiers return to their homes.

A similar anti-war theme animated Nazimova's (1879–1945)[253] film *War Brides*, which was based on her successful stage play and marked her film debut.

The plot is straightforward. A young woman's newly married husband, a soldier, is sent to the front. When she receives word of his death her first impulse is suicide. However, she is pregnant and accepts her new responsibility. When she hears that the King, who has passed an edict that women must bear more children for future wars, will pass through her village she organizes the women for a march of protest against the war. Dressed in black, she leads a long procession to meet the monarch. Soldiers try to turn her back, but she comes face to face with the monarch, then kills herself and her unborn child. The title card proclaims: "If you will not give us women the right to vote for or against war, I shall not bear a child for such a country!"

War Brides ran in New York for several months, then went on general release. In a review of the film the *New York Times* said that "she [Nazimova] knows how to express herself in terms of the film. Her marvelously mobile face, capable of indicating varying shades of emotion, especially those of sorrow, is a priceless asset [...]. So there was some reason for the word 'Success' on the floral offerings in the lobby."[254]

When America entered World War I suddenly the pacifist theme of *War Brides* became extremely unpopular. The film was withdrawn in April 1917. The censors noted that "the philosophy of this picture is so easily misunderstood by unthinking people that it has been found necessary to withdraw it from circulation for the duration of the war." Undismayed, Lewis Selznik (1870–1933), the producer, had new titles written that set the story in Germany, then sent the film back out to theaters, where it continued to make money.

Undoubtedly the most successful American anti-war film of the era was based on the 1916 novel *The Four Horsemen of the Apocalypse* (*Los Cuatro jinetes del Apocalipsis*) by the Spanish author Vincente Blasco Ibáñez (1867–1928). He had been working as a war correspondent in France when the French President, Raymond Poincaré (1860–1934), personally asked him to use the Battle of the Marne as inspiration for a novel depicting the horrors of war. *The Four Horsemen of the Apocalypse* was the result. The book became an instant best seller as well as an international success. Ibáñez became more well-known abroad than in his own native Spain.

The title of the book was taken from the Bible, the Book of Revelations 6:1–8. The four horsemen precede the beast of the Apocalypse, the end of everything. The first horseman is Plague, riding on a white steed; the second, War, astride a red charger, the third, Famine, mounted on a black stallion; and the fourth, Death, riding on a pale-colored horse. Horrid monsters and deformities were believed to swarm above their heads, "like a repulsive escort." Meanwhile, as one of the characters announces: "God is asleep, forgetting the world.... It will be a long time before he awakes, and while he sleeps the four feudal horsemen of the Beast will course through the land as its only lords."[255]

With the presence of this fourfold doom as a backdrop, Ibáñez hammered home his anti-war theme through a heart-wrenching story about a family and their unconditional love and tragic losses. There is no mistaking the author's message. A carnage has been unleashed that makes it difficult to claim that the modern world is civilized. Barbarism, depravity and destruction, both physical and moral, are the horrors facing mankind. Ibáñez wrote: "Poor Humanity, crazed with fear, was fleeing in all directions on hearing the thundering pace of the Plague, War, Hunger and Death. Men and women, young and old, were knocking each other down and falling to the ground overwhelmed by terror, astonishment and desperation."[256]

The book sold over half a million copies in the first year. The *New York Times* wrote that *The Four Horsemen of the Apocalypse* was "the greatest novel the world has seen in many years. [...] [A] thinking reader may see in it the way toward molding a new national life that will make war forever impossible. [...] [T]he most absorbing story you ever read, as the critics say. It is the one novel of the war that will be valued more and more as the years pass."[257] According to *Publishers Weekly*, *The Four Horsemen of the Apocalypse* became the most read novel in the United States in 1919.

The movie version starring Rudolph Valentino was also an immediate commercial success, one of the first films to gross more than a million dollars at the domestic box office.[258] In fact, it grossed $4.5 million and turned Valentino into a star.

It is impossible to measure the impact of the book and the film. Certainly they were read and seen by millions. This was very different from the usual anti-war fare of an impassioned speaker addressing the already converted, a politician haranguing the party faithful, or a pamphlet passed out on street corners. *The*

Four Horsemen of the Apocalypse spoke to the general public en masse. With a believable authenticity it delivered an anti-war message that was unmistakable, a warning dressed in the most melodramatic form possible, yet apparently highly effective and persuasive. Many, both men and women, left the cinema in tears as though for the first time they had experienced the terrible realities of war. Ibáñez may well have done more for the propagation of anti-war sentiment in America than any other individual.

* * *

In 1915 the song, "I Didn't Raise My Boy to Be a Soldier" appeared, another reflection of the American pacifistic mood:

> Ten million soldiers to the war have gone.
> Who may never return again.
> Ten million mothers' hearts must break,
> For the ones who died in vain.
> Head bowed down in sorrow in her lonely years,
> I heard a mother murmur thro' her tears:
>
> *Chorus*:
> > I didn't raise my boy to be a soldier,
> > I brought him up to be my pride and joy,
> > Who dares to put a musket on his shoulder,
> > To shoot some other mother's darling boy?
>
> Let nations arbitrate their future troubles,
> It's time to lay the sword and gun away,
> There'd be no war today,
> If mothers all would say,
> I didn't raise my boy to be a soldier.
>
> *(Chorus)*
>
> What victory can cheer a mother's heart,
> When she looks at her blighted home?
> What victory can bring her back,
> All she cared to call her own?
> Let each mother answer in the year to be,
> Remember that my boy belongs to me!
>
> *(Chorus)*

It became a top hit for several months, and sold more than 700,000 copies of sheet music, making it the first commercially successful anti-war song. The sheet music carried the headline "A Mother's Plea for Peace" and a color drawing of a mother and son sitting at the hearth, the son kneeling while the mother clasps him. Over their heads a troop of soldiers marches toward a chaotic battle scene. One feminist writer[259] claimed that the face of the mother bears a resemblance to Jane Addams, the famous American suffragette.

The popularity of "I Didn't Raise My Boy to Be a Soldier" roughly coincided with the campaign for the 1916 presidential election that re-elected Woodrow Wilson. His opponent, Charles Evans Hughes, although anti-war, downplayed the issue, while Wilson campaigned under the slogan: "He kept us out of war." "I Didn't Raise My Boy to Be a Soldier" is often given some of the credit for electing President Wilson, who won a very narrow victory for his second term.[260]

At the time many prominent politicians attacked the song for its obvious pacifism. Ex-President Theodore Roosevelt (1858–1919), for example, remarked that "foolish people who applaud a song entitled 'I Didn't Raise My Boy to Be a Soldier' are just the people who would also in their hearts applaud a song entitled 'I Didn't Raise My Girl to Be a Mother.'"[261]

The song was ripe for parody and many were produced, such as "I Did Not Raise My Boy to Be a Coward," "I Didn't Raise My Boy to Be a Soldier, but I'll Send My Girl to Be a Nurse," and "I Didn't Raise My Dog to Be a Sausage." Even Groucho Marx (1890–1977) got into the act with a tale about a poker game in which a card-playing mother states, "I didn't raise my boy; he had the joker!"

* * *

After several years of constant warfare most writers, wherever they were, picked up the sickening scent of battle and reacted to it, many with varying degrees of pacifism. Given the incredible carnage, whose totals were in seven figures, it was difficult not to do otherwise. Families who wore the black armbands of death had become commonplace and hundreds of thousands of walking, hobbling, blinded wounded now populated the European streets.

In Germany, once the war began, all anti-war novels and plays were suppressed by the military authorities and were not published again until after the war. Many manuscripts were smuggled into Switzerland, printed there, then the books taken back across the border into Germany, typically with false, benign title pages, advertising agricultural texts or children's novels.

Mutter (*Mother*), for example, was written by Helene Kessler (1870–1957), using the nom de plume of Hans von Kahlenberg, and published in Berne, Switzerland. As the title suggests, it focuses on the anguish of a mother whose son is killed in battle. Consumed by her memories and obsessed by the despairing cries of "Mother" that she hears constantly from thousands of voices, she curses war as an outrage to humanity and calls upon women everywhere to put an end to it.

Another "Swiss" book was *Menschen im Krieg* (Men in war) by Andreas Latzko (1876–1943), who had been an officer in the Austro-Hungarian army fighting on the Italian front. Wounded during an artillery barrage, he was sent to Switzerland to recover. While he was convalescing, the savagery of the battlefield still fresh in his mind, he wrote the six short stories that make up the book. They all focus on the protracted battles of the Isonzo front, which cost the Italians and Austro-Hungarians more than a half-million casualties. Latzko introduces his graphic and anguished account with the simple, optimistic statement dedicated "to friend and foe: I am positive the time will come when all will think as I."[262]

An impassioned reviewer declared: "It—*Menschen im Krieg* (*Men in War*)—is horrible in its fascination and so intense as to be actually painful to the reader."[263]

> A few minutes before Captain Marschner had seen the man still running— the same face still full of vitality—from heat and excitement. His knees gave way. The sight of that change, so incomprehensible in its suddenness, gripped at his vitals like an icy hand. Was it possible? Could all the life blood recede in the twinkling of an eye, and a strong, hale man crumble into ruins in a few moments? What powers of hell slept in such pieces of iron that between two breaths they could perform the work of many months of illness? [...]
>
> He looked about, shaken by nausea, his gorge rising. In a dip in the trench he saw a pile of dirty, tattered uniforms heaped in layers and with strangely rigid outlines. It took him some time to grasp the full horror of that which towered in front of him. Fallen soldiers were lying there like gathered logs, in the contorted shapes of the last death agony. Tent flaps had been spread over them, but had slipped down and revealed the grim, stony grey caricatures, the fallen jaws, the staring eyes. The arms of those in the top tier hung earthward like parts of a trellis, and grasped at the faces of those lying below, and were already sown with the livid splotches of corruption.[264]

The book was ultimately published in 19 languages, most appearing under pseudonyms. A critic wrote on the appearance of the American edition:

> It is such men as Latzko whose hands we must grasp with honor and admiration when at last the war comes to an end. It is they, working from within, who will disrupt the evil fabric of Prussianism, the cannon-lechers and the feasters on blood. It is they who, knowing the black despair of war with a bitterness beyond the fetch of words, will help us to end it. It is they who, having been duped and tricked by comfortable bureaucrats, will make the world safe for the humble. It is they who will bury the carrion emperors and general staffs deep beyond plummet's sounding—so deep that even the old scorn and hatred of them will seem but the shadow of a shade.[265]

One fervent reviewer called the book "The cry of a human soul wrung by agony and horror" and labeled it one of the best books to come from the war.[266]

Another anti-war novel that received wide acclaim was *Opfergang* (The way of sacrifice), written during the siege of Verdun by Fritz von Unruh (1885– 1970). The son of a Prussian general, he had become totally disillusioned by the war. When he was commissioned by the German War Ministry to write a book to promote the war effort and raise morale, instead he wrote *The Way of Sacrifice*, which was immediately banned. In it, a soldier speaks about duty, the sacred word of the Prussian tradition: "It is certainly a fine word and overcomes all personal feelings. But what lies behind it has degenerated. Duty is the cancer in the heart of the [German] people."[267] *The Way of Sacrifice* was clandestinely circulated during the war but not formally published until 1919.[268] Like many anti-war novels of its time, the book paints an appalling portrait of modern warfare and the death that awaits a soldier in a thousand forms. A small group of men are sent into this hell to be blinded, mutilated, gassed and killed, their suffering meaningless, their lives passionless digits in battlefield statistics. They are simply more *Kanonenfutter* (canon fodder) to be added to the millions already sacrificed. This was hardly the message that the German War Ministry wanted to hear, but it struck a responsive chord in the war-weary public.

Writing under the name of Ret Marut, B. Traven (also a nom de plume; 1882?-1969?) created the newspaper *Der Ziegelbrenner* in Bavaria as an anti-war voice to counter the chauvinistic German press. War, Traven argued, was powered by three motors: capitalism, nationalism and militarism. All three required a strong, centralized state. Do away with the state and quite simply you do away with war. Pursued by the authorities until the German defeat, the newspaper blossomed under the short-lived Bavarian Soviet Republic.[269] When the regime fell in 1919, *Der Ziegelbrenner* was once again reduced to a whisper from the underground. B. Traven became a hunted man and left Germany in 1921, disillusioned, never to return.[270] He settled in Mexico and went on to write such classics as *The Death Ship* and *The Treasure of the Sierra Madre*.

Hermann Hesse (1877–1962) had become a permanent resident in Switzerland, where he was free to think and write without censorship. In the words of Romain Rolland (1866–1944), who had also gone into exile in Switzerland, Hesse was "the one German poet who has written the serenest and loftiest words, and preserved in the midst of this demoniacal war an attitude worthy of Goethe."[271]

Early in the war Hesse had implored the artists and thinkers of Europe "to save what little peace" might yet be saved and not to join with their pens in destroying the future of Europe. He wrote an "Invocation to Peace," which he hoped would provide an inspiration to the many who felt stifled and oppressed. He would speak for them:

> *Jeder hat's gehabt*
> *Keiner hat's geschaetzt.*
> *Jeden hat der suesse Quell gelabt.*
> *O wie klingt der Name Friede jetzt!*
>
> *Klingt so fern und zag,*
> *Klingt so traenenschwer,*
> *Keiner weiss und kennt den Tag,*
> *Jeder sehnt ihn vol Verlangen her.*
>
> (Each one possessed it

> but no one prized it.
> Like a cool spring it refreshed us all.
> What a sound the word Peace has for us now!
>
> Distant it sounds, and fearful,
> And heavy with tears.
> No one knows or can name the day
> For which all sigh with such longing.)[272]

But writing almost passively about peace was as far as Hesse was willing to go. He was no peace militant and had a clear aversion to political parties, protests and propaganda. Rather, he saw himself as a peace sympathizer and advocate who represented a kind of third way, neither war nor actively agitating for peace, an almost Tolstoyan, ipsative view, what has been called the politics of "detachment,"[273] where the goal is to awaken the hidden God that dwells within each individual. According to one observer and critic, Hesse wanted "to guide the reader [...] into his innermost being," where he can see for himself "the living knowledge of peace and brotherhood"[274]: "The inner voice of one's destiny will no doubt guide one safely once it can be heard—such at least is the conclusion reached by his novels—just as Hesse claims it has shaped his own response to the great events of the day."[275]

Hesse was engaged in a quest for self-enlightenment, searching for a new definition of self, a blend of Eastern and Western philosophies, one that clearly excluded all forms of violence. At one point his protagonist Siddhartha says: "You don't force him, don't beat him, don't give him orders, because you know that soft is stronger than hard, water stronger than rocks, love stronger than force."[276]

It is of course difficult, if not impossible, to measure with any precision Hesse's influence. Certainly he was not a lone voice shouting against the wind from his exile in Switzerland. Hesse was one of the best-known German writers of his day. His persuasive, intuitive logic and perspective undoubtedly became a factor in many personal decisions, an effect that permeated Germany's intellectual class. His books were widely translated and eventually sold millions of copies in their original German-language editions.

When Germany was clearly defeated, Hesse called upon the German people to abandon "the most sacred ideals" (*die heiligsten Güter*) of the past and look toward a new future. The thing for us to do, Hesse wrote in 1918,

> is to go down like men or to continue to live on like men. Not, however, to whimper like children [...]. Our goal is not to become once again great and rich and powerful as rapidly as possible and have once again ships and armies [...]. Our goal is not a childish illusion. Have we not seen what comes of ships and armies, of power and wrath? Is all that forgotten?[277]
>
> Ahead of us lies the task of the vanquished [...] not only to bear their fate but to make it their own and to understand it, until the misfortune is no longer felt

as something alien which has suddenly come down upon us out of distant clouds but as something which belongs to us and which guides our thought [...]. Then this long war and this painful defeat will turn out to have become our good and well-deserved fate, no longer a sickness and wound from which we suffer, but a valuable promise for our future.[278]

A very efficient underground circulated these books in Germany to a growing group of people who realized that the war must end. Everywhere men and women clung to a belief in rationality, in cognition, in logical process, often with a fierce, even devout tenaciousness, as if mental coherence and discipline were the lodestone of their own sanity. This produced an incredible faith in the power of the written word, the notion that thoughts can be translated into text, pass through the medium of print, enter into the minds of other men, who then propel them into action. In essence, the word is swifter, sharper, and stronger than the sword. Words had become a way for an individual to strike back at the system, for an insignificant David to suddenly rise from nowhere and assault the Goliath of modern war. More than perhaps any previous conflict, World War One became a struggle of words fought with tracts, articles, graffiti, posters, pamphlets, handbills and even postcards.

Proof that this avalanche of words, much of it from Switzerland, did not disappear in the *foehn Wind* (wind coming off the mountains) can be found in a report by the GOC (General Office Commanding) of the Munich Garrison, which states:

> The numerous German writers in Switzerland [...], thanks to their extensive personal [...] contacts with Germany, are exerting a considerable influence on the mood and attitude of wide sections [of the population] [...]. In these circumstances a group of respected individuals determinedly putting into action their programme for the "awakening of the German people" from within German-speaking Switzerland represents a serious threat to the morale of the German people, and more especially to the essential foundation of this morale: the universal conviction of the justice of the German cause.[279]

* * *

In France *Le Feu* (Under fire), a powerful anti-war novel by Henri Barbusse (1873–1935), won the Prix Goncourt, the most prestigious French prize for fiction, as "the best and most imaginative prose work of the year" and went on to become a best seller. The book sold more than 200,000 copies the first year.[280] It is still read today in many French schools.

Invalided out of the French army three times, Henri Barbusse spent a total of 17 months at the front. By the time he left the trenches he had become a pacifist with a steadily growing hatred of militarism. He wrote with an intense passion, words his weapon of choice and the enemy anyone who could but didn't bring an immediate end to the senseless slaughter:

Morality is delightful—and they pervert it. How many crimes have they made into virtues, with a single word, by calling them "national?" They deform even truth, putting their individual national truths in place of the eternal one. They make as many truths as there are peoples, distorting and twisting Truth itself.[281]
[...]
All these people who cannot or will not make peace on earth, all those who, for one cause or another, cling to the old order of things, find or invent justifications for it, these are your enemies![282]

Barbusse wrote with a harsh naturalism that was unusual at the time. He wrote to shock but also to tell the soldiers on the line that the power to end the fighting was in their hands. The book circulated through the trenches, one of the first anti-war novels to do so. At the time, Barbusse was a populist (he became a communist later). He believed in revolution, in the power of the masses to realize that there was no nobility in modern warfare, only a monstrous human crime, an endless slaughterhouse. He claimed that "the 30 million slaves who have been thrown on top of one another by crime and error into this war of mud raise human faces in which the glimmer of an idea is forming. The future is in the hands of these slaves and one can see that the old world will be changed by the alliance that will one day be formed between those whose number and whose suffering is without end."[283]

Hélène Brion (1882–1962), a pacifist and feminist, had the dubious distinction of being the first Frenchwoman to be tried before a military tribunal. She was arrested for distributing "defeatist propaganda," sending anonymous notes to teachers and legislators with such messages as "Peace without annexation, conquest or indemnity" and "Enough men killed! Peace!" When the police entered her home they found 14 envelopes addressed to legislators containing pacifist notes. Her trial in 1917 became a cause célèbre, front-page news as the press labeled her an advocate of birth control, a defeatist, an anti-militarist, an anarchist, and a spy. Prominent feminists, writers and even Members of Parliament testified on her behalf.

Brion admitted to the court: "I am an enemy of war because I am a feminist!" If women had been allowed to participate fully in politics, she declared, "things would have come to pass differently."[284] In fact, she explained she had been acting in the best interests of the country. Hélène Brion was found guilty, sentenced to three years in prison, then freed on parole.

* * *

It was almost inevitable that out of the great abyss of war that had consumed the Continent for four years should come an intellectual void, a profound emptiness that could not be filled with thought, no matter how humanistic it might be. The result was a pan–European art movement, Dada—also known as Dadaism[285]—that essentially advocated nothingness, spreading an anti-war, anti-bourgeois message. It began in Zurich in 1916 and gathered force, rejecting the type of conservative reason and logic that had justified the carnage and praising nonsense, irrationality and intuition. Its purpose, to the extent that it could define one, was to be a revolt against war and at the same time express the chaos of the moment and ridicule the modern world through all forms of art: graphics, painting, poetry and literature.

Basically anarchistic, or occasionally socialist, in perspective, Dadaism expressed the frustration of European artists who witnessed the destructive power of the war and searched for some ways, no matter how extreme, to make their voices heard. It was never more than a fringe movement, their strident voices magnified by the attention given to them by the media.

Jean Arp (1886–1966), an Alsatian Dadaist artist, tried to define the movement: "Losing interest in the slaughterhouse of the world war, we turned to the Fine Arts [...]. While the thunder of the batteries rumbled in the distance, we pasted, we recited, we versified, we sang with all our soul. We searched for an elementary art that would, we thought, save mankind from the furious folly of these times."[286]

* * *

On the other side of the world, Japan was one of the Allies, and although it appeared that the whole country was united behind the Emperor, there was, in fact, a small group of intellectuals who challenged the cult of Bushido.

Yosano Akiko (1878–1942), for example, advocated a "philosophy of peace," condemning militarism in Japan as "barbarian thinking [that] is the responsibility of us women to eradicate [...] from our midst."[287] She had written the poem "Thou Shalt Not Die" during the Russo-Japanese War of 1904–1905. Turned into a popular song, it continued to circulate widely during the First World War. The poem begins:

> Oh, my brother, I weep for you.
> Do not give your life.
> Last-born among us,
> You are the most beloved of our parents.
> Did they make you grasp the sword
> And teach you to kill?
> Did they raise you to the age of 24,
> Telling you to kill and die?[288]

Yosano goes on to attack the Emperor, a clear taboo in traditional Japanese society:

> Brother, do not give your life.
> His Majesty the Emperor
> Goes not himself into the battle.
> Could he, with such deeply noble heart,

Think it an honor for men
To spill one another's blood
And die like beasts?[289]

Yet the government did nothing. Perhaps they weren't sure what to do. Few, if any, women had ever dared to criticize the Emperor. However, the people in the streets were outraged and stoned her house. The Japanese press threw their own stones, and they had plenty to throw. Among other things they called her "a traitorous subject, a rebel, a criminal who deserves the nation's punishment [...], a case of *lèse majesté* [...], an expression of dangerous thoughts which disparage the idea of the national family [...], a poison-tongued menace."[290]

Another Japanese with an unshakable anti-war belief was Uchimura Kanzo (1861–1930), who became perhaps the most influential pacifist in the early part of the century. In 1914 he saw war coming in Europe and published a series of essays titled *Religion and Current Events*. In them he called pacifism the "single touchstone" by which one could test the sincerity of faith.

Uchimura Kanzo is given credit for founding the Mukyokai religious movement, whose adherents eventually numbered in the tens of thousands. They rejected all formal Christian institutions, having no sacraments, liturgy, professional clergy, church buildings or memberships rolls. Instead, this non-churchism is based on independent Bible study groups centered on the traditional teacher-disciple (*sensei-deshi*) relationship. The teachers have no formal training in the Bible, establishing a group only when inspired to do so. The group thus disintegrates when its teacher dies or retires. The Mukyokai attracted people from all social strata in Japan, but it was particularly appealing to the Japanese intelligentsia—scholars, university professors, graduate students, and professionals.

According to the Mukyokai, war is the result of man's uncontrolled passions and is permitted by God to exist as a punishment for the sins of nations. War is sinful quite simply because it involves murder and cruelty. Under no circumstances, not even surprise attack or as a last resort, is war justified. Non-resistance (*muteikosbugi*) is the logical consequence, and most Mukyokai did oppose militarism in personal passive fashion and as a result they never posed a real threat to the state.

Uchimura Kanzo was the first Mukyokai Christian to reject the idolatry of the Japanese Empire openly. Known as "the *lèse majesté* incident," at a special ceremony for the reading of the Imperial Rescript he refused to bow deeply, since this could be interpreted as an act of idolatry by Christian beliefs. This inadequate bow was immediately taken as an act of contempt toward the Emperor, and Uchimura Kanzo was vilified as an "impious traitor" and an "offender of the Imperial Holyness."[291]

The attacks expanded to include all Japanese Christians, since, as a monotheistic religion, Christianity was essentially intolerant and could not coexist with the Imperial Rescript which reflected traditional Japanese devotion to the Emperor. When their beliefs were reduced to basics, Christians could not be loyal subjects of the Emperor. There were charges and countercharges, which ignited a long intellectual debate and resulted in the publication of at least 30 books and over a hundred articles. But nothing was settled. The real issues became obscured in the banter of religious polemics.

Uchimura Kanzo put a different kind of spin on Christian pacifism. The death of a Christian, he claimed, is a sacrifice of much greater value than the death of an individual who believes in war. God, Uchimura was certain, would appreciate the difference. A war could be ended only by many pacifists sacrificing themselves to atone for the sins of others.

* * *

In Australia, the peace movement was always comparatively strong. On a per capita basis it often exceeded that of the other English-speaking countries, the UK, the United States, and Canada. Certainly during World War One it was strong enough to help defeat two referenda on conscription, one in 1916 and another in 1917, a victory that no other peace movement managed to obtain.

Although William Hughes (1862–1952), the Prime Minister at the time, technically had the power to implement conscription for overseas service, he felt the need to be thoroughly democratic. He also thought he would win a plebiscite and by doing so have a stronger mandate. The first plebiscite was held on October 28, 1916. The Australian people were asked: "Are you in favour of the Government having, in this grave emergency, the same compulsory powers over citizens in regard to requiring their military service, for the term of this War, outside the Commonwealth, as it now has in regard to military service within the Commonwealth?"[292]

The conscription issue deeply divided Australia. Many people who were in favor of it took it as a sign of loyalty to Britain as well as a vote in support of those men who were already fighting. The anti-conscription forces included the farmers and trade unions who feared their workers might be replaced by cheaper foreign or female labor and the many smaller groups, some religious, who thought that the whole war was immoral and that it was unjust to force men to fight.

The women's vote was seen as vital and undoubtedly tipped the scales in favor of anti-conscription. One of the organizations in the forefront of the battle was the Women's Peace Army, an attempt to mobilize the women in Australia who opposed all war, regardless of political party membership. It was meant to be "a fighting body" that would destroy militarism "with the same spirit of self-sacrifice that soldiers showed on the battlefield." "We war against war" became their motto, their flag in the feminist colors of purple, green and white. They declared: "The time has come when the women, the mothers of the world, shall refuse to give their sons as material for shot and shell [...]. For the sake of the mothers of soldier-sons, vote!"[293]

The Australian people narrowly rejected conscription. Forty-nine percent voted "yes" and 51 percent "no." In addition, it was widely believed that the "no" vote was understated, particularly among the soldiers at the front.

A year later, after enormous casualties in Europe to the Australian troops (more than 60 percent), pressure was put on the Australian government for reinforcements. The number of men who volunteered had slowed to a trickle. Prime Minister Hughes decided to try a second plebiscite on December 20, 1917. This time the question was even more vague than the previous one, but the intention was clear: "Are you in favour of the proposal of the Commonwealth Government for reinforcing the Commonwealth Forces overseas?"[294] This time the "no" vote prevailed by an even greater margin. The people of Australia had made their intentions clear, not once but twice, against conscription, an anti-war statement louder than that of any other country.

* * *

Shortly after taking office for a second term in 1917 President Wilson asked the United States Senate for a declaration of war against Germany. Many of his supporters were outraged. A mere few months before they had campaigned for him as a peace candidate, a man who would keep America out of the European war.

In his war message President Wilson stated that there were two reasons why the United States had to enter the conflict, the first to make the world safe for democracy; and the second, to substitute cooperation for competition in international affairs.

At one point Senator James K. Vardaman[295] (1861–1930) from Mississippi set forth what he understood to be the principle of letting the people rule:

> The President [...] suggested that if the people who are now engaged in this war in Europe had been consulted there would have been no war. If I may be permitted to indulge in a little speculation I will say, Mr. President, that if the people of the United States—I mean the plain, honest people, the masses who are to bear the burden of taxation and fight the Nation's battles, were consulted—the United States would not make a declaration of war against Germany today.

Although the American Constitution clearly grants Congress the right to declare war,[296] Senator Vardaman and others were raising a critical point. Times had changed, they maintained, and democracy should change with them. When the Constitution was written it would have been physically impossible to consult "the people" of the 13 colonies on anything. But by the 20th century America had been transformed into a participatory democracy. Since "the people," that is, at that moment all white males, had the right to vote, so the argument runs, thus they should use that right to vote on such a vital issue as whether or not the country should go to war. Current history might be far different if this democratic principle had been adopted.

Although it was not explicitly mentioned, the idea of democratic control of foreign policy was a popular subject, which often surfaced when people discussed the causes of the European war. Had the foreign policy of the European nations been subject to the will of the people, so the argument ran, the war would never have begun. Although the American Congress theoretically represented the people, such a vital question as whether or not to go to war should perhaps have bypassed the elected representatives and gone directly to the people.

Were America's voters really ready to declare war? Would a referendum have passed? How would "the people" have voted? It's difficult to say. How many of the so-called hyphenated Americans, German-Americans, Austrian-Americans, Hungarian-Americans, et al., had the great Melting Pot failed to melt? How many were still loyal to the European countries of their birth?

Ernest Lundeen (1878–1940), a Congressman from Minnesota, reported that according to a poll of 54,000 voters in his district there was a ten-to-one rejection of any participation in the war.

Senator Robert M. La Follette (1855–1925) from Wisconsin, one of the six Senators who voted against the declaration of war, read into the *Congressional Record* a number of telegrams that he had received just two days after President Wilson's call for war:

> From Seattle Washington: Straw referendum signed today at public market; city streets, shows 31 for war declaration, 374 against.
>
> From Sheboygan Wisconsin: By referendum vote taken the last two days of the qualified electors [...] on the question, Shall our country enter into the European war? 4,082 voted no and 17 voted yes.
>
> Racine Wisconsin: Four thousand people assembled at the auditorium last night: lots of American sentiment: no enthusiasm for war: recruits were asked for: only seven men offered themselves for enlistment.
>
> Berkeley California: Having sounded the opinions of juniors and seniors taking electrical engineering at the University of California today, I have foundation on which to base my statement that practically none of us enthuse at all over war.
>
> New Ulm Minnesota: At an election, 485 votes were cast against war to 19 for war.[297]

Addressing the President directly, Senator La Follette went on to summarize the mail he had received: "Mr. President, [...] I have received some 15,000 letters and telegrams. They have come from some 44 states in the Union. They have been assorted according as to whether they speak in criticism or commendation of my course in opposing war. [...] [N]ine out of ten are an unqualified endorsement of my course in opposing war with Germany on the issue presented.[298]

Like Senator Vardaman, Senator La Follette challenged President Wilson to hold a referendum, to ask the country directly whether or not they wanted to engage in the European war: "Who has registered the knowledge or approval of the American people of the course this Congress is called upon to take in declaring war upon Germany? Submit the question to the people, you who support it. You who support it dare not do it, for you know that by a vote of more than ten to one the American people as a body would register their declaration against it."[299]

Fiorello La Guardia (1882–1947), then a Representative from New York (he later became mayor of the city), stated later that at least 60 percent of the House members who voted for the war believed that the United States would never send a single soldier to Europe. Apparently they accepted the logic that once America had declared war and was ready to supply the Allies that would be enough to tip the balance and force the Germans to realize that the war was lost.

Senator George William Norris (1861–1944) from Nebraska told the Senate, "I feel we are about to put the dollar sign on the American flag." Robert M. La Follette reminded his colleagues in the Senate that England was a hereditary monarchy that was hardly promoting democracy in Ireland, Egypt or India. Other members of Congress also railed against Wilson's concept of making "the world safe for democracy." Senator Warren G. Harding (1865–1923) of Ohio, later to become the 29th President of the United States, said rather succinctly that "it is none of our business what type of government any nation on this earth may choose to have." And Congressman Ernest Lundeen added rather prophetically that it was impossible to "thrust democracy with loving bayonets down the throats of unwilling peoples."[300] Another Congressman, Denver S. Church (1862–1952), alleged that 98 percent of the American population were opposed to intervention. Other Congressmen tried unsuccessfully to add amendments to the declaration, for example to prevent American soldiers being sent abroad.

When the declaration of war came to a vote in Congress, the Senate passed it 82 to 6; and the House of Representatives, 373 to 50.

Meyer London (1871–1926), a Representative from New York, was one of those 50. He addressed the Congress: "No, I shall not kill. I shall not vote to kill. I am ready to suffer injury rather than kill a fellow human being. Mr. Chairman, war is wrong, inexcusable, indefensible. Let us be strong men; let us throw away our political ambitions; let us throw away our chances of reelection [...]. Let us be free, strong men, and do what men should do in momentous times like these."

Jeanette Rankin (1880–1973), the first woman to be elected to Congress, was also among the 50. When she was called on to vote, she replied: "I want to stand by my country, but I cannot vote for war. I vote no." Later she said: "As a woman, I can't go to war and I refuse to send anyone else [...]. You can no more win a war than you can win an earthquake [...]. The world must finally understand that we cannot settle disputes by eliminating human beings."[301]

The press was aflame, especially many leftist newspapers, which were full of fiery prose and outraged that the United States had been drawn into the protracted European bloodletting. Jane Addams (1860–1935), the social reformer, called it "the lowest pit into which human nature can sink."[302] Peace organizations made their own declarations. For example, the Fellowship of Reconciliation issued a statement: "We are patriots who love our country and desire to serve her and those ideals for which she has stood [...], but we cannot believe that participation in war is the true way of service to America or to humanity. Nor can we persuade ourselves that it is right to do evil that good may come."[303] Essayist Randolph S. Bourne (1886–1918) wrote:

> We go to war to save the world from subjugation! But the German intellectuals went to war to save their culture from barbarization! And the French went to war to save their beautiful France! And the English to save international honor! And Russia, most altruistic and self-sacrificing of all, to save a small State (Serbia) from destruction.
> [...] Was the terrific bargaining power of a great neutral [the United States] ever really used? Our war followed, as all wars follow, a monstrous failure of diplomacy.[304]

President Wilson tried to answer some of this criticism. At one point he stated that the German government had declared war without the "previous knowledge or approval"[305] of the German people, implying that the United States could obviously do the same. That remark set off a firestorm of arguments that was to last for months.

Whether or not the American people would have given their approval to a declaration of war is a moot question. Accurate public opinion polling had yet to make its debut and there are few direct surrogates. One of them might be found in the rising popularity of the American Socialist Party after war was declared in April 1917.

The day following the declaration of war the Socialist Party convened an emergency convention in St. Louis and immediately proclaimed its "unalterable opposition to the war": "We brand the declaration of war by our government a crime against the people of the United States and against the nations of the world. In all modern history there has been no war more unjustifiable than the war in which we are about to engage."[306] This unequivocal stand against the war actually *increased* the Socialist Party's popularity. In the fall elections of 1917, six months after the United States declared war on the Central Powers, the socialists received unprecedented support. For example, their share of the vote in Chicago rose to 34 percent; in Toledo, 35 percent; in Buffalo, 25 percent; and in Cleveland, 20 percent. In 15 cities of the populous Northeast the socialists averaged 22 percent of the vote.

* * *

Another indication of the lack of popular support for the American declaration of war can be found in the response to President Wilson's call for an army of a million men.[307] Three weeks after war was declared in 1917 only 32,000 men, in other words, barely 3 percent of the total, had volunteered. Apparently the public had not forgotten that just a few months before the President had campaigned for re-election under the slogan "He kept us out of the war." In addition, for years politicians had been feeding the public a diet of peace and non-intervention in European affairs. It would not be simple to put the country suddenly on the opposite tack.

A Selective Service Act was passed requiring all men between the ages of first 21 and 30, then 18 and 45, to register for the draft. Many followed the dictates of their conscience and refused to report to their draft board, hoping that their action would become part of a mass movement—a nationwide protest to the American entry into the European war—and that each man who refused to register for the draft or serve in the army would become an example for the next. Often men were quite vocal about their moral stance, even taking a certain amount of pride in their disobedience and in that way encouraging others to do the same. The logic was simple. If enough men ignored the call to arms, then the army would not exist.

It is estimated that during the war about 337,000 men "dodged" the draft, that is, failed to register. No one knows how many war resisters or religious opponents of violence are included in this category. No doubt for others it was an easy way out, a quiet and unobtrusive way to avoid the whole issue, but for many registering for the draft constituted a clear first step toward picking up a deadly weapon.

All across America many men, and women, objected to conscription and went to jail for their beliefs. A group called the American Patriots Association in California issued a guide explaining how to avoid the draft, titled "Legal Opinion and Advice on Conscription Law to American Patriots" and written by Daniel O'Connell.[308] When O'Connell addressed a meeting where many draft-age men were present he was arrested, tried under the Espionage Act,[309] then sentenced to five years in prison. Kate Richards O'Hare (1876–1948), former secretary of the Socialist Party, was arrested after she spoke at a meeting in North Dakota and said that "the women of the United States are nothing but brood sows, to raise children to get into the army and be made into fertilizer."[310] William J. Head circulated a petition in South Dakota calling for the repeal of the Selective Service Act, claiming the act was unconstitutional and that "we were all damn fools" for supporting the war. He was sentenced to three years in Leavenworth Penitentiary and fined $500. In Minnesota Abraham L. Sugarman was accused of denouncing the Selective Service Act and "suggesting that if they [young men of draft age] all held together the act could not be enforced, as there were not jails enough to hold all the people."[311] He also reportedly said: "This is supposed to be a free country. Like Hell it is!"[312] Those comments earned him a sentence of three years in Leavenworth Penitentiary.

Probably the largest mass protest to the draft was the so-called Green Corn Rebellion in eastern Oklahoma. Many of the tenant farmers there, whites, blacks and some Indians, were extremely poor, most sharecroppers and indebted to banks and moneylenders. They belonged to the radical Working Class Union, which was directly connected to the IWW, the Industrial Workers of the World. The farmers knew little about the war in Europe and had no desire to go there and risk their lives for a system that had left them impoverished. They watched the comfortable commercial classes in the towns participate in patriotic movements, so quite naturally they became anti-patriotic. When a sheriff and his deputy tried to investigate the unrest in the countryside, there was a confrontation with some of the farmers and, in an exchange of fire, the deputy was killed. That provided the spark for the rebellion.

About 300 farmers decided to march to Washington and force the government to end the war. They hoped to be joined by thousands of others and thus build a protest movement of the rural poor, men who had nothing to gain by fighting someone else's battles on the other side of the ocean.

The name Green Corn came from the fact that the group intended to eat green corn, which was in season at the time as they marched to the Capitol. However, they had not gone far when they met the forces of law and order in the form of a large, well-organized posse. The farmers fled without a fight and the rebellion collapsed. Four hundred and fifty people were arrested and held in the state penitentiary. Two hundred and sixty-six were quickly released, but charges were levied against 184 participants, of whom about 150 were convicted or pled guilty, receiving prison terms ranging from 60 days to ten years. Most were freed or paroled after a short time, but at least five spent more than five years behind bars. The cost of rebellion had been high.

A Seminole Musogee Indian woman spoke about her uncle who had been one of the leaders of the rebellion:

> The full moon of late July, early August it was, the Moon of the Green Corn. It was not easy to persuade our poor white and black brothers and sisters to rise up. We told them that rising up, standing up, whatever the consequences, would inspire future generations. Our courage, our bravery would be remembered and copied. That had been the Indian way for centuries, since the invasions. Fight and tell the story so that those who come after or their descendants will rise up once again. It may take a thousand years but that is how we continue and eventually prevail.[313]

* * *

Another group of resisters contested the constitutionality of the Selective Service Act (that is, the draft) by challenging the right of the government to send them abroad. According to Article IV, Section 4, of the Constitution, Congress "shall protect each of them [the states] against Invasion." The war in Europe clearly did not constitute an invasion of the United States. The Supreme Court thought otherwise and justified the draft from other sections of the Constitution.

Those who refused to serve on religious grounds contended that their right to do so was protected by the First Amendment, which guarantees freedom of religion.[314] This included the Quakers and the Mennonites, who took an uncompromising opposition to the use of armed force and considered all types of warfare to be dehumanizing no matter how worthy its goals. For them, no international body could keep the peace. Pacifists must work to eliminate the social injustices that bred war, poverty and the capitalist system of inequities. Thus they opposed any American intervention in the European war.

The Mennonites, on the one hand, sought to withdraw from society and politics and regarded all governments as evil. Therefore, they refused any military duty, no matter how trivial it might be. The Quakers, on the other hand, were pacifists but politically active and sought to change society and government through social reform. For them, that was the means to eliminate the injustices they believed caused violence.

The exact numbers of these groups are not known, but some indication as to their size may be had from the number of Americans who registered to serve in the armed forces.

Three months after the declaration of war only 32,000 men had volunteered to serve their country, a rather poor response and far from the patriotic fervor that the announcement of war had produced in Europe in 1914. To obtain the necessary manpower for the military, Congress instituted a draft. All males aged 21 to 30 were required to register for military service. (The age limit was later changed to include all men aged 18 to 45.) Almost 9.6 million of the 10.2 million men of draft age voluntarily registered.

For those who did register, local draft boards granted CO status to 56,830. Of this number, 20,873 COs were actually inducted. All of them except 3,989, who were mostly religious objectors, decided during training to serve with their units. Of this number, one-third eventually accepted non-combatant service in the quartermaster, medical, or engineer corps and another third accepted furloughs to work in civilian industry, agriculture, or overseas relief agencies.

The rest, that is, about 1,300, were either tried and convicted for refusing to serve or awaiting trial at the time of the armistice.

In some 2,000 prosecutions under the act, however, its application broke down at all levels—judges, juries, and prosecutors. Abuses became so gross, in fact, that late in 1918 the Attorney General forbade further prosecution by district attorneys without his specific approval.

Before that happened, COs suffered horribly. They were also labeled "Yellowbacks," that is, cowards and slackers, who, it was said, were too fearful to pick up a gun.

For refusing to serve in the military 142 COs received life imprisonment and 17 were actually sentenced to death, although the sentence was never carried out. Most received prison sentences of 20 to 25 years. And when they arrived in jail, physical abuse was used to try to break their will.

Many of these COs belonged to religious sects that strictly forbade their members to wear a uniform and serve in the military. Some belonged to groups such as the Mennonites or the Hutterites, who spoke German, or the Molokans—a Russian pacifist sect—who spoke Russian, and the language barrier only served to isolate them further. Beatings were common, hard labor 15 hours a day or more the norm, and for the slightest infraction the men were chained by the wrist, then suspended from the ceiling for hours. The Eighth Amendment to the Constitution of the United States states: "Excessive bail shall not be required, nor excessive fines imposed, *nor cruel and unusual punishments* inflicted." This was widely ignored. The military authorities were convinced that given enough physical punishment a CO would break, then cooperate. The worst places for a pacifist, of any denomination or conviction, were the federal prisons at Fort Leavenworth, Fort Jay and Alcatraz. There, more likely than not, they might be condemned to "the hole," a black punishment dungeon in the subbasement of the prison.

The Hofer brothers, Joseph and David, were unfortunate examples. Hudderite pacifists, they refused not only to bear arms but to serve the military in any manner. Most COs wore a military uniform, went through parts of the training, but never carried or fired a weapon. The Hofers, however, refused to cooperate at all. They obeyed the order to appear at the induction center, but once there they would not sign any documents and ignored all commands. Their reply was always the same, that "our conscience won't allow us." Charged with disobeying a military order, they were tried by a court-martial, found guilty and sentenced to 37 years of hard labor. They were sent to Alcatraz, where once again they were ordered to put on military uniforms. When they refused, they were placed in dungeons below the surface of the water, solitary confinement out of earshot of each other. Reportedly a guard told them: "There you will stay until you give up the ghost—just like the last four we carried out yesterday!"[315] The cells were pitch-black and water dripped from the walls. Naked and wearing a ball and chain, they were hosed down daily in freezing weather, given a glass of water every day but no food. After five days they died of pneumonia. Their bodies were sent home to South Dakota, and, when their families opened the coffins they found the Hofers dressed in the uniforms that they had refused to wear in life.

The Hudderite community was so stunned by the brutal and inhuman treatment given to the young men that they sold their farms and moved the entire community to Canada.

Another "Yellowback," Ernest L. Meyer, who was imprisoned in Leavenworth, described the kind of treatment some of the COs received:

A number of Molokans were brought to the fort [Leavenworth]. [...] they refused to work under military orders and were at once put in solitary confinement in the "hole." They were manacled nine hours a day, in standing posture, to the bars of this dungeon, and at the end of nine hours each day their bonds were unloaded and they fell exhausted to the cement floor. They slept on a plank on the floor, which was crawling with vermin. The Molokans were kept in the "hole" continuously.[316]

Howard W. Moore, another CO, was sentenced to the infamous "hole" of Fort Leavenworth Penitentiary for refusing a military order. While he was chained to the wall, like a man in a medieval dungeon, word arrived that he had been awarded a Carnegie medal for bravery for rescuing a drowning woman at the risk of his own life. When the Carnegie commission learned that he was a CO, the award was withheld. Howard W. Moore was one of the last six COs released from jail on November 24, 1920.[317]

News and details of "the hole" finally traveled back to Washington and the War Department eventually abolished manacling and, to some extent, isolation in punishment cells.

* * *

On the day that the United States declared war, April 6, 1917, President Wilson received several thousand telegrams reminding him that he had been elected precisely because he had promised to keep America out of war. The volte-face caught the country off guard. No matter how well Wilson clothed the declaration of war in lofty principles, it still meant joining the primeval struggle being fought in the trenches of Europe:

> It is a fearful thing to lead this great peaceful people into war, into the most terrible and disastrous of all wars, civilization itself seeming to be in the balance. But the right is more precious than peace, and we shall fight for the things which we have always carried nearest our hearts—for democracy, for the right of those who submit to authority to have a voice in their own governments, for the rights and liberties of small nations, for a universal dominion of right by such a concert of free peoples as shall bring peace and safety to all nations and make the world itself at last free.

According to the government there were three main groups who would oppose the decision to go to war, some ethnic minorities (German-Americans, Austrian-Americans, et al.), a few religious groups (Mennonites, Quakers and the so-called sectarian pacifists), and members of the American peace movement, such as the socialists, who were perhaps the largest and most vocal of these groups.

To combat any resistance on the part of the "hyphenated Americans," suddenly America was awash with government-sponsored anti–German propaganda. This also fueled support for the war and quite intentionally contributed to a mood of intolerance. In fact, it was a massive official assault on American civil liberties. President Wilson had predicted that a wave of bigotry and fanaticism would follow a declaration of war when in April 1917 he told a New York newspaper:

> Once you lead this people into war, they'll forget there ever was such a thing as tolerance. To fight you must be brutal and ruthless, and the spirit of ruthless brutality will enter into the very fibre of our national life, infecting Congress, the courts, the policeman on the beat, the man in the street. Conformity would be the only virtue, and every man who refused to conform would have to pay the penalty.[318]

When war did come President Wilson immediately began to advocate a hard line, which was designed to intimidate anyone reluctant to support it and to crush those who would not support the war effort. The President told Congress: "There are citizens of the United States, I blush to admit […] who have poured the poison of disloyalty into the very arteries of our national life […]. Such creatures of passion, disloyalty, and anarchy must be crushed out. The hand of our power should close over them at once."[319]

Disloyalty could and would be interpreted quite simply. Anyone who refused to support the war effort, anyone who advocated peace, negotiation, or compromise, was accused of being disloyal to the congressional declaration of war. Democratic process and freedom of thought and speech were all in effect suspended. To make the world "safe for democracy," as the President pledged to do, the former professor of political science had virtually eliminated the basics of American democracy.

True to his prediction of intolerance, President Wilson championed the passage of the Espionage Act of 1917, which made it a crime for a person to convey information with the intent to interfere with the operation of the armed forces of the United States or to promote the success of its enemies. It was punishable by a maximum fine of $10,000 (about 170,000 in today's dollars) and 20 years in prison. The law was later extended by the Sedition Act of 1918, which made it illegal to use "disloyal, profane, scurrilous, or abusive language"[320] about the United States government or its flag or armed forces during war.

Many states also passed their own Sedition Acts, most of them even harsher than the federal one. In Montana, for example, a special session of the state legislature in February 1918 criminalized saying or writing just about anything negative about the government or its conduct of the war. Stiff criminal penalties—a maximum of 10 to 20 years in prison and a $20,000 (about 350,000 in today's dollars) fine—conveyed the seriousness of the crime.

Typical statements that were forbidden were: "We shouldn't be sticking our nose in there and we should get licked for doing so," and "this is a rich man's war," and "Americans had no business in that boat [the *Lusitania*]. They were hauling over munitions." Overheard in a barroom, on the street or in a casual conversation about the day's news, these comments put their speakers behind bars for years. Free speech in America had disappeared almost overnight.

Using this kind of repressive legislation, the opponents of the war were quickly silenced. "Peace" had suddenly become a dirty word. Anyone who spoke with a Germanic accent or called himself a German-American was equally suspect. The President set the tone: "Any man who caries a hyphen around with him carries a dagger that he is ready to plunge into the vitals of the republic."[321]

Speaking out against the head of the American Socialist Party, Eugene V. Debs (1855–1926), President Wilson declared: "Before the war he [Debs] had a perfect right to exercise his freedom of speech and to express his own opinion, but once the Congress of the United States declared war, silence on his part would have been the proper course to pursue."[322]

The American Postmaster General banned virtually every Socialist newspaper, magazine or other publication from the mails, effectively putting their printing presses out of action.

Pro-peace movies such as *Battle Cry for Peace* were banned while *The Beast of Berlin*, *To Hell with the Kaiser* and *Face to Face with Kaiserism* drew large audiences.

Dachshunds were renamed liberty dogs; German measles were renamed liberty measles; sauerkraut was called liberty cabbage. By the end of the war local groups had outlawed the teaching of German in schools, banned the playing of Beethoven's music, and boycotted performances by artists of German background. The City University of New York reduced by one credit every course in German. Towns such as Berlin, Iowa, changed their names (in that case to Lincoln). Cincinnati's German Street converted to English Street and German family names like Ochs and Schwartz became Anglicized as Oaks and Black.

The military adversary was thousands of miles away, but German-Americans soon became convenient local scapegoats. In Van Houten, New Mexico, an angry mob accused an immigrant miner of supporting Germany and forced him to kneel before them, kiss the flag, and shout "To hell with the Kaiser." In Illinois, a group of zealous patriots accused Robert Prager (1888–1918), a German coal miner, of hoarding explosives. Though Prager asserted his loyalty to the very end, he was lynched by an angry crowd of over 200 people. Explosives were never found.[323]

In the words of Clarence Darrow (1857–1938), the lawyer who would later achieve fame defending John T. Scopes (1900–1970) in the so-called "Monkey" Trial, in America "the pacifist speaks with a German accent."[324]

* * *

The Socialist Party and the National Civil Liberties Bureau (the wartime predecessor to the American Civil Liberties Union) mounted a legal battle testing the constitutionality of military conscription. The cases moved up rapidly through the federal courts until they finally arrived at the Supreme Court. There lawyers argued that conscription was a violation of the Thirteenth Amendment, which outlaws slavery and involuntary servitude. However, in *Arver v. United States* (1918) the court unanimously upheld conscription, relying on a decision of the Pennsylvania Supreme Court during the American Civil War, *Kneedler v. Lane* (1863), as a precedent, as well as the fact that most nations of the world at the time had some sort of compulsory military service. The *Kneedler v. Lane* case was based on a three-to-two decision of the Pennsylvania court, even though two months earlier the court had ruled that conscription was unconstitutional. After that ruling the composition of the court changed and it reversed its previous decision.

In the end, the American draft resisters had no legal recourse and were supported only by the strength of their own beliefs. A typical draft resister stood before his draft board and stated: "I am standing for my convictions, and those convictions are, that war is an unnecessary evil and the only way to end war and get a lasting peace, bring about a real democracy, is to stand up and say, 'I don't want to kill my fellowmen; I don't want to be a murderer.' Do as you please to me; I cannot be a murderer."[325] When questioned by the draft board as to how he thought he would fare if Germany won the war, the draft resister candidly replied, "Why, about the same, sir. I suppose the Germans would court-martial me, too, sir. That is what they are doing to our German comrades."[326]

Many draft resisters were forcibly inducted into the army, and then when they refused to wear a military uniform or take any orders they were courtmartialed and given severe sentences, sometimes 20 or 25 years. No one remained in prison that long. All sentences, regardless of their length, were commuted after the Armistice. Strangely enough, the first draft resister to be arrested, Otto Wangerin, was also among the last to serve a prison sentence for following his conscience. He was finally released in 1921.[327]

* * *

An atypical victim of the Espionage Act was Congressman Victor Berger, the first socialist to be elected to the House of Representatives. True to his party's platform, he vigorously opposed the war whenever he had the chance. For example, he editorialized in a Milwaukee newspaper: "And we repeat that the war was caused by the struggle between Great Britain and Germany for commercial supremacy of the world's trade. The Social-Democracy of the world stands for and demands peace! If this be treason—let them make the most of it."[328]

The House of Representatives refused to allow Berger to take his seat for violations of the Espionage Act. At the same time, the government suspended mailing privileges for his newspaper. The governor of Wisconsin then called a special election to fill Berger's vacant seat, but the voters of Milwaukee re-elected him to Congress. Once again the House of Representatives refused to let him take his seat. Berger ran for office again in 1920, but this time he was defeated. However, by then he had appealed his conviction for violations of the Espionage Act and the 20 year-jail sentence that went with it to the Supreme Court, where he won. All charges against him were dropped and his mailing privileges were returned. In 1922 Berger ran again for Congress and won. This time the House of Representatives allowed him to take his seat. He then served three successive terms.[329]

There was however, another socialist in Congress, Meyer London (1871–1926), from New York, the second socialist (and the only other) elected to Congress at the time. He was allowed to take his seat in the House of Representatives and cast a vote against the declaration of war, which he called "the democracy of the cemetery and the equality of the slaughterhouse."[330] London also voted against the Sedition Act, the only Congressman in the House of Representatives to do so. However, at that point London ceased to follow the party line. He enraged his fellow socialists by supporting the war once it was declared, refused to introduce bills that the Socialist Party suggested and urged Russia not to make a separate peace with the Central Powers. At one point he declared: "I wonder whether I am to be punished for having had the courage to vote against the war or for standing by my country's decision when it chose war."[331] In fact, he was punished for neither. But he was put in the very uncomfortable position of being attacked as a dangerous radical on the one hand and a collaborationist traitor to socialism on the other, that is, being un–American and a militarist at the same time.

The president of the American Socialist Party, Eugene Debs, was not so lucky as Victor Berger or Meyer London. Debs had been the party's presidential nominee five times and in 1916 received 6 percent of the popular vote. Three months after the declaration of war, Debs appeared at an outdoor rally in Ohio. At one point he stated with obvious sarcasm that "it is extremely dangerous to exercise the constitutional right of free speech in a country fighting to make democracy free for the world."[332] For two hours he went on to attack government policy and of course the war in Europe, saying, among other things: "The master class has always declared the wars, the subject class has always fought the battles. The master class has had all to gain and nothing to lose, while the subject class has had nothing to gain and all to lose." Debs had been well aware that federal agents were in the crowd among his listeners. He was arrested, and less than two weeks later indicted for ten separate acts of sedition that violated the Espionage Act, a victim of the conformity that President Wilson predicted would arrive. At his trial, Debs freely conceded his guilt:

> I have been accused of having obstructed the war. I admit it. Gentlemen, I abhor war [...]. Your Honor, years ago I recognized my kinship with all living beings, and I made up my mind that I was not one bit better than the meanest on earth. I said then, and I say now, that while there is a lower class, I am in it, and while

there is a criminal element I am of it, and while there is a soul in prison, I am not free.[333]

Debs received a ten-year sentence and was sent to a maximum-security federal prison. As if to underscore the vindictive nature of the punishment, Debs was denied mail and visiting privileges, leaving him incommunicado.

Nonetheless, while still in prison Debs ran for president. In the 1920 election 913,644 people voted for Eugene V. Debs, prisoner #9653. It was slightly more votes than he had received in 1912. Nonetheless, President Wilson steadfastly refused to free Debs, claiming, "The man was a traitor to his country and will never be pardoned during my administration [...]. I will never consent to the pardon of this man."[334]

And he didn't. When Warren G. Harding (1865–1923) became President in 1921, he received a petition signed by more than 300,000 Americans requesting that Debs be pardoned. Debs was never pardoned, but he was released under a general amnesty on Christmas Day, 1921. Three years later Eugene V. Debs was nominated for the Nobel Peace Prize for his work in the interests of peace during World War I.[335] He often told audiences: "I am opposed to every war but one; I am for that war with heart and soul, and that is the worldwide war of the social revolution."

FOUR

Peace—with a Vengeance

In March 1915 a document titled "Proposals for the Avoidance of War" and marked "Private and Confidential, Not for Publication," circulated at the upper levels of the British government. Prepared by a small committee headed by Lord Bryce (1838–1922), it was, in essence, a scheme for a league of nations. It eventually became a source of key concepts and language used several years later in the Covenant of the League of Nations. The point of view was unabashedly clear and purposeful. Lord Bryce was well acquainted with the horrors of the modern battlefield. "If we do not try to end war," he announced, "war will end us."[1]

He developed the same theme in the introduction to the "Proposals for the Avoidance of War": "The feeling that the present war is a disastrous failure of civilization, and that at its close all should be done, that human wisdom and foresight can devise, to prevent the recurrence of such a catastrophe, is, we believe, general, if not universal, among all the nations concerned."[2]

Lord Bryce had no illusions concerning the enormity of the task he confronted. He began by quoting John Stuart Mill (1808–1873): "Small remedies for great evils do not produce small effects. They produce no effects."[3]

Trying not to be too radical or utopian, Lord Bryce nonetheless devised a scheme that would still mark a departure from the international system that had obviously been too weak to prevent a world war. He proposed a union of Sovereign States that would include, at a minimum, all the Great Powers of Europe and the United States. The organization would, he hoped, be the germ of an international polity, but that was not its purpose.

There was little new in the contents of Lord Bryce's plan. The novelty was that, for once, the concept of world peace was coming from the top, the highest levels of British government, who realized that the old international system had fallen apart and needed to be replaced. The plan was kept "private" until its mechanisms could be tinkered with and perfected. And there would be plenty of time for that. By 1915 it was clear that the war would be a long one.

Lord Bryce's plan enshrined the concept of arbitration, which for decades had been proposed as the best way to deal with international disputes. The members of the Union, the new supranational government-to-be, would bind themselves by treaty:

1. To refer all disputes that might arise between them, if diplomatic methods of adjustment had failed, either to a court of arbitration for judicial decision or to a council of conciliation for investigation and report.

2. Not to declare war or begin hostilities until the court had decided or the council had reported.

3. To put pressure, diplomatic, economic or forcible, upon any signatory power that should act in violation of the preceding conditions.[4]

Tacitly acknowledging the failure of elitist secret diplomacy as one of the causes of the war, Lord Bryce proposed a measure of popular control over international relations by publishing the results of all inquiries and discussions. This was something the peace societies had advocated for years. Lord Bryce simply provided an echo: "Without pretending that public opinion is always and everywhere pacific, we believe that, when properly instructed, it is more likely to favour peace than do the secret operations of diplomacy."[5]

The original draft of the document had been written by Goldsworthy Lowes Dickinson (1862–1932), a political scientist at King's College, Cambridge, late in the summer of 1914 before the war fully began. In an article titled "The War and the Way Out, Preparing the Path to Peace,"[6] he argued that the existing international anarchy had left the world without a means of conflict resolution. Dickinson prescribed a peace of reconciliation based on national self-determination and backed up by a European peace league equipped with coercive sanctions to ensure that disputes were settled peacefully. He also proposed arms limitations of some kind and the democratic control of foreign policy. His ideas formed the basis of numerous plans that were circulated in both the United States and England. What he wanted to avoid was a peace whose terms were dictated by vindictive nationalists, which of course is exactly what happened after the Germans signed the Armistice ending the war.

* * *

However, at the time Dickinson formulated the plan, in the early days of the war, he was convinced that the conflict would end with a negotiated peace. A group of statesmen would gather around a table in a neutral country and amiably try to arrive at a solution that would please everyone. Should that occur, a specific plan needed to be formulated beforehand so as to be readily available when the moment came to define the new world structure. Working with Lord Bryce and others, Dickinson drafted a new document titled "When the War

Comes to an End," and that in turn, by 1915, became the "Proposals for the Avoidance of War."

The drafting committee, known as the Bryce Group, mainly scholars and statesmen, held divergent views, but they agreed on a few central points—one of which was a moratorium on war. They also agreed that all members of the league "should bind themselves by treaty, to give moral and material support to any power attacked by another in breach of the agreement." All conflicts would be referred to arbitration or to conciliation by an independent council and there should be a "cooling off" period following any arbitral award or council recommendations. Ultimately these ideas became an integral part of the League Covenant. The Bryce Group also raised and discussed other important issues, e.g., what constitutes a judiciable dispute, the supervision of arms limitations, the conduct of military operations, both on land and at sea, and who can be a member of the league.

A new version of the "Proposals" was printed and circulated, again privately, in 1915. It became the basis for a new society in England, the League of Nations Society, which announced that its principal goal was "to advocate an Agreement among civilized States, which will serve as a basis of permanent peace among them, by providing for the Peaceful Settlement of Disputes, for Mutual Defense, and the Observance of Treaties and International Law."[7]

By 1916 numerous suggestions had been made and numerous other schemes for an international organization that would monitor the peace had been suggested, but the common denominator remained the proposal formulated by the Bryce Group. The "Proposals" were finally published and made available to the public in 1917 both in the UK and in the United States.

By the time the war ended, a document existed that had been tested and amended by scholars, statesmen and diplomats on both sides of the Atlantic, and that included the American President and Secretary of State as well as the British Prime Minister and members of his War Cabinet. In the final analysis, at the drafting of the League of Nations Covenant in Paris the hand of the Bryce Group can clearly be seen in articles 12 to 17. But, perhaps more important, the "Proposals" served as a semi-official starting point, a démarche encouraging discussion, debate and discourse at the highest levels of government about how a peaceful world should be structured after the war.

* * *

In the fall of 1917, after the Bolshevik revolution, the Russian Council of Workingmen's and Soldiers' Delegates requested that the Allies draw up a set of peace terms. At the same time the council asked them to adopt the Russian formula of "no annexations and no indemnities and the self-determination of peoples." Vladimir Lenin (né Vladimir Ilyich Ulyanov, 1870–1924), now firmly in control of the government, signed the *Decree on Peace*, which was approved by the Second Congress of the Soviet of Workers', Soldiers', and Peasants' Deputies. The *Decree* stated:

> The [Russian] government proposes an immediate armistice to the governments and peoples of all the belligerent countries, and, for its part, considers it desirable that this armistice should be concluded for a period of not less than three months, i.e., a period long enough to complete the negotiations for peace with the participation of representatives of all peoples or nations, without exception, involved in or compelled to take part in the war.[8]

The Russians were proposing to meet with the Central Powers and confront them face-to-face across a negotiating table for the first time since the war began. However, the Allies categorically refused to consider a possible end to the war by a return to the *status quo ante bellum*, which is roughly what the Russian position meant to them.

At that point a number of options had been open to the Allies, for example, sending observers or using the military attachés of their respective embassies, who informally could have explored the possible terms for an armistice on the Western Front. But apparently none of these options was proposed or even seriously considered. On the one hand, the Allies let another chance for peace slip through their fingers. On the other hand, if the Allies had formally joined the Bolsheviks at Brest-Litovsk it would have given credibility to the new Russian regime, as well as strengthened their bargaining position. The basically conservative Allies made it clear that they were not about to encourage the revolutionary groundswell that seemed to be sweeping across Europe.

Less than a month later, Leon Trotsky (*né* Lev Davidovich Bronshtein, 1879–1940), then Commissar for Foreign Affairs, repeated the offer to meet with the Central Powers. When the Allies refused again, he indicated he was ready to sign a separate agreement with the Germans and bring an immediate end to the war in the east.

In fact, the Bolsheviks had no other choice. They had marched into the corridors of power under the banner of "LAND, PEACE and BREAD." If they were unable to deliver immediately the two most pressing needs, peace and bread, they knew they would not control the government for long. The Russian armies were already disintegrating, mass desertions had become commonplace and in many places the front lines had virtually ceased to exist. The new Soviet government in Petrograd had no other option but to sue for peace.

The first peace proclamation was published in *Izvestia*, the official organ of the Petrograd Soviet, shortly after the Bolsheviks seized power: "It [the Petrograd Soviet] demands an immediate truce on all fronts, announces its willingness to consider calmly and objectively all peace proposals [...]. It is not at all seeking to break with its Allies, but it has taken a defensive position."[9]

The British ambassador to Russia during the revolution, Sir George Buchanan (1854–1924), published a declaration in which he stated: "The Allied

Governments find themselves in the presence of a *fait accompli* on a subject concerning which they have not been consulted. It is furthermore impossible for the Embassy to reply to the notes of a Government which his own Government has not recognized."[10]

The French were also not ready to make peace, or, putting it in the best possible light, they were not ready to let a new revolutionary Russia take the lead and therefore the credit for ending the war. General Lavergne, head of the French mission at the Russian Staff Headquarters, informed his counterpart: "France does not recognize the power of the People's Commissars. [...] [I]t counts upon the firm resolution of the military leaders to repel every criminal *pourparler* and to keep the Russian army facing the common enemy [...]. No Government has the right to discuss separately the question of an armistice or of peace."[11]

The United States had entered the war less than six months previously, and it was also unwilling to let the new Russian government take the peace initiative. Its official position was that "the United States, an ally of Russia, pursuing with her the war [...] protests energetically and categorically against any separate armistice that might be concluded by Russia."[12]

The Germans, however, were delighted. For them, it was a clear success, undeniable proof to the public that all their sacrifices had finally produced a military victory. Foreign Secretary Richard von Kühlmann (1873–1948) told the Reichstag: "Russia has set the world ablaze [...]. Russia has swept away the culprits, and she is laboring to find through an armistice and peace an opportunity for her internal reconstruction."[13]

The Bolsheviks did what they could to force the Allies to the negotiating table; for example, they strongly hinted that if the Allies refused to join them at Brest-Litovsk the new Russian government would repudiate the Czarist debt, which was enormous. This was not an insignificant threat. By the end of the war it is estimated that Russia owed well over 300 billion contemporary U.S. dollars, a sum roughly equal to the combined current yearly military budgets of China, Russia, France and Great Britain.

Trotsky tried to hold the door open as long as possible for participation by Allies. Just before the Bolshevik delegation left Petrograd for the front to meet with the Germans he told the American military attaché, General Judson (1865–1923), that "the Allies, if they thought it advisable, might intervene at a later stage of the negotiations."[14]

While the Russians were trying to convince the Allies to take part in the peace negotiations a Bolshevik delegation passed through the front lines under a white flag, then entered Brest-Litovsk, which was occupied by the Germans. The way had been prepared by an exchange of notes and several meetings in no-man's-land by staff officers of both sides. As the Bolshevik delegation passed through the Russian lines "[t]hey were received with rounds of applause [from the army] which developed into a long ovation."[15]

Awaiting the Bolshevik delegation in Brest-Litovsk was a group of German and Austrian generals and diplomats, including the Austro-Hungarian Foreign Minister, Count Czernin (1872–1932), and Field Marshall Prince Leopold of Bavaria (1846–1930).

The Bolshevik delegation was a mixed lot, including Adolph Joffe (1883–1927), a doctor, and his associate Lev Kamenev (1883–1936), a professional revolutionary; Anastasia Bitsenko (1875–1938), recently released from 17 years in prison in Siberia for assassinating a Czarist general; and a peasant, Roman Stashkov, who was literally picked up off the street. While driving to the railway station in Petrograd the Russian delegation had realized that they needed someone to symbolically represent the peasantry. Stashkov was found on a street corner, also headed toward a train station, albeit another one. When questioned about his politics he replied, "The very leftist," and was immediately promised a small of money if he agreed to join the delegation. Reportedly Stashkov took his place at the negotiation table and sat quietly through the sessions, although he understood absolutely nothing, since all the meetings were conducted in French. But he did take a very active part in the sumptuous formal dinners, where he shoveled in as much food as possible through his long, unkempt beard. Once, when asked if he wanted red or white wine, Stashkov turned to the man seated next to him, Prinz Ernst von Hohenlohe (1863–1950), Queen Victoria's grandnephew, and asked, "Which is stronger? It makes no difference to me which one I drink. I'm only interested in the alcohol."[16]

As a first step both sides agreed upon a temporary truce for 48 hours, and that in turn was extended for another 28 days, which would be automatically renewed unless either side gave a 7-day notice. For the first time in over three years along the whole front, from the Baltic Sea to the Black Sea, not a shot was fired.

Writing later, Trotsky summarized the Bolshevik position:

> The question of peace was first put before the world in a shape which made it impossible to side-track it any longer by machinations behind the scenes. On the 22nd of November a truce was signed to discontinue military activities on the entire front from the Baltic to the Black Sea. Once more we requested our Allies to join us and to conduct together with us the peace negotiations. There was no reply, though this time the Allies did not again attempt to frighten us by threats. The peace negotiations were started December 9th, a month and a half after the peace decree was adopted [...]. For a month and a half we kept our Allies informed about every step we made and always called upon them to become a party to the peace negotiations. Our conscience is clear before the peoples of France, Italy and Great Britain [...]. We did all in our power to get all the belligerents to join the peace negotiations.[17]

At roughly the same time Trotsky announced that Russia repudiated all the previous treaties that had been signed by the Czarist government. He also declared that Russia would publish the secret treaties, which certainly did not endear him to the Allies.

Lloyd George (1863–1945) gave the reply in a speech to the British Parliament: "Her [Russia's] action will not lead, as she imagines, to universal peace. It will simply prolong the world's agony, and inevitably put her in bondage to the military dominance of Prussia."[18]

Stephen Pichon (1857–1933), French Minister of Foreign Affairs, told the Assemblée Nationale: "Russia may treat for a separate peace with our enemies or not. In either case the war will continue. An Ally has failed us [...]. But another Ally (the United States) has come from the other end of the world."[19]

The truce resulted in a signed armistice, which remained in effect over the Christmas holidays. During that time the Bosheviks tried to decide what to do. The country was in total chaos, the army, or what was left of it, mutinous or at best demoralized, and the new Soviet government was facing a strong and victorious German military force.

In early January, Trotsky returned to Petrograd and an intense debate in the Party Central Committee about how precisely to deal with the Germans. Trotsky fervently believed that Western Europe, especially Germany, was on the threshold of a revolution. If the Russian Bolsheviks could just hold out long enough, they would be rescued by the German proletariat, whose revolt and "inevitable" rise to power would virtually destroy the Kaiser's army. Trotsky told the committee: "They cannot threaten us with an offensive as they cannot be sure the German soldiers will take part in one [...], and if German imperialism attempts to crucify us on the wheel of its military machine, then [...] we shall appeal to our elder brothers in the west and say: 'Do you hear?' and the international proletariat will respond—we firmly believe this—'We hear!'"[20]

Lenin disagreed and adopted a more pragmatic approach. He felt that they had no choice but to accept whatever terms the German generals offered. He called Trotsky's proposal "political showmanship." After much debate in the Central Committee the decision was taken to accept Trotsky's "no peace, no war" proposal but to delay it as long as possible in the hope that the revolution would begin in the West, especially Germany.

Marxists had always believed that Germany, the most advanced industrial nation on the continent, was the logical place for the first truly socialist revolution. Trotsky and Lenin were devoted internationalists who had always followed theory to the letter. Even after the Bolsheviks took power Lenin wrote: "If it is necessary for us (Russia) to go under to assure the success of the German revolution, we should have to do it. The German revolution is vastly more important than ours."[21]

However, Lenin began to change and eventually took the position that Russia would be a convenient base from which to spread the revolution. Therefore, it had to be protected, no matter what the cost. Trotsky remained committed to the German revolution.

For a while the German generals also used a delaying tactic while they tried to apply the Wilsonian principle of "self-determination" for the nationalities in the east. They intended to break up the Russian Empire and create independent states in the Baltic and the border regions that could easily be controlled by Germany. But the generals needed a little time, for example, to persuade the Ukrainian politicians to sign a separate peace treaty, which they eventually did. Then the Germans would be ready to return to the negotiating table.

Meanwhile, Trotsky made a short trip to Warsaw; then, complaining about the lack of communication with Petrograd, he returned to the capital for discussions with the government.

Finally, when he could delay the negotiations no longer, Trotsky traveled back to Brest-Litovsk. But this time the Germans had decided to force the negotiations to a conclusion. They presented the Russian delegation with a map of Eastern Europe that stripped Russia of extensive territories. A new frontier put the Germans less than a hundred miles from Petrograd, then curved eastwards all the way to the Don River.

Enraged, Trotsky announced to the Germans his "no peace, no war" formula and coupled it with a stirring appeal to the workers of Europe to seize power and follow the Russian example:

> We have come to the conclusion that the hour of decision has struck [...]. We do not wish to take part any longer in this purely imperialist war, in which the claims of the propertied classes are being paid in blood. [...] [W]e are withdrawing our army and our people from the war [...]. We are informing all peoples and all Governments of this. We are issuing orders for the complete demobilization of our armies [...]. We expect and firmly believe that other peoples will soon follow our example [...]. We refuse to give our sanction to the conditions which German and Austro-Hungarian imperialism writes with the sword on the body of living peoples. We cannot put the signature of the Russian revolution to conditions which carry with them oppression, misfortune, and misery to millions of human beings.

Trotsky then left Brest-Litvosk confident that he had won a diplomatic victory and certain that the Germans would not dare to renew their offensive. However, six days later that is exactly what they did. The German army began advancing on a broad front. The "no peace, no war" solution had been a disaster. The remnants of the Russian army retreated as fast as they could walk or run, and with them, just ahead of the Germans, was a huge civilian population estimated to be about 8 million. Many perished on the way. A large percentage of the survivors were later caught in the Russian Civil War and never returned to their homes.

The Russians had no choice but to agree to the German terms. A delegation quickly returned to Brest-Litovsk. After nearly six months of negotiations the Bolsheviks signed the treaty, which effectively let the Germans keep virtually all the territory they had conquered, nearly a million square miles, an area as large as Austria-Hungary. Russia also lost roughly a quarter of the former empire's population, that is, over 50 million people, a quarter of its industry, nine-tenths of its coal mines, and in total over a quarter of its income. It was a peace at any price solution, the worst possible, but there was no alternative. The Russian army no longer had the will to resist. Lenin told the Fourth All-Russian Congress of Soviets in Moscow: "We must not deceive ourselves. We must have courage to face the unadorned, bitter truth. We must measure in full, to the very bottom, the abyss of defeat, partition, enslavement, humiliation, into which we have been thrown."[22]

Some Germans were bewildered and even slightly embarrassed that such a punitive peace had been allowed to occur. But the locus of power in Germany had shifted as the war progressed and the military assumed the role of final decision maker. The generals were determined to bring home giant territorial laurels on their spears. Viktor Bredt (1879–1940), a socialist member of the Reichstag, declared to the Reichstag Inquiry Commission: "The layman stands amazed and the scholar wonders how it was possible for the Reichstag to approve the Peace of Brest-Litovsk after it had passed the Peace Resolution.... Never in the history of the world has there been an instance of greater annexationist politics than the Treaty of Brest-Litovsk."[23]

Another member of the Reichstag, Ludwig Quessel (1872–1931), brought up the question that undoubtedly crossed many people's minds, both in Germany and in the West—should the Germans impose a peace on the West what would it look like?: "What the Supreme Command (Generals von Hindenburg [1847–1934] and Ludendorff [1865–1937]) considered to be an acceptable peace in the east, we have seen in the treaty of Brest-Litovsk. In the event of victory the peace in the west by the Supreme Command would have been of the same kind. It would have been a dictated peace just like the one we concluded at Brest-Litovsk."[24]

The Allies had remained on the distant sidelines and watched the long drama unfold. They could easily have had an observer of one sort or another at the protracted negotiations, a diplomat or staff officer, to take advantage of the many social occasions and, at a minimum, have a frank exchange of views. But when the details of the draconian peace became known, they drove the Allies even further away from the negotiating table. Any notion of German reasonableness disappeared. A German victory, then peace on the Western Front would be disastrous. President Wilson wrote with bitterness shortly after the Treaty of Brest-Litovsk was signed: "They [The Central Powers] have convinced us that they are without honor and do not intend justice. They observe no covenants, accept no principles but force and their own interests. We cannot come to terms with them."[25]

The Treaty of Brest-Litovsk lasted only from March 1918 till November 1918, when it was categorically annulled by the November 11 Armistice agreement on the Western Front. Two days later the Russians formally denounced the treaty.

* * *

While the Russians and the Central Powers were negotiating, President Wilson stood before a joint session of the American Congress and set forth his Fourteen Points or the "Wilsonian Commandments," as George Clemenceau (1841–1929), the Prime Minister of France, called them.[26] They concisely stated the war aims of the Allies and made it clear that the Entente would not be drawn into the German–Russian peace conference at Brest-Litovsk. Among other things, the Fourteen Points called for the return of Alsace-Lorraine to France, the Belgian state's restoration to what it was before the war, an independent Poland, and the dismemberment of the Austrian-Hungarian Empire. These demands were all radically different from the Russian formula of "no annexations and no indemnities."

The reaction of the Allies to President Wilson's Fourteen Points was instantly favorable, so much so that many Americans suddenly realized that there was a real chance for world peace. Even some of those who had been opposed to the intervention of the United States in the European war switched sides and supported America's new role in European affairs, hoping that the future would remake the world and create an agency of collective security that would in effect do away with war.

Two days after President Wilson's speech, the Allies formally committed themselves to the project of a league of nations to discourage future wars. In a joint note to Wilson they declared:

> They [the Allies] associate themselves with all their hopes with the project for the creation of a league of nations to insure peace and justice throughout the world. They are conscious of all the advantages to the cause of humanity and civilization which would flow from the establishment of international rules designed to avoid violent conflicts between nations, rules which must provide the sanctions necessary to insure their execution and so prevent a false security from serving simply to facilitate new aggressions.[27]

On January 15, 1917, Viscount Motono, the Japanese Minister for Foreign Affairs cabled Washington: "I have noted with interest your unremitting efforts to secure the world against a repetition of the present convulsion. All proposals directed to effect so desirable an end must be welcomed and carefully studied by every one to whom peace and good will are not empty names and who has any regard for humanity."[28]

One by one, the neutral countries agreed. Switzerland was the first, then Spain and Denmark.

* * *

Wilson's Fourteen Points speech also effectively closed the door to any possible negotiation with the Central Powers and committed the United States to join the fight in the trenches to a bitter end. Since the Germans could not possibly accept Wilson's demands, his terms simply strengthened their resolve and willingness to fight for what they believed should be theirs. The war had become a hopeless battle of wills.

The last, or the Fourteenth, of Wilson's Points echoed a goal advocated by most peace societies, as well as one that had appeared in Pope Benedict XV's peace proposal. It announced to the world that the United States stood firmly behind the concept of world government: "A general association of nations must be formed under specific covenants for the purpose of affording mutual guarantees of political independence and territorial integrity to great and small states alike."[29]

* * *

President Wilson conceived and framed the Fourteen Points together with his confidant and chief advisor, Colonel House (1858–1938). One may cast doubt on both Colonel House's motives and his principles. The man did not have the ideal profile for someone who was a broker for peace and democracy, helped to write the armistice agreement with Germany, and later became the chief American negotiator at the Paris Peace Conference.

Shortly before Woodrow Wilson had become President, Colonel House had written a futuristic novel titled *Philip Dru, Administrator: A Story of Tomorrow*. The plot is simple: the main character, Philip Dru, leads the democratic western part of the United States in a civil war against the plutocratic East and becomes the dictator of America. The book displays contempt for the democratic process, a voracious appetite for violence, and an admiration for a benevolent dictatorship.

Unfortunately, one cannot dismiss the book as pure fiction, as Colonel House went out of his way to say that the novel delivered a clear message. "Most of it," the colonel wrote, "I stand upon as being both my ethical and political faith."[30]

President Wilson was well aware of Colonel's House's anti-democratic and authoritarian beliefs. Wilson had read the novel during one of his summer vacations in Bermuda. One is confronted by a bizarre conundrum. The two men were very close. Colonel House stayed in the White House whenever he was in Washington, and President Wilson often referred to House as his "right hand" or his "second personality." Was President Wilson, the arch-democrat, in reality a crypto-authoritarian, or was it just what one journalist called it: "the strangest friendship in history?"[31]

At one point the main character of *Philip Dru: Administrator: A Story of Tomorrow* says: "Our government is, perhaps, less responsive to the will of the people than of almost any of the civilized nations. Our Constitution and our laws served us well for the first hundred years of our existence, but under the conditions of today they are not only obsolete, but even grotesque."[32]

Should there be any doubt as to how Colonel House thought the country should be governed, the author's alter ego, Dru, spoke on his behalf and made his preference for a dictatorship absolutely clear.

> General Dru now called a conference of his officers and announced his purpose of assuming the powers of a dictator, distasteful as it was to him, and, as he felt it might also be, to the people. He explained that such a radical step was necessary, in order to quickly purge the Government of those abuses that had arisen [...]. They were assured that he was free from any personal ambition, and he pledged his honor to retire after the contemplated reforms had been made, so that the country could again have a constitutional government [...]. He then issued an address to his army proclaiming himself "*Administrator of the Republic.*"[33]

Colonel House appears to have been a very strange man to be entrusted with the responsibility for, as President Wilson put it, making the "world safe for democracy."

* * *

The idea of a safer, saner, more humane world governed by some kind of global government had been common currency for many years, filling journals and providing endless grist for lectures and debates. A very vocal minority could be found in almost every country arguing and agitating for a peaceful resolution of conflict, not a fanatic fringe, but a respectable, accepted part of society. Prominent businessmen, politicians and the clergy were often members of peace groups and did not hesitate to use their position and privileges to speak out for the cause.

Bertha von Suttner (1843–1914), for example, the doyenne of the peace movement in the decades before the war, had campaigned continually for the creation of supra-state bodies like the League of Nations and a World Court to ensure peace: "As 40 million people can live at peace in one nation, so 1,700 million can live at peace in one world; as three states can form a Triple Alliance or Triple Entente, so all states can form a Federation of the World; as courts settle differences between individuals of one nation; so international courts will settle differences between nations."[34]

One of the most popular writers of his time, H. G. Wells (1866–1946), was also a staunch believer, especially toward the end of the war, in what he called "A League of Free Nations." This, he felt, would confront the most urgent problem of civilization, the constant specter of war. In fact, Wells's thinking went well beyond a "League of Free Nations." The goal he sought was not only peace in Europe but a compassionate, global peace. Almost from the moment the conflict began, he became an impassioned and uncompromising evangelist of a world state:

The only wise course before the allied European powers now is to put their national conceit in their pockets and to combine to lock up their foreign policy, their trade interests, and all their imperial and international interests into a League so big as to be able to withstand the most sudden and treacherous of blows. And surely the only completely safe course for them and mankind—hard and nearly impossible though it may seem at the present juncture—is for them to lock up into one unity with a democratized Germany and with all other states of the earth into one peace-maintaining League.[35]

For Wells, the greatest impediment to world government was nationalism, the cancerous root of war: "[Nationalism] trumpets and waves its flags, obtrudes its tawdry loyalties, exaggerates the splendors of the past, and fights to sustain the ancient hallucinations."[36] According to Wells, after nationalism was processed by the press and schools it distorted and exaggerated the facts so brutally that any rational analysis or discussion of events became virtually impossible. Truth was only a mere manipulated shadow at the service of the system that had only one real goal. The idea of the nation-state, Wells wrote, "is essentially and incurably a war-making state."[37]

Wells would eventually castigate President Wilson for "his obsession by the idea of sovereignty of 'nationalities' and his incapacity to think out what he meant by a nationality." According to Wells, "He [Wilson] thought only of nations struggling to be free. He never thought of man struggling to be free of nationality."[38]

In 1916 Wells wrote very prophetically: "This is one world and bayonets are a crop that spreads. Let them gather and seed, it matters not how far from you, and a time will come when they will be sticking up your nose. There is no real peace but the peace of the whole world, and that is only to be kept by the whole world resisting and suppressing aggression wherever it arises."[39]

But while Wells was essentially a crusading optimist, a utopian for whom nothing short of the ultimate goal really mattered, most other writers and philosophers of the time parted company with him somewhere along the way. Marie Lenéru (1875–1918), for example, ended her very popular play, *La Paix* (The peace), on an essentially pessimistic note, which unfortunately proved to be realistic. The brief truces between wars would continue, she posited, and the pacifists would struggle on, despite the failure of their resolutions and congresses and the inability to recognize their recurrent mistakes. Meanwhile the cities of Europe would be reduced to rubble and their shells would stand like headstones in giant cemeteries.[40]

* * *

Hoping to create an antidote to militarism, in 1918 Romain Rolland (1866–1944) wrote the *Declaration of the Independence of the Mind*, an apolitical and pacifist manifesto by which he hoped the world's intellectual elite would declare themselves the dedicated opponents of nationalism, ethnocentrism and warfare. In a public statement Rolland asked the opinion leaders of the Western world to affirm their solidarity and determination never to let humanity plunge again into the savagery of war.

However, once the intellectuals received the text[41] they started making suggestions to change the wording, adding phrases or indeed whole paragraphs, altering the focus, and, in general, quibbling with definitions, perspective and objectives. Max Eastman (1883–1969) insisted on transposing the entire text into Marxian terminology, Bertrand Russell (1872–1970) wrote lengthy reservations, longer than the original document, and G. B. Shaw (1856–1950) completely rewrote about a third of the text. Some intellectuals refused to have anything to do with the declaration. Anatole France (1844–1924), for example, ignored Rolland's appeal and Madame Curie (1867–1934) declared that she could not forget the sinking of the *Lusitania*.[42]

At one point an exasperated Romain Rolland wrote to Bertrand Russell: "My Declaration has received so many demands for modifications or toning down from different sides that if they were accepted, nothing would be left but the title."[43]

Finally, on June 26, 1919, two days before the Treaty of Versailles was signed, *L'Humanité* in Paris published the declaration basically as it was composed by Romain Rolland. Only one sentence had been changed. The original read: *"Nous prenons l'engagement de ne servir jamais que la Vérité"* (We pledge to serve only Truth). It was replaced by *"Nous honorons la seule Vérité"* (We honor Truth alone).[44]

Despite the squabbling over the wording, the document was signed by some of the world's leading thinkers, among them Albert Einstein (1879–1955), Hermann Hesse (1877–1962), Benedetto Croce (1866–1952), Bertrand Russell (1872–1970), Stefan Zweig (1881–1942), Maxim Gorky (1868–1936), Alfred Stieglitz (1864–1946), Upton Sinclair (1878–1968), Rabindranath Tagore (1861–1941), and Henri Barbusse (1873–1935).

Eventually over a thousand intellectuals representing several dozen countries signed the document. Encouraged, Romain Rolland proposed the creation of an Internationale de l'esprit (an International of the Mind), an organization that would be patterned after the communist "International" that had just been established in Moscow. He wanted the new union to be truly international and include philosophers from India and the Far East. The goal was grandiose, nothing less than a world-encompassing humanism that would unify mankind.

Stefan Zweig called the Internationale de l'esprit:

> The invisible republic of the spirit, the universal fatherland. [...] [I]n a world falling to ruin, it was to be the cornerstone of the invisible temple, the refuge of the disillusioned. [...] [I]ts only law is that of brotherhood; its only enemies are

hatred and arrogance between nations. Whoever makes his home within this invisible realm becomes a citizen of the world. [...] [H]e is an indweller in all tongues and in all countries, in the universal past and the universal future.[45]

However, in the halcyon days after the end of the war many other schemes that promised peace, prosperity and unity vied for the world's attention, not the least of which was the newly formed League of Nations. The Internationale de l'esprit slipped out of the headlines and was soon forgotten.

* * *

As the war drew to an end a fundamental shift in public attitudes appears to have taken place. For the first time there was an almost universal sense that the deliberate launching of a war could no longer be justified. Never again would armies march so lightheartedly to the battlefield as they did in 1914.

Particularly in the United States the end of the war produced a fork in the road toward a lasting peace, two opposing lessons based on the same appalling reality. The first reasoned that safety from conflict and strife could be found in withdrawal and seclusion, a retreat behind high walls and ever more powerful weapons, as if the cancer of war came from without and not from within the nature of human beings. The second conclusion was a tenacious, renewed optimism nourished by men and women who declared that not only "is Europe one," as Bertha von Süttner was fond of repeating, but also "the entire world is one." The rights of man must be extended to include all men and women all over the world. All deserved equal protection from the scourge of war.

The League of Nations reflected this latter opinion, a determined positive view of a future that would emerge from the despair of the trenches. Supporting it was the fervent belief that, if left to themselves, men would always opt for peace instead of war. That had been proved on the battlefield. When the opportunity presented itself, soldiers came out of the trenches, walked across the no-man's-land and, on the other side of the barbed wire, found men who were merely mirror images of themselves, equally frightened, weary, and ready to lay down their arms.

* * *

The Armistice was finally signed at 5:00 a.m. on November 11, 1918, and went into effect six hours later.

David Lloyd George (1863–1945) announced to the House of Commons: "At eleven o'clock this morning came to an end the cruelest and more terrible war that has ever scourged mankind. I hope we may say that thus, this fateful morning, came to an end all Wars."[46]

However, during those six final hours of warfare after the cease-fire agreement had been signed but had not formally taken effect, the fighting continued. As perhaps a final testament to the futility and absurdity of the war, during that last morning 2,738 men from both sides were killed and more than 8,000 wounded.

* * *

But the new world order that was supposed to emerge from the ashes of the war turned out to be flawed from the beginning. The Treaty of Versailles that officially ended the war was full of phrases like "to promote international co-operation" and "honourable relations between nations" and "international law as the actual rule of conduct." In fact, these phrases were just a verbal mask, a sop to the world's peace societies, and behind them was just another vindictive victors' decree forced upon the vanquished, a spiked collar around the neck of the German people, what one German delegate peace conference called "the victorious violence of our enemies."

After they signed the treaty the German delegates were treated like outcasts and shown to a separate exit before the general body of the conference arrived. Later they told the press that had they known that they would be treated like pariahs and second-class civilians they would never have signed the document.

In Germany the treaty was immediately labeled a diktat, a decree or an order. Instead of binding men and nations together, it drove them apart and became an open wound that festered for decades. In the German press they called it "a stab-in-the-back," "a murderous plan," and a "Cathagean peace."

Prince Lichnowsky (1860–1928), the former German ambassador to London, had been widely known as "the ambassador of peace." He had done his utmost to prevent the war. After the Armistice he emerged from obscurity and wrote in a German newspaper: "The terms of the Armistice now laid upon us are animated by a spirit for which one can find no other name than revenge; for if these terms were conscientiously observed, they would infallibly bring in their train of misery and famine, anarchy and chaos."[47]

The French Deputy Marcel Cachin (1869–1958) said: "The Allied armies fought to make this war the last. They fought for a just and lasting peace, but none of these boons has been bestowed on us. We are confronted with the failure of the policy of the one man in whom our party had put its confidence—President Wilson. The peace conditions [...] are unacceptable from various points of view, financial, territorial, economic, social, and human."[48]

Many British also realized that if harsh terms were imposed on the Germans this was likely to be planting the seeds of yet another war. When the Admiral of the British Fleet, John Fisher (1841–1920), was asked how long it would be until the next war, he replied quite accurately "20 years time." Douglas Haig (1861–1928), the senior British officer during World War One, wrote to his wife just before the Armistice: "It is important that our Statesmen should [...] not attempt to humiliate Germany as to produce the desire for revenge in years to come."[49]

Conclusion

Never had war been so total, so devastating, so consuming in human life and spirit. One is forced to pose the question—why, during the 1,566 days of warfare, did not one of the many attempts to bring the belligerents to the negotiating table succeed, or at least create a momentary cease-fire, one long enough to give public opinion a chance to fully express their feelings?

Unfortunately, a constellation of negative factors working together produced an almost insurmountable barrier that effectively blocked any movement toward peace. None of the many "peace feelers" was ever allowed to mature into a cease-fire, the first step toward a *pourparler*.

First, there was a total lack of popular control and participation in the conduct of foreign affairs. Many, if not most, of the peace attempts were never revealed to the public. Covered by layers of censorship and classified as military secrets, the contacts and discussions between belligerents were often cloak-and-dagger operations involving only a few individuals. Typically, only those in key positions knew about them. In Germany, this meant the generals of the high command, the Kaiser and a few Ministers; in Russia and Austria-Hungary the Czar, the Emperor and their top Ministers; in Italy, France and Great Britain the Prime Minister and a select group of cabinet leaders. Thus perhaps a dozen men, two or three dozen at most, controlled the destiny of the millions mired in the trenches. Most of these Kings, Presidents and Ministers never saw the brutal face of war, the armies living and fighting in mud and filth, or heard the cries of anguish from the casualties overflowing the field hospitals. War for these men of privilege was a geopolitical board game whose pieces slid effortlessly and antiseptically from one position to another.

Seldom did the forces of humanism and rationality have a chance to speak out and almost never did they directly influence the course of events. The many anti-war organizations and the millions of war-weary soldiers and civilians had little or no opportunity to make their opinions known.

When the two sides did have contact, usually through representatives or potential mediators, they both played the same well-worn, pre-war diplomatic game in which one side insists upon knowing the other's terms without revealing its own—a vicious circle that cannot possibly succeed. Neither side ever really announced what their war aims were, aside from totalistic bombast like "crush the Prussians" or "annihilate the English army."

In the corridors of power the concept of peace had become associated with weakness, the fear that a proposal for negotiation would be interpreted as the last act before surrender. When the tide of battle seemed to be ebbing for the Allies the Central Powers became intransigent and the reverse when their fortunes seemed to wane. Peace became simply another tactic and never was a real goal.

Behind this use of peace as a ploy was the fear haunting Emperors, Czars, Prime Ministers and generals that negotiations might lead to drastic compromises, which in turn might spell their own demise and rapid fall from power. Only a peace achieved by an overwhelming military victory could protect them and deliver the diplomatic and territorial spoils to justify their jingoistic rhetoric and the long, horrible years of suffering and sacrifice. H. H. Asquith (1852–1928), the wartime Prime Minister of the UK, for example, was speaking the language of total victory when he declared before Parliament: "We shall never sheath the sword which we have not lightly drawn [...] until the military domination of Prussia is wholly and finally destroyed."[1] And the German Kaiser was equally, if not more, belligerent and totalistic when he stood in front of his troops and ranted: "It is my Royal and Imperial command that you exterminate the treacherous English and march over General French's contemptible little army."[2] The generals were often even more strident. William Robertson (1860–1928), Chief of the British Imperial Staff, lectured:

> It would be a cowardly crime to accept a premature peace [...]. There are amongst us, as in all communities, a certain number of cranks, cowards and philosophers, some of who are afraid of their own skins being hurt, whilst others are capable of proving to those sufficiently weak-minded to listen to them that we stand to gain more by losing the war than by winning it [...]. We need pay no attention to those miserable members of society.[3]

In these men's minds there was no room for compromise. Victory and peace were fused into one. The end of the war would arrive only when the opposing army was totally destroyed, its generals driven to their knees.

The military command was haunted by fears of a scenario of failed peace negotiations. Should they give the order to stop fighting, what would happen if, for one reason or another, a peace conference reached an impasse and the diplomats gave up? Would the war-weary armies go back to the trenches and pick up their weapons? It might be difficult, if not impossible, to re-start the war. This had proved to be the case after the so-called Christmas truce of 1914 and the truce at Gallipoli. The soldiers in the trenches quickly learned that those facing them across the no-man's-land were just a reflection of themselves.

How would the opposition parties and organizations exploit a failed cease-fire? Would governments fall and with them the top echelon of staff officers? Would the war-weary public be willing to return to their jobs and sacrifices simply because a few diplomats were unable to agree on insignificant details? Who would be blamed? As the generals looked in the mirror of history they saw their own tarnished image. What would future generations say and write of them?

To complicate matters even further, these European and American men in positions of power, like all men, had their own, often unique, set of convictions, prejudices, idiosyncrasies, jealousies and ambitions that affected what they thought and did. German Chancellor Michaelis (1857–1936), for example, was a Protestant and very anti–Papist, which is a major reason why he failed to exploit Pope Benedict XV's (1854–1922) peace proposal. The staunch republicans Raymond Poincaré (1860–1924), Prime Minister of France, and his advisors, the Cambon brothers, Jules-Martin (1845–1935), head of the Political Section of the French Foreign Ministry, and Paul (1843–1924), French ambassador to Great Britain, undoubtedly lacked enthusiasm for Prince Sixtus (1886–1934) and his proposals because the Prince was a reactionary and an eminent Bourbon. And the well-known antipathy between Colonel House (1858–1938), President Wilson's (1856–1924) confidant and advisor, and the American Secretary of State William Jennings Bryan (1860–1925) certainly did not facilitate the Straus affair in 1914, nor did the fact that Colonel House was an Anglophile endear him to the Germans. The list of personal foibles and their consequences is almost endless.

The unfortunate truth is that if a handful of men in key positions, or just some of them, had decided to end the war by a negotiated settlement, it could have happened almost immediately. The one thing they seemed to have had in common was that they had all grown up in the school of pre-war diplomacy, a breeding ground of mutual distrust, suspicion, fear and hatred. From the beginning of the conflict they had made up their minds the peace could be won only by a victory on the battlefield. Regrettably, as history has shown us, peace through victory yields neither peace nor victory. When someone entered the corridors of power who thought otherwise, a Frenchman like Aristide Briand (1862–1932) or a German like Richard von Kühlmann (1873–1948), who was open to negotiation and compromise, he quickly found doors to negotiation slammed in his face.

In the end the will of the generals prevailed. The war became a fight to the finish, till the Central Powers were prostrate, exactly the goal the Allied military had sought from the beginning. But what the generals thought was peace was really just a protracted cease-fire, a pause long enough for Germany to recover, rearm, then strike back. They were to call it World War Two, but in reality it just another round of World War One.

Chapter Notes

Chapter One

1. Edwin Ginn was a millionaire textbook publisher and typified the American "rags to riches" success story. When he was 12 he was a cook in a logging camp and by the time he was 29 he owned his own publishing company. An idealist and internationalist, he believed in the power of the written word and created the World Peace Foundation, "which published hundreds of thousands of inexpensive peace books and distributed them to the masses." Barbara S. Kraft, "Peacemaking in the Progressive Era: A Prestigious and Proper Calling," *The Maryland Historian* 1 (Fall 1970): 128.
2. Although many sources credit the origin of the word "pacifist" to Émile Arnaud—e.g., Sandi E. Cooper, "Émile Arnaud," *Biographical Dictionary of Modern Peace Leaders*, ed. Harold Josephson (Westport, CT: Greenwood Press, 1985) 37–38—Denys P. Myers, corresponding secretary and librarian of the World Peace Foundation, writes in a letter to the editor of the *New York Times* on March 23, 1918, that "the real inspirer of the word was not Arnaud, but the Dane, Federick Bajer [...] at a meeting of the commission of the International Bureau of Peace on Oct. 1, 1900, had proposed what he termed in French a *'traité d'alliance pacigérante'*, which was based on the idea of Article 27 of the 1899 Hague Convention for the Pacific Settlement of International Disputes [...], and got into English the next year when the Universal Peace Congress was held at Glasgow."
3. A. C. F. Beales, *The History of Peace* (New York: Dial Press, 1931), 204.
4. Twenty-six of the 59 governments claiming independent sovereignty in 1899 were represented at the Hague Conference.
5. Klaus Schlichtmann, "Japan, Germany and the Idea of the Hague Peace Conferences," *Journal of Peace Research* 40.4, Special Issue on Peace History (July 2003): 383.
6. Jan Bloch's real name was Ivan Stanislavovich Blioch and the full title of his book is *The Future of War in Its Technical, Economic and Political Relations* (New York City: Doubleday and McClure, 1899).
7. "Obituary, Jean de Bloch," *New York Times*, Jan. 8, 1902.
8. Grant Dawson, "Preventing 'a Great Moral Evil': Jean de Bloch's 'The Future of War' as Anti-Revolutionary Pacifism," *Journal of Contemporary History* 37.1 (Jan. 2002): 17.
9. Peter Van den Dungen and Lawrence S. Wittner, "Peace History: An Introduction," *Journal of Peace Research* 40.4, Special Issue on Peace History (July 2003): 368.
10. Bloch had amassed a small fortune building railroads in Russia and he used it to augment the power of his pen by founding, and funding, the world's first museum of war and peace, in Lucerne, Switzerland. The museum opened in 1902, and its purpose—like that of *The War of the Future*—was to warn the world of the coming war. See: Sandi Cooper, *Patriotic Pacifism: Waging War on War in Europe, 1815–1914* (Oxford: Oxford University Press, 1991), 82. An impressive array of weapons was put on display to demonstrate their increasing lethalness, which, Bloch believed, rendered war impossible for any thinking individual. "War itself is the strongest testimony against war," he declared. But for many, the bellicose exhibits merely resembled what one would find in a war, rather than the elements of a peace museum. Bloch didn't live to see his museum open its doors, and they closed forever 18 years later, in 1920. Ironically, the museum had become a victim of the war it sought to prevent. Today the building houses a public school. See: Peter Van den Dungen, "Preventing Catastrophe: The World's First Peace Museum," *Ritsumeikan Journal of International Studies. Ritsumeikan kokusai kenkyu* 18.3 (March 2006): 449–462.
11. Arthur and Lila Weinberg, "Jean de Bloch Describes the Burdens of 'Armed Peace,'" in *Instead of Violence: Writings by the Great Advocates of Peace and Nonviolence Throughout History* (New York: Grossman, 1963), 320–324.
12. Elizabeth Sanders, *Roots of Reform* (Chicago: University of Chicago Press, 1999), 59.
13. Merle Curti, *Peace or War: The American Struggle 1636–1936* (New York: W. W. Norton, 1936), 188.

14. Curti, *Peace or War*, 15.
15. Geoffrey Best, "Peace Conferences and the Century of Total War: The 1899 Hague Conference and What Came After," *International Affairs* (Royal Institute of International Affairs, 1944) 75.3 (July 1999): 623.
16. Curti, *Peace or War*, 189.
17. "Sense and Nonsense," *Sacred Heart Review* 21.16 (April 15, 1899): 20.
18. *New York Times*, Feb. 6, 1906.
19. Curti, *Peace or War*, 190.
20. Cecilie Reid, "American Internationalism: Peace Advocacy and International Relations, 1895–1916," dissertation, Boston College, December 2005, 80.
21. John W. Foster, "The Evolution of International Law," *Yale Law Journal* 18.3 (Jan. 1909): 161. The modern mechanism of international arbitration is usually traced back to the Jay Treaty of 1794 between the United States and Great Britain, which established a joint British-American commission to settle all claims arising from the Revolutionary War. Surprisingly enough, the method worked quite effectively and was used on more than eight separate occasions over the next century to settle boundary disputes.
22. The Wadai war between French colonial forces and the Wadai Empire lasted from 1909 to 1911 and cost approximately 10,000 casualties. It took place in an area of what is today eastern Chad and central Sudan.
23. "The Old Year and the New," *New York Sun*, Jan. 1, 1910, 6.
24. "Peace Conference Opens," *New York Times*, May 9, 1910, 1.
25. "The Prophecies of Stephen Phillips," *The Independent*, Jan. 24, 1901.
26. In fact, the duel in 1900 was far from dead. It was increasing, but most of the confrontations ended with a symbolic drawing of blood. Philipp Blom, *The Vertigo Years* (New York: Basic Books, 2008), 165.
27. "A Warless World," *The Spectator*, Sept. 3, 1898.
28. *The Independent*, Jan. 3, 1901.
29. "Admiral Togo—'the Peaceful Man of the East,'" *American Journal of International Law* 5.4 (Oct. 1911): 1051–1054.
30. Kraft, "Peacemaking in the Progressive Era," 128.
31. Robert Goldsmith, *A League to Enforce Peace* (New York: Macmillan, 1917), 99.
32. For a detailed description of the fishing dispute and its consequences for the current problems of over-fishing, see: Brian Joseph Payne, "Fishing a Borderless Sea: Environmental Territorialism in the North Atlantic 1818–1910," thesis submitted in partial fulfillment for the Degree of Doctor of Philosophy, University of Maine, May, 2006.
33. Manley O. Hudson, "The Permanent Court of Arbitration," *American Journal of International Law* 27.3 (July 1933): 450–454.
34. "The Progress of the World," *Review of Reviews* 3.15 (April 1891): 277.

35. *London Times*, June 13, 1912. Frédéric Passy shared the Nobel Peace Prize in 1901 with Jean Henri Dunant (1828–1910), the founder of the Red Cross.
36. William Howard Taft and David H. Burton (ed.), *The Collected Works of William Howard Taft*, vol. 6 (Athens: Ohio University Press, 2003), 198.
37. Taft and Burton, 199.
38. "Taft Is for Peace with Reservations," *New York Times*, March 23, 1910.
39. In fact, there is at least one instance where President Taft violated his own principle: he refused to arbitrate with Great Britain over the tolls for the Panama Canal.
40. Taft and Burton, 200.
41. Sent to Europe on a six-week vacation by President Taft, Archibald Butt and his friend the painter Francis Davis Millet, went down with the *Titanic* on her maiden voyage.
42. David Henry Burton, *Taft, Holmes, and the 1920s Court: An Appraisal* (Cranbury, NJ: Associated University Presses, 1998), 83.
43. The Achaean League was a Hellenistic-era confederation of Greek city states on the northern and central Peloponnesus that existed between 280 BC and 146 BC The league was named after the region of Achaea, which is a mountainous area in the northwestern part of the Peloponnese peninsula. The capital is Patras. Homer uses the term "Achaeans" as a generic term for Greeks throughout the *Iliad*.
44. Keith Wilson, "The Agadir Crisis, the Mansion House Speech, and the Double-Edgedness of Agreements," *Historical Journal* 15.3 (1972): 513.
45. Richard "Dick" Turpin (1705–1739) was an English highwayman whose exploits as a poacher, burglar and thief were romanticized following his execution in York for horse theft.
46. Edmund Deville Morel, "The True Story of the Morocco Negotiations," *Nineteenth Century* 71 (February 1912): 246.
47. John Keiger, "Jules Cambon and the Franco-German Détente, 1907–1914," *Historical Journal* 26.3 (1983): 647.
48. Ima Christina Barlow, *The Agadir Crisis* (Chapel Hill: University of North Carolina Press, 1940), 346.
49. *Daily Chronicle*, July 22, 1911, 1.
50. *Times*, July 20, 1911, 9.
51. Philippe Millet, "The Truth About the Franco-German Crisis of 1911," *Nineteenth Century* 71 (June 1912): 1054.
52. Edmund Deville Morel, "The 'Truth' About the Franco-German Crisis," *Nineteenth Century* 72 (July 1912): 37.
53. Mark Hewitson, "Germany and France Before the First World War: A Reassessment of Wilhelmine Foreign Policy," *English Historical Review* 115.462 (June 2000): 594.
54. Genevieve R. Tabious and Charles Francis Atkinson, *The Life of Jules Cambon* (London: Jonathan Cape, 1938).
55. G. P. Gooch, *Recent Revelations of European*

Diplomacy (New York: Longmans, Green, 1930), 295.
56. G. P. Gooch, "Kiderlen-Wachter," *Cambridge Historical Journal* 5.2 (1936): 189.
57. Barlow, 369.
58. Credit for the agreement solving the Agadir Crisis is usually given to Jules Cambon, who at the time was called the Greatest Diplomatist in the World: "He remains solitary, mysterious, inscrutable, the living repository of secrets that would, according to foreign dailies, shake the world." *Current Literature* 52.2 (1912): 160.
59. Standing alongside Mussolini was Pietro Nenni, who in the 1960s would be Italy's socialist Foreign Minister.
60. R. J. B. Bosworth, *Mussolini* (New York: Oxford University Press, 2002), 85.
61. Christopher Hibbert, *Benito Mussolini* (London: Reprint Society, 1962), 33.
62. Gerald Clarke, "Two Views of a Little Caesar," *Time*, June 7, 1982.
63. Bosworth, 85.
64. Desiree Ntolo, *The Sacred and the Profane* (Bloomington, IN: Author House, 2008), 233.
65. Ntolo, 234.
66. The sole survivor of the massacre was Mary Jo Estep, who was raised by a white family and became an elementary school teacher on the Yakima Reservation in the state of Washington. She died in a nursing home in 1993, aged 82, after being given the wrong medication. The nursing home was fined $2,500.
67. Dayton O. Hyde, *The Last Free Man: The True Story Behind the Massacre of Shoshone Mike and his Band of Indians in 1911* (New York: Dial Press, 1973), 235.
68. Hyde, 235.
69. In 1933 Angell issued a new and updated edition. He changed his argument slightly. He no longer contended that economics would stop a war or prevent it but instead took the position that waging a war for economic reasons would be a futile struggle and that a nation could not enrich itself by the conquest of its neighbors. This earned him a Nobel Peace Prize in 1933.
70. Howard Weinroth, "Norman Angell and the Great Illusion: An Episode in pre-1914 Pacifism," *Historical Journal* 17.3 (September 1974): 551–574. After events and World War One proved him wrong, Angell continued to work for peace. He denounced the Treaty of Versailles but supported wholeheartedly the League of Nations and the cause of disarmament. He served briefly as a Member of Parliament. He died in 1967. *Biographical Dictionary of Modern Peace Leaders*, 27–31.
71. See chapter 2.
72. Weinroth, 554.
73. Norman Angell, *The Great Illusion* (New York: Heinemann, 1913), 381–382.
74. Roger Chickering, *Imperial Germany and a World Without War: The Peace Movement and German Society* (Princeton, NJ: Princeton University Press, 1975), 38–88.

75. In 1910 the Carnegie Endowment for International Peace was founded with a $10 million trust (about 200 million in today's U.S. dollars) "to hasten the abolition of international war, the foulest blot upon our civilization." Its first publications focused on the laws of neutrality and the causes of war in the Balkans.
76. Philip D. Supina, "The Norman Angell Peace Campaign in Germany," *Journal of Peace Research* 9.2 (1972): 161–164. The pamphlet was titled *Offener Brief und die deutschen Studentenschaft von Norman Angell* (An open letter to the German students by Norman Angell) and sent to students at seven German universities: Frankfurt, Heidelberg, Göttingen, Berlin, Leipzig, Munich and Wurzburg.
77. Supina, 161.
78. Ibid., 164.
79. Although the students were free to travel as they wished, Kahn did establish a preferred route: Paris, London, Liverpool, Marseille, Athens, Constantinople, Beirut, Damascus, Cairo, Ceylon, India, Burma, Singapore, Indonesia, Vietnam, Hong Kong, China, Japan, United States, Germany, Russia— Saint Petersburg, Moscow, Odessa—Budapest, Vienna, and finally back to Paris.
80. L. S. Stavrianos, *Global Rift: The Third World Comes of Age* (New York: Morrow, 1981), 263.
81. Jay Winter, *Dreams of Peace and Freedom* (New Haven and London: Yale University Press, 2006), 16.
82. Winter, 21.
83. Joseph O. Baylen and and Jane G. Weyant, "Vasili Vereshchagin in the United States," *Russian Review* 30.3 (July 1971): 257.
84. Merle Eugene Curti, "Pioneers of Peace," *North American Review* 229.5 (May 1930): 556.
85. HMS *Dreadnought* was a battleship that revolutionized naval power in 1906 when she entered service. She marked such an advance in naval technology that her name came to be associated with an entire generation of battleships, the "dreadnoughts." HMS *Dreadnought* was the first battleship of her era to have a uniform main battery, rather than a few large guns complemented by a secondary battery. She was the first capital ship to be powered by steam turbines, making her the fastest battleship in the world at the time of her completion.
86. John H. Maurer, "Arms Control and the Anglo-German Naval Race Before World War I: Lessons for Today?" *Political Science Quarterly* 112.2 (Summer 1997): 285.
87. Ballin had become a celebrity when he created the world's first pleasure cruise in 1891. He was the head of Hapag's passenger division. Hapag's ships were little used in the winter months. Taking advantage of this, Ballin sent the luxurious *Augusta Victoria* to the Mediterranean, where she spent 57 days cruising from one port to the next. The idea was an immediate success. He refused to support World War One and as a result ceased to enjoy the Kaiser's favor. Ballin was called "an interested party" and a "pessimist" and kept away from the Kaiser. See: [Count] Bernstorff, *My Three Years in America*

(New York: Charles Scribner's Sons, 1920), 409–410.
88. Bernhard Huldermann, *Albert Ballin*, trans. W. J. Eggers (London, New York, Toronto and Melbourne: Cassell and Company, 1922), 131.
89. Winston S. Churchill, *The World Crisis 1911-1918* (New York: Free Press, 1931), 96.
90. Ibid., 97.
91. Ballin, who for years was discredited in Berlin as a pacifist, was suddenly requested by the German General Staff to conduct the peace negotiations. Apparently he could not bear to witness the collapse of his world and his life's work. He poisoned himself as the revolution reached Hamburg and died at the age of 61, along with the German Empire, on the ninth of November 1918 about noon.
92. C. C. Aronsfeld, "Jewish Enemy Aliens in England During the First World War," *Jewish Social Studies* 18.4 (Oct. 1956): 275.
93. Huldermann, 162.
94. Ibid., 165.
95. E. L. Woodward, *Great Britain and the German Navy* (Oxford: Claredon Press, 1935), 326.
96. Schopenhauer's *The World as Will and Representation* was published between 1883 and 1886. Lord Haldane wrote several philosophical works himself, the best-known of which is *The Reign of Relativity* (1921), which dealt with the philosophical implications of the theory of relativity.
97. *The Whispering Gallery* (New York: Boni & Liveright, 1926), 72–73. The author signed the book as "Being Leaves from the Diary of an Ex-Diplomat."
98. Pearson, *The Whispering Gallery*, 85.
99. It is interesting to note that five years previously, in 1907, at the Second Hague Peace Conference, Marschall von Bieberstein had taken just the opposite position. As the representative of the German Empire, he had argued for a strong German naval policy and had been opposed to any practical discussion of the question of the restriction of armaments. Von Bieberstein died in 1912 shortly after taking the post of German ambassador to Great Britain. He was replaced by Prince Lichnowsky (1860–1928).
100. Richard Langhorne, "The Naval Question in Anglo-German Relations, 1912-1914," *Historical Journal* 14. 2 (1971): 359.
101. Alfred von Tirpitz is regarded as the father of the German navy force behind the Fleet Acts of 1898, 1900, 1908 and 1912, known collectively as the Tirpitz Plan. By 1914, the Plan had given Germany the second-largest naval force in the world (roughly 40 percent smaller than the Royal Navy).
102. Donald Kagan, *On the Origins of War and the Preservation of Peace* (New York: Doubleday, 1995), 176–177.
103. Maurer, "Arms Control and the Anglo-German Naval Race Before World War I?" 302. Prince Lichnowsky, in his *Memoirs*, states: "Haldane's mission had failed as we had required the assurance of neutrality, instead of being content with a treaty securing us against British attacks and attacks with British support." Prince Lichnowsky, *My Mission to London, 1912-1914* (New York: George H. Doran, 1918), 4.
104. E. L. Woodward, 363.
105. Ibid., 336.
106. Richard Burdon Haldane, *Before the War* (Teddington, Middlesex: Echo Press, reprint 2006), 27.
107. E. L. Woodward, 333.
108. For example, "the failure of the Haldane mission." Kagan, 177. There is an almost identical statement: "the failure of the Haldane mission" in A. J. P. Taylor, *The Struggle for Mastery in Europe 1848-1918* (Oxford and New York: Oxford University Press, 1954), 459.
109. Edward F. Willis, *Prince Lichnowsky, Ambassador of Peace* (Berkeley and Los Angeles: University of California Press, 1942), 155.
110. Huldermann, 175.
111. Haldane, 30.
112. E. L. Woodward 341. The French were, of course, extremely worried by the Anglo-German contacts and understood immediately that the German goal was to create a new entente, one that would leave the French out.
113. James Brown Scott, "Lord Haldane's Diary of Negotiation Between Germany and England in 1912," *The American Journal of International Law* 12.4 (Oct. 1918): 838.
114. Hansard, *Parliamentary Debates*, 5th series, 34.1340–41 and 35.35.
115. Langhorne, 359.
116. Ibid., 366.
117. Maurer, "Arms Control and the Anglo-German Naval Race Before World War I," 293.
118. Solomon Wank, ed., *Doves and Diplomat*. (Westport, CT, and London: Greenwood Press, 1978), 98.
119. Frederick Winston Furneaux Smith Birkenhead, *Churchill 1874-1922* (London: Harrap, 1989), 280.
120. E. L. Woodward, 420.
121. Willis, 164.
122. John H. Maurer, "The Anglo-German Naval Rivalry and Informal Arms Control," *Journal of Conflict Resolution* 36.2 (June 1992): 301–302.
123. "Mr. Churchill's Naval Holiday," *New York Times*, Nov. 4, 1913.
124. "Daniels Wants Up-to-Date Navy," *New York Times*, Dec. 1, 1913, 1.
125. "House for Naval Holiday," *New York Times*, Dec. 7, 1913, 15.
126. Ibid.
127. Ibid.
128. Woodrow Wilson never expected to become President. He was a compromise candidate chosen on the 46th ballot at the Democratic convention. He won the national election by a plurality only because the Republican vote was split between William Howard Taft, the party candidate, and Theodore Roosevelt, who formed a breakaway party.
129. Maurer, "The Anglo-German Naval Rivalry and Informal Arms Control," 302.

130. Ibid.
131. "The Christ of the Andes," *Missionary Review*, March 1906, 211–212.
132. *London Times*, Feb. 24, 1902. Holdich was regarded as the foremost authority at the time on all matters connected with frontier delimitation and demarcation, having spent 35 years studying borders in all climates and topographies. He had settled similar disputes in India and Afghanistan and had written numerous books on the subject. He was also vice president of the Royal Geographic Society. He was called out of retirement to deal with the Chile–Argentine dispute.
133. Colonel Sir T. H. Holdich, "The Patagonian Andes," *Geographical Journal* 23.2 (Feb. 1904): 156.
134. "Argentine–Chile Boundary Award," *National Geographic Magazine*, Jan. 1903, 115–116.
135. *London Times*, July 26, 1902.
136. "The First Transandine Railroad from Buenos Aires to Valparaiso," *National Geographic Magazine*, May 1910, 397–417.
137. "The Christ of the Andes," 213.
138. Carolina Huidobro, "The Christ of the Andes," *The Independent*, May 7, 1908, 1021.
139. Lewis R. Freenay, "Over the Andes" (*Cornhill Magazine*, Sept. 1923, 355.
140. "Chile–Argentina Boundary Dispute," *National Geographic Magazine*, June 1902, 220.
141. "The Story of the Erection of the Great Peace Monument on the Andean Boundary Between Chile and Argentina," *American Peace Society*, 1905. Although both countries pledged themselves not to sell any ships to nations engaged in war, one or two of the vessels were bought under disguise by a firm in New York. It, in turn, resold them to the Japanese, who used them in the siege of Port Arthur in 1904–1905.
142. Beales, 250–251.
143. Cooper, *Patriotic Pacifism*, 362.
144. "Geographical Problems in Boundary Making," *Geographical Journal* 47 (Jan./June 1916): 439.
145. Karen Larsen, *A History of Norway* (New York: Princeton University Press for the American-Scandinavian Foundation, 1950,) 488–489. At the end of the Napoleonic wars Norway had been taken from Denmark and given to Sweden.
146. Walter J. Kendall III, "Pope Paul VI's Aphorism—'If You Want Peace Work for Justice'—and the Nobel Peace Prize Winners," *The Acorn* 11.1 (Fall-Winter 2000–2001): 39.
147. Several of his books were translated into English, most notably *Is World Peace Possible?* and *The Hope of the Centuries*.
148. T. K. Derry, *A Short History of Norway* (London: George Allen & Unwin, 1957), 202.
149. Raymond E. Lindgren, *Norway—Sweden, Union, Disunion and Scandinavian Integration* (Princeton, NJ: Princeton University Press, 1959), 209.
150. Col. Karl E. Hanevik, "Norwegian Neutrality in the Inter-War Years," *Strategy Research Project*, March 16, 2006, 5.

151. David S. Patterson, "Andrew Carnegie's Quest for World Peace," *Proceedings of the American Philosophical Society* 114.5 (Oct. 20, 1970): 372.
152. Andrew Carnegie, *Autobiography of Andrew Carnegie* (Boston: Houghton Mifflin, 1920), 250.
153. In addition to the funds that he gave directly to the Hague Conferences, Carnegie also established the Carnegie Endowment for International Peace in 1910, an "organization dedicated to advancing cooperation between nations and promoting active international engagement by the United States," and the Church Peace Union (CPU) in 1914 "to mobilize the world's churches, religious organizations and other spiritual and moral resources to join in promoting moral leadership and finding alternatives to armed conflict." On the eve of the First World War, the Church Peace Union sponsored a conference on the shores of Lake Constance in Germany. As the delegates made their way to the conference by train, Germany was invading Belgium. The delegates fled to London, and the organization continued its work at the end of the war. The CPU is still in existence today, although its name has been changed to the Carnegie Council for Ethics in International Affairs.
154. Patterson, 375.
155. *New York Times*, Nov. 24, 1907.
156. Douglas R. Chambers, *A Century of Heroes* (Pittsburgh: Carnegie Hero Fund Commission, 2004), 32.
157. Chambers, 25.
158. Edwin D. Mead, *Heroes of Peace* (Boston: World Peace Foundation, 1911).
159. The Hero Fund was inspired by Selwyn M. Taylor and Daniel A. Lyle, who gave their lives in rescue attempts following a coal mine explosion in Harwick, Pennsylvania, on January 25, 1904.
160. Chambers, 12.
161. Ibid., 38, 201.
162. Ibid., 58.
163. Ibid.
164. "Carnegie Hero Fund Accepted by Kaiser," *New York Times*, Jan. 1, 1911. The German Hero Fund was taken over by the Nazis when they came to power and finally reinstated in 2005.
165. Chambers, 31, 224–226. Each of the national funds has developed a slightly different policy, although all basically reward civil bravery of one kind or another. The Swedish Carnegie Hero Fund, for example, is typical and has given more than 2,350 awards since 1912. The contemporary award consists of a gold watch, a diploma and a small sum of money. The men and women who received them performed such acts of bravery as saving a person from drowning, rescuing someone from a burning apartment, or pulling a child from the path of an oncoming train.
166. Pater Krass, *Carnegie* (Hoboken, NJ: John Wiley & Sons, 2002), 450.
167. "Chaos, Then Reform, Prof. Matthews on Change of Spelling, British Opinion Varied," *Boston Evening Transcript*, March 14, 1906, 23.
168. Carnegie cut off the $25,000 per year after four years.
169. Esperanto continues today buoyed up by the

fact that over 4,000 books have been published in it. In addition, more than 100 original novels have been written in Esperanto and currently Google offers it as an option for its search engine.
170. Patterson, 374.
171. Krass, 476.
172. "President Roosevelt's Popularity Undiminished by Critics of the Kaiser," *New York Times*, June 12, 1909.
173. Patricia O'Toole, *When Trumpets Call: Theodore Roosevelt After the White House* (New York: Simon & Schuster, 2005), 87.
174. Theodore Roosevelt, "International Peace," an address before the Nobel Committee, Christiania, Norway, May 5, 1910.
175. Joseph Bucklin Bishop, *Theodore Roosevelt and His Time, Shown in His Own Letters*, vol. 2 (New York: Charles Scribner's Sons, 1920), 254. Statements by the Kaiser of his affection for England were not uncommon. At a dinner just after the death of Queen Victoria in 1901, he declared: "We ought to form an Anglo-German alliance; you keep the seas, while we would be responsible for the land; with such an alliance, not a mouse could stir in Europe without our permission, and the nations would, in time, come to see the necessity of reducing their armaments." Tyler Whittle, *The Last Kaiser* (London: Heinemann, 1977), 193.
176. Whittle, 254.
177. Charles F. Howlett and Ian M. Harris, *Books, Not Bombs: Teaching Peace Since the Dawn of the Republic* (Charlotte, NC: Information Age Publishing, 2010) 64.
178. Clyde E. Crum, "Contributions of the American School Peace League to International Education," *History of Education Journal* 4.2 (Winter 1953): 51.
179. Curti, *Peace or War*, 210.
180. Ibid., 211.
181. Howlett and Harris, *Books, Not Bombs*, 68.
182. Ibid., 68.
183. Ian M. Harris and Mary Lee Morrison, *Peace History* (Jefferson, NC: McFarland, 2003), 19.
184. Crum, 57.
185. Robert I. Rotberg, *A Leadership for Peace* (Palo Alto, CA: Stanford University Press, 2007), 88.
186. Rotberg, 105.
187. Ibid., 87.
188. Peter Filene, "The World Peace Foundation and Progressivism: 1910–1918," *New England Quarterly* 36.4 (Dec. 1963): 481.
189. Filene, 495.
190. Ginn intended to add later Victor Hugo's description of the dead and dying on the fields of Waterloo.
191. Rotberg, 139.
192. Ibid., 138.
193. Benjamin de Jong van Beek en Donk and Dr. B. Jonkheer, "The Peace Movement," *A General View of the Netherlands* 35 (1915).
194. Both the Rijksmuseum in Amsterdam and the museum Het Prisenhof in Delft claim to have the original book chest in their collection.

195. The Dutch based their support of international peace backed up by an international force on *De jure belli ac pacis* (On the law of war and peace), a study by Grotius (1583–1645) published in 1625 in which he defines a just war (*juris exsecutio armata in armatum*).
196. See: "War Obviated by an International Police; a Series of Essays, Written in Various Countries" (The Hague: Nijhoff, 1915).
197. Theodore Roosevelt won the Nobel Peace Prize for his effort to end the Russo-Japanese War by a negotiated settlement. He was the first American to win any Nobel Prize.
198. Stefan T. Possony, "Peace Enforcement," *Yale Law Journal* 55.5 (Aug. 1946): 926.
199. Charles W. Eliot, "An International Force Must Support an International Tribunal," *American Society for Judicial Settlement of International Disputes* 19 (Dec. 1914).
200. Rotberg, 129.
201. Hyman Kublin, "The Japanese Socialists and the Russo-Japanese War," *Journal of Modern History* 22.4 (1950): 322–339.
202. Hyman Kublin, "The Origins of Japanese Socialist Tradition," *Journal of Politics* 14.2 (May 1952): 278.
203. Alfred Stead, *Great Japan, a Study of National Efficiency* (London and New York: John Lane, 1906), 238.
204. Steve Rabson, "Shimazaki Toson on War," *Monumenta Nipponica* 46.4 (Winter 1991): 459.
205. Rabson, "Shimazaki Toson on War," 459.
206. *Biographical Dictionary of Modern Peace Leaders*, 507–508.
207. Rabson, "Shimazaki Toson on War," 458–459.
208. Nolbuya Bamba and John F. Howes (eds.), *Pacifism in Japan* (Vancouver: University of British Columbia Press, 1978), 108.
209. *Biographical Dictionary of Modern Peace Leaders*, 972.
210. The Japanese fought the war using money borrowed from American and British banks. Large Jewish banks in particular, such as Kuhn, Loeb & Co., supported the Japanese, since their opponent, Russia, was identified with anti–Semitism and pogroms.
211. David Wells and Sandra Wilson (eds.), *The Russo-Japanese War in Cultural Perspective, 1904–05* (Houndmills: Macmillan, 1999), 173.
212. Kublin, "The Japanese Socialists and the Russo-Japanese War," 330.
213. Leo Tolstoy, "Bethink Yourselves," *London Times*, 10 July 1904, 13.
214. Tokutomi Roka made a pilgrimage to Tolstoy's home at Yasnaya Polyana in Russia and spent some time there. Roka became a convert to pacifism and on returning to Japan removed himself from mainstream society and lived like a semi-hermit, eventually becoming a pantheist. He was nicknamed Little Tolstoy.
215. Laurence Kominz, "Pilgrimage to Tolstoy: Tokutomi Roka's Junrei Kik," *Monumenta Nipponica* 41.1 (Spring 1986).

216. Tolstoy, "Bethink Yourselves." Tolstoy is credited with the introduction of the distinct concept of "peace" through his writings about non-violence. According to one, perhaps pedantic, Japanese academic: "In Japan, Tolstoy is even associated with the origin of the concept of 'peace' itself. Before it gained access to Western discourse, the Japanese language lacked a term corresponding to "peace" in the English sense of "freedom from, or cessation of, war or hostilities; that condition of a nation or community in which it is not at war with another" (*OED*). In 1889, a group of Quaker literati and thinkers founded a journal called *Heiwa*, which is now the standard Japanese translation for the English word "peace." To the term *heiwa*, which hitherto meant only "serenity," they ascribed a new meaning: "the condition of not having conflict with other nations" (*The Great Japanese Dictionary of Military Terms*, qtd. in Sbgb Masaaki). Takayuki Yokota-Murakami, "Tolstoy, Attila, Edison: The Triangular Construction of a 'Peace-Loving' Russian Identity Across Borders," *Slavic and East European Journal* 45.2 (Summer 2001): 221.
217. Kublin, "The Japanese Socialists and the Russo-Japanese War," 331.
218. The police probably padded the figure so as to secure a larger appropriation. San Katayama, "The Marxian Socialist Group," in *The Labor Movement in Japan*. Chicago: C. H. Kerr, 1918), 104.
219. Kublin attributes the statement to Sen Katayama. "The Japanese Socialists and the Russo-Japanese War," 337.
220. Randall, 75.
221. Shumpei Okamoto, *The Japanese Oligarchy and the Russo-Japanese War* (New York: Columbia University Press, 1970), 207.
222. Harvey Goldberg, *The Life of Jean Jaurès* (Madison: University of Wisconsin Press, 1962), 434.
223. Ruth Roebke-Berens, "Austrian Social Democratic Peace Policy and the Balkan Crisis of 1912-1913," *Peace & Change* 7.1-2 (Winter 1981): 21-22.
224. Manifesto of the International Socialist Congress in Basel, 1912.
225. Dieter Groh, "The 'Unpatriotic Socialists' and the State," *Journal of Contemporary History* 1.4 (Oct. 1966): 151-177.
226. Bertram Wolfe, "Angelica Balabanoff and V. I. Lenin: The Opposing Poles of the Socialist Movement against War," *Antioch Review* 24.2 (Summer 1964): 231.
227. Karl Liebknecht (1871-1919), for example, declared "the best foreign policy was not to have one." Groh, 164.
228. Sandi E. Cooper, "The Reinvention of the 'Just War' Among European Pacifists Before the First World War," in *The Pacifist Impulse in Historical Perspective*, eds. Harvey Leonard Dyck and Peter Brock (Toronto: University of Toronto Press, 1996), 304.
229. Roger Chickering, "A Voice of Moderation in Imperial Germany: The 'Verband fur internationale Verstandigung' 1911-1914," *Journal of Contemporary History* 8.1 (Jan. 1973): 147.

230. Ibid., 147-148.
231. Friedrich Naumann was a German politician and Protestant priest. He was a conservative nationalist who became a member of the Reichstag in 1907. After World War One he helped draft the constitution of the Weimar Republic.
232. Max Weber, a sociologist and political economist, is typically cited, with Émile Durkheim and Karl Marx, as one of the three principal architects of modern social science. His book *The Protestant Ethic and the Spirit of Capitalism* argues that ascetic Protestantism was one of the major "elective affinities" associated with the rise of capitalism, bureaucracy and the rational-legal nation-state in the Western world. Weber emphasized the importance of cultural influences embedded in religion.
233. The Hague Conventions, 1899 and 1907, were two international treaties negotiated at The Hague in the Netherlands; along with the Geneva Conventions, the Hague Conventions were among the first formal statements of the laws of war and war crimes. A third conference was planned for 1914 and later rescheduled for 1915 but never took place due to the start of World War One.
234. Chickering, "A Voice of Moderation," 157-158.
235. The Verband also took part in the campaign to spread Norman Angell's theories in German universities. Chickering, "A Voice of Moderation," 159-160. Not all of the Carnegie money was well spent. The German Kaiser reportedly remarked to a friend: "Of course, Carnegie is a nice old man and means well, but he is totally ignorant of world history. He's just advanced us five million marks for world peace. We accepted it, naturally, but, of course, we intend to continue our policy of maintaining our army and navy in full strength."Arthur N. Davis, *The Kaiser as I Know Him* (New York and London: Harper & Brothers, 1918), 46.
236. "The Anglo-German Understanding Conference," *The Advocate of Peace* 74.11 (Dec. 1912): 255.
237. Chickering, "A Voice of Moderation," 163.
238. Whittle, 251.
239. "Why London?" *Living Age* 58, reprinted in the *New York Times*, Jan. 11, 1913.
240. *New York Times*, May, 31, 1913, 6. No sooner was the treaty signed than the Balkan states, particularly Bulgaria, began to fight again. Bulgaria rapidly lost all the territory that it had won at the London conference.
241. Sean M. Lynn-Jones, "Détente and Deterrence: Anglo-German Relations. 1911-1914," *International Security* 11.2 (Autumn 1986): 130.
242. Lynn-Jones, 130.
243. Ernst Christian Helmreich, *The Diplomacy of the Balkan Wars 1912-1913* (New York: Russell & Russell, 1938), 340.
244. E. L. Woodward, 398.
245. Lynn-Jones, 131.
246. Ibid.
247. According to Lichnowsky, the German Ambassador to the Court of St. James (see: Lichnowsky, *My Mission to London*, 15), the Portuguese had pre-

viously considered selling all their African colonial possessions to the Germans.
248. Lynn-Jones, 137.
249. Ibid., 136.
250. Sir Edward Grey had problems with his vision and was forced to reduce his workload as well as take periodic vacations to rest his eyes. Francis Harry Hinsley, *British Foreign Policy Under Sir Edward Grey* (London and New York: Cambridge University Press, 1977), 537.
251. Lynn-Jones, 135.
252. Whittle, 265; Willis, 260.
253. Lynn-Jones, 141.
254. Ibid., 144.
255. The Carnegie peace endowment had launched two separate private initiatives to mediate between the warring Mexican factions. The most ambitious plan was begun by Nicholas Murray Butler (1962–1947), longtime president of Columbia University (1902–1947), president of the Carnegie Endowment for Peace (1925–1945), Nobel Peace Prize winner (1931), and an outspoken anti-Semite. Butler sent Francis Loomis (1861–1948), former Assistant Secretary of State, to Paris to form a commission composed of representatives of Holland, Switzerland, the Carnegie Endowment and carefully chosen Mexicans, which would be "an advisory council to a provisional president, and devote themselves to the task of forming and establishing a provisional government." See: Wank, 133.
256. Friedrich Katz, *Pancho Villa* (Palo Alto, CA: Stanford University Press, 1998), 337.
257. Wank, 138.
258. Ibid., 142.
259. Ibid., 143.
260. Lynn-Jones, 117.
261. Ibid., preface.
262. Michael Small, *The Forgotten Peace* (Ottawa: University of Ottawa Press, 2009).
263. Martin Ceadel, *Living the Great Illusion: Sir Norman Angell, 1872–1967* (Oxford: Oxford University Press, 2009), 157–158.
264. Sandi E. Cooper, "Pacifism in France, 1889–1914: International Peace as a Human Right," *French Historical Studies* 17.2 (Autumn 1991): 368.
265. Francis Feeley, "French School Teachers Against Militarism, 1903–1918," *The Historian* 57.2 (Winter 1994): 2.
266. Anatole France (1844–1924), born François-Anatole Thibault, was a French poet, journalist, and novelist. Some of his most famous novels are *Thaïs* (1890), *L'Île des Pingouins* (*Penguin Island*) (1908), and *Les dieux ont soif* (*The gods are athirst*) (1912). He was a member of the Académie française and won the Nobel Prize for Literature in 1921.
267. David Émile Durkheim (1858–1917) was a French sociologist whose primary goal was to establish sociology as a recognized academic discipline. He is commonly cited as the principal architect of modern social science and father of sociology. He was also France's first professor of sociology.
268. Marcel Sembat was a prominent socialist man of letters and government minister.
269. Many people produced ideas about how to cope with the sovereignty of Alsace-Lorraine. The American professor Irving Fisher (1867–1947), for example, proposed in 1914 the creation of a neutralized "District of Columbia," a kind of international seat for a union of nations.
270. Cooper, "Pacifism in France, 1889–1914," 1.
271. Malcom Brown and Shirley Seaton, *Christmas Truce, the Western Front December 1914* (Basingstoke and Oxford: Pan Books, 1994), 3.
272. Brown and Seaton, 3.
273. Georg Von Hase, *Kiel and Jutland*, trans. by Arthur Chambers and F. A. Holt (London: Skeffington & Son, 1980), 60.
274. Alfred Machin grew up in France but started the first Belgian film company, Belge-Cinéma Film, in Brussels in 1912. During the war he was drafted into the French army and became the Pathé delegate for the Société Cinématographique de l'Armée. He worked with David Griffith, the American director, in 1917 to produce the 1918 war film *Hearts of the World*. After the war Machin bought his own studio in Nice. He died there in 1929.
275. "*Chagrin d'amour dure toute la vie*" is the second line of a famous 18th-century French love song, "Plaisir d'amour."
276. Ernst Mathijs, *The Cinema of the Low Countries* (London: Wallflower Press, 2003).
277. The book had originally been published in Danish in 1892 and went through several editions before the First World War. The Danes went on to produce three more anti-war films during the war: *Ned med Vaabnene* (1914), *Verdens Undergang* (1916), and *Pax Aeterna; Den evige Fred / Peace on Earth* (1917).
278. Her own summary of the story is "the history of a young woman whose fate was closely involved with the wars fought in our own day."
279. Bertha von Süttner, *Lay Down Your Arms* (London: Longmans, Green, 1908).
280. The four women ahead of Bertha von Süttner on the European popularity list were either royalty or actresses.
281. "And Peace to All Men," *The Observer*, Dec. 16, 2001.
282. Irwin Abrams, "Bertha von Süttner and the Nobel Peace Prize," *Journal of Central European Affairs* 22 (Oct. 1962): 286–307.
283. Cortright, 44.
284. Josephson, 921–923.
285. The title "Colonel" was not military but honorific. It had been given him by Texas governor James S. Hogg (1851–1906) for helping him win an election.
286. President Woodrow Wilson once said, "Mr. House is my second personality. He is my independent self. His thoughts and mine are one." Godfrey Hodgson, *Woodrow Wilson's Right Hand: The Life of Colonel Edward M. House* (New Haven and London: Yale University Press, 2006), foreword. Sir Edward Grey (1862–1933), British Foreign Secretary, wrote: "House longed to get good accomplished and

was content that others should have the credit." Seymour, *The Intimate Papers of Colonel House*, vol. 1 (Boston and New York: Houghton Mifflin, 1926), foreword.
287. Bernstorff, 70.
288. The Schrippenfest, literally the "White Roll Feast"—a *Schrippe* being a roll of white bread—was the one occasion of the year when the common soldier received white instead of black bread and was treated to such luxuries as a meat course, stewed prunes and wine. The feast was given by the Kaiser and the highlight of the ceremony was the Kaiser's presence, sitting in the midst of his troops eating their white rolls and drinking from a glass already used by one of the common soldiers. Seymour, vol. 1, 252.
289. Seymour, vol. 1, 255.
290. Ibid., 256.
291. E. L. Woodward, 436.
292. Hodgson, 92.
293. Seymour, vol. 1, 264.
294. E. L. Woodward, 437.
295. The journalist was George Sylvester Viereck (1884–1962), a German-American poet and author, who is thought to have been the illegitimate son of the Kaiser. Viereck spent most of his life in America, where he later became a Nazi apologist.
296. Hodgson, 91.
297. F. W. Foerster, *Europe and the German Question* (London: George Allen & Unwin, 1941), 93.
298. Mark Aldanov, "Count Witte," *Russian Review* 1.1 (Nov. 1941): 64.
299. Aldanov, 101.
300. Michael Florinsky, "The Russian Mobilization of 1914," *Political Science Quarterly*, 42.2 (June 1927): 213–214.
301. Bernadotte E. Schmitt, "July 1914: Thirty Years After," *Journal of Modern History* 16.3 (Sept. 1944): 188.
302. Schmitt, 188.
303. Lichnowsky, 35.
304. Schmitt, 188.
305. Ibid.
306. Florinsky, 225.
307. Those acquainted with Nicholas II often observed that he spoke English better than he did Russian.
308. Sidney B. Fay, "The Kaiser's Secret Negotiations with the Tsar, 1904–1905," *American Historical Review* 24.1 (Oct. 1918): 49.
309. The full text of the Treaty of Björkö (see: Fay, 67–68):

Their Imperial Majesties, the Emperor of All the Russias on the one side, and the German Emperor on the other, in order to insure the peace of Europe, have placed themselves in accord on the following points of the herein treaty relative to a defensive alliance:

Art.I. If any European state attacks one of the two empires the allied party engages to aid the other contracting party with all *his military and naval forces."

Art.II. The high contracting parties engage not to conclude with any common enemy a separate peace.

Art.III. The present treaty will become effective from the moment of the conclusion of the peace between Russia and Japan and may be denounced with a year's previous notification.

Art.IV. When this treaty has become effective Russia will undertake the necessary steps to inform France of it and to propose to the latter to adhere to it as an ally.

[Signed] Nicholas. William. [Countersigned] Von Tschirschky. Count Benkendorf. Naval Minister Birilev.

310. Fay, 59.
311. Ibid., 71.
312. Florinsky, 220.
313. "Count Tolstoi's Way," *New York Times*, April 17, 1899.
314. Philippe Alexandre, "Messianisme et américanisation du monde. Les États-Unis et les organisations pacifistes de France et d'Allemagne à la veille de la Première Guerre mondiale" (1911–1914), *Themenportal Europäische Geschichte*, 2007.
315. "Anna B. Eckstein Collected Papers," Swarthmore College Peace Collection.
316. The Kellogg-Briand Pact, which is also called the World Peace Act, was signed in 1928 by the United States, the UK, France, Italy and others. It outlawed war.
317. "To the Governments Represented at the Third Hague Conference," no. 14193, Swarthmore College Peace Collection.
318. R. P. Neuman, "Working Class Birth Control in Wilhelmine Germany," *Comparative Studies in Society and History* 20.3 (July 1978): 413.
319. The League was named after Spartacus, leader of the largest slave rebellion of the Roman Republic.
320. Sir Edward Grey, *Twenty Five Years*, vol. 2 (London: Hodder and Stoughton, 1925), 223.
321. *"On n'humanise pas le carnage, on le condamne parce qu'on s'humanise."* Frédéric Passy, *L'avenir de l'Europe: Conférence faite le 14 février 1895, à la mairie du VIe arrondissement de Paris, au nom de la Société française pour l'arbitrage entre nations* (Paris: Société française pour l'arbitrage, 1895).
322. Goldberg, 386.
323. Ibid., 388.
324. David E. Sumler, "Opponents of War Preparedness in France, 1913–14," in *Doves and Diplomats*, ed. Salomon Wank (Westport, CT, and London: Greenwood Press, 1978), 117.
325. Goldberg, 437.
326. Eugene Debs, "When I Shall Fight," *The Appeal to Reason*, Sept. 11, 1915.
327. Theodore Ruyssen, "The Final Efforts of the European Pacifists to Prevent the War," *The Advocate of Peace* 76.10 (Nov. 1914): 237.
328. Ibid., 238.
329. Goldberg, 466.
330. Ibid., 467.
331. Raoul Villain spent the First World War in

jail. He was brought to trial in 1919 and acquitted by a popular jury. Anatole France wrote in *L'Humanité*: "Workers! A monstrous verdict brings in that assassinating Jaurès is not a crime." Jaurès's wife, who was the plaintiff, had to pay the court costs. Fighting for Franco, Villain died in Spain at the beginning of the Spanish Civil War in 1936.

332. Goldberg, 466. Meanwhile the nationalist paper *La France militaire* declared: "It will be a beautiful war which will deliver all the captives of Germanism." L. C. F. Turner, *Origins of the First World War* (London: Edward Arnold, 1980), v.

333. Adam Hochschild, *To End All Wars: A Story of Protest and Patriotism in the First World War* (London: Pan Books, 2011), 95.

334. Bob Holman, *Keir Hardie, Labour's Greatest Hero?* (Oxford: Lion Hudson, plc., 2010), 176.

335. Iain McLean, *Keir Hardie* (London: Allen Lane, 1975), 157.

336. William Stewart, *J. Keir Hardie* (London: Independent Labour Party Publications Department, 1921), 240.

337. Stewart, 286.

338. Ibid.

339. Hochschild, 91.

340. Douglas J. Newton, *European Socialism and the Struggle for Peace 1889–1914* (Oxford: Clarendon Press 1985), 251.

341. Beales, 279.

342. Albert de Mun, "L'Europe toute entière, incertaine et troublée, s'apprête pour une guerre inévitable, dont l'heure lui est cachée, dont la cause lui demeure encore ignorée, mais qui s'avance vers elle avec l'implacable sûreté du destin," *L'Écho de Paris*, Jan. 18, 1913.

343. Norman Stone, "Moltke-Conrad: Relations Between the Austro-Hungarian and German General Staffs, 1909–14," *Historical Journal* 9.2 (1966): 213.

344. *Outbreak of the World War. German Documents Collected by Karl Kautsky*, ed. Max Montgelas and Walter Schuecking (New York: Oxford University Press, 1924), 307–308.

345. Robert A. Friedlander, "Who Put Out the Lamps?: Thoughts on International Law and the Coming of World War I," *Duquesne Law Review* 20.4 (Summer 1982): 569.

Chapter Two

1. Article #2: "In case of serious disagreement or dispute, before an appeal to arms, the Contracting Powers agree to have recourse, as far as circumstances allow, to the good offices or mediation of one or more friendly Powers." And in Article #3: "Independently of this recourse, the Contracting Powers deem it expedient and desirable that one or more Powers, strangers to the dispute, should, on their own initiative and as far as circumstances may allow, offer their good offices or mediation to the States at variance."

2. Seymour, vol. 1, 283. Also: Frank B. Lord and James William Bryan, *Woodrow Wilson's Administration and Achievements* (Project Gutenberg Ebook, August 29, 2009 [eBook #29850]), 30. Also: *New York Times*, August 6, 1914.

3. Luke 14:18: "But they all alike began to make excuses."

4. Kent Forster, *The Failures of Peace* (Washington, DC: American Council on Public Affairs, 1941), 14. Also: Arthur S. Wilson Link, *The Struggle for Neutrality 1914–1915* (Princeton, NJ: Princeton University Press, 1960), 191–192. Also: *Foreign Relations of the United States,* 1914 Supplement: *The World War* (Washington DC: United States Government Printing Office, 1928), 37, 48, 49, 50, 60, 78.

5. David Cortright, *Peace: A History of Movements and Ideas* (Cambridge: Cambridge University Press, 2008), 53.

6. Ralph D. Nurnberger, "Bridling the Passions," *Wilson Quarterly (1976)* 11 (New Year's 1987): 96.

7. Seymour, vol. 1, 284.

8. Johan Den Hertog and Samuel Kruizingza, *Caught in the Middle, Neutral, Neutrality and the First World War* (Amsterdam: Amsterdam University Press, 2011), 63.

9. A self-made man, Hans Niels Andersen began his career as a cabin boy on a sailing ship in the Far East. While in Siam, in the 1880s, he was also the owner of the now famous Oriental Hotel in Bangkok.

10. W. B. Fest, "British War Aims and German Peace Feelers During the First World War," *Historical Journal* 15.2 (June 1972): 292.

11. Fest, 22. Also: Harry Hanak, Review of Wolfgang Steglich, *Die Friedensversuche der kriegführenden Mächte im Sommer und Herbst 1917. Quellenkritische Untersuchungen, Akten und Vernehmungsprotokolle* (Stuttgart: Franz Steiner, 1984), *English Historical Review* 104.411 (April 1989): 436–438. Also: Kay Lundgreen-Nielsen: Review of Wilhelm Ernst Winterhager, *Mission für den Frieden, Europäische Mächtepolitik und dänische Friedensvermittlung im Ersten Weltkrieg: vom August 1914 bis zum italienischen Kriegseintritt Mai 1915,* (Stuttgart: Franz Steiner, 1984), *International History Review* 9.3 (Aug. 1987): 509–511.

12. Forster, 22–23.

13. Maurice Paléologue, *An Ambassador's Memoirs*, trans. F. A. Holt (New York: George H. Doran, 1924), December 30, 1915.

14. Paléologue, December 30, 1915.

15. Forster, 23–24.

16. Ibid., 16.

17. Although the Vatican pledged its neutrality, the papal nuncio in Paris allegedly said in a meeting at the Institut Catholique "to fight against France is to fight against God." The Pope, Benedict XV, was said to have once exclaimed that he was sorry not to have been born a Frenchman.

18. The name Benedict was not an idle choice. Benedict XV later claimed that he was influenced by the founder of that renowned monastic order, Saint Benedict of Nursia (San Benedetto da Norcia) (c. 480–547), and his search for peace.

19. John F. Pollard, *The Unknown Pope: Benedict XV (1914–1922) and the Pursuit of Peace* (London: Geoffrey Chapman, 1999), 86.
20. John F. Pollard, "The Unknown Pope: Benedict XV (1914–1922) and the Pursuit of Peace," *Historical Journal* 43.3 (Sept. 2000): 910.
21. Benedict XV may have been the most pacifistic Pope in recent history, but he was not the first modern Pope to espouse the cause of peace. Leo XIII (1810–1903) issued the groundbreaking encyclical *Rerum Novarum*, which called for a new international order based on peace, justice and love rather than military might. In 1900 he performed a symbolic example of disarmament by melting down old swords and selling them as scrap iron. Pope Pius X (1903–1914), who preceded Benedict XV, wrote that working to avoid war "conforms to the precepts of the Gospel." See: Cortright, 200–203. Also: Thomas J. Massaro, S.J., and Thomas A. Shannon, *Catholic Perspectives on War and Peace* (Lanham, MD: Rowman & Littlefield, 2003), 19.
22. Beales, 301.
23. Walter H. Peters, *The Life of Benedict XV* (Milwaukee: Bruce, 1959), 113.
24. Malcolm Brown, "The Christmas Truce 1914: The British Story," in *Meetings in No Man's Land, Christmas 1914 and Fraternization in the Great War*, ed. Marc Ferro, Malcolm Brown, Rémy Cazals and Olaf Mueller (London: Constable & Robinson, 2007), 21.
25. Brown, "The Christmas Truce 1914: The British Story," 22.
26. Although the Vatican cultivated this peaceful image, at the same time it was directly involved in supporting the Easter Uprising in Ireland and paying for the shipment of 22,000 Russian rifles, which ultimately fell into British hands. Etic Frattini, *The Entity: Five Centuries of Secret Vatican Espionage*, trans. Dick Cluster (London: JR Books, 2009), 188–191.
27. Peters, 117.
28. Ibid., 114.
29. Ibid., 124.
30. Bernstorff, 68–69.
31. Ibid., 10–11.
32. Richard Hofstadter, *The American Political Tradition: And the Men Who Made It* (New York: Alfred Knopf, 1948), 260.
33. Bernstorff, 63.
34. Joachim Von Kürenberg, *The Kaiser: A Life of Wilhelm II, Last Emperor of Germany*, trans. H. T. Russell and Herta Hagen (New York: Simon & Schuster, 1955), 348.
35. Thomas C. Kennedy, The Hound of Conscience: A History of the No-Conscription Fellowship, 1914–1919 (Fayetteville: University of Arkansas Press, 1981), 51.
36. J. A. Thompson, Albion: A Quarterly Journal Concerned with British *Studies* 14.1 (Spring 1982): 93.
37. Joe P. Dunn, *Military Affairs* 46.2 (April 1982): 104.
38. Peter Brock and Nigel Young, *Pacifism in the Twentieth Century* (Syracuse, NY: Syracuse University Press, 1999), 26.
39. Thomas C. Kennedy, "Public Opinion and the Conscientious Objector," *Journal of British Studies* 12.2 (May 1973): 110.
40. Ibid., 109.
41. Some sources report the number sentenced to death as 34, e.g., Brock Millman, "HMG and the War Against Dissent, 1914–1918," *Journal of Contemporary History* 40.3 (July 2005): 430.
42. Brock, 430.
43. Hochschild, 189.
44. Max Arthur, *Forgotten Voices of the Great War* (London: Ebury Press, 2002), 108–109.
45. CO Project, *Conscientious Objection in Britain in World War One* (London: Peace Pledge Union).
46. Kennedy, "Public Opinion and the Conscientious Objector," 119.
47. Hochschild, 190.
48. Mrs. Henry Hobhouse, *I Appeal unto Caesar: The Case of the Conscientious Objector* (London: George Allen & Unwin, 1917), 28–29.
49. Hochschild, 191.
50. Martin Caedel, *Pacifism in Britain, 1914–1945: The Defining of a Faith* (Oxford: Clarendon Press, 1980), 45.
51. As an MP, Trevelyan wrote articles for newspapers and gave a series of lectures on the need to negotiate a peace with Germany. He was attacked in the popular press as being a "pro–German, unpatriotic, and a scoundrel." Like other anti-war MPs, he was defeated in the 1918 General Election.
52. Phillip Snowden was not a pacifist, but he campaigned against the war and conscription. His stance was unpopular and, like the other anti-war MPs, he lost his seat in Parliament in the 1918 General Election. He regained it in 1922 and became Chancellor of the Exchequer in 1924.
53. Ramsay MacDonald also resigned his government post at the beginning of the war. The press accused him of cowardice and treason for his support of the pacifist cause. After the war he became the first Labour Party Prime Minister.
54. Thompson, 93.
55. Kennedy, *The Hound of Conscience*, 52–53. The NCF, jointly with the Fellowship of Reconciliation and the Friends Service Committee, issued a Christmas message in 1918. The leaflet called for forgiveness and goodwill. It warned against harsh treatment of a defeated Germany and added, prophetically, that unless a positive path was found in the future, "the very militarism against which we have been fighting will dominate our lives, and ere long the sun of western civilization will be set in a sea of blood."
56. Sidney Webb, "Conscience and the Conscientious Objector," *North American Review* 205.736 (March 1917): 420.
57. Jo Vellacott, "The No-Conscription Fellowship," review of "The Hound of Conscience: A History of the No-Conscription Fellowship, 1914–19" by Thomas C. Kennedy, *Russell: The Journal of the*

Bertrand Russell Archives, new series, 1.2 (Winter 1981–1982): 158–161. The end of the war removed the NCF's raison d'être and it was dissolved in 1919.
58. Bertrand Russell, "Barbarism," in *Twentieth Century Protest*, ed. Brian MacArthur (London: Penguin Group, 1998), 42.
59. Jeanne Larson and Madge Micheels-Cyrus, *Seeds of Peace: A Catalogue of Quotations* (Philadelphia and Santa Cruz: New Society, 1987), 8.
60. Bertrand Russell, "War and Non-Resistance," *Atlantic Monthly*, August 1915, 266–274.
61. Ibid.
62. Ibid.
63. Russell, *Autobiography* (London and New York: Routledge, 1998), 290.
64. *Times*, May 17, 1916, in Russell, *Autobiography* 291.
65. Roger P. Chickering, "The Peace Movement and the Religious Community in Germany, 1900–1914," *Church History* 38.3 (September 1969): 301.
66. Ibid., 302.
67. The Gratry Society was named after Alphonse Gratry (1805–1872), a French priest, mystic, philosopher and advocate of world peace. He was a member of La Ligue internationale de la paix and participated in the 1867 Congrès de la paix universelle. He wrote extensively and his last book, *La Paix*, appeared in 1869 just before the Franco-Prussian war.
68. Paul Sabatier, *France Today: Its Religious Orientation*, trans. Henry Bryan Binns (New York: E. P. Dutton, 1913), 61.
69. Martin Luther supported a non-religious war against the Turks. In 1526, he argued in *Whether Soldiers Can Be in a State of Grace* that national defense is reason for a just war. He actively urged Emperor Charles V and the German people to fight a secular war against the Turks. At the time of the Siege of Vienna, Luther wrote a prayer for national deliverance from the Turks, asking God to "give to our emperor perpetual victory over our enemies."
70. Chickering, "The Peace Movement and the Religious Community in Germany, 1900–1914," 307.
71. James C. Juhnke, "World War (1914–1918)," *Global Anabaptist Mennonite Encyclopedia Online*, 1989.
72. Caroline Moorehead, *Troublesome People* (Bethesda, MD: Adler & Adler, 1987).
73. Chickering, "The Peace Movement and the Religious Community in Germany, 1900–1914," 300–311.
74. Fried was merely the propagandist or popularizer of a theory developed by the Russian sociologist Jacques Novicow (1849–1912). Novicow called himself "a European" and believed that the survival of an ancient form of violence, such as warfare, utterly contradicted the productive forces in society and was opposed to cultural advances. He regarded the nation-state as a transitory stage that would eventually be supplanted by a federation of states on a global level.
75. Wank, 21–37.
76. Ibid., 34. It should be noted that Fried's "scientific pacifism" was based mainly on the theories of a contemporary Russian sociologist, Jakob Novikow.
77. Martin Wolf, "Will the Nation-State Survive Globalization?" *Foreign Affairs*, January/February 2001. Also: R. E. Rowthorn and S. N. Solomu, "The Macroeconomic Effects of Overseas Investment on the UK Balance of Trade, 1870–1913," *Economic History Review* 44.4 (Nov. 1991): 654–664.
78. James D. Shand, "Doves Among the Eagles: Pacifists and Their Government During World War I," *Journal of Contemporary History* 10.1 (Jan. 1975): 101.
79. Alfred H. Fried, "Pacifism Will Survive...," in *Instead of Violence*, ed. Arthur and Lila Weinberg, 270–273. Alfred H. Fried had received the Nobel Peace Prize in 1911 and in the pre-war years was regarded as a pillar of the international peace movement. Strangely enough, initially he supported the war effort of the Central Powers, but then he retreated to Switzerland, where he tried to rekindle the anti-war movement.
80. Karl's Liebknecht's father, Wilhelm, was a personal friend and comrade of Karl Marx from the days of the 1848 revolution.
81. Karl Liebknecht, "Votes 'No' in the Reichstag," in *Instead of Violence*, ed. Arthur and Lila Weinberg), 285–287.
82. Liebknecht's party, the German Social-Democratic Party (SPD), voted against him. At a parliamentary meeting 78 of the 92 members voted in favor of granting the government the so-called war credits. Other socialist parties in Europe also supported the war efforts of their respective governments, with the sole exception of the Italian socialist party, who in 1915 voted against the granting of war credits. Groh, 151–177.
83. James D. Young, *Socialism Since 1889: A Biographical History* (Totowa, NJ: Barnes & Noble Books, 1988), 71.
84. Karl Liebknecht, *Militarism* (New York: B. W. Huebsch, 1917), 174–175.
85. Liebknecht, *Militarism*, 176–177.
86. James D. Young, *Socialism Since 1889*, 72.
87. Whittle, 291.
88. Leon Trotsky, *Political Profiles* (London: New Park, 1972), 132.
89. Ebba Dahlin, *French and German Public Opinion on Declared War Aims, 1914–1918* (Palo Alto, CA: Stanford University Press, 1933), 50–51.
90. Philip S. Foner, *May Day: A Short History of the International Workers' Holiday* (New York: International, 1986), 84.
91. Liebknecht, *Militarism*, introduction, x–xi.
92. Walter I. Trattner, "Julia Grace Wales and the Wisconsin Plan for Peace," *Wisconsin Magazine for History* 44.3 (Spring 1961): 204.
93. Ibid., 204.
94. Burnet Hershey, *The Odyssey of Henry Ford and the Great Peace Ship* (New York: Taplinger, 1967) 64.
95. The idea that the United States should call a

conference of neutral nations was not new. Several Senators had introduced bills in the Senate asking the President to do so, and at least one country, Venezuela, had made a formal recommendation to that effect.

96. Julia Grace Wales, *Continuous Mediation Without Armistice* (Chicago: Woman's Peace Party, 1917), 13.

97. Wales, 13.

98. Ibid., 9.

99. Hershey, 66.

100. Beales, 299.

101. The only "festivities" were a trip to Haarlem to see the tulips and a visit to the hyacinths at the end of the congress.

102. Aletta Jacobs was the first woman to complete a university course in the Netherlands and the first female physician.

103. Jane Addams, Emily G. Balch and Alice Hamilton, *Women at The Hague: The International Congress of Women and Its Result* (Urbana and Chicago: University of Illinois Press, 2003), xvi.

104. The congress also marked the foundation of the Women's International League for Peace and Freedom (WILPF), an organization that still exists today, its goals being social justice, sustainable development, women's equality and disarmament.

105. Adams, Balch, and Hamilton, 44.

106. Barbara S. Kraft, *The Peace Ship* (New York: Macmillan, 1978), 22–23.

107. Trattner, 212.

108. Kraft, *The Peace Ship*, 30.

109. John Hall, *That Bloody Woman: The Turbulent Life of Emily Hobhouse* (Truro, UK: Truan, 2008), 235.

110. Only one other member of the House of Commons, John Burns, resigned in protest to the British entry into the war. Burns, known as an independent radical, refused to publicly account for his resignation and completely withdrew from politics.

111. A. J. A. Morris, *C. P. Trevelyan 1870–1958, Portrait of a Radical* (Belfast: Blackstaff Press, 1977), 118.

112. Morris, *C. P. Trevelyan 1870–1958*, 127.

113. A. J. A. Morris, "C. P. Trevelyan's Road to Resignation 1906–1914: The Odyssey of an Antiwar Liberal," in *Doves and Diplomats: Foreign Offices and Peace Movements in Europe and America in the Twentieth Century*, ed. Solomon Wank (Westport, CO, and London: Greenwood Press, 1978), 98.

114. The National Peace Council was founded in 1908 and finally disbanded in 2000. It acted as the coordinating body for almost 200 groups across the UK.

115. Morris *C.P. Trevelyan 1870–1958*, 101.

116. See chapter 1.

117. E. D. Morel became famous for leading the protest against slavery in the Congo Free State. At the outbreak of World War One he campaigned for neutrality. When that fight was lost, he helped create the Union of Democratic Control. He was secretary of the UDC until his death in 1924.

118. The UDC continued to exist after the First World War and in the 1930s joined the anti-fascist struggle. The membership declined drastically after the Second World War and the organization ceased to exist sometime in the 1960s.

119. The Union of Democratic Control (UDC) had three main objectives: (1) that in future to prevent secret diplomacy there should be parliamentary control over foreign policy; (2) that there should be negotiations after the war with other democratic European countries in an attempt to form an organization to help prevent future conflicts; (3) that at the end of the war the peace terms should neither humiliate the defeated nation nor artificially rearrange frontiers, as this might provide a cause for future wars. The concept of popular control of foreign policy was not new. It had been demanded by the Universal Peace Conference of 1890 in London, the Manchester Peace Congress of 1904 and the Edinburgh Peace Congress of 1911.

120. Morris, *C. P. Trevelyan 1870–1958*, 133.

121. Ibid., 133.

122. The one person in the *Times* survey who mentioned foreign news was a lady who wanted more news about India, as she had a son there working on a tea plantation.

123. *War and Peace* was founded in 1913 by the Garton Foundation, which in turn had been founded by Norman Angell. After May 1917 it was published as a supplement to *The Nation*, a pacifist journal.

124. Hanak, Harry, *Great Britain and Austria-Hungary During the First World War* (London: Oxford University Press, 1962), 157.

125. Ibid., 152.

126. Ibid., 156.

127. The UK Military Service Act specified that men from 18 to 41 years old were liable to be called up for service in the army unless they were married, widowed with children, serving in the Royal Navy, ministers of religion, or working in one of a number of reserved occupations. A second Act in May 1916 extended liability for military service to married men, and a third Act in 1918 extended the upper age limit to 51.

128. Michel L. Martin, "France: A Statute but No Objections," in *The New Conscientious Objection: From Sacred to Secular Resistance*, ed. Charles S. Moskos and John Whiteclay Chambers III (New York: Oxford University Press, 1993), 80.

129. Ibid., 14.

130. Michael Clinton, "Coming to Terms with 'Pacifism': The French Case, 1901–1918," *Peace & Change* 26.1 (Jan. 2001): 8.

131. "The People Want War," *The Advocate of Peace* 78.3 (March 1916): 65.

132. Romain Rolland, *Above the Battle*, trans. C. K. Ogden (Chicago: Open Court, 1916), 37–38.

133. Gerhart Hauptmann (1862–1946) was a German dramatist and novelist. A pacifist during World War One, he received the Nobel Prize for Literature in 1912 "in recognition of his fruitful, varied and outstanding production in the realm of dramatic art."

134. Ibid., 56.
135. Josephson, 815. The phrase "moral conscience of Europe" was apparently coined by Romain Rolland's good friend the Austrian author, Stefan Zweig.
136. René Fueloep-Miller, "Tolstoy, the Apostolic Crusader," *Russian Review* 19.2 [Special Issue: Leo Tolstoy] (April 1960): 116.
137. Romain Rolland, "Calls for an End of the Homicidal fury in Europe," in *Instead of Violence*, ed. Arthur and Lila Weinberg, 282–285.
138. Clinton, 18.
139. Stefan Zweig, *Romain Rolland: The Man and His Work*, trans. Eden and Cedar Paul (New York: Thomas Seltzer, 1921), 293.
140. Ibid., 297.
141. Rolland, 41.
142. Ibid., 78.
143. Leo Tolstoy, *The Complete Works of Count Tolstoy*, vol. 23, ed. and trans. Leo Wiener (London: G. J. Howell, 1905), 126.
144. Fueloep-Miller, 121. Yasnaya Polyana, in Russian literally "Clear Glade," the place where Tolstoy was born, wrote *War and Peace* and *Anna Karenina*, and is buried, is located about 200 kilometers (120 miles) from Moscow.
145. Tolstoy's vegetarianism would be called vegan today since he refused to eat animal products such as eggs and milk.
146. Colm McKeogh, *Tolstoy's Pacifism* (Amherst, NY: Cambria Press, 2009), 123.
147. Ibid., 195.
148. Leo Tolstoy, *What Is Religion? And Other New Articles and Letters*, trans. V. Tchertkoff and A. C. Field (Hants: Free Age Press, 1902), 170–172.
149. In England John Coleman Kenworthy (1863–1948) founded a colony based on Tolstoyan principles at Purleigh, Essex in 1896. This community closed a few years later, but its residents moved on to create the Whiteway Colony in Gloucestershire and the Stapleton Colony in Yorkshire, both of which still exist today.
150. The Christian Commonwealth Colony in Georgia was established in 1896 by a number of Christian socialists who followed Tolstoyan principles and comprised 932 acres. When their cotton mill and towel production failed, the colonists successfully printed a periodical called *The Social Gospel*, which reached at least 2,000 readers. The income was not sufficient to maintain the colony. In 1900, after a typhoid epidemic killed several members, the property was sold and the proceeds were used to settle debts.
151. In 1904 Augusto D'Halmar, nom de plume for Augusto Goemine Thomson (1882–1950), a well-known writer, formed Colonia Tolstoyana, a collective of peasants, which failed in a few years. Another Tolstoyan colony was founded in Santiago and published the newspaper *La Protesta Humana* (The human protest).
152. Mohandas Gandhi (1869–1948) established a colony called the Tolstoy Farm near Johannesburg, South Africa, having been inspired by Tolstoy's ideas.

The colony, about 1,100 acres, was funded by Gandhi's close friend Herman Kallenbach (1882–1950). Gandhi called the farm a "cooperative commonwealth" and he lived there for about four years. The last resident caretaker left the farm in 1970.
153. Many of these Tolstoyan communities survived into the Soviet era, and as late as World War Two over 100 Tolstoyans were shot for refusing military service.
154. Tolstoy, *The Complete Works of Count Tolstoy*, 196–197.
155. The word "Doukhobor" was originally applied to the sect by an Orthodox archbishop in anger to signify that they fought against the Holy Spirit.
156. George Woodcock and Ivan Avakumovic, *The Doukhobors* (London: Faber and Faber, 1968) 19.
157. Ibid., 95.
158. Ibid., 267.
159. Ibid., 103.
160. One source puts the number of Doukhobors who originally arrived in Canada at 7,427, with 417 others arriving between 1900 and 1929. See: Harry B. Hawthorn, ed., *The Doukhobors of British Columbia* (London: University of British Columbia and J. M. Dent & Sons, 1955), 7.
161. Today perhaps 20 to 40,000 people of Doukhobor descent live in Canada, but no more than 4,000 claim "Doukhobor" as their religious affiliation. Perhaps another 30,000 live in Russia and the former Russian colonies. Five thousand more live in the United States along the Canadian border.
162. McKeogh, 157.
163. Ibid., 158.
164. Josephson, 953. Gandhi was full of contradictions. During World War One Gandhi had yet to fully accept the doctrine of non-resistance. He first helped recruit an ambulance corps in the UK and then later, in India, traveled extensively recruiting soldiers to fight in the British army. It was only later that he became non-violent. Romain Rolland wrote about him: "Gandhi is a Tolstoy in a more gentle, appeased, and, if I dared, I would say, in a more Christian sense, for Tolstoy is not so much a Christian by nature as by force of will." Janko Lavrin, "Tolstoy and Gandhi," *Russian Review* 19.2 [Special Issue: Leo Tolstoy] (Apr. 1960): 133–134.
165. Fueloep-Miller, 120–121.
166. "Tolstoy on Disarmament," *New York Times*, Jan. 16, 1899.
167. McKeogh, 122.
168. Ibid., 209.
169. Gandhi recognized that political organization was necessary for the coordination of community life. However, he wished to be rid of the coercive element, what he called "the body force," and replace it by a "soul force," a faith in the superiority of the soul to the body. See: Mulford Q. Sibley, "The Political Theories of Modern Religious Pacifism," *American Political Science Review* 37.3 (June 1943): 441.
170. Sibley, 210.

171. Ibid.
172. "Mr Roosevelt's Attack on Tolstoy," in *Current Literature* (New York: 1909), 64–65.
173. "The Czar Sees Tolstoi," *New York Times*, Jan. 17, 1899.
174. "Count Tolstoy on the War—'Bethink Yourselves!'" *New York Times*, July 10, 1904.
175. Leo Tolstoy, *On Patriotism*, chapter 14 (Moscow: March 17, 1894), transcribed and edited by www.nonresistance.org, 24–25.
176. Barnett Singer, "From Patriots to Pacifists: The French Primary School Teachers, 1880–1940," *Journal of Contemporary History* 12 (1977): 417.
177. Singer, 418. Of the 35,000 schoolmasters mobilized during the war, 8,419, nearly a quarter, were killed on the field of battle.
178. Ibid.
179. Feeley, 19.
180. Ibid., 20.
181. Ibid.
182. Ibid.
183. Ruth Roach Pierson, *Women and Peace: Theoretical, Historical, and Practical Perspectives* (London: Routledge Kegan & Paul, 1987), 107.
184. Feeley, 21.
185. Josephson, 838–839.
186. Evelyne Morin-Rotureau, *Combat de femmes 1914–1918* (Paris: Autrement Memoires/Histoire, 2004), 227.
187. *La Paix* was written between 1914 and 1917, but the Comédie Française had found it to be too inflammatory to be produced during the wartime. Lenéru died during the influenza epidemic of 1918. Nancy Sloan Goldberg, "Women, War, and H. G. Wells: The Pacifism of French Playwright Marie Lenéru," *WLA* 14 (2002): 165.
188. By the beginning of the First World War, 1914, H. G. Wells had already written some of his most famous novels, for example, *The Time Machine* (1895), *The Island of Dr. Moreau* (1896), *The Invisible Man* (1897), and *The War of the Worlds* (1898). Over 10 million volumes of his work had been sold.
189. H. G. Wells, *War and the Future*. (London: Cassel and Company, 1917) 8–9.
190. The phrase was the title of a book: H. G. Wells, *The War That Will End War* (London: Frank & Cecil Palmer, Red Lion Court, 1914). On page 11, Wells wrote: "For this is now a war for peace. It aims straight at disarmament. It aims at a settlement that shall stop this sort of thing forever. Every soldier who fights against Germany now is a crusader against war. This, the greatest of all wars, is not just another war, it is the last war!"
191. Intellectuals in other countries replied with similar statements. The Russian intelligentsia, for example, published a declaration titled "To Our Country and to the Whole of the Civilized World." It was signed by 1,100 Russian intellectuals. French academics published a "Declaration by French Academics to the Universities of Neutral Countries." Even Portuguese, Spanish and Scandinavian intellectuals issued their statements, most anti–German but also some in favor.

192. Giuseppe Castagnetti, Hubert Goenner, Jürgen Renn, Tilman Sauer, and Britta Scheideler, "Foundation in Disarray: Essays on Einstein's Science and Politics in the Berlin Years," Max Planck-Institut für Wissenschaftsgeschichte. Reprint 63, 1997, 15.
193. "Some Germans Tried to Fight Fairly; Professor Nicolai One of Many Who Suffered for Disobeying General Staff," *New York Times*, June 8, 1919, 26.
194. *Journal of the American Medical Association*, Jan. 26, 1918, quoted in a Feb. 10, 1918, *New York Times* article, "Truth About Dr. Nikolai; German Professor Jailed Despite Berlin's Official Denials."
195. C. E. Playne, *German Pacifism During the War* (London: National Peace Council, 1919), 8.
196. Wolf Zuelzer, *The Nicolai Case* (Detroit: Wayne State University Press, 1982), 16.
197. Ibid., 43.
198. Ibid.
199. Ibid., 44.
200. Woodbridge N. Ferris, "Review of Biology of War" (Ferris Library for Information, Technology and Education, 1919).
201. Ibid.
202. Strangely enough, after the war Nicolai was one of the first Germans to set foot on French soil. He went there to establish contact with French pacifists.
203. Zuelzer, 211.
204. Franklin H. Giddings, *Political Science Quarterly* 34.1 (March 1919): 149–151.
205. Zuelzer, 222.
206. The flight out of Germany was not Professor Nicolai's first attempt to leave. Previously he tried to cross the Swiss border on foot but ran into a German patrol and was arrested. Luckily he was released with only a warning, and he didn't try again.
207. Zuelzer, 230–231.
208. After the war Professor Nicolai led a nomadic existence in Uruguay, Argentina and the Soviet Union. He finally settled in Chile.
209. Foerster had previously founded the German Society for Ethical Culture and had been one of the founding members of the Deutsche Friedensgesellschaft (the German Peace Society). He had also been one of the few German intellectuals to oppose the annexation of Alsace-Lorraine in 1871.
210. Hans Kohn, *The Mind of Germany* (New York: Charles Scribner's Sons, 1960), 325.
211. Ibid.
212. Ibid.
213. "Mr. Angell's Plea for a League of Nations," *New York Times*, Aug. 18, 1918.
214. Ebba Dahlin, 90.
215. Hermann Fernau, *Because I Am a German*. (New York: E. P. Dutton, 1916), 156.
216. During the German revolution of 1918–1919 Fernau advocated a "Third Way," that is, a path toward democracy that rejected both the *ancien régime* and a Bolshevik or communist future.
217. Fernau, 158–159.
218. Josephson, 356.

219. A German (nom de plume for Richard Grelling), *I Accuse!* trans. Alexander Gray (New York: George H. Doran, 1915), 34.
220. Friedrich Herneck, *Einstein und Weltbild: Aufsätze und Vorträge* (Berlin: Der Morgen, 1979) 37.
221. Larson and Micheels-Cyrus, 180.
222. Otto Nathan and Heinz Norden, *Einstein on Peace* (New York: Simon & Schuster, 1960), vii.
223. Hubert Goenner and Guiseppe Castagnetti, "Albert Einstein as Pacifist and Democrat During World War I," *Science in Context* 9.4 (1996): 326–327.
224. Ibid., 340.
225. Ibid.
226. Josephson, 250–251.
227. Goenner and Castagnetti, 343.
228. Ibid., 369.
229. The German Goethebund was a cultural association founded against censorship and for the free development of intellectual life.
230. Goenner and Castagnetti, 348.
231. Josephson, 276.
232. Sébastien Faure, *Vers la paix. Appel aux socialistes, syndicalistes, révolutionnaires & anarchistes* (Imprimerie Sébastien Faure [La Ruche], 1915).
233. In addition, Minister Malvy promised that he would destroy the records of those soldiers who read Faure's tracts, but this was never done.
234. Larson and Micheels-Cyrus, 161.
235. Sylvain Garel, *Louis Lecoin: An Anarchist Life* (London: Kate Sharpley Library, 2000), 24.
236. Pierre Ruff died in a Nazi concentration camp.
237. Josephson, 549.
238. "Kings Going Forth to War," *New York Times*, Aug. 2, 1914.
239. Hamilton Holt was also a founding member of the NAACP (National Association for the Advancement of Colored People) and the president for 25 years of Rollins College in Florida. He openly advocated a policy whereby students could approve or disapprove of faculty hirings.
240. Andrew Carnegie was probably the first to use the phrase "A League for Peace." He did so in an address to the students of St. Andrew's University in 1905. See: Hamilton Holt, "The League to Enforce Peace," *Proceedings of the Academy of Political Science in the City of New York* 7.2 (July 1917): 65.
241. The first paragraph of Hamilton Holt's "The Way to Disarm: A Practical Proposal" reads: "In his famous essay, 'Perpetual Peace,' published in 1795, Emmanuel Kant, perhaps the greatest intellect the world has ever produced, declared that we can never have universal peace until the world is politically organized and it will never be possible to organize the world politically until the people, not kings, rule." Hamilton Holt, "The Way to Disarm: A Practical Proposal," *The Independent* 79 (Sept. 28, 1914): 427. Kant's essay "Perpetual Peace: A Philosophical Sketch" (*Zum ewigen Frieden: Ein philosophischer Entwirf*), written in 1795, describes his proposed program for perpetual peace. It is typically viewed as the starting point of contemporary liberal thought. Among other things, Kant posits three definitive articles that would provide a foundation for peace: "The civil constitution of every state should be republican. The law of nations shall be founded on a federation of free states. And the law of world citizenship shall be limited to conditions of universal hospitality."
242. Beales, 292.
243. Ibid., 293.
244. Theodore Marburg, *League of Nations: A Chapter in the History of the Movement*, foreword by William Howard Taft (New York: Macmillan, 1917), viii.
245. Ibid., 40.
246. In fact, the first step toward a system of world or European peace was taken almost 1,000 years ago by the now forgotten Bishop Guy d'Anjou. He proclaimed a truce of God limiting the use of arms and mobilizing the spiritual power of Christianity against the scourge of war. To the surprise of many, the bishop succeeded in curbing violence in his diocese. Other French bishops followed his example. In the year 1000, at the council at Poitiers, the motto "*Guerre à la guerre*" was adopted, which forced the princes of the Church to oppose war by the intervention of troops under religious leadership. Later at a synod in Limoges in 1031, it was resolved to ex-communicate violators of the peace. It was also decided that military force was to be used against any breakers of God's truce. In 1038 the synod of Bruges also swore to take military measures against violators of the ecclesiastic peace laws. The Archbishop Aimon carried out several punitive expeditions against rebellious knights. The archbishop may, in fact, be considered the earliest commander of a modern, international armed peace force. Unfortunately, Aimon's peace force was annihilated by a group of knights who were more expert in the art of war than the 700 clerks whom they killed.

Taft's scheme also bears a certain similarity to a resolution passed by the Council of Toulouse in the early 13th century, which demanded that: (1) every person over 14 years of age was to pledge with a solemn oath not to violate the truce of God and not to assist any violator of the peace; (2) this oath was to be repeated every three years, and a person refusing to renew the pledge was to be treated as a breaker of the law; (3) alliances between nobles were forbidden; (4) any violator of the peace was to be attacked forthwith by all the others who had pledged themselves to maintain peace; his territory was to be cut off from communications and traffic; his stronghold was to be besieged and stormed; the aggressor and his men were to be punished severely and their property confiscated; (5) the violator of the peace was to be excommunicated (a sanction that frequently entailed economic ruin and even physical destruction); (6) the subjects of the aggressor were formally ordered to revolt against their master and to obstruct his aggression. See: Possony, 910.
247. Holt, "The League to Enforce Peace," 67–68.

248. Ibid., 68.
249. A typical example is cited by Lucia Ames Mead, reporting a conversation with a Massachusetts Senator who said: "I believe in arbitration, of course [...]. I've worked to promote that [...], but when you peace people talk about ending war, I can't follow you. I think you will have to wait until the millennium; for so long as there is sin in the world there must needs be force." John Whiteclay Chambers II, in *The Eagle and the Dove: The American Peace Movement and United States Foreign Policy 1900–1922*, ed. John Whiteclay (Syracuse, NY: Syracuse University Press, 1991), 8.
250. Holt, "The League to Enforce Peace," 68.
251. Chambers, 10.
252. Ruhl J. Bartlett, *The League to Enforce Peace* (Chapel Hill: University of North Carolina Press, 1944), 54.
253. Bartlett, 55.
254. "The President on the Enforcement of Peace," *The Independent* 86 (June 5, 1916): 357.
255. Marburg, 88.
256. Holt, "The League to Enforce Peace," 66.
257. Goldsmith, 275.
258. "Our Duty to Move for Peace at Once, Says Jacob Schiff," *New York Times*, Nov. 25, 1916, 1, 4.
259. Beales, 294.
260. "Taft as Envoy for World Peace," *New York Times*, Nov. 6, 1916.
261. Beales, 294.
262. Ibid., 294–295.
263. Ibid.
264. Charles DeBenedetti, *The Peace Reform in American History* (Bloomington: Indiana University Press, February 22, 1984), 98.
265. Curti, *Peace or War*, 239–240.
266. Nicholas Murray Butler was also instrumental in persuading Andrew Carnegie to provide the initial $10 million funding for the Carnegie Endowment for International Peace. Butler would later become the president of the Endowment and be awarded the Nobel Peace Prize in 1931.
267. Howlett, "Nicholas Murray Butler's Crusade for a Warless World," *Wisconsin Magazine of History* 67.2 (Winter, 1983–1984): 106.
268. Ibid., 109.
269. Ibid., 111.
270. Ernesto Teodoro Moneta founded the Lombard Association for Peace and Arbitration (Unione Lombarda per la pace e l'arbitrato) in 1887. The organization called for total disarmament and sought to create a League of Nations. He shared the Nobel Peace Prize in 1907 with Louis Renault.
271. Sandi E. Cooper, "The Guns of August and the Doves of Italy: Intervention and Internationalism," *Peace & Change* 7.1–2 (Winter 1981): 29.
272. Cooper, "The Reinvention of the 'Just War' Among European Pacifists Before the First World War," 305.
273. The Lombard Society, perhaps the most influential of the Italian peace societies. Cooper, "The Reinvention of the 'Just War' Among European Pacifists Before the First World War," 309.

274. Martin Ceadel, "Ten Distinctions for Peace Historians," in *The Pacifist Impulse in Historical Perspective*, ed. Dyck and Brock), 35.
275. Thus far, Ernesto Teodoro Moneta is the only Italian to have won the Nobel Peace Prize.
276. Ceadel, "Ten Distinctions for Peace Historians" 35.
277. James A. Young, "The Consulta and the Italian Peace Movement, 1914–18," in *Doves and Diplomats*, ed. Salomon Wank (Westport, CT, and London: Greenwood Press, 1978), 165.
278. The letter was answered in the spring of 1915 by 155 Germanic feminists and titled "Open Letter in Reply to the Open Christmas Letter from Englishwomen to German and Austrian Women":

To our English sisters, sisters of the same race, we express in the name of many German women our warm and heartfelt thanks for their Christmas greetings [...]. This message was a confirmation of what we foresaw—that women of the belligerent countries, with all faithfulness, devotion, and love to their country, can go beyond it and maintain true solidarity with the women of other belligerent nations, and that really civilized women never lose their humanity.

279. Hochschild, 188–189.
280. John Ellis, *Eye-Deep in Hell: Trench Warfare in World War I* (Baltimore: Johns Hopkins University Press, 1989), 170.
281. Malcolm Brown and Shirley Seaton, *Christmas Truce: The Western Front December 1914* (Basingstoke and Oxford: Pan Macmillan, 1994), 17–18.
282. "War Notes, a Broken Truce," *London Times*, Nov. 26, 1914), 7e.
283. Stanley Weintraub, *Silent Night: The Remarkable Christmas Truce of 1914* (London: Simon & Schuster, 2001), 14–15.
284. Rémy Cazals, "Good Neighbors," in *Meetings in No Man's Land: Christmas 1914 and Fraternization in the Great War*, 99–100.
285. Brown and Seaton, 51.
286. Arthur, 56.
287. Brown, "The Christmas Truce 1914: The British Story," 29.
288. Ibid., 38–39
289. Ibid., 36–37.
290. Brown and Seaton, 143.
291. Weintraub, 36.
292. Cazals, "Good Neighbors," 131.
293. Ibid., 88.
294. Gabriel Chevallier is best known for the anti-war novel *Clochemerle*, which has been translated into 26 languages and sold several million copies. He was wounded during World War I, was awarded the Croix de Guerre and became *Chevalier de la Légion d'honneur*.
295. Olaf Mueller, "Brother Boche," in *Meetings in No Man's Land: Christmas 1914 and Fraternization in the Great War*, 198.
296. Mueller, 160.
297. Ibid., 171.
298. Jay Winter, *The Great War and the Shaping of the 20th Century* (London: BBC Books, 1996), 96.

299. Brown and Seaton, 94.
300. Ibid., 61–62.
301. Ibid., xxi.
302. Weintraub, 53.
303. Ibid., 146.
304. Modris Eksteins, *Rites of Spring: The Great War and the Birth of the Modern Age* (Boston: Houghton Mifflin, 1989), 97.
305. Brown, "The Christmas Truce 1914: The British Story."
306. Nearly half a million Christmas parcels were sent from Britain to France and Belgium, and the Germans made a similar effort supported by a national campaign to send *Liebesgaben* (love gifts) to the men on the fighting front.
307. On August 6, 1914, Lord Asquith said in a speech to the House of Commons:
Unhappily, if—in spite of all our efforts to keep the peace, and with that full and overpowering consciousness of the result, if the issue be decided in favour of war,—we have, nevertheless, thought it to be the duty as well as the interest of this country to go to war, the House may be well assured it was because we believe, and I am certain the country will believe, we are unsheathing our sword in a just cause.
308. Brown, "The Christmas Truce 1914: The British Story," 48.
309. Eksteins, 112.
310. Brown, "The Christmas Truce 1914: The British Story," 48.
311. Ibid., 154.
312. The Peninsular War was between France and the allied powers of Spain, the UK, and Portugal for control of the Iberian Peninsula during the Napoleonic Wars. It began in 1807 and lasted until Napoleon was finally defeated in 1814. Many stories of fraternization have emerged, e.g., troops sharing the same water source, even drinking and playing cards together.
313. Brown, "The Christmas Truce 1914: The British Story," 17–18.
314. Weintraub, 160–161.
315. Ibid., 184, 193. Although the men on the front may have been ready to end the conflict once and for all with the Christmas truce, the politicians and generals were certainly not in agreement. In January 1915 the lead article in *Vanity Fair*, a popular American magazine of the time, provided a rough idea of what the Germans would expect from a truce at that point in the war: "the elimination of Belgium; the withdrawal from Russia of her Baltic provinces, the creation of a United Poland, under Austro-Hungary; the addition to Germany of Northeastern France, the temporary occupation of London; the neutralization of the English Channel, etc.," all points the Allies would certainly not have accepted.
316. Ibid., 53.
317. Ibid., 183.
318. Martin Gilbert, *The First World War* (London: Phoenix, 2008), 117.
319. Weintraub, 168–169.
320. Brown and Seaton, 169.
321. Ibid., 164.
322. Brown, "The Christmas Truce 1914: The British Story," 63.
323. Ibid.
324. Weintraub, 99.
325. Correspondence from the front was also censored. A regiment's letters were inspected and read one day a month. Roughly 180,000 letters were read each week. Each censor had to read, on the average, 280 letters a day. Their reports on the contents were sent to the General Staff, where they were analyzed as an indicator of morale. See: Cazals, "Good Neighbors," 100.
326. Eksteins, 134.
327. Cazals, "Good Neighbors," 115.
328. On Christmas Eve temperatures all along the Western Front dropped below freezing and in some places snow fell. Winter, 96.
329. Gilbert, 118.
330. Weintraub, 122.
331. Brown and Seaton, xxv.
332. Ibid., xxi–xxii.
333. John Richard Stephens, *Weird History 101* (Holbrook, MA: Adams Media Corporation, 1997), 78.
334. Weintraub, 166.
335. Ibid., 202.
336. Brown and Seaton, 201–202.
337. Weintraub, 199.

Chapter Three

1. Oswald Garrison Villard, *Fighting Years: A Memoir* (New York: Harcourt, Brace, 1939), 247.
2. Kraft, *The Peace Ship*, 33–34.
3. Ibid., 75.
4. Carol Gelderman, *Henry Ford, the Wayward Capitalist* (New York: Dial Press, 1981), 105. The phrase "Out of the trenches by Christmas" was actually coined by Ford's "peace secretary," Theodore Delavigne, a former Detroit newspaperman. Hershey, 18.
5. Allan Nevins and Frank Ernest Hill, *Ford—Expansion and Challenge 1915–1933* (New York: Charles Scribner's Sons, 1957), 27.
6. Hershey, 24.
7. A number of jokes circulated. A typical one was: "Why did Ford close down all his automobile factories? Because he took all the nuts to Europe." A prominent newspaper called the voyage of the *Oscar II* the "strangest assortment of living creatures since Noah's Ark," and another suggested they hold their meetings in the Zoological Gardens. Reynold M. Wik, *Henry Ford and Grass-Roots America* (Ann Arbor: University of Michigan Press, 1972), 166.
8. Nevins and Hill, 31.
9. James Brough, *The Ford Dynasty: An American Story* (Garden City, NY: Doubleday, 1977), 23.
10. Brough, 24.
11. Wik, 167.
12. Nevins and Hill, 27.
13. Kraft, *The Peace Ship*, 91.
14. Nevins and Hill, 41.

15. Gelderman, 100. It was Ford's first trip across an ocean. Hershey, 18.
16. The stowaway, Jacob Greenberg, posed as a Western Union delivery boy to get on board. Once the ship had sailed he presented himself to Henry Ford and offered to work for his passage. For several days he peeled potatoes in the hold; then he was put on the office staff.
17. Kraft, *The Peace Ship*, 117.
18. Nevins and Hill, 40.
19. It can be argued that the *Oscar II* was not the first peace ship but the second. Eight months before, in April 1915, the *Noordam*, a Dutch ship, had sailed from New York to The Hague carrying a delegation from the American Woman's Peace Party, the WPP, to the International Congress of Women, which was largely devoted to ending the war.
20. Nevins and Hill, 41.
21. Hershey, 31.
22. Kraft, *The Peace Ship*, 141.
23. Nevins and Hill, 45.
24. Keith Sward, *The Legend of Henry Ford* (New York: Rinehart, 1948), 93.
25. Gelderman, 137.
26. Charles DeBenedetti, *The Peace Reform in American History* (Bloomington: Indiana University Press, 1984), 94. Some of the bills were astronomical by any standard. For example, the delegates managed to spend $2,000 (approximately $40,000 in today's dollars) on taxis in Oslo in two days, $56,000 (approximately a million in today's dollars) on a Norwegian "Christmas binge," and $10,000 (approximately $200,000 in today's dollars) on telegrams while on board the *Oscar II*. Hershey, 126–128.
27. Moorehead, 28.
28. Nevins and Hill, 53.
29. Kraft, *The Peace Ship*, 297.
30. Hertog and Kruizingza 63.
31. Ibid., 22. Also: Harry Hanak, Review of Wolfgang Steglich, ed., *Die Friedensversuche der kriegführenden Mächte im Sommer und Herbst 1917. Quellenkritische Untersuchungen, Akten und Vernehmungsprotokolle* (Stuttgart: Franz Steiner, 1984), *English Historical Review* 104.411 (April 1989): 436–438. Also: Kay Lundgreen-Nielsen: Review of Wilhelm Ernst Winterhager, *Mission für den Frieden, Europäische Mächtepolitik und dänische Friedensvermittlung im Ersten Weltkrieg: vom August 1914 bis zum italienischen Kriegseintritt Mai 1915* (Stuttgart: Franz Steiner, 1984), *International History Review* 9.3 (Aug., 1987): 509–511.
32. Joyce Marlow, ed., "The Standard, 8 July 1915," in *The Virago Book of Women and the Great War, 1914–1918* (London: Virago Press, 1998), 109.
33. Marlow, 109.
34. Fest, 295.
35. Hall, 222.
36. John V. Crangle and Joseph O. Baylen, "Emily Hobhouse's Peace Mission, 1916," *Journal of Contemporary History* 14.4 (Oct. 1979): 733.
37. Asquith was obviously quite fond of the twittering sparrows analogy. He also used it to refer to Colonel House's peace mission of 1915, which Asquith called "the twittering of sparrows amid the storms and tumult of a tempest which is shaking the foundations of the world." George H. Cassar, *Asquith as War Leader* (London: Hambledon Press, 1994), 173.
38. Crangle and Baylen, 734.
39. Hall, 236.
40. Ibid., 248.
41. Ibid., 249; Crangle and Baylen, 736.
42. Hall, 250. It is easy to understand how she arrived at such a benign image of the camp. The German authorities adhered to the Geneva Convention and basically allowed the detainees to administer their own internal affairs. A kind of mini-society evolved in the camp. Letters, books, sports equipment and a printing press were all allowed, and the detainees organized their own police force, magazine, library and postal service, which handled over 6,000 pieces of mail per month. The camp detainees also arranged their own entertainment. Among them were several musicians, including Ernest MacMillan, who later became the conductor of the Toronto Symphony Orchestra. The Ruhleban Musical Society produced *The Mikado*, a pantomime version of *Cinderella*, *Othello*, *Twelfth Night* and *The Importance of Being Earnest*. In addition, a number of independent businesses, including a casino, also developed within the camp.
43. Ibid., 255.
44. Crangle and Baylen, 741.
45. Hall, 257.
46. Ibid., 258.
47. Kate Sharpley married in 1922 and dropped out of sight. The British anarchist library is named after her. Albert Meltzer, *I Couldn't Paint Golden Angels* (Edinburgh: AK Press, 1996), 291–292.
48. Hochschild, 187.
49. Tom Bell, *John Maclean, a Fighter for Freedom* (Glasgow: Communist Party, Scottish Committee, 1944), 45.
50. Douglas Newton, "The Lansdowne 'Peace Letter' of 1917 and the Prospect of Peace by Negotiation with Germany," *Australian Journal of Politics and History* 48.1 (Dec. 2002): 17.
51. David Stevenson, *The First World War and International Politics* (Oxford: Clarendon Press, 1988), 110.
52. Hugo Stinnes built a huge industrial empire centered in Germany and made enormous profits from the war. In the 1920s he owned 4,500 companies and 3,000 manufacturing plants. The American magazine *Time* called him "The New Emperor of Germany."
53. Marlow, 99.
54. Goenner and Castagnetti, 351–352.
55. Other countries had also suggested Wilson step forward as a mediator. At the beginning of the conflict the Spanish King, Alfonso XIII, had offered to jointly mediate with the American President.
56. Bernstorff, 275.
57. Esther Caukin Brunaur, "The Peace Proposals of December 1916–January 1917," *Journal of Modern History* 4.4 (Dec. 1932): 563.

58. Brunaur, 315.
59. Forster, 50.
60. Whittle, 282.
61. Forster, 50.
62. Ibid., 51.
63. Ibid.
64. Mueller, "Brother Boche," in *Meetings in No Man's Land: Christmas 1914 and Fraternization in the Great War*, 191.
65. Forster, 52.
66. Ibid., 55–56.
67. Ibid., 56
68. Ibid.
69. Ibid., 58.
70. Martin Gilbert, *A History of the Twentieth Century*, vol. 1 (New York: William Morrow, 1997), 394–395.
71. Brock and Young, 59–60.
72. Maksimilian Voloshin, *Anno mundi ardentis. 1915.* (Moscow: Izdatel'stvo Zerna, 1916).
73. The Old Believers began as a protest against church reforms introduced by Patriarch Nikon between 1652 and 1666 and include different sects. By the 1910s, according to the last Imperial Russian census, approximately 25 percent of the population of the Russian Empire said that they belonged to one of the Old Believer sects.
74. Juhnke, *Global Anabaptist Mennonite Encyclopedia Online*.
75. With incredible clarity, Camille Huysmans had seen the war coming and since 1911 had been trying desperately to bring Europe's Social Democratic parties together.
76. The Logan Act was named after Dr. George Logan, a pacifist and a state legislator, later Senator, from Pennsylvania. During the so-called Quasi-War (1798–1800) between the United States and France, Dr. Logan went to Paris and met with many officials of the French government. He suggested ways to improve relations between the two countries, and the French almost immediately took action to correct a number of objectionable policies. Despite the fact that Logan was largely successful in reducing the tension between the two countries, his interference was deeply resented by the American government. The Logan Act forbidding unauthorized persons from negotiating with foreign government is the result.
77. Stéphanie Dalbin, *Visions Croisées, Franco-Allemandes de la Première Guerre Mondiale* (Berne: Peter Lang S.A., 2007), 129.
78. Forster, 12.
79. The Joint Socialist Statement on the Refusal of Passports to Stockholm, *New York Call*, Sept. 1917, the World War I Document Archive.
80. Forster, 125.
81. Joe H. Kirchberger, *The First World War: An Eyewitness History* (New York: Facts on File, 1992), 228–229.
82. John Williams, *Mutiny 1917* (London: Heinemann, 1962), 87.
83. Williams, 77.
84. Ibid., 115.
85. The name *Le Bonnet Rouge* (The red cap) draws its inspiration from the *bonnet phrygien*, a Roman symbol of liberty. *Le Bonnet Rouge* was a sign of revolutionary allegiance dating from 1789 and became an official emblem of the Revolution in August 1792. To this day the national emblem of France, Marianne, wears a Phrygian cap.
86. Williams, 99.
87. Charles-Louis de Secondat, Baron de La Brède et de Montesquieu (1689–1755), generally referred to as Montesquieu, was a French philosopher who lived during the Age of the Enlightenment. He is famous for clarifying the separation of powers, which has been implemented in many constitutions throughout the world.
88. Williams, 12.
89. Ibid., 70.
90. Ibid., 154.
91. Ibid., 3.
92. Other sources, such as Guy Pedroncini, *Les Mutineries de 1917* (Paris: Publications de la Sorbonne, Presse Universitaires de France, 2nd ed., 1983), have different statistics: 629 death penalties, resulting in 43 executions, and 2,878 soldiers sentenced to hard labor.
93. Corporal Moulin not only missed the rest of the First World War, but he also missed the Second World War. He was last seen in Spain after the close of World War II.
94. At one meeting between the British and French generals, General Pétain told General Haig that 2 French divisions had refused to go into battle. The real figure was closer to 50 divisions.
95. Charles I had never expected to inherit the throne. However, after the suicide of Archduke Rudolph, the assassination of Francis Ferdinand and the premature death of his own father, he was next in line.
96. William Martin, "Peace on the Way," in *Statesmen of the War* (New York: Minton, Balch, 1928), 10.
97. James and Joanna Bogle, *A Heart for Europe: The Lives of Emperor Charles and Empress Zita of Austria-Hungary* (Leominster, UK: Fowler Wright Books, 1991), 77–78.
98. Reportedly on the day of his wedding he told his wife, the Empress Zita, "Now we must help each other to get to Heaven."
99. Forster, 96.
100. Bogle, 77.
101. Beatification requires that a miracle has occurred. It is the penultimate step on the path to full sainthood. According to the Vatican, Emperor Karl cured a Brazilian nun of varicose veins.
102. William Martin later became active in the League of Nations, the editor of the *Journal de Genève*, and a professor of the diplomatic history of Switzerland and international law at the University of Genève.
103. Cedric James Lowe and F. Marzari, *Italian Foreign Policy, 1870–1940* (London: Routledge, 1975), 257.
104. "Text of Letter Given Out; Paris Makes

Public Austrian Ruler's Autograph Message on Peace," *New York Times*, April 12, 1918. The letter was communicated by Prince Sixtus to President Poincaré on March 31, 1917.
105. Bogle, 79.
106. Forster, 97.
107. Davis, 97.
108. Lamar Cecil, *Wilhelm II*, vol. 2: *Emperor and Exile, 1900–1941* (Chapel Hill and London: University of North Carolina Press, 1996), 242.
109. Cecil, 242
110. Martin, 17.
111. Cecil, 100 fn.
112. Edward Benes, *My War Memoirs* (Manchester, NH: Ayer, 1970), 319–322.
113. Count Reverrera and Count Armand were, in fact, cousins, but it is unclear how well they knew each other.
114. From the French perspective, the affair began in Vienna.
115. Bogle, 89.
116. Ibid., 95.
117. F. W. Foerster, "A Voice from Germany: Why German Peace Declarations Fail to Convince," *International Conciliation* 129, New York: American Association for International Conciliation (Aug. 1918): 451, 453.
118. Foerster, "A Voice from Germany," 452.
119. Taylor, 554, n. 1.
120. Brunaur, 552.
121. *Norddeutsche Allgemeine Zeitung*, Nov. 10, 1915, 1–2.
122. David R. Woodward, "Britain's 'Brass-Hats' and the Question of a Compromise Peace, 1916–1918," *Military Affairs* 35.2 (April 1971): 66.
123. Except for a short period of uncertainty during the winter of 1917–1918, the British high command was strongly opposed to any settlement less than the crushing defeat of Germany.
124. "Peace Overtures of the Central Powers and Reply of Entente Powers," *American Journal of International Law* 11.4, Supplement: "Diplomatic Correspondence Between the United States and Belligerent Governments Relating to Neutral Rights and Commerce" (Oct. 1917): 273.
125. Robert Lansing (American Secretary of State; 1864–1928), "Suggestions Concerning the War Made by President Wilson December 18, 1916, and Replies of Belligerents and Neutrals," *American Journal of International Law* 11.4, Supplement: "Diplomatic Correspondence Between the United States and Belligerent Governments Relating to Neutral Rights and Commerce" (Oct. 1917): 290.
126. Charles Seymour, *The Intimate Papers of Colonel House*, vol. 2 (Boston and New York: Houghton Mifflin, 1926), 404.
127. Burián's list of basic conditions were: the territorial integrity of the Central Powers, restoration of Belgium to a sovereign state, recognition of the Kingdom of Poland, Russia's loss of Courland and Lithuania, extensive changes in the Balkans, freedom of the seas, free passage through the Straits for Russia, restoration of Germany's colonies, restoration of the Belgian Congo, and no indemnities.
128. General von Hindenburg (1847–1934), Chief of the German General Staff, made several modifications; for example, if guarantees could not be secured by King Albert (1875–1934), then Germany should annex Liège and France should pay an indemnity for the return of the German-occupied territory. In the colonies the general was willing to give up Kiaochow (on the southern coast of the Shandong peninsula in China), as well as the Carolinas and the Mariana Islands.
129. Brunaur, 565.
130. Speech by Abraham Lincoln, June 16, 1864, in Philadelphia.
131. Sterling Kernek, "The British Government's Reaction to President Wilson's 'Peace' Note of December 1916," *Historical Journal* 13.4 (1970): 732–733.
132. Kraft, *The Peace Ship*, 263.
133. Seymour, vol. 2, 418.
134. Naomi W. Cohen, *Jacob H. Schiff: A Study in American Jewish Leadership* (Hanover, NH: University Press of New England, 1999), 199.
135. Seymour, vol. 2, 420.
136. Johann von Bernstorff was completely at home in the Anglo-Saxon world. Although German by origin, he was born in London and served there in the German diplomatic corps from 1902 to 1906. He married a woman of German-American extraction.
137. Bernstorff, 10.
138. Ibid., 425.
139. Brunaur, 552.
140. Seymour, vol. 1, 45.
141. Seymour, vol. 2, 455.
142. Bernstorff, 382.
143. Ibid., 383.
144. Count Tarnowski was appointed to the Austro-Hungarian Embassy in Washington D.C., in 1899 and remained there until 1901, when he was transferred to Paris.
145. Pollard, 117.
146. Other sources give the credit for establishing the link between the French and the Germans to the Countess de Mérode or to the Belgian industrialist Coppée and his son. See: Forster, 106–112.
147. Baron von der Lancken had also been the Civil and Political Governor of Brussels during the German occupation. He had achieved some notoriety when he refused worldwide appeals to save nurse Edith Cavell from execution for "treason." After the war, when Baron von der Lancken was appointed by the German government to negotiate with the Commission for Relief in Belgium, Herbert Hoover, then the chairman, refused to meet von der Lancken and publicly told him "to go to hell." "Hoover Rebuffs Germans' Plea; Sends Caustic Message for Lancken Implicated in Cavell Execution and Rieth," *New York Times*, Dec. 28, 1918.
148. Aristide Briand was often called the Great Pacifier and after the war, in 1926, was awarded the Nobel Peace Prize. At one time he proposed a United States of Europe.

149. "France: Death of Briand," *Time*, March 14, 1932.
150. See note 147.
151. Forster, 109.
152. Ibid., 111.
153. Ibid., 112.
154. The Vatican also tried unsuccessfully to stop the Armenian genocide by acting through Turkey's allies, Germany and Austro-Hungary.
155. William E. Rappard, *The Quest for Peace Since the World War* (Cambridge, MA: Harvard University Press, 1940), 41.
156. Later Benedict XV also called for an international agreement outlawing conscription.
157. Charles J. Herber, "Eugenio Pacelli's Mission to Germany and the Papal Peace Proposals of 1917," *Catholic Historical Review* 65.1 (Jan. 1979): 31.
158. Erich Ludendorff, *The General Staff and Its Problems: The History of the Relations Between the High Command and the German Imperial Government as Revealed by Official Documents*, vol. 2, trans. F. A. Holt (London: Hutchinson, 1920), 479–480.
159. Admiral Georg Alexander von Müller, *The Diaries, Note Books and Letters of Admiral Georg Alexander von Müller, Chief of the Naval Cabinet, 1914–1918*, ed. Walter Görlitz (New York: Harcourt, Brace & World, 1964), 279.
160. Von Kürenberg, 347.
161. Wilhelm II (Emperor of Germany 1888–1918), *The Kaiser's Memoirs*, trans. Thomas R. Ybarra (New York and London: Harper & Brothers, 1922), 270–271.
162. Foerster, *Europe and the German Question*, 245.
163. For example, the American Secretary of State, Robert Lansing, insisted that "no effort was made by him (Benedict XV) till the possibility of victory by the Central Powers seemed remote." Dragan Zivojinovic, "Robert Lansing's Comments on the Pontifical Note of August 1, 1917," *Journal of American History* 56.3 (Dec. 1969): 558. And Colonel House, Wilson's closest advisor, thought that "the Pope's peace overture was inspired by Austria." Zivojinovic, 560.
164. Some observers feel that London actually feared a clear statement from Germany concerning their war aims and reparations for France and Belgium. Such a declaration might have greatly reduced popular support for a "war to the finish."
165. Taking a purely Catholic point of view, the Vatican's paramount goal was to keep intact the Austro-Hungarian Empire, where Catholicism was the state religion. The Vatican concluded that if the war was carried through till one side or the other triumphed, no matter who won, Austria-Hungary would be in a worse condition than if peace was negotiated before an end arrived. Should the Central Powers lose, disintegration of the empire would almost certainly follow, and should the Central Powers win, Austria-Hungary would become a vassal state of Germany.
166. Pollard, 126.
167. It should be noted that some of the Pope's specific terms would reappear about six months later included in Wilson's Fourteen Points.
168. Zivojinovic, 558.
169. Joseph P. Tumulty, *Woodrow Wilson as I Know Him* (Whitefish, MT: Kessinger, 2010), 184.
170. "Letter of Reply to the Pope," Aug. 27, 1917 (American Presidency Project). The letter was actually signed by Robert Lansing.
171. Whittle, 287.
172. Matthias Erzberger was a Catholic with close contacts to the Vatican. One source has gone so far as to call him "the Vatican's white hope." Pollard, 124.
173. Playne, 4.
174. Ibid.
175. Ibid.
176. "Text of the *Reichstag* Peace Resolution," *New York Times*, July 16, 1917, taken from the *Berlin Tageblatt*.
177. Koppel S. Pinson, *Modern Germany, Its History and Civilization* (New York: Macmillan, 1954), 334.
178. Thomas Rhodes, *The Real von Kühlmann* (London: Noel Douglas, 1925). Part of the purpose of the book is to prove that von Kühlmann was devoted to the cause of peace and opposed to the cabal of generals who persuaded the Kaiser to declare war in 1914.
179. Rhodes, 84.
180. E. Eyck, "The Generals and the Downfall of the German Monarchy, 1917–1918," *Transactions of the Royal Historical Society*, 5th series, 1952, 2, 60.
181. Ibid.
182. Von Kürenberg, 348.
183. Russell, *Autobiography*, 255.
184. Patrick Bridgwater, "German Poetry and the First World War," *European History Quarterly* 1 (1971): 149. One German newspaper, for example, the *Berliner Tageszeitung*, apparently received 500 poems daily in August 1914.
185. Nancy Blaine, ed., *Western Civilization: Ideas, Politics, and Society* (Boston: Houghton, Mifflin, Harcourt, 2009) 741.
186. Julian Grenfell, "Into Battle," in *A Treasury of War Poetry, British and American Poems of the War, 1914–1917*, ed. George Herbert Clarke (Boston: Houghton Mifflin, 1917), 82.
187. Siegfried Sassoon, *Counter-Attack, and Other Poems* (New York: E. P. Dutton, 1918).
188. Louis Untermeyer, ed., *Modern British Poetry* (New York: Harcourt, Brace and Howe, 1920), 224.
189. Isaac Rosenberg, *The Selected Poems of Isaac Rosenberg* (London: Cecil Woolf, 2003).
190. Louis Untermeyer, ed., *Modern American Poetry* (New York: Harcourt, Brace and Howe, 1919), 121.
191. Herbert Read, *Naked Warriors* (London: Art & Letters, 1919), preface.
192. Robert Giddings, *The War Poets* (London: Bloomsbury, 1990), 111.
193. John Stuart Roberts, *Siegfried Sassoon*,

1886–1967 (London: Richard Cohen Books, 1999), 113.
194. Jean Moorcroft Wilson, *Siegfried Sassoon: The Making of a War Poet* (London: Duckworth, 1998), 403.
195. Roberts, 74.
196. Jean Moorcroft Wilson 406.
197. Sassoon, "The General," in *Counter-Attack, and Other Poems*, 125.
198. Sassoon, "Base Details," in *Counter-Attack, and Other Poems*.
199. Charles Sorley, "When You See Millions of the Mouthless Dead"; Bridgwater, 175.
200. Siegfried Sassoon, "Suicide in the Trenches," *Cambridge Magazine* (23 Feb. 1918).
201. It was Sassoon who provided the final title. Jon Stallworthy, *Wilfred Owen* (London: Oxford University Press and Chatto and Windus, 1974), 221.
202. Bridgwater, 163.
203. The couplet appeared under the title, "Common Form" in "Epitaphs of the War, 1914–1918." The poem was written soon after Kipling's son's death in France in 1915.
204. René Arcos, "Les Morts."
205. Genold, "Aux Hommes," *Notre Voix* (June 1919). Delong was the chief editor of *Notre Voix*, a pacifist journal published in 1919–1920.
206. Georg Heym, "The War" ("Der Krieg"), trans. Walter A. Aue.
207. Bridgwater, 165. Whitman saw no victory or honor in war. He once said "that whole damned war business is about 990 parts diarrhoea to one part glory."
208. Gerrit Engelke, "To the Soldiers of the Great War," *Poetry Magazine* 9 (Oct. 1998).
209. Elizabeth A. Marsland, *The Nation's Cause: French, English and German Poetry of the First World War* (New York: Routledge, 1991), 186.
210. Bertram Lloyd, ed. and trans, *The Paths of Glory: A Collection of Poems Written During the War, 1914–1919* (London: George Allen & Unwin, 1919), 72–73.
211. Marsland, 49.
212. Paul Betts and Greg Eghigian, eds., *Pain and Prosperity: Reconsidering Twentieth-Century German History* (Palo Alto, CA: Stanford University Press, 2003), 113. Lersch's strongly nationalist poetry at the beginning of the war was resurrected later by the Nazis.
213. Martin Stephen, *Never Such Innocence: Poems of the First World War* (London: J. M. Dent, Everyman, 1988), 185.
214. The Gallipoli Campaign is also known as the Dardanelles Campaign or the Battle of Gallipoli. It took place between April 25, 1915, and January 9, 1916. It was a joint British and French operation whose objective was to capture the Ottoman capital of Constantinople and secure a sea route to Russia. The attempt failed, and the campaign is considered to be a major victory for the Turks.
215. Tony Ashworth, *Trench Warfare 1914–1918: The Live and Let Live System* (London: Pan Books, 1980), 213.

216. Aubrey Herbert, *Mons, Anzac & Kut: A British Intelligence Officer in Three Theatres of the First World War 1914–18* (UK: Leonaur Books, 2010), 84. The line "The Assyrian came down like the wolf on the fold" was taken from Lord Byron's (1788–1824) *The Destruction of Sennacherib*. The idea behind Herbert's previous sentence: "It was as if God had breathed in their faces," was undoubtedly a paraphrase of two other lines that appear later in the same poem: "For the Angel of Death spread his wings on the blast, / And breathed in the face of the foe as he passed."
217. Robert Rhodes James, *Gallipoli* (New York: Macmillan, 1965), 186.
218. Herbert, 85.
219. Michael Hickey, *Gallipoli* (London: John Murray, 1995).
220. Richard Ned Lebow, "The Morgenthau Peace Mission of 1917," *Jewish Social Studies* 32.4 (Oct. 1970): 270.
221. While he was the American ambassador in Turkey, Henry Morgenthau did what he could to stop the genocide of the Armenians. To no avail. He argued and even pleaded with the Turkish Pashas, whom he described as "still reeking with the blood of nearly a million human beings." In his book *Ambassador Morgenthau's Story* (chapter 24: "The Murder of a Nation" (New York: Doubleday, Page, 1918), he wrote that the English-speaking public cannot understand precisely what this nation is which we call Turkey. [...] [A] complete narration of the sadistic orgies of which these Armenian men and women were the victims can never be printed in an American publication. Whatever crimes the most perverted instincts of the human mind can devise, and whatever refinements of persecution and injustice the most debased imagination can conceive, became the daily misfortunes of this devoted people. I am confident that the whole history of the human race contains no such horrible episode as this.
222. Technically, the United States never went to war with the Ottoman Empire.
223. For example, F. W. Brecher, "Revisiting Ambassador Morgenthau's Turkish Peace Mission of 1917," *Middle East Studies* 24.3 (July 1988): 360.
224. Brecher, 360.
225. Lebow, 271.
226. Ibid.
227. Felix Frankfurter later became an Associate Justice of the United States Supreme Court in 1938. He was the court's most outspoken advocate of judicial restraint, the idea that courts should not interpret the Constitution in such a way as to impose sharp limits upon the authority of the legislative and executive branches. On the voyage to Gibraltar, Frankfurter brought along his assistant, Max Lowenthal (1888–1971), who later became an advisor to several United States senators, including Harry S. Truman. Lowenthal was also the chief advisor on Palestine to Clark Clifford, who himself advised President Truman from 1947 to 1952. President Truman credited Lowenthal as being the primary force behind the United States' recognition of Israel.

228. Eliahu Lewin-Epstein was the treasurer of the Zionist Provisional Executive Committee in New York City.
229. Arshag K. Schmavonian worked for the United States embassy in Istanbul for over 16 years as a legal advisor and translator. He accompanied Ambassador Morgenthau on almost every official visit and attended meetings with American businessmen and missionaries. Schmavonian was later transferred to Washington, where he worked as a "Special Advisor" to the U.S. State Department.
230. Lebow, 281–282.
231. Kennerley Rumford (1870–1959), a singer and for the war years an intelligence officer, was sent with Weizmann as liaison officer.
232. Jehuda Reinharz, "His Majesty's Zionist Emissary: Chaim Weizmann's Mission to Gibraltar in 1917," *Journal of Contemporary History* 27.1 (April 1992): 267.
233. Lebow, 282.
234. According to another version of the events in Gibraltar, one told to William Yale after the war was over, a banquet was hosted by the British commander at Gibraltar on the evening of Morgenthau's arrival. After the meal was over the British officers withdrew, leaving Morgenthau, Weizmann, and the French representative, Mr. Weyl, alone. At that point in blunt terms Dr. Weizmann explained the situation and apparently Morgenthau agreed. William Yale, "Ambassador Henry Morgenthau's Special Mission of 1917," *World Politics* 1.3 (April 1949): 315.
235. Ibid., 267.
236. Ibid., 271.
237. Ibid., 310.
238. Jonathan Schneer, *The Balfour Declaration* (London: Bloomsbury Publishing Plc., 2011), 283.
239. Ibid.
240. *Greenmantle* first appeared in 1916, the second of five novels that feature the character Richard Hannay, soldier and master spy. Hannay is sent to investigate rumors of a Moslem uprising in the Middle East and, after a difficult and dangerous trip, ends up in Constantinople. He and a few friends try to prevent German plans to use religion as an arm of warfare. Of course, they succeed.
241. There have been four films based on *The 39 Steps*, one of them in 1935, directed by Alfred Hitchcock. There have also been a number of theatrical adaptations, as well as many for the radio, among them one by Orson Welles and two by the BBC.
242. Basil Zaharoff was a Greek self-made man, who rose from the streets of Constantinople to become a wealthy arms merchant and a citizen of France. He was officially decorated by both France and Great Britain. His Russian-sounding name was adopted by the family while they were in exile in Odessa. According to his own account, he began his career when still a child as a guide to the red-light district of Constantinople.
243. Schneer, 292.
244. *The Records of the Permanent Under-Secretary's Department, Liaison 1873–1939* (Foreign & Commonwealth Office, March 2005), 32.
245. Schneer, 295. Lloyd George and Zaharoff had known each other since the days of the Boer War. Their relationship contained an odd bond: Zaharoff's first wife, Emily Burrows, had earlier had a brief liaison with Lloyd George. A mutual friend commented that he was certain that Zaharoff had told Lloyd George that he knew what had happened. It disconcerted Lloyd George, but as Mrs Zaharoff was dead (she died about 1900), there was not much anyone could do about it. Donald McCormick, *Pedlar of Death* (London: MacDonald, 1965), 148–149.
246. Schneer, 296.
247. *The Records of the Permanent Under-Secretary's Department, Liaison 1873–1939*, 33.
248. Ibid., 34.
249. Schneer, 359.
250. Milton Meltzer, *Ain't Gonna Study War No More: The Story of America's Peace Seekers* (New York: Random House, 2002), 134.
251. Ibid., 135.
252. Robin Andersen, *A Century of Media, a Century of War* (New York: Peter Lang, 2006), 6.
253. Nazimova's first name was Alla, but she used only her last name.
254. "Nazimova in Film of War Brides Play," *New York Times*, Nov. 13, 1916.
255. Vincente Blasco Ibáñez, *The Four Horsemen of the Apocalypse*, trans. Charlotte Brewster Jordan (UK: Dodo Press, 1916), 138.
256. Ibáñez, 137–138.
257. "With Authors and Publishers," *New York Times Book Review*, Dec. 22, 1918.
258. Ibáñez was offered $200,000 (about $2.2 million in today's dollars) for the film rights. Directed by Rex Ingram (1895–1969) and starring Rudolph Valentino (1895–1926), the film was released in 1921 and was soon a commercial and critical success. In an early scene, Valentino dances the tango in an Argentine tavern displaying a grace and nimbleness he had acquired over years as a dance master. For the first time audiences were exposed to "the Latin Lover." The movie was a megasuccess, and Valentino became the screen's first sex symbol. *The Four Horsemen of the Apocalypse* was the top overall film of the year in 1921, beating *The Kid* by Charles Chaplin (1889–1977) and prompting Ibáñez to allegedly say: "I earn more than Rudyard Kipling [...]. I am the most famous writer in the world." César Domínguez, "Making a Career of the Arrière-garde: Vincente Blasco Ibáñez as World Author," *European Review* 19.2 (2011): 311.
259. Susan Zeiger, "She Didn't Raise Her Boy to Be a Slacker: Motherhood, Conscription, and the Culture of the First World War," *Feminist Studies* 22.1 (Spring 1996): 11.
260. The presidential election of 1916 was one of the closest in American history. With 266 electoral votes needed to win, Wilson won 30 states for 277 electoral votes, while Hughes won 18 states and 254 electoral votes. The key state was California, which Wilson won by only 3,800 votes out of nearly a million cast. If Hughes had carried California and its 13 electoral votes, he would have won the election.

261. Russell Buchanan, "Theodore Roosevelt and American Neutrality," *American Historical Review* 43.4 (July 1938): 784. Roosevelt detested pacifists and didn't hesitate to say so. Rejecting a suggestion that he debate with one, Roosevelt wrote: You might exactly as well propose a joint debate between some leading Black-hander and a Superintendent of the police force as a joint debate between any man who takes the views I take, which are those that every patriotic American should take, and any man who stands for disarmament or for the silly and mischievous peace-at-any-pricer modern Copperhead policies of the average pacifist of today [Buchanan, 784].

262. Andreas Latzko, *Menschen im Krieg* (Zurich: Rascher-Verlag, 1917), trans. As *Men in War* (New York: Boni and Liveright, 1918), 41.

263. "An Austrian Officer's Gruesome Pictures of War," *Current Opinion* 64.6 (June 1918): 424.

264. Latzko, 84, 95–96.

265. C. D. M., *Boston Transcript*, March 20, 1918, 8.

266. Thomas C. Schneider and Hans Wagner, *"Huns" vs. "Corned Beef": Representations of the Other in American and German Literature and Film in World War One* (Osnabruck: Universitatsverlag, 2007), 133.

267. Hans Kohn, 326.

268. Ariela Halkin, *The Enemy Reviewed: German Popular Literature Through British Eyes Between the Two Wars* (Westport, CT: Praeger, 1995), 50.

269. The Bavarian Soviet Republic, sometimes called the Munich Soviet Republic (Bayerische Räterepublik or Münchner Räterepublik), was a short-lived government that sought to replace the fledgling Weimar Republic in its early days.

270. B. Traven was essentially an anarchist and followed the philosophy of Max Stirner (1806–1856), who espoused a kind of "individual anarchism," an open-minded recognition of the world as one finds it coupled with an awareness that there is no soul, no personal essence of any kind. B. Traven ended up in Mexico, where he wrote a series of novels, often with anti-war themes. Among his most famous are *The Death Ship* and *The Treasure of the Sierra Madre*. Biographical Dictionary of Modern Peace Leaders.

271. Rolland, 156.

272. Ibid., 156–157.

273. Robert Galbreath, "Hermann Hesse and the Politics of Detachment," *Political Theory* 2.1 (Feb. 1974): 65.

274. Ibid., 70.

275. Ibid.

276. Hermann Hesse, *Siddhartha* (London: Penguin, 2008), 70.

277. Pinson, 348.

278. Hans Kohn, 259–260.

279. Bridgwater, 181.

280. Proceeds from the sales of *Le Feu* went directly into the creation of a veterans' organization, the ARAC (Association Républicaine des Anciens Combattants), which became one of the earliest elements in the French veterans' movement.

281. Henri Barbusse, *Under Fire*, trans. Robin Buss (London: Penguin Modern Classics, 2003), 316.

282. Barbusse, 316.

283. Ibid., 6.

284. Mona Siegel, "To the Unknown Mother of the Unknown Soldier: Pacifism, Feminism, and the Politics of Sexual Difference Among French Institutrices Between the Wars," *French Historical Studies* 22.3 (Summer 1999): 438.

285. The word "Dada" reportedly arrived when during a meeting of artists in a café someone stuck a paper knife into a French-German dictionary and it happened to point to the French word "dada"—hobbyhorse.

286. Steve Edwards and Paul Wood, *Art of the Avant-Garde* (London: Yale University Press, 2004), 340.

287. Yosano's anti-war poem continued be well-known even after World War II when it was sewn into the fabric of *noren* curtains, the traditional Japanese fabric dividers, hung between rooms, on walls, in doorways, or in windows.

288. Steve Rabson, "Yosano Akiko on War: To Give One's Life or Not: A Question of Which War," *Journal of the Association of Teachers of Japanese* 25.1., Special Issue: "Yosano Akiko (1878–1942)" (April 1991): 45.

289. Ibid., 46.

290. Ibid., 51.

291. Carlo Caldarola, "Pacifism Among Japanese Non-Church Christians," *Journal of the American Academy of Religion* 41.4 (Dec. 1973): 510.

292. Bobbie Oliver, *Peacemongers* (Fremantle: Fremantle Arts Centre, 1997), 44.

293. Malcolm Saunders and Ralph Summy, *The Australian Peace Movement: A Short History* (Canberra: Australian National University, 1986), 21.

294. Oliver, 44.

295. In addition to being opposed to the war, Vardaman also advocated a policy of racism against African-Americans, even to the point of supporting lynching in order to maintain his vision of white supremacy. John V. Denson, *Reassessing the Presidency: The Rise of the Executive State and the Decline of Freedom*, ed. John V. Denson (Auburn, AL: Ludwig von Mises Institute, 2001), 734. He was known as the "Great White Chief."

296. Article I, Section 8, Clause 11 of the American Constitution, the so-called war powers clause, states: "[Congress shall have Power...] [t]o declare War, grant Letters of Marque and Reprisal, and make Rules concerning Captures on Land and Water."

297. *Congressional Record* (Senate, April 4, 1917), 224–225.

298. Denson, 738.

299. Ibid., 743.

300. Justus D. Doenecke, *Nothing Less Than War: A New History of America's Entry into World War 1* (Lexington: University Press of Kentucky, 2011), 295.

301. Larson and Micheels-Cyrus 5. Also: Lynne E. Ford, *Encyclopedia of Women and American Politics* (New York: Facts on File, 2008), 376.
302. Curti, *Peace or War*, 255–256.
303. Charles Chatfield, *For Peace and Justice, Pacifism in America 1914–1941* (Boston: Beacon Press, 1971), 30.
304. Bourne, Randolph S., in Martin S. Sheffer, ed., *In Search of a Democratic America: The Writings of Randolph S. Bourne* (Lanham, MD: Lexington Books, 2002), 88.
305. Lars Nelson, *President Wilson* (Stockholm: P. A. Norstedt, 1919), 128.
306. Michael Head, *Crimes Against the State, from Treason to Terrorism* (Farnham, UK: Ashgate, 2011), 119.
307. When the United States declared war barely 200,000 men were in uniform.
308. *California Women and Politics: From the Gold Rush to the Great Depression*, ed. Robert W. Cherny (Lincoln: University of Nebraska Press, 2011), 328.
309. A total of 2,188 persons were prosecuted under the Espionage and Sedition Acts; 1,055 were convicted.
310. H. C. Peterson and Gilbert C. Fite, *Opponents of War 1917–1918* (Seattle: University of Washington Press, 1957), 35.
311. Ibid., 37.
312. Ibid.
313. Davis D. Joyce, *Alternative Oklahoma: Contrarian Views of the Sooner State* (Norman: University of Oklahoma Press, 2007), 224.
314. Most COs in World War I in the United States were religious objectors, belonging to so-called peace churches: Mennonites, the Society of Friends (Quakers), the Church of the Brethren and many Pentecostal groups.
315. John A. Hostetler, *Hutterite Society* (Baltimore, MD: Johns Hopkins Press, 1974), 129.
316. Ernest L. Meyer, *"Hey! Yellowbacks!"* (New York: John Day, 1930), 138.
317. Howard W. Moore lived to become the nation's oldest pacifist and CO. He died in 1993 at the age of 104. He wrote in the last sentence of his autobiography: "Unless the human species arrives at a spiritual and intellectual awareness of our interdependence and establishes a world community using the earth's resources for the benefit of all, we are headed for extinction." *Daily Star*, Nov. 24, 2001.
318. Frank Irving Cobb, *Cobb of the World, a Leader in Liberalism* (Freeport, NY: Libraries Press, 1924), 270.
319. David M. Kennedy, *Over Here* (Oxford: Oxford University Press, 2004), 24.
320. *The United States at Large*, vol. 40 (April 1917–March 1919) (Washington, DC: U.S. Government Printing Office, 1919), 553.
321. Michele Wucker, *Lockout* (New York: Public Affairs, 2006), 61.
322. Tumulty, 295.
323. Twelve men were tried for the murder of Robert Prager, but all were acquitted.
324. Brock and Young, 29.
325. William R. Douglas, "'The Germans Would Court Martial Me, Too': St. Paul's World War I Socialist Draft Resisters," *Minnesota History* 55.7 (Fall 1997): 299.
326. Douglas, 299.
327. Douglas, 301. Wangerin originally received a 15-year sentence to be served at the federal prison at Leavenworth, Kansas. In his sentencing statement Wangerin "claimed to be an internationalist and a follower of Thomas Paine." He probably quoted Paine's credo, "My country is the world." From Leavenworth Wangerin was sent to Alcatraz, where he was finally paroled shortly after the Armistice. However, he still faced a civil federal sentence for refusing to register for the draft. He finally became a free man late in 1921.
328. Peterson and Fite, 163.
329. While in Congress Victor Berger introduced the first bill for unemployment insurance as well as one for old-age pensions and public housing.
330. Cohen, 205.
331. Melech Epstein, *Profiles of Eleven* (Lanham, MD: University Press of America, 1987), 183.
332. Stephen Martin Kohn, *American Political Prisoners: Prosecutions Under the Espionage and Sedition Acts* (Westport, CT: Praeger, 1994), 77.
333. Howard Zinn and Anthony Arnove, *Voices of a People's History of the United States* (New York: Seven Stories Press, 2011), 297.
334. Tumulty, 295.
335. In 1924 two people were nominated for the Nobel Peace Prize, Eugene Debs and Edmund Dene Morel. No prize was awarded.

Chapter Four

1. Sylvester John Hemleben, *Plans for World Peace Through Six Centuries* (Chicago: University of Chicago Press, 1943), 138.
2. Viscount Bryce, *Proposals for the Avoidance of War with a Prefatory Note by Viscount Bryce* (Marked "Not for Publication. As revised up to February 24, 1915," available at openlibrary.org), 7–8.
3. John Stuart Mill, *Principles of Political Economy*, vol. 1 (New York: Cosimo, 2006), 368. In fact, Bryce misquoted Mill, but the meaning was correct. Mill actually wrote that " small means do not merely produce small effects, they produce no effects at all."
4. Ibid., 368.
5. Bryce, 12.
6. Martin James Dubin, "Toward the Concept of Collective Security: The Bryce Group's 'Proposals for the Avoidance of War,' 1914–1917," *International Organization* 24.2 (Spring 1970): 288.
7. Hemleben, 143.
8. V. Lenin, *Collected Works*, vol. 26 (September 1917–February 1918) (Moscow: Progress Publishers, 1964), 251.
9. Judah L. Magnes, *Russia and Germany at Brest-Litovisk* (New York: Rand School of Social Science, 1919), 8–9.
10. Ibid., 14.

11. Ibid., 15.
12. Ibid.
13. Ibid., 17.
14. Ibid., 20.
15. Ibid.
16. David R. Woodward, *World War I Almanac* (New York: Facts on File, 2009), 268.
17. Leon Trotsky, *From October to Brest-Litovsk* (authorized translation from the Russian) (New York: Socialist Publication Society, 1919).
18. Magnes, 26.
19. Ibid., 40.
20. Geoff Swain, *Trotsky* (Edinburgh: Pearson Education, 2006), 80.
21. Pinson, 337.
22. Magnes, 174.
23. Pinson, 336.
24. Ibid.
25. John W. Wheeler-Bennett, *Brest-Litovsk: The Forgotten Peace, March 1918* (New York: St. Martin's Press, 1966), 368.
26. Clemenceau once quipped: "Fourteen Points! To think God Himself needed only ten!"
27. Marburg, 118–119.
28. Ibid., 120.
29. Charles Howard-Ellis, *The Origin, Structure and Working of the League of Nations* (Boston: Houghton Mifflin, 1929), 72.
30. Hodgson, 48.
31. George Sylvester Viereck, *The Strangest Friendship in History: Woodrow Wilson and Colonel House* (London: Duckworth, 1933).
32. Edward M. House, *Philip Dru: Administrator: A Story of Tomorrow* (New York: B. W. Huebsch, 1912), 222.
33. Ibid., 153.
34. Clifford E. Gates, "The Pacifistic Trend in German Literature," *German Quarterly* 5.1 (Jan. 1932): 40.
35. Nancy Sloan Goldberg, 167.
36. Edward Mead Earle, "H. G. Wells, British Patriot in Search of a World State," *World Politics* 2.2 (Jan. 1950): 186.
37. Ibid., 191.
38. Ibid., 191–192.
39. Earle, 208.
40. Ibid., 174.
41. Romain Rolland, *The Forerunners*, trans. Eden and Cedar Paul (New York: Harcourt, Brace and Howe, 1920), 209. The full text of the Declaration of the Independence of the Mind by Romain Rolland is as follows:

Brain workers, comrades, scattered throughout the world, kept apart for five years by the armies, the censorship and the mutual hatred of the warring nations, now that barriers are falling and frontiers are being reopened, we issue to you a call to reconstitute our brotherly union, but to make of it a new union more firmly founded and more strongly built than that which previously existed. The war has disordered our ranks. Most of the intellectuals placed their science, their art, their reason, at the service of the governments. We do not wish to formulate any accusations, to launch any reproaches. We know the weakness of the individual mind and the elemental strength of great collective currents. The latter, in a moment, swept the former away, for nothing had been prepared to help in the work of resistance. Let this experience, at least, be a lesson to us for the future! First of all, let us point out the disasters that have resulted from the almost complete abdication of intelligence throughout the world, and from its voluntary enslavement to the unchained forces. Thinkers, artists, have added an incalculable quantity of envenomed hate to the plague which devours the flesh and the spirit of Europe. In the arsenal of their knowledge, their memory, their imagination, they have sought reasons for hatred, reasons old and new, reasons historical, scientific, logical, and poetical. They have worked to destroy mutual understanding and mutual love among men. So doing, they have disfigured, defiled, debased, degraded Thought, of which they were the representatives. They have made it an instrument of the passions; and (unwittingly, perchance) they have made it a tool of the selfish interests of a political or social clique, of a state, a country, or a class. Now, when, from the fierce conflict in which the nations have been at grips, the victors and the vanquished emerge equally stricken, impoverished, and at the bottom of their hearts (though they will not admit it) utterly ashamed of their access of mania—now, Thought, which has been entangled in their struggles, emerges, like them, fallen from her high estate. Arise! Let us free the mind from these compromises, from these unworthy alliances, from these veiled slaveries! Mind is no one's servitor. It is we who are the servitors of mind. We have no other master. We exist to bear its light, to defend its light, to rally round it all the strayed sheep of mankind. Our role, our duty, is to be a centre of stability, to point out the pole star, amid the whirlwind of passions in the night. Among these passions of pride and mutual destruction, we make no choice; we reject them all. Truth only do we honour; truth that is free, frontierless, limitless; truth that knows nought of the prejudices of race or caste. Not that we lack interest in humanity. For humanity we work, but for humanity as a whole. We know nothing of peoples. We know the People, unique and universal; the People which suffers, which struggles, which falls and rises to its feet once more, and which continues to advance along the rough road drenched with its sweat and its blood; the People, all men, all alike our brothers. In order that they may, like ourselves, realise this brotherhood, we raise above their blind struggles the Ark of the Covenant—Mind which is free, one and manifold, eternal.

42. The *Lusitania* was a Cunard liner in service between England, Ireland and New York. During the First World War (May 7, 1915), the ship was torpedoed by the German U-boat *U-20* and sank in 18 minutes 11 miles from Ireland. Of the 1,959 people

aboard 1,198 were killed, leaving 761 survivors. The sinking turned public opinion in many countries against Germany and probably contributed to the American entry into World War I. The *Lusitania* became an iconic symbol in military recruiting campaigns of why the war was being fought.

43. Michael W. Pharand, "Above the Battle? Bernard Shaw, Romain Rolland, and the Politics of Pacifism," in *Shaw*, vol. 11: *Shaw and Politics* (University Park: Penn State University Press, 1991), 174.

44. Ibid., 178.

45. Zweig, 351.

46. Speech in the House of Commons, Nov. 11, 1918.

47. Willis, 302.

48. *L'Écho de Paris*, May 12, 1919.

49. Adam Hochschild, *To End All Wars* (London: Pan Books, 2011), 341.

Conclusion

1. David R. Woodward, "Britain's 'Brass-Hats' and the Question of a Compromise Peace, 1916–1918," 65.

2. Arthur Posonby, *Falsehood in War-Time: Containing an Assortment of Lies Circulated Throughout the Nations During the Great War* (Newport Beach, CA: Institute for Historical Review, 1991), 85.

3. David R. Woodward, "Britain's 'Brass Hats' and the Question of a Compromise Peace, 1916–1918, 65. Also: David R. Woodward, *Lloyd George and the Generals* (London: Routledge, 2003), 114.

Bibliography

Abrams, Irwin. "Bertha von Süttner and the Nobel Peace Prize." *Journal of Central European Affairs* 22 (Oct. 1962): 286–307.
Addams, Jane, Emily G. Balch, and Alice Hamilton. *Women at The Hague: The International Congress of Women and Its Results.* Urbana and Chicago: University of Illinois Press, 2003.
"Admiral Togo—'The Peaceful Man of the East.'" Editorial comment. *American Journal of International Law* 5.4 (Oct. 1911): 1051–1054.
Aldanov, Mark. "Count Witte," *Russian Review* 1.1 (Nov. 1941): 56–64.
Andersen, Robin. *A Century of Media, a Century of War.* New York: Peter Lang, 2006.
Angell, Norman. *The Great Illusion.* New York: Heinemann, 1913.
"The Anglo-German Understanding Conference," *The Advocate of Peace* 74.11 (Dec. 1912): 254–255.
Aronsfeld, C. C. "Jewish Enemy Aliens in England During the First World War." *Jewish Social Studies* 18.4 (Oct. 1956): 275–283.
Arthur, Max. *Forgotten Voices of the Great War.* London: Ebury Press, 2002.
Ashworth, Tony. *Trench Warfare 1914–1918: The Live and Let Live System.* London: Pan Books, 1980.
Bamba, Nolbuya, and John F. Howes, eds. *Pacifism in Japan.* Vancouver: University of British Columbia Press, 1978.
Barbusse, Henri. *Under Fire.* Trans. Robin Buss. London: Penguin Modern Classics, 2003.
Barlow, Ima Christina. *The Agadir Crisis.* Chapel Hill: University of North Carolina Press, 1940.
Bartlett, Ruhl J. *The League to Enforce Peace.* Chapel Hill: University of North Carolina Press, 1944.
Baylen, Joseph O., and Jane G. Weyant. "Vasili Vereshchagin in the United States." *Russian Review* 30.3 (July 1971): 250–259.
Beales, A. C. F. *The History of Peace.* New York: Dial Press, 1931.
Bell, Tom. *John Maclean, a Fighter for Freedom.* Glasgow: Communist Party, Scottish Committee, 1944.
Benes, Edward. *My War Memoirs.* Manchester, NH: Ayer, 1970.
Bernstorff [Count]. *My Three Years in America.* New York: Scribner's, 1920.
Best, Geoffrey. "Peace Conferences and the Century of Total War: The 1899 Hague Conference and What Came After." *International Affairs* (Royal Institute of International Affairs 1944) 75.3 (July 1999): 620–634.
Betts, Paul, and Greg Eghigian, eds. *Pain and Prosperity: Reconsidering Twentieth-Century German History.* Palo Alto, CA: Stanford University Press, 2003.
Birkenhead, Frederick Winston Furneaux Smith. *Churchill 1874–1922.* London: Harrap, 1989.
Bishop, Joseph Bucklin. *Theodore Roosevelt and His Time, Shown in His Own Letters.* Vol. 2. New York City: Scribner's, 1920.
Blaine, Nancy, ed. *Western Civilization: Ideas, Politics, and Society.* Boston: Houghton, Mifflin, Harcourt, 2009.

Blioch, Ivan Stanislavovich (aka Jean de Bloch). *The Future of War in Its Technical, Economic and Political Relations.* New York: Doubleday and McClure, 1899.
Blom, Philipp. *The Vertigo Years.* New York: Basic Books, 2008.
Bogle, James, and Joanna Bogle. *A Heart for Europe: The Lives of Emperor Charles and Empress Zita of Austria-Hungary.* Leominster, UK: Fowler Wright Books, 1991.
Bosworth, R. J. B. *Mussolini.* New York: Oxford University Press, 2002.
Bourne, Randolph S. *In Search of a Democratic America: The Writings of Randolph S. Bourne.* Edited by Martin S. Sheffer. Lanham, MD: Lexington Books, 2002.
Brecher, F. W. "Revisiting Ambassador Morgenthau's Turkish Peace Mission of 1917." *Middle East Studies* 24.3 (July 1988).
Bridgwater, Patrick. "German Poetry and the First World War." *European History Quarterly* 1 (1971): 147–186.
Brock, Peter, and Nigel Young. *Pacifism in the Twentieth Century.* Syracuse, NY: Syracuse University Press, 1999.
Brough, James. *The Ford Dynasty: An American Story.* Garden City, NY: Doubleday, 1977.
Brown, Malcolm, and Shirley Seaton. *Christmas Truce: The Western Front December 1914.* Basingstoke and Oxford: Pan Books, 1994.
Brunauer, Esther Caukin. "The Peace Proposals of December 1916–January 1917." *Journal of Modern History* 4.4 (Dec. 1932): 544–571.
Bryce (Viscount). *Proposals for the Avoidance of War with a Prefatory Note by Viscount Bryce.* N.p.: n.p, 1915. http://openlibrary.org/books/OL14036310M/Proposals_for_the_avoidance_of_war.
Buchanan, Russell. "Theodore Roosevelt and American Neutrality." *American Historical Review* 43.4 (July 1938): 775–790.
Burton, David Henry. *Taft, Holmes, and the 1920s Court: An Appraisal.* Cranbury, NJ: Associated University Presses, 1998.
Caldarola, Carlo. "Pacifism Among Japanese Non-Church Christians." *Journal of the American Academy of Religion* 41.4 (Dec. 1973): 506–519.
Carnegie, Andrew. *Autobiography of Andrew Carnegie.* Boston: Houghton Mifflin, 1920.
Cassar, George H. *Asquith as War Leader.* London: Hambledon Press, 1994.
Castagnetti, Giuseppe, Hubert Goenner, Jürgen Renn, Tilman Sauer, and Britta Scheideler. "Foundation in Disarray: Essays on Einstein's Science and Politics in the Berlin Years." Max Planck-Institut für Wissenschaftsgeschichte (Max Planck Institute for the History of Science). Reprint 63, 1997.
Ceadel, Martin. *Living the Great Illusion: Sir Norman Angell, 1872–1967.* Oxford: Oxford University Press, 2009.
———. *Pacifism in Britain, 1914–1945: The Defining of a Faith.* Oxford: Clarendon Press, 1980.
Cecil, Lamar. *Wilhelm II*, vol. 2: *Emperor and Exile, 1900–1941.* Chapel Hill: University of North Carolina Press, 1996.
Chambers, Douglas R. *A Century of Heroes.* Pittsburgh: Carnegie Hero Fund Commission, 2004.
Chambers, John Whiteclay, II, ed. *The Eagle and the Dove: The American Peace Movement and United States Foreign Policy 1900–1922.* Syracuse, NY: Syracuse University Press, 1991.
Chatfield, Charles. *For Peace and Justice: Pacifism in America 1914–1941.* Boston: Beacon Press, 1971.
Cherny, Robert W., ed. *California Women and Politics: From the Gold Rush to the Great Depression.* Lincoln: University of Nebraska Press, 2011.
Chickering, Roger P. *Imperial Germany and a World Without War: The Peace Movement and German Society.* Princeton, NJ: Princeton University Press, 1975.
———. "The Peace Movement and the Religious Community in Germany, 1900–1914." *Church History* 38.3 (Sept. 1969): 300–311.
———. "A Voice of Moderation in Imperial Germany: The 'Verband fur internationale Verstandigung' 1911–1914." *Journal of Contemporary History* 8.1 (Jan. 1973): 147–164.
"Chile–Argentina Boundary Dispute." *National Geographic Magazine*, June 1902.
"The Christ of the Andes." *Missionary Review*, March 1906, 211–213.
The Christ of the Andes: The Story of the Erection of the Great Peace Monument on the Andean Boundary Between Chile and Argentina. Boston: American Peace Society, 1905.

Churchill, Winston S. *The World Crisis 1911–1918*. New York City: Free Press, 1931.
Clarke, George Herbert, ed. *A Treasury of War Poetry: British and American Poems of the War, 1914–1917*. Boston: Houghton Mifflin, 1917.
Clarke, Gerald. "Two Views of a Little Caesar." *Time* (June 7, 1982).
Clinton, Michael. "Coming to Terms with 'Pacifism': The French Case, 1901–1918." *Peace & Change* 26.1 (Jan. 2001): 1–30.
CO Project. *Conscientious Objection in Britain in World War One*. London: Peace Pledge Union.
Cobb, Frank Irving. *Cobb of the World: A Leader in Liberalism*. Freeport, NY: Libraries Press, 1924.
Cohen, Naomi W. *Jacob H. Schiff: A Study in American Jewish Leadership*. Hanover, NH: University Press of New England, 1999.
Cooper, Sandi. "Émile Arnaud." In *Biographical Dictionary of Modern Peace Leaders*. Edited by Harold Josephson. Westport, CT: Greenwood Press, 1985. 37–38.
_____. "The Guns of August and the Doves of Italy: Interventions and Internationalism." *Peace & Change* 7.1-2 (Winter 1981): 29–44.
_____. "Pacifism in France, 1889–1914: International Peace as a Human Right." *French Historical Studies* 17.2 (Autumn 1991): 359–386.
_____. *Patriotic Pacifism: Waging War on War in Europe, 1815–1914*. Oxford: Oxford University Press, 1991.
Cortright, David. *Peace: A History of Movements and Ideas*. Cambridge: Cambridge University Press, 2008.
Crangle, John V., and Joseph O. Baylen. "Emily Hobhouse's Peace Mission, 1916." *Journal of Contemporary History* 14.4 (Oct. 1979): 731–744.
Crum, Clyde E. "Contributions of the American School Peace League to International Education." *History of Education Journal* 4.2 (Winter 1953): 51–57.
Curti, Merle. *Peace or War: The American Struggle 1636–1936*. New York: W. W. Norton, 1936.
_____. "Pioneers of Peace." *North American Review* 229.5 (May 1930): 553–560.
Dahlin, Ebba. *French and German Public Opinion on Declared War Aims, 1914–1918*. Stanford, CA: Stanford University Press, 1933.
Dalbin, Stéphanie. *Visions Croisées: Franco-Allemandes de la Première Guerre Mondiale*. Berne: Peter Lang S.A., 2007.
Davis, Arthur N. *The Kaiser as I Know Him*. New York and London: Harper & Brothers, 1918.
Dawson, Grant. "Preventing 'A Great Moral Evil': Jean de Bloch's 'The Future of War' as Anti-Revolutionary Pacifism." *Journal of Contemporary History* 37.1 (Jan. 2002): 5–19.
DeBenedetti, Charles. *The Peace Reform in American History*. Bloomington: Indiana University Press, 1984.
Debs, Eugene. "When I Shall Fight." *The Appeal to Reason* (Sept. 11, 1915).
De Jong van Beek en Donk, Benjamin, and Dr. B. Jonkheer. "History of the Peace Movement in the Netherlands." *A General View of the Netherlands*, vol. 25. Leiden: Commercial Department of the Netherlands Ministry of Agriculture, Industry and Commerce, 1915.
Denson, John V., ed. *Reassessing the Presidency: The Rise of the Executive State and the Decline of Freedom*. Auburn, AL: Ludwig von Mises Institute, 2001.
Derry, T. K. *A Short History of Norway*. London: George Allen & Unwin, 1957.
Doenecke, Justus D. *Nothing Less Than War: A New History of America's Entry into World War 1*. Lexington: University Press of Kentucky, 2011.
Domínguez, César. "Making a Career of the Arrière-garde: Vincente Blasco Ibáñez as World Author." *European Review* 19.2 (2011): 307–320.
Douglas, William R. "'The Germans Would Court Martial Me, Too': St. Paul's World War I Socialist Draft Resisters." *Minnesota History* 55.7 (Fall 1997): 286–301.
Dubin, Martin James. "Toward the Concept of Collective Security: The Bryce Group's 'Proposals for the Avoidance of War,' 1914–1917." *International Organization* 24.2 (Spring 1970): 288–318.
Dunn, Joe P. *Military Affairs* 46.2 (April 1982).
Dyck, Harvey Leonard, and Peter Brock, eds. *The Pacifist Impulse in Historical Perspective*. Toronto: University of Toronto Press, 1996.
Earle, Edward Mead. "H. G. Wells, British Patriot in Search of a World State." *World Politics* 2.2 (Jan. 1950): 181–208.

Edwards, Steve, and Paul Wood. *Art of the Avant-Garde.* London: Yale University Press, 2004.
Eksteins, Modris. *Rites of Spring: The Great War and the Birth of the Modern Age.* Boston: Houghton Mifflin, 1989.
Eliot, Charles W. *An International Force Must Support an International Tribunal.* Baltimore, MD: American Society for Judicial Settlement of International Disputes, Dec. 19, 1914.
Ellis, John. *Eye-Deep in Hell, Trench Warfare in World War I.* Baltimore: Johns Hopkins University Press, 1989.
Epstein, Melech. *Profiles of Eleven.* Lanham, MD: University Press of America, 1987.
Eyck, E. "The Generals and the Downfall of the German Monarchy, 1917–1918." *Transactions of the Royal Historical Society,* 5th series, 1952.
Faure, Sébastien. *Vers la paix. Appel aux socialistes, syndicalistes, révolutionnaires & anarchistes.* Imprimerie Sébastien Faure [La Ruche], 1915.
Fay, Sidney B. "The Kaiser's Secret Negotiations with the Tsar, 1904–1905." *American Historical Review* 24.1 (Oct. 1918): 48–72.
Feeley, Francis. "French School Teachers Against Militarism, 1903–1918." *The Historian* 57.2 (Winter 1994): 315–328.
Fernau, Hermann. *Because I Am a German.* With an introduction by T. W. Rolleston. New York: E. P. Dutton, 1916.
Ferris, Woodbridge N. "Review of C. F. Nicolai's *Biology of War.*" Ferris Library for Information, Technology and Education. Big Rapids, MI: Grand Rapids Press, 1919.
Ferro, Marc, Malcolm Brown, Rémy Cazals, and Olaf Mueller, eds. *Meetings in No Man's Land: Christmas 1914 and Fraternization in the Great War.* London: Constable & Robinson, 2007.
Fest, W. B. "British War Aims and German Peace Feelers During the First World War." *Historical Journal* 15.2 (June 1972): 285–308.
Filene, Peter. "The World Peace Foundation and Progressivism: 1910–1918." *New England Quarterly* 36.4 (Dec. 1963): 478–501.
Florinsky, Michael. "The Russian Mobilization of 1914." *Political Science Quarterly* 42.2 (June 1927): 203–227.
Foerster, F. W. *Europe and the German Question.* London: George Allen & Unwin, 1941.
———. "A Voice from Germany: Why German Peace Declarations Fail to Convince." *International Conciliation* 129 (New York: American Association for International Conciliation) (Aug. 1918): 447–461.
Foner, Philip S. *May Day: A Short History of the International Workers' Holiday.* New York: International, 1986.
Foreign Relations of the United States, 1914 supplement: The World War. Washington, D.C.: United States Government Printing Office, 1928.
Forster, Kent. *The Failures of Peace.* Washington, D.C.: American Council on Public Affairs, 1941.
Foster, John W. "The Evolution of International Law." *Yale Law Journal* 18.3 (Jan. 1909): 149–164.
Frattini, Eric. *The Entity: Five Centuries of Secret Vatican Espionage.* Translated by Dick Cluster. London: JR Books, 2009.
Freenay, Lewis R. "Over the Andes." *Cornhill Magazine* (Sept. 1923): 355.
Friedlander, Robert A. "Who Put Out the Lamps?: Thoughts on International Law and the Coming of World War I." *Duquesne Law Review* 20.4 (Summer 1982): 569.
Fueloep-Miller, René. "Tolstoy, the Apostolic Crusader." *Russian Review* 19.2 [Special Issue: Leo Tolstoy] (April 1960): 99–121.
Galbreath, Robert. "Hermann Hesse and the Politics of Detachment." *Political Theory* 2.1 (Feb. 1974): 62–76.
Garel, Sylvain. *Louis Lecoin: An Anarchist Life.* London: Kate Sharpley Library, 2000.
Gates, Clifford E. "The Pacifistic Trend in German Literature." *German Quarterly* 5.1 (Jan. 1932): 37–44.
Gelderman, Carol. *Henry Ford: The Wayward Capitalist.* New York: Dial Press, 1981.
"Geographical Problems in Boundary Making." *Geographical Journal* 47 (Jan./June 1916): 421–436.
German, A (nom de plume for Richard Grelling). *I Accuse!* Translated by Alexander Gray. New York: George H. Doran, 1915.

Giddings, Franklin H. *Political Science Quarterly* 34.1 (March 1919).
Giddings, Robert. *The War Poets.* London: Bloomsbury, 1990.
Gilbert, Martin. *The First World War.* London: Phoenix, 2008.
_____. *A History of the Twentieth Century.* Vol. 1. New York: William Morrow, 1997.
Goenner, Hubert, and Guiseppe Castagnetti. "Albert Einstein as Pacifist and Democrat During World War 1." *Science in Context* 9.4 (1996): 325–386.
Goldberg, Harvey. *The Life of Jean Jaurès.* Madison: University of Wisconsin Press, 1962.
Goldberg, Nancy Sloan. "Women, War, and H. G. Wells: The Pacifism of French Playwright Marie Lenéru." *WLA (War, Literature & the Arts)* 14 (2002): 165–177.
Goldsmith, Robert. *A League to Enforce Peace.* New York: Macmillan, 1917.
Gooch, G. P. "Kiderlen-Wachter." *Cambridge Historical Journal* 5.2 (1936): 178–192.
_____. *Recent Revelations of European Diplomacy.* New York: Longmans, Green, 1930.
Grey, Sir Edward. *Twenty Five Years.* Vol. 2. London: Hodder and Stoughton, 1925.
Groh, Dieter. "The 'Unpatriotic Socialists' and the State." *Journal of Contemporary History* 1.4 (Oct. 1966): 151–177.
Haldane, Richard Burdon. *Before the War.* 1920. Teddington, UK: Echo Press, reprint 2006.
Halkin, Ariela. *The Enemy Reviewed: German Popular Literature Through British Eyes Between the Two Wars.* Westport, CT: Praeger, 1995.
Hall, John. *That Bloody Woman: The Turbulent Life of Emily Hobhouse.* Truro, UK: Truan, 2008.
Hanak, Harry. *Great Britain and Austria-Hungary During the First World War.* London: Oxford University Press, 1962.
_____. Review of: *Die Friedsversuche der kriegführenden Mächte im Sommer und Herbst 1917. Quellenkritische Untersuchungen, Akten und Vernehmungsprotokolle.* Edited by Wolfgang Steglich. Stuttgart: Franz Steiner, 1984.
Hanevik, Col. Karl E. "Norwegian Neutrality in the Inter-War Years." *Strategy Research Project*, March 16, 2006.
Hansard. *Parliamentary Debates*, 5th series, xxxiv, cols. 1340–1341, and xxxv, col. 35.
Harris, Ian M., and Mary Lee Morrison. *Peace History.* Jefferson, NC: McFarland, 2003.
Hawthorn, Harry B., ed. *The Doukhobors of British Columbia.* London: University of British Columbia and J. M. Dent, 1955.
Head, Michael. *Crimes Against the State: From Treason to Terrorism.* Farnham, UK: Ashgate, 2011.
Helmreich, Ernst Christian. *The Diplomacy of the Balkan Wars 1912–1913.* New York: Russell & Russell, 1938.
Hemleben, Sylvester John. *Plans for World Peace Through Six Centuries.* Chicago: University of Chicago Press, 1943.
Herber, Charles J. "Eugenio Pacelli's Mission to Germany and the Papal Peace Proposals of 1917." *Catholic Historical Review* 65.1 (Jan. 1979): 20–48.
Herbert, Aubrey. *Mons, Anzac & Kut: A British Intelligence Officer in Three Theatres of the First World War 1914–18.* UK: Leonaur Books, 2010.
Herneck, Friedrich. *Einstein und Weltbild: Aufsätze und Vorträge.* Berlin: Der Morgen, 1979.
Hershey, Burnet. *The Odyssey of Henry Ford and the Great Peace Ship.* New York: Taplinger, 1967.
Hertog, Johan Den, and Samuel Kruizingza. *Caught in the Middle: Neutral, Neutrality and the First World War.* Amsterdam: Amsterdam University Press, 2011.
Hesse, Hermann. *Siddhartha.* London: Penguin, 2008.
Hewitson, Mark. "Germany and France Before the First World War: A Reassessment of Wilhelmine Foreign Policy." *English Historical Review* 115.462 (June 2000): 570–606.
Hibbert, Christopher. *Benito Mussolini.* London: Reprint Society, 1962.
Hickey, Michael. *Gallipoli.* London: John Murray, 1995.
Hinsley, Francis Harry. *British Foreign Policy Under Sir Edward Grey.* London and New York: Cambridge University Press, 1977.
Hobhouse, Mrs. Henry. *I Appeal Unto Caesar: The Case of the Conscientious Objector.* London: George Allen & Unwin, 1917.
Hochschild, Adam. *To End All Wars: A Story of Protest and Patriotism in the First World War.* London: Pan Books, 2011.

Hodgson, Godfrey. *Woodrow Wilson's Right Han: The Life of Colonel Edward M. House*. New Haven and London: Yale University Press, 2006.
Hofstadter, Richard. *The American Political Tradition: And the Men Who Made It*. New York: Alfred Knopf, 1948.
House, Edward M. *Philip Dru: Administrator: A Story of Tomorrow*. New York: B. W. Huebsch, 1912.
Ibáñez, Vincente Blasco. *The Four Horsemen of the Apocalypse*. Translated by Charlotte Brewster Jordan. UK: Dodo Press, 1916.
Hochschild, Adam. *To End All Wars*. London: Pan Books, 2011.
Holdich, Colonel Sir T. H. "The Patagonian Andes." *Geographical Journal* 23.2 (Feb. 1904): 153–173.
Holman, Bob. *Keir Hardie, Labour's Greatest Hero?* Oxford: Lion Hudson, plc., 2010.
Holt, Hamilton. "The League to Enforce Peace." *Proceedings of the Academy of Political Science in the City of New York* 7.2 (July 1917): 65–69.
———. "The Way to Disarm: A Practical Proposal." *The Independent* 79 (Sept. 28, 1914): 427–429.
Hostetler, John A. *Hutterite Society*. Baltimore, MD: Johns Hopkins Press, 1974.
Howard-Ellis, Charles. *The Origin, Structure and Working of the League of Nations*. Boston: Houghton Mifflin, 1929.
Howlett, C. F. "Nicholas Murray Butler's Crusade for a Warless World." *Wisconsin Magazine of History* 67.2 (Winter 1983–1984): 99–120.
Howlett, Charles F., and Ian M. Harris. *Books, Not Bombs: Teaching Peace Since the Dawn of the Republic*. Charlotte, NC: Information Age, 2010.
Hudson, Manley O. "The Permanent Court of Arbitration." *American Journal of International Law* 27.3 (July 1933): 440–460.
Huidobro, Carolina. "The Christ of the Andes." *The Independent*, May 7, 1908, 1021.
Huldermann, Bernhard. *Albert Ballin*. Translated by W. J. Eggers. London, New York, Toronto and Melbourne: Cassell, 1922.
Hyde, Dayton O. *The Last Free Man: The True Story Behind the Massacre of Shoshone Mike and his Band of Indians in 1911*. New York: Dial Press, 1973.
James, Robert Rhodes. *Gallipoli*. New York: Macmillan, 1965.
Josephson, Harold, ed. *Biographical Dictionary of Modern Peace Leaders*. Westport, CT: Greenwood Press, 1985.
Joyce, Davis D. *Alternative Oklahoma: Contrarian Views of the Sooner State*. Norman: University of Oklahoma Press, 2007.
Juhnke, James C. "World War (1914–1918)." *Global Anabaptist Mennonite Encyclopedia Online*, 1989.
Kagan, Donald. *On the Origins of War and the Preservation of Peace*. New York: Doubleday, 1995.
Kant, Immanuel. "Perpetual Peace: A Philosophical Sketch." 1795. Indianapolis and Cambridge: Hackett, 2003.
Katayama, Sen. "The Marxian Socialist Group." *The Labor Movement in Japan*. Chicago: C. H. Kerr, 1918.
Katz, Friedrich. *Pancho Villa*. Palo Alto, CA: Stanford University Press, 1998.
Kavanagh, P. J., and James Michie, eds. *Oxford Book of Short Poems*, new ed. Oxford: Oxford University Press, July 24, 2003.
Keiger, John. "Jules Cambon and the Franco-German Détente, 1907–1914." *Historical Journal* 26.3 (1983): 641–659.
Kendall III, Walter J. "Pope Paul VI's Aphorism—'If You Want Peace Work for Justice'—and the Nobel Peace Prize Winners." *The Acorn* 11.1 (Fall-Winter 2000–2001): 36–52.
Kennedy, David M. *Over Here*. Oxford: Oxford University Press, 2004.
Kennedy, Thomas C. *The Hound of Conscience: A History of the No-Conscription Fellowship, 1914–1919*. Fayetteville: University of Arkansas Press, 1981.
———. "Public Opinion and the Conscientious Objector." *Journal of British Studies* 12.2 (May 1973): 113–114.
Kernek, Sterling. "The British Government's Reaction to President Wilson's 'Peace' Note of December 1916." *Historical Journal* 13.4 (1970): 732–733.

Kirchberger, Joe H. *The First World War: An Eyewitness History.* New York: Facts on File, 1992.
Kohn, Hans. *The Mind of Germany.* New York City: Scribner's, 1960.
Kohn, Stephen Martin. *American Political Prisoners: Prosecutions under the Espionage and Sedition Acts.* Westport, CT: Praeger, 1994.
Kominz, Laurence. "Pilgrimage to Tolstoy: Tokutomi Roka's Junrei Kik." *Monumenta Nipponica* 41.1 (Spring 1986): 51–101.
Kraft, Barbara S. *The Peace Ship.* New York: Macmillan, 1978.
_____. "Peacemaking in the Progressive Era: A Prestigious and Proper Calling." *Maryland Historian* 1 (Fall 1970): 121–144.
Krass, Peter. *Carnegie.* Hoboken, NJ: John Wiley, 2002.
Kublin, Hyman. "The Japanese Socialists and the Russo-Japanese War." *Journal of Modern History* 22.4 (Dec. 1950): 322–339.
_____. "The Origins of Japanese Socialist Tradition." *Journal of Politics* 14.2 (May 1952): 257–280.
Langhorne, Richard. "The Naval Question in Anglo-German Relations, 1912–1914." *Historical Journal* 14.2 (1971): 359–370.
Larsen, Karen. *A History of Norway.* New York: Princeton University Press for the American-Scandinavian Foundation, 1950.
Larson, Jeanne, and Madge Micheels-Cyrus. *Seeds of Peace: A Catalogue of Quotations.* Philadelphia and Santa Cruz: New Society, 1987.
Latzko, Andreas. *Menschen im Krieg (Men in War).* Zurich: Rascher-Verlag, 1917.
Lavrin, Janko. "Tolstoy and Gandhi." *Russian Review* 19.2 [Special Issue: Leo Tolstoy] (April 1960): 132–139.
Lebow, Richard Ned. "The Morgenthau Peace Mission of 1917." *Jewish Social Studies* 32.4 (Oct. 1970): 267–285.
Lenin, V. *Collected Works.* Vol. 26 (Sept. 1917–Feb. 1918). Moscow: Progress, 1964.
Lichnowsky, Prince. *My Mission to London, 1912–1914.* New York: George H. Doran, 1918.
Liebknecht, Karl. *Militarism.* New York: B. W. Huebsch, 1917.
Lindgren, Raymond E. *Norway-Sweden: Union, Disunion and Scandinavian Integration.* Princeton, NJ: Princeton University Press, 1959.
Link, Arthur S. Wilson. *The Struggle for Neutrality 1914–1915.* Princeton, NJ: Princeton University Press, 1960.
Lloyd, Bertram, ed. and trans. *The Paths of Glory: A Collection of Poems Written During the War, 1914–1919.* London: George Allen & Unwin, 1919.
Lord, Frank B., and James William Bryan. *Woodrow Wilson's Administration and Achievements.* Project Gutenberg Ebook, August 29, 2009 [eBook #29850].
Lowe, Cedric James, and F. Marzari. *Italian Foreign Policy, 1870–1940.* London: Routledge, 1975.
Ludendorff, Erich. *The General Staff and Its Problems: The History of the Relations Between the High Command and the German Imperial Government as Revealed by Official Documents.* Vol. 2. Translated by F. A. Holt. London: Hutchinson., 1920.
Lynn-Jones, Sean M. "Détente and Deterrence: Anglo-German Relations. 1911–1914." *International Security* 11.2 (Autumn 1986): 121–150.
Magnes, Judah L. *Russia and Germany at Brest-Litovisk.* New York: Rand School of Social Science, 1919.
Marburg, Theodore. *League of Nations: A Chapter in the History of the Movement.* Foreword by William Howard Taft. New York: Macmillan, 1917.
Marlow, Joyce, ed. "The Standard, 8 July 1915." In *The Virago Book of Women and the Great War, 1914–1918.* London: Virago Press, 1998.
Marsland, Elizabeth A. *The Nation's Cause: French, English and German Poetry of the First World War.* New York: Routledge, 1991.
Martin, Michel L. "France: A Statute but No Objections." In *The New Conscientious Objection: From Sacred to Secular Resistance*, edited by Charles S. Moskos and John Whiteclay Chambers III. New York: Oxford University Press, 1993, 80–97.
Martin, William. "Peace on the Way." *Statesmen of the War.* New York: Minton, Balch, 1928.
Massaro, Thomas J., S.J. and Thomas A. Shannon. *Catholic Perspectives on War and Peace.* Lanham, MD: Rowman & Littlefield, 2003.

Mathijs, Ernst. *The Cinema of the Low Countries.* London: Wallflower Press, 2003.
Maurer, John H. "The Anglo-German Naval Rivalry and Informal Arms Control, 1912–1914." *Journal of Conflict Resolution* 36.2 (June 1992): 284–308.
———."Arms Control and the Anglo-German Naval Race Before World War I: Lessons for Today?" *Political Science Quarterly* 112.2 (Summer 1997): 285–306.
McCormick, Donald. *Pedlar of Death.* London: MacDonald, 1965.
McKeogh, Colm. *Tolstoy's Pacifism.* Amherst, NY: Cambria Press, 2009.
McLean, Iain. *Keir Hardie.* London: Allen Lane, 1975.
Mead, Edwin D. *Heroes of Peace.* Boston: World Peace Foundation, 1911.
Meltzer, Albert. *I Couldn't Paint Golden Angels.* Edinburgh: AK Press, 1996.
Meltzer, Milton. *Ain't Gonna Study War No More: The Story of America's Peace Seekers.* New York: Random House, 2002.
Meyer, Ernest L. *"Hey! Yellowbacks!"* New York: John Day, 1930.
Mill, John Stuart. *Principles of Political Economy.* Vol. 1. New York: Cosimo, 2006.
Millet, Philippe. "The Truth About the Franco-German Crisis of 1911." *Nineteenth Century* 71 (June 1912): 1054.
Millman, Brock. "HMG and the War Against Dissent, 1914–1918." *Journal of Contemporary History* 40.3 (July 2005): 430.
Montgelas, Max, and Walter Schuecking, eds. *Outbreak of the World War. German Documents Collected by Karl Kautsky.* New York: Oxford University Press, 1924.
Moorehead, Caroline. *Troublesome People.* Bethesda, MD: Adler & Adler, 1987.
Morel, Edmund Deville. "The True Story of the Morocco Negotiations." *Nineteenth Century* 71 (Feb. 1912): 246.
———. "The 'Truth' About the Franco-German Crisis." *Nineteenth Century* 72 (July 1912): 37.
Morgenthau, Henry. *Ambassador Morgenthau's Story.* New York, Doubleday, Page, 1918.
Morin-Rotureau, Evelyne. *Combat de femmes 1914–1918.* Paris: Autrement Mémoires/Histoire, 2004.
Morris, A. J. A. *C. P. Trevelyan 1870–1958: Portrait of a Radical.* Belfast: Blackstaff Press, 1977. 85–108.
———. "C. P. Trevelyan's Road to Resignation 1906–1914: The Odyssey of an Antiwar Liberal." In *Doves and Diplomats*, edited by Solomon Wank. Westport, CT, and London: Greenwood Press, 1978, 85–108.
Nathan, Otto, and Heinz Norden. *Einstein on Peace.* New York: Simon & Schuster, 1960.
Nelson, Lars. *President Wilson.* Stockholm: P. A. Norstedt, 1919.
Neuman, R. P. "Working Class Birth Control in Wilhelmine Germany." *Comparative Studies in Society and History* 20.3 (July 1978): 408–428.
Nevins, Allan, and Frank Ernest Hill. *Ford—Expansion and Challenge 1915–1933.* New York: Scribner's, 1957.
Newton, Douglas J. *European Socialism and the Struggle for Peace 1889–1914.* Oxford: Clarendon Press, 1985.
———. "The Lansdowne 'Peace Letter' of 1917 and the Prospect of Peace by Negotiation with Germany." *Australian Journal of Politics and History* 48.1 (Dec. 2002): 16–39.
Ntolo, Desiree. *The Sacred and the Profane.* Bloomington, IN: Author House, 2008.
Nurnberger, Ralph D. "Bridling the Passions." *Wilson Quarterly (1976)* 11 (New Year's 1987): 96–107.
Okamoto, Shumpei. *The Japanese Oligarchy and the Russo-Japanese War.* New York: Columbia University Press, 1970.
Oliver, Bobbie. *Peacemongers.* Fremantle: Fremantle Arts Centre, 1997.
O'Toole, Patricia. *When Trumpets Call: Theodore Roosevelt After the White House.* New York: Simon & Schuster, 2005.
Paléologue, Maurice. *An Ambassador's Memoirs.* Translated by F. A. Holt. New York: George H. Doran, 1924.
Passy, Frédéric. *L'avenir de l'Europe: Conférence faite le 14 février 1895, à la mairie du VIe arrondissement de Paris, au nom de la Société française pour l'arbitrage entre nations.* Paris: Société française pour l'arbitrage, 1895.

Patterson, David S. "Andrew Carnegie's Quest for World Peace." *Proceedings of the American Philosophical Society* 114.5 (Oct. 20, 1970): 371–383.
Payne, Brian Joseph. "Fishing a Borderless Sea: Environmental Territorialism in the North Atlantic 1818–1910." PhD diss., University of Maine, 2006.
"Peace Overtures of the Central Powers and Reply of Entente Powers." *American Journal of International Law* 11.4. Supplement: "Diplomatic Correspondence Between the United States and Belligerent Governments Relating to Neutral Rights and Commerce" (Oct. 1917): 272–287.
Pearson, Hesketh. *The Whispering Gallery*. New York: Boni & Liveright, 1926.
Pedroncini, Guy. *Les mutineries de 1917*, 2nd ed. Paris: Publications de la Sorbonne, Presse Universitaires de France, 1983.
"The People Want War." *The Advocate of Peace* 78.3 (March 1916): 65.
Peters, Walter H. *The Life of Benedict XV*. Milwaukee: Bruce, 1959.
Peterson, H. C., and Gilbert C. Fite. *Opponents of War 1917–1918*. Seattle: University of Washington Press, 1957.
Pharand, Michael W. "Above the Battle? Bernard Shaw, Romain Rolland, and the Politics of Pacifism." In *Shaw*, vol. 11: *Shaw and Politics*. University Park: Penn State University Press, 1991, 169–183.
Pierson, Ruth Roach. *Women and Peace: Theoretical, Historical, and Practical Perspectives*. London: Routledge Kegan & Paul, 1987.
Pinson, Koppel S. *Modern Germany: Its History and Civilization*. New York: Macmillan, 1954.
Playne, C. E. *German Pacifism During the War*. London: National Peace Council, 1919.
Pollard, John F. *The Unknown Pope: Benedict XV (1914–1922) and the Pursuit of Peace*. London: Geoffrey Chapman, 1999.
Posonby, Arthur. *Falsehood in War-time: Containing an Assortment of Lies Circulated Throughout the Nations During the Great War*. Newport Beach, CA: Institute for Historical Review, 1991.
Possony, Stefan T. "Peace Enforcement." *Yale Law Journal* 55.5 (Aug. 1946): 910–949.
"The Progress of the World." *Review of Reviews* 3.15 (April 1891).
Rabson, Steve. "Shimazaki Toson on War." *Monumenta Nipponica* 46.4 (Winter 1991): 453–481.
_____. "Yosano Akiko on War: To Give one's Life or Not: A Question of Which War." *Journal of the Association of Teachers of Japanese* 25.1 (April 1991): 45–74.
Rappard, William E. *The Quest for Peace Since the World War*. Cambridge, MA: Harvard University Press, 1940.
Read, Herbert. *Naked Warriors*. London: Art & Letters, 1919.
The Records of the Permanent Under-Secretary's Department, Liaison 1873–1939. London: Foreign & Commonwealth Office, March 2005.
Reid, Cecilie. "American Internationalism: Peace Advocacy and International Relations, 1895–1916." PhD diss., Boston College, 2005.
Reinharz, Jehuda. "His Majesty's Zionist Emissary: Chaim Weizmann's Mission to Gibraltar in 1917." *Journal of Contemporary History* 27.1 (April 1992): 259–277.
Rhodes, Thomas. *The Real von Kühlmann*. London: Noel Douglas, 1925.
Roberts, John Stuart. *Siegfried Sassoon, 1886–1967*. London: Richard Cohen Books, 1999.
Roebke-Berens, Ruth. "Austrian Social Democratic Peace Policy and the Balkan Crisis of 1912–1913." *Peace & Change* 7.1–2 (Winter 1981): 17–27.
Rolland, Romain. *Above the Battle*. Translated by C. K. Ogden. Chicago: Open Court, 1916.
_____. *The Forerunners*. Translated by Eden and Cedar Paul. New York: Harcourt, Brace and Howe, 1920.
Roosevelt, Theodore. "International Peace." An Address before the Nobel Committee, Christiania, Norway, May 5, 1910.
Rosenberg, Isaac. *The Selected Poems of Isaac Rosenberg*, London: Cecil Woolf, 2003.
Rotberg, Robert I. *A Leadership for Peace*. Palo Alto, CA: Stanford University Press, 2007.
Rowthorn, R. E., and S. N. Solomu. "The Macroeconomic Effects of Overseas Investment on the UK Balance of Trade, 1870–1913." *Economic History Review* 44.4 (Nov. 1991): 654–664.

Russell, Bertrand. *Autobiography*. London and New York: Routledge, 1998.
———. "Barbarism." In *The Penguin Book of Twentieth Century Protest*, edited by Brian MacArthur. London: Penguin Group, 1998.
———. "War and Non-Resistance." *Atlantic Monthly*, Aug. 1915, 266–274.
Ruyssen, Theodore. "The Final Efforts of the European Pacifists to Prevent the War." *The Advocate of Peace* 76.10 (Nov. 1914): 236–238.
Sabatier, Paul. *France Today: Its Religious Orientation*. Translated by Henry Bryan Binns. New York: E. P. Dutton, 1913.
Sanders, Elizabeth. *Roots of Reform*. Chicago: University of Chicago Press, 1999.
Sassoon, Siegfried. *Counter-attack, and Other Poems*. New York: E. P. Dutton, 1918.
Saunders, Malcolm, and Ralph Summy. *The Australian Peace Movement: A Short History*. Canberra: Australian National University, 1986.
Schlichtmann, Klaus. "Japan, Germany and the Idea of the Hague Peace Conferences." *Journal of Peace Research* 40.4, Special Issue on Peace History (July 2003): 377–394.
Schmitt, Bernadotte, E. "July 1914: Thirty Years After." *Journal of Modern History* 16.3 (Sept. 1944): 169–204.
Schneer, Jonathan. *The Balfour Declaration*. London: Bloomsbury, 2011.
Schneider, Thomas C., and Hans Wagner. *"Huns" vs. "Corned Beef": Representations of the Other in American and German Literature and Film in World War One*. Osnabruck: Universitatsverlag, 2007.
Scott, James Brown. "Lord Haldane's Diary of Negotiation Between Germany and England in 1912." *American Journal of International Law* 12.4 (Oct. 1918): 589–596.
Seymour, Charles. *The Intimate Papers of Colonel House*. Vol. 1 and Vol. 2. Boston and New York: Houghton Mifflin, 1926.
Shand, James D. "Doves Among the Eagles: Pacifists and Their Government During World War I." *Journal of Contemporary History* 10.1 (Jan. 1975): 95–108.
Sibley, Mulford Q. "The Political Theories of Modern Religious Pacifism." *American Political Science Review* 37.3 (June 1943): 439–454.
Siegel, Mona. "To the Unknown Mother of the Unknown Soldier: Pacifism, Feminism, and the Politics of Sexual Difference Among French *Institutrices* Between the Wars." *French Historical Studies* 22.3 (Summer 1999): 421–451.
Singer, Barnett. "From Patriots to Pacifists: The French Primary School Teachers, 1880–1940." *Journal of Contemporary History* 12 (1977): 413–434.
Small, Michael. *The Forgotten Peace*. Ottawa: University of Ottawa Press, 2009.
Stallworthy, Jon, ed. *The Oxford Book of War Poetry*, Oxford: Oxford University Press, 1984.
———. *Wilfred Owen*. London: Oxford University Press and Chatto and Windus, 1974.
Stavrianos, L. S. *Global Rift: The Third World Comes of Age*. New York: Morrow, 1981.
Stead, Alfred. *Great Japan: A Study of National Efficiency*. London and New York: John Lane, 1906.
Stephen, Martin. *Never Such Innocence: Poems of the First World War*. London: J. M. Dent (Everyman), 1988.
Stephens, John Richard. *Weird History 101*. Holbrook, MA: Adams Media Corporation, 1997.
Stevenson, David. *The First World War and International Politics*. Oxford: Clarendon Press, 1988.
Stewart, William. *J. Keir Hardie*. London: Independent Labour Party Publications Department, 1921.
Stone, Norman. "Moltke-Conrad: Relations Between the Austro-Hungarian and German General Staffs, 1909–14." *Historical Journal* 9.2 (1966): 201–228.
"Suggestions Concerning the War Made by President Wilson December 18, 1916, and Replies of Belligerents and Neutrals." *American Journal of International Law* 11.4, Supplement: "Diplomatic Correspondence Between the United States and Belligerent Governments Relating to Neutral Rights and Commerce" (Oct., 1917): 288–317
Sumler, David E. "Opponents of War Preparedness in France, 1913–14." In *Doves and Diplomats*, edited by Salomon Wank. Westport, CT, and London: Greenwood Press, 1978, 109–126.
Supina, Philip D. "The Norman Angell Peace Campaign in Germany." *Journal of Peace Research* 9.2 (1972): 161–164.

Swain, Geoff. *Trotsky*. Edinburgh: Pearson Education, 2006.
Sward, Keith. *The Legend of Henry Ford*. New York: Rinehart, 1948.
Swarthmore College Peace Collection, http://www.swarthmore.edu/library/peace/.
Tabious, Genevieve R., and Charles Francis Atkinson. *The Life of Jules Cambon*. London: Jonathan Cape, 1938.
Taft, William Howard. *The Collected Works of William Howard Taft*. Edited by David H. Burton. Vol. 6. Athens: Ohio University Press, 2003.
Taylor, A. J. P. *The Struggle for Mastery in Europe 1848–1918*. Oxford and New York: Oxford University Press, 1954.
Thompson, J. A. *Albion: A Quarterly Journal Concerned with British Studies* 14.1 (Spring, 1982).
Tolstoy, Leo. "Bethink Yourselves." *London Times*, July 10, 1904.
———. *The Complete Works of Count Tolstoy*. Edited and translated by Leo Wiener. Vol. 23. London: G. J. Howell, 1905.
———. *On Patriotism*. Transcribed and edited by www.nonresistance.org. Moscow, March 17, 1894.
———. *What Is Religion? And Other New Articles and Letters*. Translated by V. Tchertkoff and A. C. Field. Hants: Free Age Press, 1902.
Trattner, Walter I. "Julia Grace Wales and the Wisconsin Plan for Peace." *Wisconsin Magazine for History* 44.3 (Spring 1961): 203–213.
Trotsky, Leon. *From October to Brest-Litovsk*. Authorized translation from the Russian. New York: Socialist Publication Society, 1919.
———. *Political Profiles*. London: New Park Publications, 1972.
Tumulty, Joseph P. *Woodrow Wilson as I Know Him*. Whitefish, MT: Kessinger, 2010.
Untermeyer, Louis, ed. *Modern British Poetry*. New York: Harcourt, Brace and Howe, 1920.
Van den Dungen, Peter. "Preventing Catastrophe: The World's First Peace Museum." *The Ritsumeikan Journal of International Studies. Ritsumeikan kokusai kenkyu* 18.3 (Mar. 2006): 449–462.
———, and Lawrence S. Wittner. "Peace History: An Introduction." *Journal of Peace Research* 40.4, Special Issue on Peace History (July 2003): 363–375.
Vellacott, Jo. "The No-Conscription Fellowship. Review of Thomas C. Kennedy, *The Hound of Conscience*." *Russell: The Journal of the Bertrand Russell Archives*, new series 1.2 (Winter 1981–1982): 158–162.
Viereck, George Sylvester. *The Strangest Friendship in History: Woodrow Wilson and Colonel House*. London: Duckworth, 1933.
Villard, Oswald Garrison. *Fighting Years: A Memoir*. New York: Harcourt, Brace, 1939.
Von Hase, Georg. *Kiel and Jutland*. Translated by Arthur Chambers and F. A. Holt. London: Skeffington, 1980.
Von Kürenberg, Joachim. *The Kaiser: A Life of Wilhelm II, Last Emperor of Germany*. Translated by H. T. Russell and Herta Hagen. New York: Simon and Schuster, 1955.
Von Müller, Admiral Georg Alexander. *The Diaries, Note Books and Letters of Admiral Georg Alexander von Müller, Chief of the Naval Cabinet, 1914–1918*. Edited by Walter Görlitz. New York: Harcourt, Brace & World, 1964.
Von Süttner, Bertha. *Lay Down Your Arms*. London: Longmans, Green, 1908.
Wales, Julia Grace. *Continuous Mediation Without Armistice*. Chicago: Woman's Peace Party, 1917.
Wank, Solomon, ed. *Doves and Diplomats: Foreign Offices and Peace Movements in Europe and America in the Twentieth Century*. Westport, CT: Greenwood Press, 1978.
War Obviated by an International Police: A Series of Essays, Written in Various Countries. The Hague: Nijhoff, 1915.
Webb, Sidney. "Conscience and the 'Conscientious Objector.'" *North American Review* 205.736 (March 1917): 403–420.
Weinberg, Arthur and Lila. *Instead of Violence: Writings by the Great Advocates of Peace and Nonviolence throughout History*. New York: Grossman, 1963.
Weinroth, Howard. "Norman Angell and the Great Illusion: An Episode in Pre-1914 Pacifism." *Historical Journal* 17.3 (Sept. 1974): 551–574.
Weintraub, Stanley. *Silent Night: The Remarkable Christmas Truce of 1914*. London: Simon & Schuster, 2001.

Wells, David, and Sandra Wilson, eds. *The Russo-Japanese War in Cultural Perspective, 1904–05*. Houndmills: Macmillan, 1999.
Wells, H. G. *War and the Future*. London: Cassel, 1917.
———. *The War That Will End War*. London: Frank & Cecil Palmer, Red Lion Court, 1914.
Wheeler-Bennett, John W. *Brest-Litovsk: The Forgotten Peace, March 1918*. New York: St. Martin's Press, 1966.
Whittle, Tyler. *The Last Kaiser*. London: Heinemann, 1977.
"Why London?" *Living Age* 58, reprinted in the *New York Times*, Jan. 11, 1913.
Wik, Reynold M. *Henry Ford and Grass-Roots America*. Ann Arbor: University of Michigan Press, 1972.
Wilhelm II (Emperor of Germany). *The Kaiser's Memoirs*. Translated by Thomas R. Ybarra. New York and London: Harper & Brothers, 1922.
Williams, John. *Mutiny 1917*. London: Heinemann, 1962.
Willis, Edward F. *Prince Lichnowsky, Ambassador of Peace*. Berkeley and Los Angeles; University of California Press, 1942.
Wilson, Jean Moorcroft. *Siegfried Sassoon: The Making of a War Poet*. London: Duckworth, 1998.
Wilson, Keith. "The Agadir Crisis, the Mansion House Speech, and the Double-Edgedness of Agreements." *Historical Journal* 15.3 (1972): 513–532.
Winter, Jay. *Dreams of Peace and Freedom*. New Haven and London: Yale University Press, 2006.
———. *The Great War and the Shaping of the 20th Century*. London: BBC Books, 1996.
Winterhager, Wilhelm Ernst. *Mission für den Frieden, Europäische Mächtepolitik und dänische Friedensvermittlung im Ersten Weltkrieg: vom August 1914 bis zum italienischen Kriegseintritt Mai 1915*. Stuttgart: Franz Steiner, 1984.
Wolf, Martin. "Will the Nation-State Survive Globalization?" *Foreign Affairs* (Jan./Feb. 2001): 178–190.
Wolfe, Bertram. "Angelica Balabanoff and V. I. Lenin: The Opposing Poles of the Socialist Movement Against War." *Antioch Review* 24.2 (Summer 1964): 223–236.
Woodcock, George, and Ivan Avakumovic. *The Doukhobors*. London: Faber and Faber, 1968.
Woodward, David R. "Britain's 'Brass-Hats' and the Question of a Compromise Peace, 1916–1918." *Military Affairs* 35.2 (April 1971): 63–68.
———. *Lloyd George and the Generals*. London: Routledge, 2003.
———. *World War I Almanac*. New York: Facts on File, 2009.
Woodward, E. L. *Great Britain and the German Navy*. Oxford: Claredon Press, 1935.
Wucker, Michele. *Lockout*. New York: Public Affairs, 2006.
Yale, William. "Ambassador Henry Morgenthau's Special Mission of 1917." *World Politics* 1.3 (April 1949): 308–320.
Yokota-Murakami, Takayuki. "Tolstoy, Attila, Edison: The Triangular Construction of a 'Peace-Loving' Russian Identity Across Borders." *Slavic and East European Journal* 45.2 (Summer 2001): 217–229.
Young, James A. "The Consulta and the Italian Peace Movement, 1914–18." In *Doves and Diplomats*, edited by Salomon Wank. Westport, CT, and London: Greenwood Press, 1978, 154–177.
Young, James D. *Socialism Since 1889: A Biographical History*. Totowa, NJ: Barnes & Noble Books, 1988.
Zeiger, Susan. "She Didn't Raise Her Boy to Be a Slacker: Motherhood, Conscription, and the Culture of the First World War." *Feminist Studies* 22.1 (Spring 1996): 6–39.
Zinn, Howard, and Anthony Arnove. *Voices of a People's History of the United States*. New York: Seven Stories Press, 2011.
Zivojinovic, Dragan. "Robert Lansing's Comments on the Pontifical Note of August 1, 1917." *Journal of American History* 56.3 (Dec. 1969): 556–571.
Zuelzer, Wolf. *The Nicolai Case*. Detroit: Wayne State University Press, 1982.
Zweig, Stefan. *Romain Rolland: The Man and His Work*. Translated by Eden and Cedar Paul. New York: Thomas Seltzer, 1921.

Index

ABC Peace Treaty 57
Abdul Kerim Bey 208–211
Addams, Jane 4, 100, 155, 228
Adler, Victor 49
Agadir Crisis 8, 13–15, 23, 69
Alfonso XIII 78, 152, 189
Allen, Clifford 89
American Federation of Labor (AFL) 6
American Friends Service Committee 4
American Patriots Association 229
American Peace Society 125
American School Peace League 39–42
American Socialist Party 228, 235, 237
American Society of International Lawyers 3
American Union Against Militarism 4
American Woman's Peace Party 4, 126, 147
Andersen, Hans Niels 78–79
Andrews, Fannie Fern 39–41
Angell, Norman 18–20, 43, 58, 101
Anglo-German Understanding Conference 52
arbitration 7, 8, 10, 11, 12, 19, 30–33, 39, 51, 59;
 International Court of Arbitration 11, 38, 44, 68, 70, 101, 184, 240–241, 250
Archduke Franz Ferdinand 55, 60, 61
Les Archives de la planète 21; *see also* Kahn, Albert
Arcos, René 197
Armand, Abel 173
Arnaud, Émile 104
Arnoldson, Klas Pontus 32–33
Arp, Jean *see* Dadaism
Asquith, H.H. 24, 139, 154, 256
Atwood, Ernestine F. 35
Austrian Social Democratic Party 49

Baghdad–Basra railway 54–55
Balkan Wars 52
Ballin, Albert 23–24, 26, 60
Barbusse, Henri 220–221, 252
Basel Congress 49–50
Baumann, Louis A., Jr. 35
Bebel, August 74
Benckendorff, Count 202
Benedict XV 82, 174–175, 181–182, 183–187, 249, 257

Berger, Victor 236–237
Bergson, Henri 20
Bertrand, Julia 113
Bethink Yourselves see Tolstoy, Leo
Bethmann-Hollweg, Chancellor Theobald von 26, 54, 76, 79, 81, 100, 122, 128, 129, 160, 177, 178, 180, 184, 188
The Biology of War see Nicolai, Georg Friedrich, *Die Biologie des Krieges*
Bismark, Otto von 23
Bitsenko, Anastasia 244
Bloch, Jan: *The Future of War* 5, 43
Boer War 22, 132, 153, 154
Bourne, Randolph S. 228
bourses de voyage autour du monde see Kahn, Albert
Boxer Rebellion 47
Bredt, Viktor 247
Brett, Reginald, Second Viscount Esher 172
Briand, Aristide 129, 160, 182–183, 257
Brion, Hélène 211
British Royal Geographical Society 32
Brockway, Fenner 86
Brusilov, General 163
Bryan, William Jennings 77, 84, 257
Bryce, Lord 239–241
Buchan, John 207
Buchanan, Sir George 242
Buck, Ott 115
Burián von Rajecz, Baron Stephan 174, 178
Burns, John 101
Butler, Nicholas Murray 129–130
Butt, Archibald 12

Cachin, Marcel 254
Cambon, Jules 14, 15, 65, 66, 257
Cardishian, Vahan 202
Carnegie, Andrew 4, 34–38, 40, 125, 130; *see also* education, simplified spelling
Carnegie Endowment for International Peace 4, 19, 52, 129, 130, 211
Carranza, Venustiano 56, 57
Cassel, Sir Ernest 23–24
Cavell, Edith 182

299

Cecil, Robert, Lord 155
Çemal Pasha 202
censorship 45, 48, 89–90, 92, 94, 96, 114, 117, 120, 121, 142–143, 167, 213, 216, 255
Charles I 169–170, 172–174
Chesterton, G.K. 87
Chevallier, Gabriel 137
Christ of the Andes 31
Christian X 78
Christians 48, 82, 86, 92, 107–109, 112, 136, 163, 223–224; see also Benedict XV
Christmas truce see fraternization
Church, Denver S. 227
Church Peace Union 4, 211
Churchill, Winston 23–24, 27–29, 54, 60–61
Clemenceau, Georges 82, 85, 172, 186, 209, 248
colonialism 8, 13, 15, 24, 54, 59, 112, 183, 210
Comte, Auguste 117
Conan Doyle, Arthur 37, 144
conscientious objectors see draft
Creel, George 130
Croce, Benedetto 252
The Cuckoo see Tokutomi, Roka
Curie, Marie 252
Czarina see Romanova, Alexandra Feodorovna
Czernin, Count 244

Dadaism 222
Daniels, Josephus 28
Darrow, Clarence 235
de Bloch, Jean see Bloch, Jan
de Brocqueville, Charles 182–183
Debs, Eugene V. 72, 174, 235, 237–238
Delbrück, Hans 122
Délong, Eugène Camille 197–198
de Mérode, Werner 182
de Mun, Albert 76
Dernburg, Bernhart 122
Despard, Charlotte 190
de Villalobar, Marquis 189
Dewey, Melvil 37
Dickinson, Goldsworthy Lowes 240
disarmament 6, 74, 101, 112, 184
Doukhobors 108–110
draft 231, 236; conscientious objectors 86–89, 231–233; draft dodgers 229; Green Corn Rebellion 230; see also Selective Service Act
dreadnought 22, 27, 60
Dunlop, Hendrik 44
Durkheim, David Émile 59
Dutch Peace Society 44, 98

Easter Sunday truce see fraternization
Eastman, Max 252
Eckstein, Anna B. 68
education 39–44, 59; literacy 3; simplified spelling 37–38
Edward VII 24, 30, 39, 152
Einstein, Albert 115, 118, 121–123, 252
Elkus, Abraham 203
Emperor Karl see Charles I
Engelke, Gerrit 198

Enver Pasha 203, 208–210
Erdody, Count Thomas 170–171
Erzberger, Matthias 187
Esperanto 3, 37–38
Espionage Act 229, 234, 236–237
Eternal Peace see Kant, Immanuel
eugenics 43

Faure, Sébastien 123
Fellowship of Reconciliation 4, 156, 211, 228
Fernau, Hermann 120
First National Peace Congress 39
Fisher, Adm. John 254
Foerster, Friedrich Wilhem 115, 119–120, 174
Ford, Henry 148–151
The Four Horsemen of the Apocalypse 214–215
France, Anatole 59, 169, 252
Frankfurter, Felix 204
Franz Josef I 79
fraternization: Christmas truce 74, 82, 132–146, 161, 165; Easter Sunday truce 162–163; Gallipoli 201–202, 256
French, Sir John 141
Fried, Alfred H. 93, 95
The Future of War see Bloch, Jan

Gallieni, General 104
Gandhi, Mohandas 110–111
Genold see Délong, Eugène Camille
George V 55, 78, 152
German Peace Society 51, 92–95, 120
Ginn, Edwin 4, 10, 42–45, 129
Giretti, Eduardo 130
Gompers, Samuel 6
Gorky, Maxim 252
The Great Illusion see Angell, Norman
Green Corn Rebellion see draft dodgers
Grelling, Richard 120–121; *Because I Am a German* 120–121
Grenfell, Julian 191
Grey, Sir Edward 22, 25, 26, 27, 29, 53, 54, 55, 64, 66, 69, 76, 81, 100, 128, 176, 180
Grotius, Hugo 44

The Hague: Convention 30; International Court 34, 38, 65; Peace Conferences 5, 6, 34, 38, 39, 51, 60, 68, 112, 132; Peace Palace 34
Haig, Field Marshal Douglas 177, 254
Haldane, Lord 23–27
Hardie, Keir 72, 73–75
Harding, Warren G. 227, 238
Harwich Frenchmen 88
Haywood, Bill 56
Head, William J. 229
Herbert, Col. Aubrey 201, 206–208
Hero Fund 35–36; see also Moore, Howard W.
Herron, George D. 173–174
Hesse, Hermann 218–219, 252
Heym, Georg 198
Hobhouse, Emily 101, 132, 153–156, 158
Hobson, Florence Edgar 132
Hobson, John A. 132
Hofer brothers 232

Holdich, Thomas, Sir 30
Holliday, William 157
Holt, Hamilton 124–126
Hopwood, Francis, Sir 152, 153
House, Colonel 63–65, 84–86, 160, 175–176, 177–180, 205, 249–250, 257
Huerta, General 56–58
Hughes, Charles Evans 211, 216
Hughes, William 224, 225
Huysmans, Camille 164

"I Didn't Raise My Boy to Be a Soldier" 215
Ibáñez, Vincente Blasco see The Four Horsemen of the Apocalypse
Ince, Thomas H. 212
Industrial Workers of the World (IWW) 56, 230
International Court 5, 12, 126, 250; see also The Hague
International Peace Bureau 58, 72
International School for Peace 10, 42
International Women's Suffrage Alliance 76
Inter-Parliamentary Union 3

Jacobs, Aletta 99
Japanese Ladies Peace Association 5
Jaurès, Jean 49, 70–71, 73
Joffe, Adolf 244
Jordan, David Starr 43

Kahn, Albert 20–22
Kaiser William II 14, 22–25, 29, 36, 38–39, 55, 60, 61, 63–65, 66–67, 73, 78, 79, 152, 171, 173, 174, 178, 185, 186, 189, 255, 256
Kamenev, Lev 244
Kant, Immanuel 59; *Eternal Peace* 43
Katayama, Sen 71
Kellog-Briand Pact 68
Kessler, Helene 216
King of Spain see Alfonso XIII
Kinoshita, Naoe: *Pillar of Fire* 46
Kipling, Rudyard 197
Komura, Marquis Jutaro 48
Kotoku, Shusui 46
Kropotkin, Peter 110
Kulishov, Anna 16

La Follette, Robert M. 226–227
La Guardia, Fiorello 227
Lammash, Professor 173–174
Lansdowne, Lord 103, 157–158
Lansing, Robert 203–204
Latzko, Andreas 216–217
Lavergne, General 250
Law, Bonar 164
Lay Down Your Arms (film) 61; see also von Süttner, Bertha
League of Nations 7, 78, 85, 118, 127, 129, 152, 160, 175, 176, 239, 241, 248, 250, 253
League to Enforce Peace 125–129, 147
Lecoin, Louis 123–124
Lenéru, Marie 114, 251
Lenin, Vladimir 241, 245–246, 247
Leopold of Bavaria, Prince, Field Marshall 244

Lersch, Heinrich 199
Lewin-Epstein, Eliahu 204
Lichnowsky, Prince Karl Max 23, 52, 66, 254
Liebknecht, Karl 95–97
Lincoln, Abraham 178–179
Lloyd George, David 13, 128, 153, 161, 178, 179, 190, 208, 209, 245, 253
London, Meyer 227, 237
Lowell, A.L. 125, 126
Lundeen, Ernest 226, 227
Ludendorff, Gen. Erich 82, 158, 171, 188, 189, 247
Lusitania 100–101, 234, 252
Luther, Martin 92
Luxemburg, Rosa 69
Lybia, conquest of 15–16
Lyttelton, Rev. Edward 191

MacDonald, Ramsay 90, 101
Machin, Alfred: *Maudite soit la guerre* 61
MacLean, John 157
Macpherson, Ian 194
Malvy, Jean-Louis 123
Marburg, Theodore 128–129
Maria Antonia of Bourbon Parma, Archduchess 170
Marx, Groucho 216
Maudite soit la guerre see Machin, Alfred
Mayo, Henry T. 56
Mayoux, François 113
Mayoux, Marie 113
Mead, Edward D. 35
Mead, Lucia Ames 125
mediation 57–58, 65–66, 77–78, 85, 100, 130, 147, 150–152, 160
Mennonites 93, 163, 231, 232, 233
Mensdorff-Pouilly, Count 152
Meyer, Ernest L. 232–233
Michaelis, Georg 185, 187, 257
Mill, John Stuart 239
Moneta, Ernesto Teodoro 130
Moore, Howard W. 233
Morel, E.D. 101, 102–103
Morgenthau, Henry 203–206, 208
Motono, Viscount 248
Mussolini, Benito 15–16
mutiny 165–169

National Council for Prevention of War 4
Naumann, Friedrich 51
"naval holiday" 27–29
Nazimova 213
neo-Malthusianism 69
Nernst, Walter 115
Neutrality League 58
Niagara Falls conference 57–58
Nicholas II of Russia, Czar 5, 6, 7, 65–67, 73, 78, 79, 80, 81, 111, 171, 255
Nicolai, Georg Friedrich 115–119; *Die Biologie des Krieges* 116–118
Nicolson, Arthur 55
Nicolson, Harold 26
Nippold, Otfried 52

Nivelle, General 165
Niven, Frederick 146
No-Conscription Fellowship (NCF) 86, 157
Nobel, Alfred 4, 34, 62
Nobel Peace Prize 5, 31, 33, 38, 51, 62, 68, 130, 238
non-resistance 107, 111, 223
non-violence 110, 111–112, 119, 122
Norris, George William 227
Norway: neutrality 33; separation from Sweden 32–33
Noureddin Bey, Dr. 206–207

O'Connell, Daniel 229
Oliviera Cezar de Costa, Angela 30–31
Ottoman League for Peace 206
Owen, Wilfried 196–197

Pacelli, Eugenio 182, 184, 185
La Paix par le droit 59
Paléologue, Maurice 80
Pan-American Conferences: Mexico 30
Passy, Frédéric 4, 11, 31, 70
patriotism 19, 41, 46, 51, 67, 75, 82, 87, 90, 91, 95, 104, 106, 111, 113, 163–164, 175, 191, 193, 199, 208, 228–231, 235, 259, 263, 265, 268, 273, 283, 289, 291, 296, 297
Peace Day 40
peace ship *see* Ford, Henry
Peace Society 10
Pétain, General 168
Pichon, Stephen 245
Pillar of Fire see Kinoshita, Naoe
Pius XII *see* Pacelli, Eugenio
Planck, Max 115
Plekhanov, Valentinovich 71
Poincaré, Raymond 170, 182, 214, 257
Pope 138, 148; *see also* Benedict XV; Pius XII
Prager, Robert 235
Protopopov, Alexander 158–159

Quakers 89, 110, 231, 233
Queen Mary 157
Quessel, Ludwig 247
Quidde, Ludwig 51

Rankin, Jeanette 227
Raspoutin 159
Read, Sir Herbert 193, 194
Reichstag 28, 49, 51, 72, 95, 96, 159, 160, 174–175, 183, 185, 187–190, 243, 247
Revertera, Count Nicholas 173
Rhodes, Cecil 21
Ribot, Alexandre 164, 172, 182, 183
Richards O'Hare, Kate 229
Richet, Dr. Charles 131
Rif War 8
Robertson, General 158, 256
Rock Well Mike's band *see* Shoshones
Roentgen, Wilhelm 115
Rolland, Romain 67, 105–106, 107–108, 118, 122, 218, 251
Romanova, Alexandra Feodorovna 80, 159

Roosevelt, Theodore 8, 11, 12, 37, 38–39, 44, 111, 125, 129, 149, 216
Rosenberg, Isaac 192
Roussel, Nelly 69
Ruff, Pierre 124
Rumbold, Horace 206
Russell, Bertrand 90–92, 190, 193, 252
Russo-Japanese War 8, 22, 45, 47, 59, 65, 70, 71, 222
Russo-Turkish War 22
Ruyssen, Théodore 59, 60

Salisbury, Lord 5
Sassoon, Siegfried 191, 193–196
Saumoneau, Louise 113
Sazonov, Sergey Dmitrievich 65, 67, 79
Scavenius, Erik 78
Schiff, Jacob H. 129
Schmavonian, Arshag K. 204
Schwimmer, Rosika 155
Second International 19, 71, 72, 73, 163
Seeger, Alan 192
Selective Service Act 229, 230–231
Selznik, Lewis 213
Sembat, Marcel 59
Sharpley, Kate 156–157
Shaw, George Bernard 87, 89, 252
Shoshones 17–18
Sinclair, Upton 252
Sino-Japanese War 46
Sixtus of Bourbon Parma, Prince 170, 257
slavery 9, 236
Smuts, Gen. Jan 153
Snowden, Phillip 90
Société d'éducation pacifique 59
Sonnino, Sydney 172
Sorley, Charles 191, 196
Sozialdemokratische Partei Deutschlands (SPD) 49, 50, 51
Spartacus League 69, 96
SPD *see* Sozialdemokratische Partei Deutschlands
Spencer, Herbert 34
Speyer, James 83
Stashkov, Roman 244
Stinnes, Hugo 158
Straus, Oscar S. 83–84, 257
Sugarman, Abraham L. 229
Süttner, Bertha von 4, 6, 62–63, 250, 253; *Lay Down Your Arms* (book) 61–62; *Memoirs* 43
Swedish Association for Peace and Arbitration 32
Swinburne, Charles 37
Swing, Raymond Gram 81

Taft, William Howard 11–13, 19, 125, 126, 129
Tagore, Rabindranath 252
Talaat Pasha 206
Tarnowski von Tarnów, Count Adam 181
Tennyson, Lord Alfred 13
Terruzzi, Regina 130
Thucydides 8
Togo, Admiral 10
Tokutomi, Roka: *The Cuckoo* 47

Tolstoy, Leo 67, 106, 107, 109–112; *Bethink Yourselves* 43, 47–48
Traven, B. 218
Treaty of Portsmouth 48
Trevelyan, Charles P. 90, 101–102
Trotsky, Leon 96, 187, 242, 243, 244–246
Twain, Mark 7

Union of Democratic Control (UDC) 101–103
union sacrée 73, 82, 104
United Nations 7
United States Section of the Women's International League for Peace and Freedom 4
Universal Peace Congress 59
Ushimura, Kanzo 46, 223–224

Valentino, Rudolph 214
Vardaman, Sen. James K. 225, 226
Vassiltchikov, Marie Alexandrovna 79–81
Vehir Bey 206
Verband für internationale Verständigung 51–52
Vereshchagin, Vasily 22
Vernet, Madeleine 114
Villa, Pancho 56, 57
Villard, Oswald Garrison 147
Viviani, René 64, 104
Voloshin, Maximilian 163
von Bernstorff, Count Johann 83, 85, 160, 179–180, 181
von Bieberstein, Baron Marschall 25
von Burián *see* Burián von Rajecz, Baron Stephan
von der Lancken, Baron 182–183
von Hindenburg, Gen. Paul 188, 189, 247
von Hohenlohe, Prince Gottfried 79
von Hötzendorf, Franz Conrad 76
von Jagow, Gottlieb 79–80, 100, 155, 158
von Kiderlen, Alfred 14, 15
von Kühlmann, Richard 183, 185, 189–190, 243, 257

von Moltke, Helmuth 76
von Müller, Adm. Georg Alexander 185
von Tirpitz, Admiral 25, 26, 28, 60, 190
von Unruh, Fritz 217
von Willamowitz Moellendorff, Ulrich 115
Vrede door Recht see Dutch Peace Society

Wadai War 8
Wales, Julia Grace 97–98, 100, 147–148, 151
Walker brothers 88
Wangerin, Otto 236
War Against War 7
Warburg, Max 158–159
Weber, Max 51
Weizmann, Dr. Chaim 205, 206, 208
Wells, H.G. 114–115, 250–251
White, Andrew D. 7
Whitman, Walt 198
William II *see* Kaiser William II
Wilson, Woodrow 29, 56, 57, 63, 73, 77, 84, 98–101, 117, 127–128, 129, 147, 150, 151, 160, 176, 177, 178, 180, 181, 186, 204, 211, 212, 225, 226, 228, 233, 234, 237, 238, 247, 248, 249, 251, 254
Wiseman, William, Sir 162
Witte, Count 65
Wolfe, Bertram 50
Woman's Peace Army 224
Woman's Peace Party 4, 125, 149, 211
World Peace Foundation 4, 35, 42, 211

Yanushkevich, Gen. Nikolai 67
Yosano Akiko 222–223

Zaharoff, Basil 207–211
Zamenhof, Ludoviko 37; *see also* Esperanto
Zetkin, Klara 69
Zimmermann, Arthur 184
Zweig, Stefan 106, 252

www.ingramcontent.com/pod-product-compliance
Lightning Source LLC
Chambersburg PA
CBHW051209300426
44116CB00006B/493